TO JOHN,

MANY THANKS FOR THE
GREAT DAY AT SENECA FALLS.

BEST, DOUG EGERTON

YEAR OF METEORS

YEAR OF METEORS

*Stephen Douglas, Abraham Lincoln, and the
Election That Brought on the Civil War*

DOUGLAS R. EGERTON

BLOOMSBURY PRESS

New York   Berlin   London

Published by Bloomsbury Press, New York

All papers used by Bloomsbury Press are natural, recyclable products made from wood grown in well-managed forests. The manufacturing processes conform to the environmental regulations of the country of origin.

LIBRARY OF CONGRESS CATALOGING-IN-PUBLICATION DATA
Egerton, Douglas R.
Year of meteors : Stephen Douglas, Abraham Lincoln, and the election that brought on the Civil War / Douglas R. Egerton. —1st ed.
p. cm.
Includes bibliographical references and index.
ISBN 978-1-59691-619-7 (alk. paper)
1. Presidents—United States—Election—1860. 2. Lincoln, Abraham, 1809–1865—Political and social views. 3. Douglas, Stephen A. (Stephen Arnold), 1813–1861—Political and social views. 4. Lincoln, Abraham, 1809–1865—Political career before 1861. 5. United States—Politics and government—1857–1861. 6. United States—History—Civil War, 1861–1865—Causes. I. Title.
E440.E43 2010
973.7'11—dc22
2010004965

First U.S. Edition 2010

1 3 5 7 9 10 8 6 4 2

Typeset by Westchester Book Group
Printed in the United States of America by Worldcolor Fairfield

For my daughters Kearney and Hannah,
who always make me smile

Year of meteors! brooding year!
I would bind in words retrospective, some of your deeds and signs;
I would sing your contest for the 19th Presidentiad;
I would sing how an old man, tall, with white hair, mounted the
    scaffold in Virginia;
(I was at hand—silent I stood, with teeth shut close—I watch'd;
I stood very near you, old man, when cool and indifferent,
    but trembling with age and your
    unheal'd wounds, you mounted the scaffold;)
I would sing in my copious song your census returns of The States,
The tables of population and products—I would sing of your ships
    and their cargoes,
The proud black ships of Manhattan, arriving, some fill'd with
    immigrants, some from the
    isthmus with cargoes of gold;
Songs thereof would I sing—to all that hitherward comes would I
    welcome give;
And you would I sing, fair stripling! welcome to you from me,
    sweet boy of England!
Remember you surging Manhattan's crowds, as you pass'd
    with your cortege of nobles?
There in the crowds stood I, and singled you out with attachment;
There in the crowds stood I, and singled you out with attachment;
Nor forget I to sing of the wonder, the ship as she swam up my bay,
Well-shaped and stately the *Great Eastern* swam up my bay,
    she was 600 feet long,
Her, moving swiftly, surrounded by myriads of small craft,
    I forget not to sing;
Nor the comet that came unannounced out of the north,
    flaring in heaven;

Nor the strange huge meteor procession, dazzling and clear,
    shooting over our heads,
(A moment, a moment long, it sail'd its balls of unearthly
    light over our heads,
Then departed, dropt in the night, and was gone;)
Of such, and fitful as they, I sing—with gleams from them would
    I gleam and patch these chants;
Your chants, O year all mottled with evil and good! year of
    forebodings!
Year of comets and meteors transient and strange! lo—
    even here one transient and strange!
As I flit through you hastily, soon to fall and be gone,
    what is this chant,
What am I myself but one of your meteors?

—WALT WHITMAN, 1859–1860

CONTENTS

"Let Us Press On"

April–June, 1861

RESIDENTS DUBBED SOUTHERN Illinois as Little Egypt, not only because the flat terrain resembled the Nile delta but also because the region exhibited the proslavery attitudes of its ancient namesake. Although the Northwest Ordinance of 1787 allowed "neither slavery nor involuntary servitude" in the region, settlers who had carried their slaves into the territory before the ordinance were permitted to retain their unwaged laborers. A resident of the aptly named Cairo could gaze east across the Ohio River into Kentucky, while another might face west and spy Missouri. Boatmen sailing down the Mississippi River reached the Tennessee border after forty-three miles. So it was no surprise that public opinion in lower Illinois was bitterly divided following the Confederate bombardment of Fort Sumter on the morning of April 12, 1861. The *Golconda Weekly Herald* warned residents to arm themselves against "black Republican" armies, and several city leaders in Cairo threatened to turn the town into an independent city-state. "Many who profess to be Union men," fretted one Democrat, "hesitate about coming out boldly against treason, fearing hereafter to be classed as Republicans." The state assembly was preparing to go into special session on April 23, and worried legislators peppered Stephen A. Douglas, the state's Democratic senior senator, with urgent requests to "stand by our Government, and sink party feeling for the present." Douglas's health, damaged by a lifetime's fondness for whiskey and cigars, had yet to recover from the grueling fall campaign and a bruising winter legislative session in Washington. But vowing, "Let us press on," he resolved to "come home to arouse the people in favor of the Union."[1]

On April 20, Douglas and his second wife, Adele, left the besieged national capital by rail; across the river in Virginia, the Stars and Bars, the first of several Confederate flags, flapped in the spring breeze. The Baltimore and Ohio Railroad passed through portions of western Virginia, and when his train reached the arsenal town of Harpers Ferry, southern militiamen boarded the car and threatened to arrest the senator as a prisoner of war. With more courage than realism, the diminutive Little Giant, as the senator was known, warned the soldiers that if they did so, they would have to answer to the "largest army" that Virginia had yet seen. Cooler heads prevailed, and the senator was sent on his way. On the morning of April 25, Douglas's party pulled into Springfield, the Illinois state capital. Although exhausted from his journey, Douglas promptly met with Governor Richard Yates, Republican Illinois senator Lyman Trumbull, and Orville Hickman Browning, a former Whig whom Douglas had bested in an 1843 congressional race. The time for partisanship had passed, Douglas insisted, and together the group forged "an understanding" regarding the various militia bills pending in the state assembly.[2]

That evening, as legislators and curious residents of the city shoved their way into the packed statehouse, Douglas delivered one of the most important speeches of his career. Once capable of speaking for hours, the weary senator kept his remarks short. But his words were both blunt and emotional, and as he spoke, some in the audience began to weep openly. Uncharacteristically, Douglas began by confessing an error. He had devoted his career to compromise and sectional reconciliation, he admitted, and had "lean[ed] too far to the southern section of the Union against my own." As had many northern Democrats, Douglas had once believed that appeasement was the wisest response to southern demands regarding slavery in the western territories. But the fruits of his munificence, he fumed, were a "piratical flag" unfurled near the White House and the obstruction of Illinois's commerce along "our great river." A "wide-spread conspiracy exists to destroy the best government the sun of heaven ever shed its rays upon," Douglas shouted, for a "war of aggression and extermination [was] being waged" against the republic by proslavery forces. As Douglas paused to catch his breath, somebody entered the rear of the chamber waving an American flag, and the tears in the hall transformed into cheers and applause.[3]

On May 1, Douglas reached Chicago. Journalists waiting at the depot marveled at the crowd of thousands that met his car with a resounding roar. Judging from the throng, one might never have known that the politician returning home had finished fourth in the Electoral College during the previous November's presidential election. An impromptu parade escorted Douglas through the streets toward the Wigwam, the cavernous pine auditorium constructed only the preceding year to house the Republican National Convention. According to one reporter, Douglas's "words rolled out in unbroken cadences of patriotic devotion as they never rolled before." Clutching the podium unsteadily, Douglas assured the "ten thousand persons" who had elbowed their way into the hall that the election of Abraham Lincoln was merely the excuse for secession. Returning to the theme he had first advanced in Springfield, Douglas charged that the Confederacy was the product of "an enormous conspiracy" devised months before the fall election. "There are only two sides to the question," Douglas thundered in conclusion. "Every man must be for the United States or against it. There can be no neutrals in this war, *only patriots—or traitors*." It was to be his last speech.[4]

For the past eighteen years, Douglas had called Washington his home, and he owned no house in Illinois. He and Adele checked in to the Tremont House, on East Chestnut, Chicago's finest hotel. For the next few days, the senator continued to receive visitors, and despite Adele's concerns, Douglas and his guests habitually washed down their conversations with copious amounts of whiskey. By May 4, what he described as a "slight cold" had settled into a low fever. The senator sent for several doctors, who pronounced his illness to be "acute rheumatism" of a "typhoid character" complicated by "an ulcerated sore throat." Within days, Douglas could not use his arms, but he continued to dictate letters denouncing "the Cotton States" and calling on Democrats to "rally to the support of our common country." Determined to continue his efforts on behalf of his longtime foe who now served as president, Douglas insisted that he be carried outside "into open air," and by May 19 his doctors were hoping for a complete recovery. But three days later, his "torpor of the liver"—that is, cirrhosis—worsened, and the physicians warned Adele that he "could not recover."[5]

Adele sent for their young sons, Robert and Stephen Jr., who attended a private school in the Georgetown section of Washington, and she was joined by her brother, James Madison Cutts Jr. A devout Catholic, Adele brought in Bishop James Duggan, who attempted to perform a long-overdue baptism and administer last rites. Douglas declined both offers, and when a stunned Duggan raised the issue a second time, the senator roused himself to bark in a "strong, full voice" that the bishop "perhaps, did not understand me," adding that when he "desire[d] it," he would "communicate with [Duggan] freely." When Douglas continued to deteriorate, Duggan returned the following day with an offer of extreme unction, only to be rebuffed again by the senator, who snapped that he had "no time to discuss these things now."[6]

The senator began to sink "rapidly" just before dawn on Monday, June 3. Lying with his eyes partially closed, Douglas slowly muttered, "Death! Death! Death!" Adele asked if he had any messages for their sons, who had yet to arrive in Chicago. A politician even in the shades, Douglas replied, "Tell them to obey the laws and support the Constitution of the United States." For the next several hours, he slept quietly and said nothing more. As morning broke, Adele leaned across the bed and said, "Husband, do you know me? Will you kiss me?" Douglas opened his eyes and smiled, and the muscles of his mouth twitched as if in an attempt to comply. According to his doctors, Douglas gave one final "quick, convulsive shudder." They pronounced him dead "at ten minutes past nine o'clock." Douglas was forty-eight years old.[7]

Chicago plunged into "the deepest sorrow" at the news of Douglas's death. Although word had spread that the senator was gravely ill, city residents had prayed that he would rally, and when his doctors emerged from the Tremont to announce his passing, the several hundred people waiting at the hotel "bowed in awe and sorrow." Once-hostile reporters were equally stunned. As is often the case, editors "forgot past differences and spoke only of his many virtues." Yet for once, such journalistic post-mortems were more than polite embellishment. Since Abraham Lincoln's inauguration three months before, Douglas had ceased to be the bitter partisan as he had labored to rally his party and the nation behind the new Republican administration. The mayor of the city ordered that flags be lowered to half-mast and public buildings be "draped in mourning." The city's board of trade adjourned when its members heard the news, and most banks closed their doors as well. The Masonic fraternity quickly organized a procession to Bryan Hall, where "their departed member" was to lie in state for the next two days.[8]

At the offices of the Magnetic Telegraph Company, R. J. Mernick tapped the news along to President Lincoln and to the Capitol. A stunned Lincoln instructed Secretary of State William Henry Seward to drape the White House and the State Department in black crepe. The following day, Secretary of War Simon Cameron—like Seward and Douglas, an unsuccessful contender for the presidency just months before—ordered "the Colonels of the different Regiments" to likewise drape their colors in mourning. Douglas was "a Senator who forgot all prejudices in an earnest desire to serve the Republic," Cameron wrote, a man "whose last mission on earth was that of rallying the people of his own State of Illinois" to the cause "of the Union."[9]

Although Lincoln was well aware of Douglas's injurious personal habits, he was staggered by the news. Several years before, Lincoln had been asked when he and Douglas had first met, and it had been such a distant memory that he had only been able to guess at 1834. Lincoln had been twenty-five at the time, and the younger Douglas but twenty-one. For nearly three decades the two attorneys had been rivals, first in Illinois law and politics and then on the national stage. But each had respected the other's considerable talents, and even when locked in bitter contests in 1858 and 1860, Lincoln and Douglas had rarely engaged in personal barbs but had kept the focus on their ideological differences. Douglas had often praised Lincoln during the final days of the 1860 campaign, and since Inaugural Day the two had spent long hours discussing secession and the war. If sometimes given to severe bouts of melancholia that were obvious to all, Lincoln generally preferred to keep his inner thoughts private, and he said almost nothing about the death of his longtime adversary. The fact that Lincoln put even fewer words to paper about Douglas's decease suggests the depth of the president's sorrow, as

This brief telegram, sent from Chicago and dated June 3, 1861, informed a stunned President Abraham Lincoln of the death of his longtime rival and recent supporter. Courtesy Library of Congress.

does the fact that he remained solicitous about Adele and the senator's children.[10]

Adele Douglas wished her husband to be buried in Washington alongside their previously deceased infant daughter. Governor Yates and Senator Trumbull, however, urged her to reconsider in hope of preserving the symbolism of Douglas's last crusade. Concerned that the unionist sentiments of Illinois Democrats might perish along with their leader,

Yates cabled Adele that he and Trumbull were "unwilling that one whose life has been closely identified with the interests of the state should in death be separated from it." Adele gave way on this point, but not on another. Although the senator had never revealed any interest in "any particular faith," Adele was determined that he would be interred a Catholic, and Bishop Duggan, twice rebuffed by the dying Douglas, was invited to speak at the funeral. For once, the pugnacious Douglas did not have the last word.[11]

The senator was not mourned everywhere. When told the news, black abolitionist Frederick Douglass bluntly observed that "in the death of Stephen A. Douglas, a most dangerous man has been removed. No man of his time has done more to intensify hatred of the negro." And if northern activists could not forgive Douglas's racist past, white southerners detested his staunch unionism. The senator's first wife, Martha Denny Martin of North Carolina, had brought to her marriage a not-uncommon southern dowry of a twenty-five-hundred-acre cotton plantation in Mississippi along the river, together with 150 slaves. Douglas had declined the wedding present but remained manager of the property on paper, which granted him a 20 percent share of all profits each year. Upon their marriage in 1856, Adele became guardian of the senator's young sons, and shortly after his death she was dismayed to discover that as a final act of vengeance, Mississippi intended to confiscate their property. Her brother encouraged her, "against her inclination," to send the boys into the Confederacy to plead their case. The widow, only twenty-four years old, called on Lincoln for advice. The president assured Adele that he doubted even President Jefferson Davis would seize "the property of minor children," but he warned her not to publicize their meeting. "Nothing would more certainly excite the secessionists to do the worst they can against the children," Lincoln observed, than if his name was "connected with the matter." Adele accepted Lincoln's counsel and remained in the North.[12]

Douglas's death at a too-early age was symbolic of the demise of the young republic, just as his belated support for Lincoln's unionist policies was emblematic of the national reclamation soon to arrive with the Emancipation Proclamation. Yet even biographers and historians who find much to admire in the senator's belated fury at the southern planter class little know what to make of his final, angry claims that his career and nation had fallen victim to "an enormous conspiracy" hatched a year before in the early spring of 1860. In both of his final speeches, and again in his last correspondence, Douglas charged that "leaders of the secession movement" had engineered a Republican victory "by a sectional vote, to demonstrate that the Union was divided," so that they could at long last "break up" the republic. During the last months of his life, Douglas had come to believe that the "election of Lincoln [was] but a pretext," and that he, as the leader of the northern faction of a willfully "divided" Democratic Party, had been the unwitting tool of this "grand conspiracy" bent on disunion.[13]

Never shy about naming names, Douglas identified two "fire-eating" secessionists as the leaders of this plot as early as May of 1860. Speaking in the Senate shortly after the Democratic National Convention in Charleston adjourned without making a nomination, Douglas attributed the plot to South Carolina publisher Robert Barnwell Rhett and former Congressman William Lowndes Yancey of Alabama. A retired Democratic senator and the owner of the *Charleston Mercury* (which was edited by his son Robert Jr.), Rhett had endorsed secession ten years before at the Nashville Convention, while Yancey had begun to publicly call for "a Southern Confederacy" in 1858. The two secessionists met and schemed on several occasions, but no ongoing, secret collaboration was necessary. Both recognized that the best chance for a slaveholding South united in separation was a Republican victory in 1860. The Republicans remained a minority, sectional party, and a united Democratic Party might well retain control of the White House. If enough southern delegates to the Charleston convention refused to endorse front-runner Douglas and his policy of popular sovereignty in the territories, however, a fractured party would hand the election to New York senator and Republican front-runner Seward, an alleged antislavery radical, and so justify secession. Their "plan," Douglas charged, "was to keep in the Democratic party until the proper moment came for revolution," then "break up the party, and with the party" the nation. Modern political observers assume that winning candidates control elections, but 1860 was unique in that a small number of southern reactionaries manipulated the process. As one

Alabama journalist conceded on the eve of the Charleston meeting, "the true designs of such men as Yancey" were the "dissolution of the Union." Yancey and other like-minded delegates to the national convention, "although being a minority," planned to "throw the dust into the eyes of nearly all the Democracy."[14]

Normally, candidates rejoice over chaos in their opponent's camp, but while Lincoln privately suspected that the dissolution of the Democratic Party signaled a Republican victory, he also feared that the handiwork of those whom even Republicans dubbed "the conspirators" would mean a different sort of trouble in the near future. "R.B. Rhett, editor of the Charleston Mercury was the presiding genius," one Republican explained to Lincoln, and knowing that "Mr. Douglas would not be particularly favorable to their extreme views on slavery," a small group of radicals known as fire-eaters determined "to break up the Convention in a row, disrupt the party, run Douglas in the north and a favorite of their own in the south." The intention "of the Yancey school of politicians," another Republican warned Lincoln in the summer of 1860, was "to disrupt this union." Having traveled throughout the South on business, the writer assured Lincoln "that many residents of the South will rejoice when the lightning shall announce that Abraham Lincoln is elected President of these United States," but only because it would give them an excuse for secession. "Your election," he cautioned, "will be the easiest part of the struggle for you."[15]

A few years later, after the Civil War, Douglas's allegations found support in books by John Minor Botts of Virginia, yet another candidate for the presidency in 1860, and by Illinois congressman John Alexander Logan, both constitutional Unionists. In 1866, Botts alleged that it was not merely a few "reckless and desperate" politicians who led the "unsuspecting people of the South" astray, but rather "the leaders of [the] Democracy." Logan agreed and traced the "history of the Great Conspiracy" to the "evil days of Nullification" in the early 1830s. Such elaborations and exaggerations have made it easy for modern scholars to dismiss Douglas's charges as the last, angry ruminations of a defeated and dying politician. Even the words "enormous conspiracy" have little helped Douglas's case, since the men who labored to dissolve the Democratic Party were neither large in number nor secretive about their objectives.

But Douglas was right enough in thinking that there were those in the South who sought to forge a new nation of "the slave holding race," as one of then–Mississippi senator Davis's correspondents phrased it. These activists regarded Douglas's stubborn refusal to quit the presidential contest even after the party split as welcome news, as it guaranteed the election of Lincoln and ensured the secession "of all the slaveholding states." Those southern radicals who desired a Republican victory, complained Democratic congressman Alexander H. Stephens, the future Confederate vice president and one of Douglas's few supporters in Georgia, "intended from the beginning 'to rule or ruin.' " But Stephens was wrong. Yancey and the "seceders" who used Douglas's ambitions against him were not motivated by "envy, hate, jealousy, [or] spite." Their calculations were eminently rational; they planned to ruin so they could rule.[16]

Justly famous for his oratorical skills, Yancey's appeal lay in his brutal honesty. Mainstream southern Democrats, who opposed Douglas as insufficiently firm on slavery in the West and hoped to unite the party behind Davis or Vice President John C. Breckinridge of Kentucky, well understood that Yancey intended to destroy the party. As George Hunter of Louisiana charged in early 1860, Yancey and most of the Alabama delegates "wished to go out of the Union" and regarded "the disorganization of the Democratic party" as the first step toward that goal. Rhett Jr. trumpeted their plans in the pages of the *Mercury*. "The election of Breckinridge may serve to protract for a few years a feverish and therefore dangerous existence," he warned. But a Democratic victory would only lull the planter class into four or eight years of imprudent confidence while the northern states grew in population and industrial might. And so, Rhett Jr. regarded the election of a Republican "as the best thing that can happen to the Southern States." As Yancey lectured the Charleston convention, he had long ago reached the "deep-seated conviction that the South, with her institutions, [was] unsafe in the Union." It was "upon these premises" that the Alabama delegates "proceed[ed]" after arriving in South Carolina.[17]

For the sixty-year-old Rhett, disunion was "a matter which has been gathering head for thirty years." Somewhat younger at forty-six, Yancey had also opposed the national Compromise of 1850, crafted by Senator

Henry Clay and, later, Stephen Douglas. But his real labors on behalf of secession began in 1858 with the creation of the League of United Southerners, designed to organize "Committees of Safety" among southern planters in imitation of the Revolution-era committees of correspondence. Yancey hoped that by "concerted action, we can precipitate the Cotton States into a revolution." With its motto, "A Southern Republic is our only safety," Yancey's league counseled that any further attempts by slaveholders to control a national Democratic Party were not merely pointless but dangerous. Although he initially planned to boycott the Charleston convention, by 1859 he realized that if the fire-eaters did so, they would simply hand the nomination to Douglas. Far better, he concluded, for them to attend and press for a territorial slave code in the party platform. If denied, they could then run a sectional candidate of their own. But as northern Democrats charged, Yancey's threats to bolt the convention scarcely masked his "deliberate intention of helping the Republicans in electing a sectional President" so as to provide "justification for their premeditated plan of separating the South from the North."[18]

White southerners were rarely united on any course of action, and even in Yancey's Alabama, unionists denounced his schemes to force the state into the radical "position claimed for her by the Charleston *Mercury*," which was "to force the other *thirty-two* States to conform exactly" to his proslavery demands or "to leave the Convention." But for those who believed the time was long past for planters to abandon the republic, the Charleston convention, as Douglas later realized, posed the perfect opportunity. Rhett and Yancey correctly predicted that a majority of Democratic delegates consisting of Douglas men would dominate but not control the convention. Because the party machinery was organized in a way that allowed a resolute minority to capture select committees, a few dedicated secessionists enjoyed the ability to encourage quick-tempered southern delegates—many of them otherwise-dedicated unionists—to bolt the conference. As the northern representatives were sure to be unwilling to agree to a repudiation of their candidate's long-held position on popular sovereignty in the territories, the secession of southern delegates from the convention, Douglas observed, was consciously devised to destroy "the only political party in existence" that might hold the country together.[19]

Much of Douglas's fury, both before and after the Democratic convention, was fueled by the fact that Yancey and Rhett were completely open in their machinations. Yet a vast majority of southern party members consistently proved willing to play into their hands. For most slave-state delegates, the nomination of a states' rights planter would have kept them in the party. "The great and paramount object," insisted one Montgomery, Alabama, editor, was "to beat the Black Republicans, and to this every other policy or expedient must yield." But hypersensitive to their perceived rights and terrified by the specter of abolitionist John Brown, slaveholding delegates could be counted upon, as one Texan predicted, to assist in the "disintegration of the Democratic party, and even the disruption of the Union." With the one remaining national party fractured into pieces, an Alabama journalist agreed, "the triumph of Seward would be vastly less difficult," and with a Republican victory, the white South would stand united in secession.[20]

This does not mean that Yancey or Rhett desired or even expected war. Despite later assertions that enslaved southerners might assist in a Confederate victory by providing labor while young farmers took to the battlefield, no sane slaveholder wished for hostilities, as the economic risks were enormous. Yet so convinced were they that Yankees were but a nation of clerks that southern politicians easily brushed aside any fears that secession would mean war. "You may slap a Yankee in the face and he'll go off and sue you," sneered one fire-eater, "but he won't fight." The younger Rhett echoed those sentiments in the *Mercury*. That the "people of the North, prone to civil pursuits and money-making, should get up and carry out the military enterprise of conquering eight million people," he wrote, "is one of those absurdities which none but a professed panic-maker could be capable of announcing." Democratic senator James Chesnut of South Carolina, whose mansion would be partly burned during the war, agreed. He proclaimed that he would drink all of the blood shed should his state secede.[21]

To the extent that the Democrats who engineered the destruction of their own party expected their departure to be peaceful, historians have traditionally examined the Republicans when explaining the outbreak of hostilities. "To understand why the war came," Phillip S. Paludan observed nearly forty years ago, "we must look not at secession but at the

Northern response to it." More recently, Russell McClintock concurred, adding that the fighting began at Fort Sumter "not when the Southern states seceded but when the Northern states acted forcibly to stop them." Admittedly, the Lincoln administration's refusal to compromise on the territories during the secession winter of 1860–61 or to abandon federal property like Sumter ultimately forced the hand of the new Confederate government. But the fighting that began in April of 1861 cannot be divorced from Yancey's machinations in Charleston. Lincoln's refusal to bend was based on his unwillingness to turn his back on an electorate that had just elevated him into the White House, and for fire-eaters like Yancey and the Rhetts, serious concessions on the western territories were unwanted, for if reunion were achieved, all of their efforts would have been for naught.[22]

The election of 1860 serves as a reminder not just of the centrality of slavery's westward expansion in American politics, but also of the centrality of race in American life. During the campaign, Yancey denounced the Republicans as the "negro party, or mixed negro and white party, making it the mulatto party." When the younger Rhett advocated "the formation of a *Slave* Republic" in his newspaper, he spoke not only of the need to protect "domestic slavery," but also of the profound differences "between the *two forms of society* which have become established, the one at the North and the other at the South." White abolitionists and black Americans, of course, well understood that racism was an American tragedy and not simply a southern phenomenon, and no better example existed, ironically, than Stephen Douglas himself. When campaigning against Lincoln three years before his death, Douglas sarcastically told one audience that if they agreed with "Black Republicans [that] the negro ought to be on a social equality with [their] wives and daughters," they had "a perfect right to do so." So if the senator's adherence to popular sovereignty on the frontier cost him the support of southern expansionists, his incessant race-baiting earned him the enmity of such black activists as Frederick Douglass.[23]

The less than subtle allusions to race are only one feature of 1860 that modern observers of the political scene might find sadly familiar. In both major parties, the candidate who began the season as the front-runner either failed to secure the nomination or fared badly in the general election.

As the year 1860 dawned, seasoned spectators and wizened political handlers confidently predicted that Douglas would become the Democratic nominee, and that, as in 1856, the Democrats would edge the Republican candidate. Speaking on January 29, 1860, Republican editor and activist Horace Greeley assured an Iowa audience "that Stephen A. Douglas will be the nominee of the Charleston Convention, and most of the slave States will give him their votes." When asked why the South, so hostile to the senator's position on the territories, would swallow his nomination, Greeley responded that a "National Convention always nominates to win." Greeley, of course, failed to account for strategists like Yancey, who prayed his fellow Democrat would lose. Of the four major (and one minor) candidates in 1860, Douglas would place second in the popular vote but a distant fourth in the electoral count.[24]

Whereas powerful Democrats labored to ensure their party's defeat, influential Republicans desperately sought victory for their minority party. And here, Douglas's inability to capture the presidency was mirrored by Seward's failure to obtain his party's nomination. As with the Democratic front-runner, veterans of the political wars took it for granted that the former governor and longtime senator would be the Republican candidate. And as has often been the case in American politics, supporters of the defeated candidate threatened to stay home on Election Day or even support another ticket. One furious Republican, in a strangely familiar-sounding phrase, wondered how the Chicago Republican convention could have denied the selection to the "most experienced & most competent Statesman," while another informed Seward that he "shed bitter tears" over the news of Lincoln's nomination. "Mr. Lincoln's nomination is a cause of so much regret to us here in Massachusetts," reported a third.[25]

Certainly the New York senator had believed that the nomination was his for the asking. Educated at Union College, at a time when many politicians lacked formal education, Seward had made his reputation as a reformer even before election into the state assembly. A term in the governor's chair earned him the praise of abolitionists when he successfully advocated legislation guaranteeing fugitive slaves the right of jury trial. The Senate beckoned, and after Seward abandoned the rapidly collapsing Whig Party for the newly formed Republicans, he quickly emerged as the leading voice of the party. He considered accepting the Republican nomination in 1856 but suspected that the party was too new and disorganized to win, and Thurlow Weed, his longtime manager, urged him to wait for 1860. This time around, most editors, as one New York journalist said, believed the "coast [was] clear for Mr. Seward." Defeating Douglas and a unified Democratic Party would have been no easy task, but his devoted followers remained optimistic. Although blacks could not vote in Illinois, William Bonner wrote on behalf of "the Colored people of Chicago" to insist that Seward did "not alone belong to the Empire State" but was "the acknowledged Champion and Leader of Freedom" in all "the States north of Slavery." However, if the central story for the first part of 1860 was Douglas's failure to capture his party's united support, by late spring journalists instead were beginning to focus on the failure of the other front-runner to prevail.[26]

As spring turned to summer, journalists began to flock toward Springfield; by then, the dark horse candidacy of Abraham Lincoln dominated the news. But Lincoln was never supposed to be president, and with the exception of the candidate himself and his handler, David Davis, nobody, before the Chicago convention, thought he could aspire to anything higher than the second spot on the ticket. The lanky Illinois attorney, however, promised to run better in Indiana, Illinois, and the lower North than John C. Frémont had in 1856, and at the convention Davis talked up Lincoln's electability compared with that of the far-better-known New York senator. "Why shouldn't [Lincoln] be the 'Polk of 1860'?" wondered one Illinois journalist, in a reference to the unexpected Democratic nominee of 1844. Yet even as the year progressed, Lincoln remained so little known outside of his state that politicians and editors had a difficult time keeping his name straight. Feminist Susan B. Anthony was hardly alone when she urged a Seneca Falls, New York, audience to "inaugurate Abram Lincoln" the following spring.[27]

Voters today complain that the election season appears endless, but that too is nothing new. Having received a handful of convention votes in 1852 and then having barely lost the nomination to the aged James Buchanan in 1856, Douglas worked tirelessly thereafter in his quest for the White House. Lincoln began to consider a run shortly after his defeat by Douglas in the Illinois senatorial race in 1858. General Winfield

Scott, who earned the Whig nomination in 1852, hinted in 1860 that he was willing to run at the head of the Constitutional Union ticket. And for television viewers who marvel at the number of candidates who crowd the stage in modern debates, no less than twenty-six Democrats floated their names shortly before the Charleston Democratic convention. Ten more candidates received votes at Baltimore's Constitutional Union convention, and six men had their names placed in contention at the Republican meeting in Chicago. Given the number of candidates and positions, as well as the heated divisions over policy options, it is little surprise that politicians tried the patience of newspaper readers by holding four major conventions as well as four smaller protest gatherings.[28]

A voter's choice is often difficult. Since most Republicans were not abolitionists but free-soil advocates, devout antislavery voters faced a dilemma not uncommon today among political activists. Nothing in the Republican platform advocated an early end to slavery; it simply called for a ban on its extension into the frontier. Some abolitionists even refused to vote on the grounds that the Constitution denied freedom to runaway slaves who reached northern states. Yet Lincoln eloquently denounced slavery, whereas Douglas's popular sovereignty platform allowed for the theoretical possibility of slavery expanding into the western territories from Washington to New Mexico. When supporters of Douglas and Tennessee senator John Bell, the nominee of the Constitutional Union Party, labored to create a fusion ticket in New York State— and so toss the election into the House, where southern Democratic nominee Breckinridge stood a chance—radical voters along the Erie Canal, rather like modern supporters of minor protest candidates, had to decide whether to vote with their heads or their hearts. Several times in the past, abolitionists had thrown their votes away by backing New York congressman Gerrit Smith, but if Lincoln lost New York, he would probably also lose the election. In Boston, abolitionist William Lloyd Garrison conceded that a Republican victory might "do no slight service to the cause of freedom," but he seethed as voters paraded about the city bearing signs reading, "WE ARE REPUBLICANS BUT NOT ABOLITIONISTS."[29]

The fact that those marchers once assumed the contest would come down to a close match between Douglas and Seward serves as a reminder that nothing is inevitable in national politics—or in history. But as 1860 dawned and the American political system began to unravel, even seasoned journalists realized that there was no way of knowing how the race would finish, or who among the forty-two candidates from the various parties would be the one sworn in on March 4, 1861. (The Twentieth Amendment, ratified in 1933, moved the inaugural forward to January 20.) One of the most critical years in American history, 1860 truly was a "year of meteors." Like the poet Walt Whitman, many Americans fearfully thought it a "year of forebodings" and potential civil war. As they pondered "the 19th Presidentiad," most understood it to be "all mottled" with both "evil and good," and they wondered which was to prevail.

CHAPTER ONE

A Nation with Its "Hands Full"

The Republic on the Eve of 1860

FRIEND AND FOE alike agreed that Stephen A. Douglas's most striking feature was his enormous head. Republican Charles Francis Adams Jr. thought the five-feet-three-inches-tall Little Giant a "squab, vulgar little man," but he was fascinated by the senator's "immense, frowsy head." Journalist Murat Halstead sneered that the stocky Douglas required "a large vest," and that "his waist [was] becoming still more extensive." But Halstead too was drawn to the cranium. He "*has* an immense head—in height, and breadth and depth," he marveled, "you cannot find its equal in Washington." In a time when phrenologists believed that personality traits were determined by cranial size and shape, what lay behind the senator's "splendidly developed" forehead was a subject of speculation. But few observers outdid H. M. Flint, a supporter and early biographer. "His massive head rivets undivided attention," Flint gushed. "It is a head of the antique, with something of the infinite in its expression of power: a head difficult to describe, but better worth description than any other in the country."[1]

If Douglas's prodigious skull housed "a brain of unusual size," as Flint bragged, it also housed a mind quite capable of political error and miscalculation. To explain why the man who virtually everyone conceded would one day grace the president's chair instead gasped out his last breath in a

Chicago hotel requires a digression of eight years and a detour into the gravest error of the senator's career. It is, oddly, the story of a railroad. Yet rarely has a single politician wrought so much havoc, and the blunder would reshuffle the nation's two-party system, bring a longtime foe out of political retirement, and cost Douglas the republic's highest office.[2]

In 1853, Douglas chaired the Senate Committee on Territories. As Illinois was then considered the West, logic dictated that Illinois Democrat William A. Richardson occupy the same position in the House of Representatives. Both men were champions of the westward movement and typified an age in which the majority of the United States believed the republic was destined to one day stretch from coast to coast and pole to pole. But Douglas also wished to guide the development of the frontier in a way that enriched both his state and his own purse. The senator had already obtained a federal land grant on which to construct a rail line south from Chicago to Mobile, Alabama. As a major investor in real estate just west of Chicago, Douglas now hoped to organize a second line toward San Francisco. The Windy City could thus trade with California and beyond, and the previously near-worthless prairie lands he and his associates owned would quadruple in value. To that end, in March 1853, Douglas and Richardson crafted legislation to organize what remained of the 1803 Louisiana Purchase region into one vast Kansas Territory (which required extinguishing Native American property claims there). But senators from Texas and Mississippi rose to express their opposition to the proposal. A stunned Douglas watched as every southern senator joined in the vote to table his bill. Congress then adjourned until the late fall.[3]

Before returning to Illinois, Douglas paid a call on the so-called F Street Mess, a Washington boardinghouse that served as home to a quartet of powerful Democratic southern senators, David R. Atchison of Missouri, Andrew Butler of South Carolina, and two Virginians, James M. Mason and Douglas's future presidential rival Robert M. T. Hunter. Douglas had already guessed why they opposed his plan, and it had nothing to do with a sudden solicitude for Indian rights. When California had entered the Union as part of the Compromise of 1850, the South had lost parity in the Senate, its check on northern power implicitly granted thirty years earlier during the Missouri debates. Moreover, the 1820 Missouri agreement had divided the Louisiana Purchase region just above the thirty-sixth parallel, so that all lands west and north of Missouri were permanently closed to slavery. Should Douglas, as Atchison bluntly put it, get his "railroad to the Pacific Ocean," settlers would soon follow its track west, and within a few years the already free territories might have the requisite population to apply for admission as free states. Northern influence, the slaveholding Atchison insisted, already slightly enhanced in the Senate—although California's two senators typically voted with the South—would render their "species of property [increasingly] insecure."[4]

When Congress resumed its deliberations in December 1853, Douglas initially hoped to satisfy Atchison's demands that "slaveholder and non-slaveholder" be placed "upon terms of equality" in the Kansas Territory by saying as little as possible about unfree labor in the region. As one of the architects of the Compromise of 1850, in which most of the Mexican Cession of 1848 was settled without reference to slavery on the basis of "popular sovereignty"—a solution first advanced by Michigan Democratic senator Lewis Cass—Douglas was content to allow white settlers, as opposed to distant legislators, to resolve the question when the time came for statehood. On January 4, 1854, Douglas introduced a second version of his bill, which divided the region into two territories, Kansas in the south and Nebraska in the north. Settlers had the option to retain or abolish slavery, "as their constitution may prescribe at the time of admission." As chairman, the senator also produced a report questioning the constitutionality of the 1820 prohibition on slavery north of 36° 30' and endorsing the conciliatory "language of the Compromise Measures of 1850." For politicians anxious to avoid taking a public position on the explosive question of slavery expansion, popular sovereignty had the virtue of appearing to follow the revered tradition of Jeffersonian localism. "Our chief source of safety is found in the doctrine of the inviolability of states' rights," observed one supportive editor.[5]

Although northern critics of popular sovereignty regarded the concept as a cowardly effort to pawn the slavery issue off on distant pioneers to resolve at some future date, Douglas quickly discovered that his intentionally vague language still failed to appease southern men. Not for the last time was Douglas to realize that his attempt to skirt the slavery issue had led only to scorn on both sides of the question; it was, in fact, a tendency that Douglas abandoned only after the firing on Fort Sumter. Once again, Atchison led the charge. In a drunken tirade on the floor of the Senate, the Missourian observed that no prudent slaveholder would carry his human property into a territory if it appeared likely that anti-slavery settlers could later pack a constitutional convention and abolish the slaveholder's capital investment. He hoped to see Kansas "sink into hell" before letting it become a free state. Senator Archibald Dixon, a Kentucky Whig who thought it unwise to allow southern Democrats to outflank him on the matter, seconded Atchison and insisted that Douglas could not evade the question. Unless the bill explicitly repealed the Missouri Compromise ban, Dixon threatened, he would feel compelled to draft a rival bill that did. Douglas was astute enough to understand the dilemma, but he saw no way out. Without southern votes, his bill could never pass. Yet overturning a thirty-four-year-old prohibition on slavery in the American Midwest, Douglas warned Atchison, could cause "a hell of a storm" in the North.[6]

Faced with this impasse, Douglas, having previously failed with ambiguity, now sought refuge in utter duplicity. Still hoping to avoid writing the explosive term "repealed" into his bill, he instead drafted a third version, which slyly suggested that the doctrine of congressional restriction adopted in 1820 had been "superceded by the principles" of popular sovereignty embedded in the Compromise of 1850 and so was "inoperative and void." In truth, as the agreement of 1850 pertained only to the spoils of the Mexican-American War, while the Missouri accord dealt only with the Louisiana Purchase region, there was no geographic overlap between the two compromises. Moreover, the idea that politicians who had grudgingly voted for popular sovereignty four years before had understood themselves to be erasing a decades-old pact defied credulity. Yet Douglas moved ahead. On January 10, one week after his bill had been twice printed and read, the senator quietly added clauses that he insisted had been omitted through a "clerical error." The new sections explicitly

Even ardent supporters privately thought that Stephen A. Douglas's head appeared too large for his short, stocky frame, but his fierce gaze reflects his pugnacious nature. Courtesy Library of Congress.

permitted territorial settlers to decide upon slavery, and the earlier state-ment regarding the popular sovereignty sections of the 1850 compro-mise was moved from his report into the bill itself.[7]

The final touch necessary was the endorsement of President Franklin Pierce. Washington insiders knew that the New Hampshire Democrat, still mourning the death of his son Benjamin, who had been killed in a railway accident just after the 1852 election, was so easily persuaded on any course of action that his support was worthless unless put into writ-ing. Early on the morning of Sunday, January 21, Douglas, Atchison, and Democratic congressman John C. Breckinridge of Kentucky called on the president. Since Pierce and his devout wife, Jane, rarely accepted visitors on the sabbath, Douglas also urged Secretary of War Jefferson Davis to join the group. After a meeting of several hours in the White House library, Pierce agreed to support the repeal of the 1820 ban, but he emphasized the seriousness of Congress doing so. Douglas bluntly insisted that the president endorse their course of action in writing. A coldly formal Pierce did so but declined to use the term "repeal." Even so, the final version of the bill, revised yet again with the assistance of Breck-inridge and introduced on January 23 as the Kansas-Nebraska Act, was now a Democratic Party measure and officially required the support of all party members.[8]

Douglas's worries of a political firestorm in the North proved well-founded. One friendly Wisconsin editor admitted that Douglas was not only "widely and vehemently denounced" but also, in many places, "hanged and burned in effigy." Several Chicago ministers condemned the bill from the pulpit. When Douglas returned to Chicago to shore up his base and defend what he had taken to calling the "principle of non-intervention by Congress with slavery in the States and Territories," he was "threatened by a mob." Douglas attempted a major address, but the crowd of eight thousand repeatedly interrupted him with boos and hisses until he finally gave up, shouted for the audience to "go to hell," and quit the stage.[9]

The suspicions, even in the Vermont-born Douglas's adoptive state, that he was clandestinely friendly to slave-state interests had much to do with his first wife's property. As one distrustful New England newspaper put it, thanks to his 1847 marriage he had "obtained a large fortune in land and personal [slave] property." Martha Douglas died in 1853, just as the senator was beginning to consider the question of a Pacific railroad, and the grieving widower thought it "shameless" that his political enemies hinted at a connection between his deceased wife's estate and his readiness to open western lands to slave labor. Yet the fact remained that as executor of the Mississippi assets, and as the father of Martha's two sons, Douglas had several times traveled to the South on family business, and as senator he continued to draw an annual income of one fifth of the profits from the Martin family lands and slaves.[10]

The senator, of course, stood to make far greater sums from investments around the Chicago area should his dream of a western railroad come to pass. Douglas's willingness to accept money earned from the toil of enslaved southerners reveals much about the moral blindness of the decade, but in the end he agreed to Atchison's demands not because he wished to see slavery expand westward, but because he regarded the 1820 prohibition as an unnecessary nuisance. Recognizing that his proslavery critics had attracted needless hostility to their cause with the stipulation that his bill explicitly repeal the Missouri ban—when the popular sovereignty clauses in the third version of the bill provided slave property with no more or less security than his second draft had—Douglas in fact quietly hoped that his formula would result in free territories and states. He privately assured one supporter that he regarded slavery as "a curse beyond computation to both white and black." Yet he regarded the three veiled references to slavery in the Constitution as protections he could not legally "violate." Nor did he wish to. Like many northern Democrats, Douglas did not, he explained, "believe in the equality of the negro, socially or politically." As he told an approving Illinois audience in language that earned him the permanent enmity of Frederick Douglass, "Our people are a white people; our State is a white State; and we mean to preserve the race pure, without any mixture with the negro."[11]

For the next two months, the pugnacious Douglas hammered away at his free-state critics. Aware that more than his western investments was at stake—for Democratic senator Albert Gallatin Brown of Mississippi had warned that the Kansas question "must enter into the next Presidential contest"—Douglas routinely took to the Senate floor. He confidently expected to win over enough northern Democrats to combine with a

solid, bipartisan South and ensure passage of his bill. When a prescient Senator Salmon P. Chase of Ohio warned that the measure could
precipitate a "reorganization of parties," Douglas responded that only
"northern Whigs and abolitionists" opposed "this great measure of paci-
fication." Peppered with enough "God damn's" and "by God's" to drive
genteel ladies from the galleries, the racist rhetoric in Douglas's speeches
prompted an irritated William Henry Seward to retort, "Douglas, no man
who spells Negro with two gs will ever be elected President of the United
States." Pierce, however, continued to portray the bill as "a test of Democratic orthodoxy," and the measure finally passed in the Senate on March
3 by a margin of 37 to 14. Two months later, Douglas's Georgia ally,
Congressman Alexander H. Stephens, "applied whip and spur" and led
the House to approve it by a vote of 159 to 75. Southerners celebrated
their victory by firing cannons from the terrace of the Capitol building.[12]

Proslavery politicians rejoiced, and with good reason. Although enslaved Missourians comprised only 13 percent of the population, slaveholders had settled the southwestern part of the state. If plantation
agriculture could thrive below the Missouri River, there was no reason
why it might not do the same on contiguous Kansas lands. Kansas's "climate [is] peculiarly healthy to the negro," insisted Missouri attorney
general Benjamin F. Stringfellow. "Nature intended it for a slaveholding
state." Making this conquest simpler yet was the fact that Douglas, although once a state judge, had drafted his law so sloppily that any white
man within the territory on voting day—as opposed to those who intended
to become permanent residents—might cast a ballot. Atchison recognized this flaw early on and promised to lead enough men across the
state line on the first Election Day, set for March 30, 1855, "to kill every
God damned abolitionist in the Territory." Atchison was as good as his
word, judging by the final tally, which revealed that 4,968 "one-day
Kansans" had overwhelmed the 1,210 legitimate settlers. The senator
later conceded that less than one third of the proslavery voters had intended to remain in Kansas but added that he was "playing for a mighty
stake." If proslavery forces could hold Kansas, they might "carry slavery to the Pacific Ocean." Territorial Governor Andrew Reeder denounced the fraud but did nothing to overturn it. As a Pierce appointee,
he understood that the president was determined to conciliate southern

Democrats. Few settlers actually brought slaves with them, and many of those who did so imported children, but Kansans were right in bragging that "slavery does now exist there, in fact."[13]

During the battle over his bill, Douglas had insisted that leaving the matter up to the sovereignty of the settlers "would put a final extinguisher upon Abolitionism" by hushing the debate in Washington. Not only had he failed to accomplish the latter, but he had actually expanded the zone of combat into the territories. If Douglas had privately believed that popular sovereignty would result in a free Kansas, he had miscalculated yet again. And if antislavery northerners feared that slavery was about to move into the nation's heartland, it was because southern politicians made their intentions all too apparent. "It is next to impossible to procure white laborers in the west," one Missourian insisted, and "the only labor which can be hired is slave." Only congressional restriction in the Northwest Ordinance of 1787 had kept "the monster" out of Indiana and Illinois, argued the *Chicago Tribune*, and even then slaveholders had routinely sought to overturn the ban. If Congress abandoned its responsibility and left the question to Atchison's "border ruffians," the result would be further proslavery "outrages." As former Illinois Whig Congressman Abraham Lincoln observed, the Kansas-Nebraska Act was "conceived in violence, passed in violence, is maintained in violence, and is being executed in violence."[14]

For more than three decades, most politicians had struggled to avoid sectional issues in favor of a vigorous debate over economic policies. Terrified by the way old bisectional political alliances had collapsed into dangerous sectional divisions during the Missouri debates, moderates had resolutely ignored the issue of slavery, an avoidance only possible so long as the question was that of slavery where it already existed, in the South. As President Martin Van Buren, a Democrat, had famously put it, "We must always have party distinctions, and the old [economic] ones are the best." For years thereafter, the Whigs pursued a pro-business agenda, while the Jacksonian Democrats backed low-tariff policies on behalf of the farmer and the urban laborer. But just as southern men of both parties had opposed Douglas's original bill, many northern Democrats and northern Whigs alike could no longer maintain their silence as slavery expanded into the rich agricultural lands of Kansas. "The more I look at it the more enraged I become," Whig senator William P. Fessenden of Maine admitted, adding that the bill had made him "an out & out abolitionist." Congressman James H. Duncan of Massachusetts, who had supported the Compromise of 1850, expressed similar sentiments. "I now advocate the freedom of Kansas under all circumstances and at all hazards, and the prohibition of slavery in all territories now free."[15]

It did not take long for this growing radicalism among northern voters and politicians to dissolve old political affiliations. In early January of 1854, even before the final vote on the bill, Ohio's Senator Chase, a future presidential aspirant who had been elected on a Democratic–Free Soil fusion ticket, announced himself a man "without a party." Unable to remain in the party of Pierce, Davis, and Douglas, Chase contacted Charles Sumner of Massachusetts, a senator of abolitionist tendencies. With the assistance of New York abolitionist congressman Gerrit Smith and Ohio congressman Joshua R. Giddings, Chase drafted an indictment of the Kansas-Nebraska Act, "The Appeal of the Independent Democrats in Congress to the People of the United States." Published in the antislavery newspaper *National Era* on January 22, the remonstrance accused the Democrats of "a plot against humanity" designed to spread the "blight of slavery [across] the land." One week later, former congressman David Wilmot, the Pennsylvania Democrat who had fought in 1846 to keep slavery out of the Mexican Cession, organized a public meeting designed to transform Chase's protest into a political platform. A group of anti-Nebraska activists meeting at a church in Ripon, Wisconsin, were evidently the first to suggest the label of Republican for the dissenters. On May 9, a conference of thirty congressmen in Washington ratified the proposal that those antislavery Americans who wished to fight for the ideals of 1776 should hereafter "be known as Republicans."[16]

Like many southern planters, Mississippi's Jefferson Davis habitually referred to the Republicans as "the Abolition party." The reality, however, was far more complicated. Although its founding members loudly denounced slave labor as morally unsound and economically wrongheaded, the sole reason for the new party's existence was to reverse Kansas-Nebraska and deny fresh lands in the territories to the institution. Few early adherents called for emancipation in the states where slavery was

entrenched, and most agreed that the Constitution protected unfree labor where sovereign states chose to maintain it. As Lincoln was to explain
in 1858, many party members were only dedicated to banning slavery
from the frontier "during the territorial existence of any one given Territory." When it came time for that territory to draft a constitution and
apply for statehood, the residents could, if they so wished, opt to legal-
ize slavery. But that free-soil settlers might do so would be "an extraor-
dinary thing." The result, Lincoln hoped, was that following congressional
restriction, "there would never be another slave State admitted into the
Union." As Seward explained to a Rochester, New York, audience, a labor
system in which workers drew no wages contained "elements of weakness that must inevitably produce its final extinction." If isolated within
the South, slavery would finally collapse from its economic inefficiency.
The institution, Seward observed, "must either advance or recede—and
that the special business of the republican party was to withstand its ag-
gressions."[17]

Because Democrats in all sections of the nation charged that Republicans not only hoped to abolish slavery but secretly wished to integrate
liberated blacks into white society, party activists replied that they spoke
for the right of *white* pioneers to settle the territories as yeomen farmers.
"We, the Republican party," insisted Illinois senator Lyman Trumbull,
"are the white man's party." The *Hartford Courant* was blunter yet in assuring its readers that Republicans intended to shield the West "from the
pestilential presence of the black man." Free-soil Republicans, of course,
needed to court the voters, whereas abolitionist activists such as Frederick Douglass saw no reason to pander to racist northern sensibilities. But
Republican orators employed the word "white" often enough to make it
clear that most party leaders were not simply appealing to the base instincts of the electorate. As Wilmot explained, he felt "no morbid sympathy for the slave." Rather, his objective was to "preserve to free white
labor a fair country, a rich inheritance, where the sons of toil, of my own
race and color, can live without the disgrace which association with negro slavery brings upon free labor." That the man whose famous 1846
proviso—the unsuccessful 1846 effort to exclude slavery from any Mexican cession lands—had supplied the new party with its core platform
publicly confessed "no squeamish sensitiveness upon the subject of slav-

ery" suggests the depth of racism among party organizers. Wilmot's big-
otry struck a chord. When one Republican minister decided to relocate to
the territories to fight against slavery, he made his goal all too plain. "I kem
to Kansas to live in a free state," he admitted, "and I don't want niggers
a-trampin' over my grave."[18]

Especially among former Whigs, the idea that freed blacks should be
encouraged to emigrate to Liberia, in West Africa, found support among
Republicans. Henry Clay, the longtime Whig standard-bearer and Kentucky slaveholder, had conceded that slavery was evil but doubted that,
once liberated, former slaves could live in harmony among their former
masters. As a young politician, Lincoln had been active in the Illinois
State Colonization Society, and in his 1852 eulogy to his "idol" Clay, he
again argued that the removal of African Americans remained the wisest
answer to the nation's race problems. By the 1850s, however, as Lincoln admitted, there was "not surplus shipping and surplus money enough" to
liberate nearly four million American-born blacks and ferry them across
the Atlantic. Despite its impracticality, "a very large proportion" of Republicans continued to endorse black colonization, and Lincoln all but
admitted that party support for racial "separation" was little more than a
rebuttal to the persistent charge that Republicans wished to eliminate state
laws that forbade "the marrying of white people with negroes."[19]

If racists most of them were, Republicans nonetheless refused to endorse the biological excuses advanced by white southerners in defense
of slavery. By comparison, Georgia's Congressman Stephens thought
it a "great truth, that the negro is not equal to the white man; that
slavery—subordination to the superior race—is his natural and normal
condition." Although advocates of free wage-labor capitalism criticized
the South as economically backward, they blamed the institution of
slavery rather than black workers for southern poverty. A system that
provided laborers with neither wages nor incentives reduced the slave,
Seward charged, to "a brute" incapable of surviving in a modern, diversi-
fied economy. Denied literacy by most southern states, uneducated
slaves doomed the South to remain a rural, agricultural colony of Europe
and the industrializing northern states, Seward added, since mechanized
societies required a labor force "perfected by knowledge and skill." So
when Lincoln discussed the "physical difference between the white and

black races," he was referring not to an impenetrable physiological barrier to African American advancement, but rather to the long history of racism in America that even liberation could not erase. Few Republicans knew blacks intimately or cared to reform existing social or political divisions that existed across the North. But their critique of unwaged labor was unmistakable. Slave or free, blacks, Lincoln insisted, were "entitled to all the natural rights enumerated in the Declaration of Independence, the right to life, liberty, and the pursuit of happiness." When it came to "the right to eat the bread, without the leave of anybody else, which his own hand earns," Lincoln told one audience, "*he is my equal.*"[20]

A few Republicans, moreover, did rise beyond the free-soil standards of the party to earn the label of abolitionists (in that they demanded the immediate emancipation of slaves throughout the nation). Especially in safe political districts, Republicans with no higher aspirations than the Senate or House seat they currently held were free to speak openly. In Pennsylvania, former congressman Thaddeus Stevens (who would resume his career in 1859) advocated black social equality as well as liberation, as did Senator Chase of Ohio. Senator Sumner also hoped that once the "profane assumptions of race" disappeared, black Americans could eventually assume "all the political duties of an American citizen." In the Massachusetts assembly, future governor John Andrew pushed through legislation that opened the state's public schools to all children regardless of race, and in Michigan, DeWitt Leach argued that if all Americans were heirs to the ideals of the Declaration, African Americans were "naturally entitled to all the [political] rights" that any member "of the white race can claim." More prudent Republicans winced at such blunt assertions, so far in advance were they of northern public opinion. But white southerners grasped the implications of even the mildest Republican orations, all of which breathed profound hostility to the planters' way of life. As Lincoln remarked when discussing slavery's expansion into the frontier, there were two sides to the debate, and one of them was simply "in the wrong."[21]

The incessant Republican talk of the virtues of white laboring people proved a powerful draw to northern voters. Evangelical abolitionists in New England called upon white Americans to love African Americans as brothers and sisters, but most Republicans required only that voters reject the planters' refusal to respect "the dignity of labor." Because "agricultural labor is the chief employment of slaves in the South," one observer commented, haughty planters expressed "a contempt" for all labor. As another Republican added, in the North hard work was "held honorable by all" because it was "the vocation of freemen." So where the South maintained a caste system based upon race in which those on the bottom were "always to remain laborers," in the free states industrious young men enjoyed the ability to rise in the world. Although the reality was that many northerners and immigrants would never do so, the theory of free-labor capitalism held obvious attractions for middle-class voters. As Lincoln, born into poverty in Kentucky, lectured one audience, the North forced no class of people "to remain laborers." The "prudent, penniless beginner" who owned nothing more than "the two strong hands that God ha[d] given him, [and] a heart willing to labor" would within a few years "hire others to labor for him." Abolitionists regretted the willingness of Republicans to ignore the real victims of American slavery, yet it was their emphasis on whiteness that made free-soil antislavery politicians infinitely more dangerous to the South. "While the South cannot hear of the abolition plan of Garrison without a shudder," editorialized one Democratic newspaper, "they cannot think of the more stealthy programme of Seward without feeling that it is in reality the same thing, and only the more dangerous in being covered up."[22]

As the election year of 1856 approached, few members of the young party expected to capture the White House. But all hoped to lay the basis for a victory four years hence by contesting the Democrats across the North. Nearly one thousand delegates shoved into Philadelphia's Musical Fund Hall on the morning of June 17. In part because party leaders expected the Democrats, who remained the nation's last bisectional party, to win, bosses such as Thurlow Weed of New York advanced the name of John C. Frémont. Born in Savannah, the tall, handsome Frémont had spent most of his life as an adventurer and an army officer in the West. A former Democrat due to his wife's political connections, he had served as military governor and then senator of California. Weed was a longtime advocate of New York's Seward, who after initially resisting "dissolving the Whig party," had finally joined the Republicans, as had former congressman Lincoln the previous May. But Weed advised Seward to wait until the party was better situated to win a national contest, and so at forty-three Frémont became the youngest man yet nominated for the presidency. The convention briefly considered Lincoln for the vice presidency before settling on William Dayton, a former Whig senator from New Jersey. As the convention reached its final day, delegates Wilmot and Giddings crafted the party's alliterative slogan: "Free Soil, Free Speech, Free Men, and Frémont."[23]

When the Democrats met in Cincinnati that June, they unceremoniously dumped incumbent Franklin Pierce in favor of James Buchanan of Pennsylvania, who had had the good fortune of being stationed abroad as minister to Britain during the fight over Kansas-Nebraska. As he was a "doughface" (a northern man of southern sympathies), convention delegates hoped he might hold the South in place while appealing to northern moderates. Although Douglas received 118 votes to Buchanan's 168 on the convention's tenth ballot, it became clear that the Pennsylvanian was the only candidate capable of achieving the two thirds necessary for a nomination. Douglas did, however, win the consolation prize of having the party platform endorse his doctrine of "congressional noninterference"—a term he had come to favor over the discredited phrase "popular sovereignty"—as the proper formula for settling the territories. In the election, Frémont captured 38 percent of the electoral vote, including the important states Ohio and New York. (The third-party Americans, a nativist, anti-Catholic party commonly known as the Know Nothings, ran former president Millard Fillmore and took only Maryland but received what remained of the old Whig vote in a number of border states.) For Republican bosses, the outcome suggested that those two states would be safe for 1860, and that if the party wished to win in four years, it would have to add the lower North states of Pennsylvania, Indiana, and especially Illinois.[24]

Douglas assuaged the pain of his loss to Buchanan by getting married again, this time to twenty-one-year-old Adele Cutts, the vivacious daughter of a government clerk and the grandniece of Dolley Madison. Although the twenty-two-year difference in their ages was beyond the custom of the day, Douglas's friends thought Adele "unselfish, warm-hearted, unaffected, [and] sincere." A devout Catholic—daguerreotypes of Adele show her wearing a large cross around her neck—she might also be counted on, his supporters hoped, to curtail the senator's fondness for tobacco and alcohol. James Shields, who stood as best man at the wedding, pronounced her "a great benefit" as a political wife. He was right. Within weeks, old friends noticed that Douglas's shabby clothes had been exchanged for tailor-made frock coats, his oily hair was trimmed and washed, and his recently sprouted beard had vanished, never to return. Douglas's heavy drinking, however, continued unabated.[25]

It was not only white voters who followed the events of 1856. Like the men who owned them, slaves were increasingly aware that the Republican Party might one day affect their futures. Denied literacy and access to information, enslaved Americans valued news all the more for it, and those bondpersons who found ways to obtain hearsay shared it with others in the quarters and the fields. South Carolina mistress Mary Boykin Chesnut once pondered the dangers of discussing politics while domestic slaves brought food and cleared the table. Noticing the "profoundly indifferent" Lawrence standing in the doorway, Chesnut suddenly realized the folly of talking "before them as if they were chairs and tables." Were slaves "stolidly stupid or wiser than we are," she wondered, "silent and strong, biding their time?" Waiting for the right moment, of course, was something slaves spent most of their lives learning to do. According to the slave William Webb, other bondmen on his Mississippi plantation prayed that Frémont's election might mean their liberation. "They put all their trust in Frémont to deliver them from bondage," Webb later wrote. When word arrived that the Republicans had lost, a few talked "about rebelling and killing," but several older slaves spoke up to counsel, "Wait for the next four years."[26]

Many southern fire-eaters had less use for patience. Senator Mason of Virginia, a member of the F Street Mess, swore that if Frémont won, the only sane course for his state would be "immediate, absolute, and eternal separation." Republicans might pledge to fight slavery only in the territories, but since their success at capturing governors' chairs and senators' seats reflected "the *growth* of the Anti-slavery feeling at the North," observed fellow messmate Senator Robert M.T. Hunter, would their animosity be satisfied with a mere ban on the frontier? Since Republicans clearly had every intention of surrounding the slave South with free soil, marginalizing its economy and slowly eradicating its style of life, southern whites correctly regarded the "Black Republican party," as Georgia's Howell Cobb dubbed it, as an enemy far more deadly than the nonpartisan supporters of William Lloyd Garrison. Cobb, the secretary of the treasury under Buchanan and a future Confederate general, noted that although the Constitution was explicit on the question of runaway slaves, Republicans had passed a series of state "personal liberty" laws designed to assist the human "property of a citizen of a sister State." If Republicans were prepared to "annul a plain provision of the Constitution," what else might "this party do on the subject of slavery whenever they have the power to act?"[27]

With good reason, planters worried about the inroads Republicans might make in the South with nonslaveholding whites, especially the urban businessmen who had voted Whig prior to the dissolution of that party after the 1852 election. Presidents enjoyed the power of patronage, and once in office an executive such as Seward could appoint southern judges, federal marshals, and especially postmasters who might deliver antislavery literature, currently banned. Rural slaveholders consistently fretted about the loyalty of merchants and traders, who might be drawn to the Whiggish economic policies of a Republican administration. Even if Republicans failed to capture either chamber of Congress in 1860, broad executive powers, one Carolinian worried, could reduce the slave states to a position "of colonial vassalage, stripped of power in the Federal Government." Georgia senator Robert Toombs agreed. The victory of "*any Black Republican*," he warned Stephens, "would abolitionize Maryland in a year, [and] raise a powerful abolition party in Va., Kentucky and Missouri in two years." By 1864, a viable "free labour party" could exist within the "whole South," and agitation currently found only in the free states would "be transferred from the North" into the South. "Then security and peace in our borders," he argued, "is gone forever."[28]

An even greater concern for lowcountry planters was the loyalty of the up-country yeomanry. Despite the economic ties and similarity of pigmentation that yoked the two classes together, politicians like Daniel H. Hamilton worried that Republican rhetoric regarding the virtue of hard labor might appeal to the "3,000,000 of non-slaveholders at the South." Should the Republicans succeed at winning over farmers in the southern states as they had in the Midwest, "the contest for slavery," cautioned the Rhetts' *Charleston Mercury*, would "be in the South, between the people of the South." In hopes of dampening class tensions, elected officials emphasized white privilege. So long as most blacks remained an enslaved underclass, even "the poor white laborer," as Georgia governor Joseph E. Brown argued, belonged "to the only true aristocracy, the race of white men." New England states allowed black men to vote, one southern essayist noted, but "we would keep the white citizen far, far above the black slave." Just in case appeals to racial solidarity were not enough to keep yeomen safely within Democratic ranks, politicians stressed the dangers Republicans posed in a region that was home to four million slaves. Alabama congressman Jabez L. M. Curry warned his constituents that if victorious in 1860, Seward intended to "amalgamate the poor man's daughter and the rich man's buck nigger."[29]

For men like Toombs, the conflict concerning the future of the territories was no abstract debate over constitutional rights. Since masters extracted labor from their unwaged workers only by force—usually with a whip—slavery did not allow for the sort of agricultural diversity that was increasingly the hallmark of the rural North. Although few planters cared to admit it, the Republican free-labor critique of the South accurately emphasized the economic handicaps under which slave societies functioned. African Americans carried on a persistent campaign of sabotage against tools and animals, which forced masters to eschew faster horses for mules and oxen and mechanized reapers for specially made hoes. If cotton did not deplete the soil as had tobacco, the single-crop production mandated by the South's export-based economy did exhaust the land. In short, masters could either transform their unpaid workers into wage-earning laborers and diversify their economy or carry their antiquated mode of production into the western territories. As Rhett Jr. insisted, "expansion shall be the law of the South, as of the North." Unlike New England immediatists, Republicans demanded no abrupt end to slavery in the states where it existed, but their insistence on a free West spelled the doom of slavery within decades. Allow the "bad men" of the free states to move into the northwestern territories, argued Georgia's Herbert Fielder, but leave the Southwest and lands below the Rio Grande to "the institution of African slavery." Southern interests were "radically different from [those] of the Northern people," he added,

"[and] in every aspect in which the Union can be viewed, it is a permanent evil to the South."[30]

Southern imperialists had every expectation of growing cotton in the
New Mexico Territory (which included present-day Arizona), but planters
never restricted their western dreams to a single crop. Louisiana's James
De Bow, publisher of the entrepreneurial *De Bow's Review*, gushed over
the "iron, gold, and diamonds" carried out of Brazilian mines by "30,000
negroes." Like the Rhetts, who routinely emphasized this point in the
Mercury, he saw no reason why the same could not be done with southwestern silver and copper. Although California had entered the Union in
1850 as a free state, much of its coast remained uninhabited, and S. D.
Moore of Alabama thought the southern part of the state "admirably
adapted to the institution of African slavery." Even in frontier Missouri,
the enslaved population increased by more than 30 percent in the 1850s,
from 87,422 slaves to 114,931. Republicans, every bit as much as their
southern counterparts, understood that legislative battles over slavery in
the West had nothing to do with theoretical notions of southern honor
and everything to do with actually keeping unfree labor limited to its
present geography.[31]

Even with its rapidly growing black population, expanding the
empire of slavery would require not just land but also labor. By the late
1850s, many southern whites were beginning to agitate for the reopening
of the Atlantic slave trade, which had been banned by an act of Congress
in 1807. Perhaps because New Orleans had become the southern hub for
young bondpersons sold away from the Chesapeake, De Bow was one of
the leading voices for enlarging this traffic by once again embarking for
African shores. Since West Africans were "but the chattels of their chiefs
and conquerors," he editorialized in his *Review*, "emigration to the soil
of Louisiana would not only be a relief but a positive blessing." Critics
of the Atlantic trade scheme noted that its most enthusiastic advocates
were disunionists, and the fact that Alabama's William Lowndes Yancey
endorsed De Bow's essays did the cause little good among southern
moderates. Since the trade could not be resumed "so long as Alabama
and the other Southern States remained in the Union," observed one disapproving editor, Yancey required "a dissolution of the Union." But
whether the question was a lever to pry the South out of the republic or a

crucial labor requirement for the settling of the West that necessitated secession, proslavery writers like De Bow understood that condemnation of the international trade implied a moral denunciation of the internal sale of blacks. White southerners, De Bow charged, who objected "to the transfer of the rude, benighted, degraded native African to the soil of Louisiana on the score of humanity" implicitly took "the side of our Abolition enemies of the North."[32]

If given access to the fresh lands of the West, and if allowed to import more African captives to break the soil and mine for ore, the nearly four hundred thousand slaveholders of the South could regain their parity in the Senate and protect their capital investment in humans. Modern historians might argue that since most Republicans were not abolitionists, planters should not have responded to their rise with such alarm. But South Carolina senator James Henry Hammond did not care to debate the point. Was there ever a society "persuaded by arguments, human or divine, to surrender, voluntarily, two billion dollars?" he asked. If slavery was allowed to spread into the New Mexico Territory, one southerner anticipated, "Mexico and Cuba would inevitably, with Central America, form a part of the Union," and with the protection of the federal government a pioneer might enter "this new territory with his slaves."[33]

For men such as Hammond, vindication arrived shortly after the election, on March 6, 1857, in the Supreme Court case of Dred and Harriet Scott. Born a slave in Virginia around 1800, Dred Scott had resided in Alabama and Missouri, where in 1832 he had been sold to Dr. John Emerson, a surgeon with the U.S. Army. As he was transferred about the Midwest, Emerson brought Scott with him as his manservant. Emerson and Scott lived for a time at Fort Armstrong, in Illinois, and then at Fort Snelling, then part of the Wisconsin Territory, where Dred married Harriet Robinson, the slave of a federal Indian agent. While still a territory, Illinois had seen slave labor banned under the 1787 Northwest Ordinance, and Fort Snelling rested within the lands prohibited to slavery by the Missouri Compromise. Evidently believing that his position with the military exempted him from regional antislavery laws, Emerson not only purchased Harriet while on free soil, but also hired the Scotts out as domestics and for several months left the territory without them. When the doctor died in St. Louis in 1843, the Scotts hired an attorney, and in 1846 they filed suit against Irene Emerson, John's widow. Since they had not "escap[ed]" from enslaved "labor in one state," Article 4, Section 2, of the Constitution did not apply to them, they argued, and their long residence in free states and territories had effectively liberated them. So began their eleven-year journey through state and federal courts, as the case made its way toward the Supreme Court.[34]

President-elect Buchanan hoped the Court might resolve the question of slavery in the West, and he quietly lobbied Justices John Catron of Tennessee and Robert C. Grier of Pennsylvania to forge a solid consensus so as not to give the appearance that the issue had been settled along sectional lines. (Southern men held a slim five to four majority on the Court.) He need not have bothered. When the decision was handed down on March 6, two days after Buchanan's inauguration, six justices (writing separately) concurred with the "Opinion of the Court" crafted by Chief Justice Roger B. Taney of Maryland. First, over the course of twenty-four pages, Taney explained why the Constitution granted Scott, as a black American, "no rights which the white man was bound to respect," also noting that since the founders believed that blacks could not be citizens, Scott was not eligible to sue in federal court. Having denied Scott legal standing, Taney might have stopped there, but consistent with Buchanan's wish, he hoped to settle the dilemma that had bedeviled a series of presidents and Congresses. Over the next twenty-one pages, Taney ruled that any attempt by Congress to ban slavery from any territory violated a white citizen's Fifth Amendment right to carry his property— whether cattle or humans—into federal lands in the West. As territorial legislatures were inferior to Congress, Taney added, western assemblies could not deny a slaveholder's "right" to enjoy the labor of his slaves either.[35]

Outraged Republicans denounced both sections of the ruling. As Taney had denied the constitutionality of the Northwest Ordinance and the Missouri Compromise (the latter already overturned by the Kansas-Nebraska Act), the Court had effectively ruled the Republican Party's central plank, a congressional ban on slavery in the West, to be unconstitutional. Critics charged that the decision was part of a larger Democratic plot to extend slavery throughout the nation. Democrat Stephen Douglas had opened the lands of Kansas to slavery, Lincoln observed, then Democrat Franklin Pierce had signed the legislation, and now Democrat Roger Taney had provided the Court's stamp of approval. Although Taney had said nothing regarding the right of states to abolish slavery within their boundaries, the Court's lack of precision on this point, in Lincoln's mind, was possibly "a mere omission; but who can be quite sure." Although in fact there was no conspiracy on Douglas's part to do anything more than create a western railroad, Republicans were rightly alarmed by the decision. Many feared that the Court would soon move to reestablish slavery in "Massachusetts and New Hampshire," and Washington's *Union* newspaper, the official mouthpiece of the Buchanan administration, went so far as to editorialize that "*the emancipation of the slaves*" by northern states was "*a gross outrage on the rights of property* [through acts] of coercive legislation."[36]

Northern Democrats laughed at such fears. Yet if Illinois had become a free state largely because it had been set aside in 1787 as a free territory, its state assembly had later passed laws reinforcing the prohibition, and Republicans pointed out that Scott had resided in the state for as long as two years. Moreover, a case that stood a good chance of becoming the "next Dred Scott decision" was then pending in New York. Several years before, Virginian Jonathan Lemmon had brought eight young slaves into the port of Manhattan while preparing to relocate to Texas. Discovering the slaves living in a hotel, a black activist named Louis Napoleon successfully petitioned Superior Court Judge Elijah Paine for a writ of habeas corpus on the grounds that slavery was illegal in the Empire State. Although New York conservatives promptly compensated Lemmon for his losses, the state of Virginia appealed Paine's actions to the New York Supreme Court. In December 1857, that court upheld Paine's decision, writing that when Lemmon carried his slaves to New York he did "not carry there the laws of Virginia." As alarmed by this ruling as Republicans were by Dred Scott, Virginia threatened to appeal to the U.S. Supreme Court if necessary. Lemmon's slaves had been in Manhattan for only three days, yet New York had passed its act of gradual emancipation decades before, in 1799, and for antislavery politicians even the right of brief transit posed a dangerous precedent. "If a man can hold a slave one day in a free state," worried one Republican editor, "why not one month, why not one year?"[37]

It was not just Republicans, however, who were discomfited by Taney's ruling. Since the chief justice, in one of the many curiously unnecessary asides in his decision, had seen fit to deny that even a territorial legislature could ban slavery, the ruling had implicitly gutted Douglas's popular sovereignty argument fully as much as it had explicitly proscribed the Republicans' territorial prohibition. Taney had ruled not just that Congress lacked the power to restrict slavery in a territory, but also that slaves as property could not *be restricted* by any legislative body besides a sovereign state assembly. Recognizing that the decision was unpopular in his home state, Douglas sought to shift the focus to Taney's more accepted dictum that black Americans were not proper candidates for federal citizenship. African Americans belonged to "an inferior race, who in all ages, and in every part of the globe [had] shown themselves incapable of self-government," Douglas lectured one Illinois audience, before adding that the real danger was not Taney's ruling, but rather Republicans who favored the "amalgamation between superior and inferior races."[38]

If Douglas hoped to sidetrack the debate by resorting to racism, he received little help from the new president. Although born in the free state of Pennsylvania, Buchanan had grown up in Mechanicsburg, only ten miles away from Taney's Maryland, a slave state. As a young man, he had bought and freed two female slaves, yet he had retained them for seven years as unpaid domestics, and his long career had been dedicated to conciliating the South. Upon settling into the White House, Buchanan promptly moved to quell the Kansas debate by calling for the creation of a popularly supported constitution, which was part of the normal application process for statehood. But when proslavery settlers met in the town of Lecompton that fall, they crafted a document that revealed the influence of Dred Scott. The "right of an owner of a slave to such slave and its increase," read the first section of the proposed constitution, "is the same and as inviolable as the right of the owner of any property whatever." The Lecompton convention scheduled a vote on the constitution for December 21, 1857, but it stipulated that territorial voters could only choose between the "Constitution with slavery" or the "Constitution without slavery." Contrary to previous practice in other territories, the constitution as a whole would not be submitted to the electorate. The delegates also announced that the vote could only halt the further introduction of slaves into Kansas, and that the small number of bondpersons (or their children) already there would not be affected by the December outcome.[39]

Buchanan's stubborn determination to push for the Lecompton constitution placed Douglas in an impossible position. For the past three years, the senator had assured skeptical Illinois voters that popular sovereignty in the territories would result in a free Kansas. But his legislative handiwork had produced fraud and violence on the frontier and, now, the very real possibility of yet another slave state. Douglas insisted that the proper course was to ignore both the Lecompton document and a rival, free-state Topeka constitution and call for yet another convention, this time with federal protection to ensure a fair election. That the proslavery constitution did not "embody the will of that Territory," Douglas told one correspondent, was obvious to all of Washington. The best defense one could make for popular sovereignty as a concept was that it allowed the voters a choice, but the Lecompton convention, Douglas told another, was a "violation of the fundamental principles of free government." As always, Douglas swore that he cared little whether slavery was "voted down or voted up in Kansas," even as he was keenly aware that it mattered a great deal to his constituents. Since proslavery forces held a slight advantage in the territory, a fair vote might well produce another Lecompton constitution, but Buchanan was unwilling to take that gamble. Instead, the president announced that support for the constitution was a party test for loyal Democrats, adding that Kansas was "at this moment as much a slave state as Georgia or South Carolina."[40]

Since the chaos in Kansas was largely of Douglas's creation, the president assumed that the senator could be counted on to endorse the December 21 vote. For Douglas to do so, however, would mean the end of his career in Illinois and perhaps hurt him with northern voters in 1860. He was up for reelection in just eleven months, and fifty-five of fifty-six home-state papers had announced their opposition to Lecompton. Even loyal Democratic editors blamed Douglas for the mess. Hoping to convince the president to back down, Douglas called at the White House on the morning of December 3. Buchanan, angry but controlled, let Douglas make his case at length before replying. "Mr. Douglas," he warned, "I desire you to remember that no Democrat ever yet differed from an administration of his own choice without being crushed." Comparing himself to Old Hickory, Buchanan cautioned Douglas to "beware the fate of Tallmadge and Rives," two renegade Democrats of the 1830s. "Mr. President," Douglas retorted, "I wish you to remember that General Jackson is dead." Douglas stalked out, and the break was complete.[41]

Six days later, Douglas rose in the Senate to formally announce his opposition. The Lecompton constitution was such a "flagrant violation of popular rights in Kansas" that he felt compelled to "resist to the last." One week later, territorial governor Robert J. Walker, who had accepted the post only after receiving assurances from Buchanan that he would be allowed to lead "an impartial administration," resigned and charged the president with betrayal. As both Douglas and Walker had feared, the December 21 election produced a lopsided vote of 6,266 to 567. Despite the fact that the free-soil forces had boycotted the election, Buchanan declared himself satisfied with the results and urged Congress to consent to statehood. With Douglas in the minority, the Senate concurred, but in the House a coalition of Republicans and northern Democrats defeated the bill. Indiana Democrat William H. English produced a new measure that called for another territorial referendum on Lecompton, and this time, on August 2, 1858, the proslavery constitution lost handily. Kansas was to remain a territory until 1861.[42]

Douglas knew that his battle against Lecompton could jeopardize his presidential dreams. Saving his career in Illinois and holding on to his Senate seat required defying the president and powerful southern Democrats. But Douglas calculated—incorrectly, as usual—that southern memories might begin to fade and southern hearts begin to forgive. The *Charleston Herald*, normally a milder journal than the Rhetts' *Mercury*, denounced the Little Giant. "That Douglas has shown himself a traitor to the South," it editorialized, "there remains no longer room to doubt." By fighting to keep slavery out of Kansas after first raising proslavery hopes by getting the Missouri Compromise repealed, Douglas had "gone over to the Black Republicans" and wore Cain's "black mark of Abolitionism upon [his] brow." Southern whites had every expectation of winning in Kansas, but thanks to Douglas's "betray[al]," one Georgian snarled, "our victory is turned to ashes." As more and more northern Democrats abandoned their party or went down to defeat in election after election, the party's base increasingly lay in the South; as the *Herald* aptly remarked, "the Democratic party is a proslavery party." Douglas yet hoped to win the South back and secure the nomination, but Carolinians announced that they needed "no alliance with those who are polluted with the leprosy of Abolitionism."[43]

For Yancey, the failure of the Democratic president and party to secure Kansas as slave soil meant not that a Douglas candidacy had to be avoided, but rather that white southerners had to be made to understand that "no National Party can save us." After contacting Edmund Ruffin, Virginia's most dogmatic fire-eater, Yancey launched his League of United Southerners. In lengthy essays published in the *Montgomery Advertiser* and *De Bow's Review* in the late spring and early summer of 1858, Yancey proposed the creation of "Committees of Safety all over the cotton States" in which like-minded secessionists could "fire the Southern heart—instruct the Southern mind—[and] give courage to each other." Organized along the lines of northern labor unions, regional associations would be instructed to select delegates to a general council, and those delegates—no more than one for each thirty members—could take their seats on the council for a twenty-dollar fee. The council would then create executive committees and name a league president, vice president, and executive secretary. After enough southern Democrats came to the realization that their way of life was imperiled by union with northern men, the league, "by one organized, concerted action," could "precipitate the cotton States into revolution."[44]

As ever, Yancey was utterly candid regarding his intentions. One Virginia unionist charged that the league's conventions were chiefly designed to "bring together" the most active "politicians and secessionists as would enable them to make their organization more complete and more perfect for dissolution." Yancey was particularly blunt when promoting his league in Columbia, South Carolina. He described a proslavery republic that stretched as far south as the Isthmus of Panama, but for that to occur, he reminded his audience, they needed a new influx of African slaves. That stood little chance of success so long as the Carolinas remained within the United States. To uphold southern rights, the forty-four-year-old orator shouted, proslavery forces needed to "make a contest in the Charleston Convention" and defeat the candidacy of Douglas.

Elevating a southern Democrat into the White House might buy time, he admitted, but if a "Black Republican" won the election, the slave-holding states should secede before a Seward or a Chase could take the oath of office. If a Democrat carried the day, the South should demand the immediate repeal of all laws that hindered the advance of slavery, such as the 1807 prohibition on the Atlantic slave trade, and if that failed to happen, it should retire from the Union.[45]

For Douglas, 1858 dawned as the most troubled year yet in a career that had once held such promise. Despite his successful battle against the Lecompton constitution, he remained trapped by the consequences of his own territorial program. Try as he might to distance himself from an increasingly unpopular president and an ancient, equally unpopular chief justice, northern voters justly blamed the Democratic Party for restoring slavery to the national agenda after the Compromise of 1850 had briefly buried the question. Douglas yet hoped to replace Buchanan in 1860, but if he publicly admitted what he privately told Illinois supporters—that he had always believed that popular sovereignty would result in free soil—he would only further infuriate already livid southern Democrats. He realized, however, that he might have to do just that. Having conceded Illinois to Buchanan in 1856, the Republicans regarded the state, the *New York Times* observed, as "the most interesting political battle-ground in the Union." If Douglas lost his seat, his party might look elsewhere for a northern champion. Yet to remain viable with the southern base of the party in 1860, he could not afford to alienate proslavery advocates as he attempted to win back suspicious free-state Illinoisans. Walking this tightrope, Douglas knew, would be no easy task.[46]

Douglas's job was further complicated by the fact that several power-ful Chicago Democrats remained loyal to Buchanan, and in Springfield—in a troublesome harbinger of things to come—Democrats splintered into two rival conventions as they struggled to select a senatorial nominee. A few Republicans, more interested in winning than in ideological purity, briefly considered endorsing Douglas if he lost his party's nomination, on the grounds that he was no longer a Buchanan man. But former congressman Lincoln, who also coveted the seat, responded that while the senator might have had "a little quarrel with the present head of the dynasty," he did "not *promise* to *ever*" become a Republican. With the move

toward fusion beaten back, both Douglas and Lincoln obtained their respective party's nomination. Jubilant Democrats crowed over the Republican selection, regarding Lincoln as easy prey. Douglas thought
otherwise. "I shall have my hands full," he confided to one supporter.
"He is as honest as he is shrewd, and if I beat him my victory will be
hardly won."[47]

Lincoln also understood the difficulty of his quest. He had first met
Douglas twenty-two years before, in the fall of 1834 in the then–state
capital of Vandalia. Mary Todd Lincoln had known the young Douglas,
with whom she had flirted before recognizing that he was not yet interested in matrimony. But winning Mary's hand was the sole victory for
Lincoln in what was to become a lifelong contest between the two men.
He watched as the younger Douglas won election to the state legislature,
served as Illinois's secretary of state, and at the age of twenty-seven was
appointed to the state Supreme Court. Two terms in the national House
elevated Douglas into the Senate in 1847, and in 1853 he was reappointed
to the seat by the state assembly. Lincoln was also hobbled by his own
views on racial equality, which were progressive by midwestern standards (if conservative in comparison to positions held by New England
abolitionists). Whereas Douglas agreed with Taney that the Declaration
of Independence was never intended to apply to African Americans,
Lincoln insisted that the founding generation "meant" what "they said"
when it came to the inalienable rights of life, liberty, and the pursuit of
happiness. Twenty members of Springfield's small black community
resided within three blocks of Lincoln, and if he and Mary knew most of
them as domestics, he never shared the Democratic view that blacks were
"a nuisance, to the people of Illinois." However, as a clever attorney who
had learned how to play to a jury, Lincoln avoided fiery polemics in favor of humor and logic, and as a moderate he had grudgingly endorsed
the hated Fugitive Slave Act of 1850. The perennially race-baiting
Douglas might try, but depicting the witty, self-effacing Lincoln as a
radical abolitionist would prove difficult.[48]

As the clear front-runner, Douglas planned a safe campaign. He
intended to travel the state, delivering vague, carefully crafted speeches
that extolled the "sacred" democratic principles embedded within popular sovereignty, while charging that unnamed Republicans wished "to

vote, and eat, and sleep, and marry with Negroes." Instead of scheduling a rival tour, however, Lincoln initially chose to shadow Douglas across Illinois, often speaking in the same venues as had his opponent the day before. In one instance, Lincoln arrived at a lecture hall just as Douglas was finishing his address; he stood on the stairway and shouted that he would respond to Douglas's speech the next evening. But Democrats seldom remained to listen, and on July 24, Lincoln wrote to his old adversary to suggest that they "divide time and address the same audiences during the present canvass." Douglas was annoyed that Lincoln had "waited until after" he had finalized his schedule to make the request. But, regarded as one of the party's leading orators, he could not decline the challenge. Compared to the complicated negotiations that precede modern debates, the arrangement was simplicity itself. Douglas recommended a total of seven confrontations and agreed to Lincoln's proposal that they "alternately open and close the discussion." Each debate was set for three hours. For the first, in Ottawa, Douglas was to speak for the first hour; Lincoln could reply for "an hour and a half, and [Douglas would] then follow for half an hour." The two agreed to "alternate in like manner at each successive place."[49]

Debates rarely change many minds, but in their second meeting, held in the town of Freeport on August 27, Lincoln cornered his opponent in a fashion that further clouded Douglas's presidential prospects. Lincoln spoke first, and during his opening comments the lanky attorney challenged Douglas to explain how popular sovereignty might be reconciled with the hated Dred Scott decision. Forced into elaborating a point that he had hinted at the previous summer, Douglas angrily replied that, Taney notwithstanding, "the people of a Territory can, by lawful means, exclude slavery from their limits prior to the formation of a State Constitution." As Jonathan Lemmon had discovered, enslaved property tended to slip away, especially when aided by free blacks and radical whites. "Slavery cannot exist a day or an hour anywhere, unless it is supported by local police regulations," Douglas reminded the audience. Before planters would carry their expensive unfree workers into frontier lands, they required security in the form of the extensive slave codes that had existed for nearly two centuries in the Atlantic seaboard states. If settlers opposed to slavery failed to pass the necessary legislation, they could "effectually prevent the introduction of it into their midst," and so it "matters not what the Supreme Court may hereafter decide."[50]

What came to be known as the Freeport Doctrine quite possibly saved Douglas's career in Illinois. Because the legislature (rather than a popular vote) decided who would represent the state in Washington, however, that remains in some doubt. When Election Day came, Republican candidates for the assembly actually outpolled their Democratic rivals by a vote of 125,430 to 121,609, but because of the way the districts were gerrymandered, the Democrats retained a majority of state seats. When the legislature met on January 9, 1859, to select the winner, it chose Douglas by a tally of fifty-four to forty-six. When informed of his victory, Douglas, with less than complete accuracy, responded, "Let the voice of the people rule." But his triumph was short-lived. Southern Democrats, already furious over the senator's battle against Lecompton, were now more determined than ever to deny Douglas the presidential nomination and to defend their Court-granted rights in the territories (which they regarded as much the same thing). As for the loser, two days after the election ended, the Lacon *Illinois Gazette* ran a banner headline: ABRAHAM LINCOLN FOR PRESIDENT IN 1860.[51]

Not that the troubled year that preceded the presidential contest did not hold perils for the Republicans as well. Southern fire-eaters already had trouble distinguishing between mainstream free-soil politicians and so-called physical-force abolitionists, and that confusion was only increased by one activist determined to carry the struggle into the heart of Virginia. Funded by a handful of wealthy abolitionists, including New York's Gerrit Smith, John Brown and an interracial band of twenty men planned to seize the federal arsenal at Harpers Ferry. Located at the northern end of the Shenandoah Valley, the rail exchange was home to twenty-five hundred people, including 1,251 free blacks and 88 slaves. Although the gorge carved by the upper Potomac was inhospitable to large plantations, nearby Jefferson and Clarke counties contained 7,300 slaves. Brown hoped to liberate enough men to set up an impregnable guerrilla base in the Allegheny Mountains, from which they could stage further raids and spark a revolution that might roll southward. "If I could conquer Virginia," Brown explained, "the balance of the Southern states would nearly conquer themselves, there being such a large amount of slaves in them."[52]

Harpers Ferry awoke on the morning of October 17 to discover the telegraph wires cut, the trains halted, and the town occupied by Brown's small force. His raiders brought with them two hundred breech-loading .52-caliber Sharps carbines, and they expected to hand out the nearly one hundred thousand muskets and rifles stored in the armory. Understanding that slaves would have to learn to use complicated weapons, the invaders also carried a thousand pikes, long spears with razor-sharp bowie knives attached to each end. But the slaves, never notified of the plot, failed to rally to Brown's cause. Arriving instead was a company of marines, led by Colonel Robert E. Lee and Lieutenant J. E. B. Stuart. After a brief but bloody battle in the brick engine house of the arsenal, the marines killed two of the raiders and captured Brown and six others. Within days, Brown, "cut thrust and bleeding and in bonds," was tried on charges of insurrection and conspiracy and sentenced to hang on De cember 2 in nearby Charlestown.[53]

Militant slaves across the state responded to Brown's capture using the only method available to them, burning barns and plantation buildings. One editor, with perhaps a bit of hyperbole, reported that Jefferson County "was illuminated by the lurid glare of burning property." A correspondent of Governor Henry A. Wise assured Richmond officials that "three stockyards" had "been burnt in this county alone since [Brown's] capture and trial." Wise rushed five hundred militiamen to the county, but frightened whites applied their own kind of terror by lynching free blacks. Virginia fire-eater Ruffin, a member of Yancey's league, had one of the captured pikes sent to each southern state capital as a tangible reminder of what Brown had hoped to do to slaveholders.[54]

Concerned that white southerners regarded Brown as a typical Yankee, Republicans stumbled over one another in their haste to denounce the raid. Charles Sumner insisted that "of course [Brown's] act must be deplored." Lincoln criticized the action as "so absurd" that even nearby slaves "saw plainly enough it could not succeed." But northern reformers did little to quiet southern fears. The mayor of Albany, New York, organized a one-hundred-gun salute timed to coincide with the moment of Brown's death. Church bells tolled from Iowa to Boston, and at public prayer meetings in Syracuse, Rochester, and Manhattan speakers praised the martyred saint. In Concord, Massachusetts, Henry David Thoreau delivered a speech in honor of the "crucified hero," and at the close of his remarks William Lloyd Garrison, normally the most pacific of abolitionists, rose to charge the cheering crowd: "Success to every slave insurrection at the South, and in every slave country."[55]

Befitting his role as Republican front-runner, Seward received most of the abuse from planters and their northern allies. South Carolina's James Chesnut rose in the Senate to charge that Seward's rhetorical allusions to free-labor capitalism "invading" the border South had inspired "much of the violence we have seen in the country." One furious Virginian placed an advertisement in a Richmond newspaper offering fifty thousand dollars for the "head of that traitor William H. Seward." The New Yorker responded that he had met Brown only once in his life, but that did little to put a damper on Democratic fury. Hoping to regain the goodwill of southern Democrats, Douglas alleged that the raid was the "natural, logical, inevitable result of the doctrines and teachings of the Republican party." As if Brown had not been sufficiently hanged by the state of Virginia, Douglas introduced a Senate resolution demanding a law that would make it a federal crime to conspire "with intent to steal or run away [with] negroes or horses." He indicated that such legislation should be effective in both states and territories, which came close to nullifying his own Freeport Doctrine. Few, if any, angry southern Democrats noticed the contradiction.[56]

This furor all transpired with the Republican National Convention a short four months away. By election's eve, the white South was more convinced than ever that theirs was a society under siege. Outnumbered in the general population and thus in the House of Representatives, slaveholders could expect to retain no more than 83 of 233 congressional seats in the upcoming election. In past years, planters had relied on such supportive doughfaces as Pierce and Buchanan to protect their interests, but after Lecompton and Freeport few trusted Douglas to do them a similar favor. Whether Republican or northern Democrat, fretted South Carolina planter William Elliott, free-state supporters of John Brown wished them "such security as is found in St. Doming[ue]," the site of the massive 1791 Caribbean slave revolt. For more than a decade, secessionists like Rhett and Yancey had fought for their cause, but with scant success. With his raid, Brown changed that dynamic, but he did not do so alone. The person who set events in motion by tearing open the precarious peace achieved by the Compromise of 1850 was no abolitionist. It was Douglas, and rarely has a single politician helped produce such national chaos. Unless Douglas and the Democrats "recognized the constitutional rights of the South," declared South Carolina planter John Townsend in early 1860 in his aptly titled *The South Alone Should Govern the South and African Slavery Should Be Controlled by Those Only Who Are Friendly to It*, it would be the duty of "the Southern States, to take their destinies under their own control." They must "prepare, without delay, to organize for themselves a separate and independent Confederacy." Townsend urged his readers to consider his words, and then send the pamphlet along "to your Neighbor."[57]

CHAPTER TWO

"Douglas or Nobody"

The Democrats

AT AGE TWENTY-FOUR, William Lowndes Yancey killed a man. While visiting in South Carolina, he murdered his wife's uncle in a brawl. Convicted of manslaughter and sentenced to one year in prison, Yancey was pardoned by the governor after just three months. The unarmed victim, Dr. Robinson Earle, had insulted the young Yancey, who, as bad luck would have it, had been armed with a pistol, a knife, and a sword. But as Yancey saw it, he had fulfilled his "duty as a man, & he who grossly insulted [him] lies now, with a clod upon his bosom." Less than a decade later, then–Congressman Yancey fought a bloodless duel with a politician who opposed the annexation of Texas. (Both deliberately shot to miss, but honor was satisfied.) As 1860 dawned, Yancey was not yet fifty, but chronic neuralgia had bleached his hair gray and left him "with a decided stoop in his shoulders." Much to the surprise of one northern observer, though, there was "not the slightest symptom of the fanatic about him." So sure was Yancey in his quest for slaveholders' rights that his "convictions" were never "disturbed for a moment." He habitually wore a smile, and with good reason. In the South he was usually surrounded by "a multitude of admirers." But even were he to face a howling mob, the same observer marveled, his smile "would hardly darken a shade." Now Yancey intended to execute the same service on his Democratic Party that he had once performed on Dr. Earle.[1]

One may well wonder if there was a connection between Yancey's stormy personal history and his detestation of antislavery activists. Born in Georgia, the son of a former South Carolina state legislator, Yancey lost his father before he was three. His mother, Caroline Bird Yancey, remarried to Nathan Beman, a Presbyterian minister who demanded the sale (rather than the liberation) of his wife's slaves. The family then moved to Troy, New York, where William's stepfather became active in the abolitionist movement. But the household was not happy, and young William witnessed constant, bitter arguments between his parents, as well as emotional and perhaps physical abuse visited upon his mother. Yancey grew to despise Beman, whom he regarded as the hypocritical personification of all religiously inspired northern reformers.[2]

In 1833, Yancey decided to return to the world he admired and understood. He quit Williams College before graduating and settled in Greenville, South Carolina, where he read law. Marriage to Sarah Caroline Earle, the daughter of a wealthy planter, brought him thirty-five slaves and restored to him the privilege his stepfather had abandoned. Horrified by this news, Beman first demanded that his wife sever all contacts with her son and then, when she failed to do so, ordered her to return to the South (but not before seizing her assets). Beman's cruelty completed Yancey's political maturation, and upon gaining a seat in Congress in 1844, the young fire-eater eschewed all compromise in favor of absolute southern privilege. His rigid positions won him few allies in Washington, and in 1846 he resigned his seat but remained the leader of Alabama's dogmatic states' rights faction.[3]

Despite his occasional bouts of ill health, Yancey was indefatigable after founding his League of United Southerners. Although he insisted that the Republicans were positioned to capture the White House in 1860, a Democratic Party united behind a northern candidate would most likely have prevailed. The simple truth is that Yancey, like Robert Barnwell Rhett, believed that slaveholding interests were no longer safe within the republic no matter how pro-southern a president might be. As the *Wisconsin Patriot* editorialized in 1860, Yancey had been a "disunionist" for at least twelve years, having marched out of the 1848 Democratic convention in protest of candidate Lewis Cass's advocacy of popular sovereignty. Just one delegate had joined Yancey's otherwise solitary remonstration, and the editor prayed, futilely, as events were to show, that southern Democrats would not this time "follow [him] into the dismal bogs and mephitic vapors of fanaticism."[4]

To ensure that they would, Yancey began his machinations early; he had no desire to wait until the national convention in April to dismantle his party. Delegates for the national meeting were chosen in state conventions, and as leader of Alabama's fire-eaters, Yancey was guaranteed a seat when the body convened on January 11. Determined to force a unified

Dubbed "the prince of the fire-eaters" by journalist Murat Halstead,
former Alabama congressman William Lowndes Yancey advocated secession
as early as 1850. His haughty expression masked a lifetime of poor health;
Yancey would die in July 1863 at the age of forty-eight.
Courtesy Library of Congress.

southern response to Douglas's Freeport Doctrine, Yancey submitted
nine resolutions designed to protect slavery in the territories. The articles held that neither Congress nor territorial legislatures could "abolish
slavery or prohibit the introduction of the same, or impair by unfriendly
legislation, the security" of slave property. Should territorial assemblies
attempt to do so, "the principles enunciated by Chief Justice Taney" required the federal government to step in and "protect the rights of the
owner of such property." The final resolution required Alabama's entire
delegation to withdraw from the convention if this proposed platform
was not adopted. When retired diplomat John Forsyth jumped to his feet
to insist that the resolutions were designed to dissolve the party and
the Union, Yancey merely smiled thinly and called for a vote, which
carried.[5]

The demand for federal protection of slavery on the frontier did more
than worry Yancey's critics in Alabama. It placed other southern Democrats in an untenable position. Possible presidential candidates Jefferson
Davis of Mississippi and Robert M.T. Hunter of Virginia opposed Yancey's
divisive tactics, understanding full well that he hoped to fracture their
party. Yet as sound proslavery men, they shared his concerns regarding
Republican clout, and more to the point, they recognized that their constituents shared his fears. Those who wished to keep the Democrats intact could only hope that enough delegates in Charleston might rally
behind a southern candidate who embraced Yancey's Alabama Platform. Should a northern candidate refuse to do so and the party splinter
into pieces, Yancey would achieve his goal of throwing "off the shackles
both of parties and of the government, and assert[ing] their independence in a Southern Confederacy."[6]

Other southern Democrats, however, welcomed Alabama's tactics on
the grounds that the Charleston convention would have to repudiate
Douglas as a candidate as well as his Freeport "heresy." Fully aware that
Douglas would never consent to run at the head of a ticket burdened
with a proslavery platform, Senator Robert Toombs of Georgia expected
Yancey's "mischief" to result in Douglas's defeat in the convention
while leaving the party intact. During the previous year, Douglas had
warned that no nominee could "ever carry any one Democratic State of
the North" with a platform that forced slavery on settlers "when they do

not want it." Yet Douglas's battle against the Lecompton constitution, James De Bow observed, made southerners determined to ensure "his defeat in the nominating convention," and Yancey's demands for a federal slave code in the territories tore open this unhealed wound. As Louisiana senator (and future Confederate secretary of state) Judah P. Benjamin charged, Douglas was little more than a Republican in disguise, and his policy of "squatter sovereignty" marked him as the party's "fallen star."[7]

In hopes of regaining control of the increasingly disunion-minded party, Davis sought to soften Yancey's platform and make it his own. Rising in the Senate on February 2, Davis reframed Alabama's demands as six resolutions. Far more theoretical than Yancey's original platform, Davis's motion provided the constitutional groundwork for the expansion of slavery into the territories. But Davis, normally the most practical of politicians, did not expect senatorial approval of his positions. Rather, he hoped to impose a doctrinal test on northern Democrats. By calling for a "vote upon them severally," Davis intended to force each party member to take a formal position on what the white South now regarded as the most critical issue of the day—the expansion of slavery—while highlighting candidate Douglas's opposition to this core demand. Just to make sure that the Democracy stood for slaveholders' rights, Davis also paid a call on Buchanan, despite the unpopular president's lame-duck status.[8]

Davis's theoretical positions amounted to nothing new. His claim that the territories were "the common possession" of all of the states—which meant that Congress could not "give advantage to the citizens of one State" and their forms of chattel over the human property owned by residents "of every [southern] State"—had been advanced years before by South Carolina's long-deceased John C. Calhoun. Davis also softened Yancey's demand for immediate federal protection in the West, asserting that the federal government should step in only if the courts failed "to insure adequate protection" for slave property. But the Mississippian cautioned that southern masters had grown weary of the personal liberty laws passed by northern legislatures, which were designed to provide runaway slaves with the modicum of legal protection denied them by the Fugitive Slave Act of 1850. Should the North continue to "nullify" federal law, "the States injured by such breach" of their constitutional rights would have to consider secession as the "proper mode and measure of redress." States' rights southerners, of course, had denounced invasive federal might and sought refuge in nullification since the 1830s, so Davis's demands for federal authority in the West and condemnation of state legislation protecting the rights of accused runaways fueled northern claims that slaveholders routinely shifted their ideological ground in the name of protecting unfree labor.[9]

As was his style, Douglas fought back hard. For the most part, Republicans in the Senate left the debate to Democrats, content to observe as their opponents ripped their party asunder. As tempers frayed, members of Congress began to hide guns and knives within their waistcoats. "I believe every man in both houses is armed with a revolver," admitted South Carolina's James Henry Hammond, "some with two & a bowie knife." Davis's resolutions never reached the floor, but on March 1 the Democratic caucus adopted a modified version of his three key declarations. The revised statement clarified when the federal government would be compelled to take action by adding the words "territorial government" to the list of offices that might fail to pass or enforce legislation necessary to protect slavery in the West. Understanding that the caucus had adopted the three resolutions in expectation of including them in the party's platform come April, Douglas's backers angrily announced that they refused to be bound by the vote and criticized the caucus for its "tyranny and usurpation." But as Buchanan and a majority of Democratic senators had endorsed the resolutions, Douglas could not claim he had not been warned. And the Charleston convention was but seven weeks away.[10]

Truculent as ever, Douglas had no interest in altering course, and Davis and the caucus notwithstanding, most American voters regarded the Illinoisan as the front-runner for his party's nomination. Douglas had announced his candidacy early in the previous fall, and before Congress had reconvened in December 1859 he had delivered major speeches in Columbus and Cincinnati, Ohio. A lengthy essay defending his popular sovereignty platform was published in *Harper's Magazine*, and as the most viable northern Democrat in the race, Douglas continued to hammer away at the idea that only he could defeat Seward and the "Black

Republicans." Although Douglas injured the truth by insisting that the compromisers of 1850 had intended to repeal previous restrictions on slavery in other territories, he was right enough in observing that popular sovereignty in the Southwest had been "ratified by the people in the Presidential election of 1852" and "incorporated into the Cincinnati platform in 1856," which had elevated Buchanan into the White House. Republican editor Horace Greeley confidently predicted that Douglas would "be the nominee of the Charleston Convention." The senator remained, "in the eyes of the Democratic masses in the Free States, the champion and embodiment of the principle of Popular Sovereignty," which struck many voters as the only middle ground left to an increasingly polarized electorate.[11]

As far as most northern Democrats were concerned, their party had paid too high a price for its long-standing willingness to give way to southern demands. Before the 1854 elections, northern Democrats had held ninety-two congressional seats, while their southern counterparts had possessed sixty-seven. But Kansas-Nebraska, Dred Scott, and Lecompton had cost northerners dearly, and as they faced 1860, northern Democrats retained only thirty-two seats (while southern Democrats had picked up just two, for a total of sixty-nine). If the candidate to emerge from Charleston was a southern planter or a northern doughface, nervous northern Democrats could expect another round of losses at the polls. So when Douglas announced that he had no intention of making "peace with [his] enemies" or conceding "one iota of principle" to the southern wing of the party, northern Democrats took heart. As his official campaign biography boasted, Douglas's policies were "equally remote from the fanaticism of the North and the fanaticism of the South."[12]

The fact that Douglas saw no moral distinction between the two sectional groups he denounced as equally "fanatical"—one of whom wanted to immediately eradicate human bondage, while the other wished to perpetuate it where it existed and carry it into the West—earned the senator a handful of supporters in the South. Southern unionists accepted the argument that Douglas was the only candidate who enjoyed enough bisectional support "to defeat the Black Republicans and to save us from their dreaded domination." Unwilling to concede that some fire-eaters actually prayed for a Republican victory, a handful of editors from Georgia to Texas decried the "ungrateful, suicidal [hostility] of Southern men towards Mr. Douglas." They emphasized how the senator's commitment to "manifest destiny" benefited slaveholders not merely in Kansas but also in the Caribbean. "He is an ardent friend of the acquisition of Cuba," one Macon, Georgia, newspaper observed, "negroes and all, and of keeping it a slave State." A second one added that Douglas had voted to retain the Gag Rule, which prohibited Congress from accepting antislavery petitions, and noted also that he was one of the first to speak against "the foul injustice" of the Wilmot Proviso. "Douglas has fought a hundred battles for the South, and not one against her," added still another. In writing this, the editor tactfully declined to mention the Lecompton fight, but then, supporting the lesser of two evils was already an old practice in American politics.[13]

An angry and ideologically driven southern majority, however, stubbornly refused to accept Douglas's inevitability. Some southern Democrats suspected that Douglas's decision to oppose the Lecompton constitution had less to do with his need to preserve his career in Illinois than it did with preparing "the road for deserting the [Democratic] camp and openly joining the enemy." And since Douglas had hinted on more than one occasion that he expected popular sovereignty in Kansas to result in free soil, even those southern voters who did not believe he planned to switch parties saw little to distinguish his policies from those of his 1858 opponent in the senatorial race. Why should they bother to remain loyal to a party, some wondered, if a Douglas presidency differed from a Seward presidency only on "this abstract question" of means? The planter class was determined to carry slavery into the West, and if Douglas's Freeport Doctrine kept it from doing so, he was "no better than a Black Republican, at whose election the Union should be dissolved."[14]

Those Democrats determined to find another candidate had more than a few options. As early as the summer of 1859, the editor of the *Boston Courier* marveled that there were "now twenty-four known [Democratic] candidates for the Presidency." The *New York Herald* raised the figure to twenty-six. Some, such as Jefferson Davis and Senator Andrew Johnson of Tennessee, were serious contenders. Treasury Secretary Howell Cobb of Georgia and Vice President John C. Breckinridge of Kentucky made the list owing to their visibility within the Buchanan administration, while Sam Houston, Henry A. Wise, and Horatio Seymour were the current or former governors of Texas, Virginia, and New York, respectively. Other potential candidates were more obscure or eccentric; failed president Franklin Pierce appeared on the *Herald*'s roll. Yet antebellum conventions were notorious for deadlocking over the front-runners and producing dark horse candidates, such as James K. Polk, who had gone on to victory. Seasoned political observers assumed that delegates pledged to the lesser candidates would unite in opposition to Douglas. After numerous ballots, Douglas's handlers might concede defeat, and the delegates in Charleston, "untrammeled by [previous state] instructions," could then "take counsel together as they have heretofore done" and unite around the candidate with the least political baggage.[15]

For many southerners, the most obvious candidate was the very man determined to deny Douglas the presidential nod. Davis, nearly fifty-two, was a staunch proslavery man but never an "ultra." Born in Kentucky, the planter had an impressive résumé: congressman, secretary of war under Pierce, senator (with a hiatus during his cabinet term) since 1847, and chairman of the Senate Committee on Military Affairs. After a string of northern presidential candidates—Cass of Michigan, Pierce from New Hampshire, and Buchanan of Pennsylvania—slaveholding Democrats believed that the South was "*entitled* to the candidate" in 1860. Realistic delegates understood that a fire-eater could not carry a single northern county, but Davis, a tall, reserved West Point graduate who had served with distinction in the Mexican-American War, "might be the man," as one Alabama paper editorialized, "to beat the Black Republicans." Fearful that a Republican victory would mean disunion, some conservative northern editors gushed over Davis's "eminent abilities and distinguished services." Even in Garrison's Massachusetts, talk was rife that a fusion ticket of Davis and Edward Everett, a former Whig governor and senator in the state, could secure enough electoral votes to prevent a Republican triumph.[16]

In a century when it was regarded as unseemly to openly desire political power, American statesmen, and particularly southerners, had mastered the art of advancing their interests while appearing utterly uninterested in public office. Davis advocated the renomination of

Pierce, but although the New Englander had supported slaveholders' rights, no serious person thought his nomination likely. Andrew Johnson, who opposed Davis's Senate resolutions as unnecessarily divisive and was himself interested in a spot on the ticket, believed that Davis was "burning up with ambition." Two years before, Davis had journeyed to New England to test the political waters. A speech at Boston's Faneuil Hall—where he shared the stage with Everett—made a "profound impression," if only because he carefully glossed over sectional differences. Among those Davis courted was Massachusetts's Caleb Cushing, whom he had known when the latter was attorney general in the Pierce administration. Cushing judged it unlikely that Douglas could obtain the nomination after his public break with Buchanan, and rumor had it that he and Davis had discussed a possible Cushing vice presidency.[17]

Within the cabinet, Secretary Cobb hoped his dutiful service might win him the endorsement of Buchanan, and he was not above providing Washington editors with lucrative printing contracts with the Treasury Department in exchange for positive reporting. But the president declined to endorse anyone before the convention (apart from insisting that the nominee should not be Douglas). Neither did former president John Tyler, who fantasized that the party might reward him for acquiring Texas with a second, nonconsecutive term. Upon realizing that "the whole South," in fact, would not "rally with a shout" were his name to be placed in contention, the Virginian, who at fifty-one had been the country's youngest president, instead endorsed Breckinridge, who at thirty-six had become the nation's youngest vice president. Like Davis, the handsome Breckinridge enjoyed considerable support in the North. Because of his formal deportment and the lack of rhetorical fireworks in his oratory, Breckinridge was widely perceived to be more moderate than his positions might suggest. There "will be, virtually, no contest if Mr. Breckinridge be nominated," insisted one Pennsylvania editor. Although no "fire-eater," the editor added, Breckinridge was a good proslavery man who "detests fanaticism and [the] absurdities into which it has driven Seward Republicans."[18]

If Senator Johnson regarded Davis as overly striving, it was in part because he recognized that defect in himself. Born into poverty in North Carolina, Johnson lacked the national stature enjoyed by fellow senators

Douglas and Davis. Yet he could claim better bisectional support. A former governor and congressman, Johnson had advocated a homestead bill, and the possibility of free land in the West appealed to the farmers who comprised a majority of voters in both sections. When queried by the editor of the Chattanooga *Advertiser*, Johnson provided the bland answer required of any interested candidate. He did not seek higher office, yet neither could he decline the honor. Given the large number of potential candidates and the nearly unanimous southern enmity toward Douglas, Johnson's chances, mused another editor, were at least on par with the Illinois senator's. Yet Johnson, who had risen from the "humble position of tailor," had never become a planter, and the two adult slaves (and their three children) he owned were domestics. De Bow denounced the undereducated Johnson as a "socialist" and charged that his "free-farm [policies fixed] him in the class of the demagogues." Johnson's occasional hints that farm and plantation interests were not synonymous marked him as unreliable as to slavery, De Bow added, and left "him with few adherents at the South."[19]

Like most southern candidates, Johnson was aware that bisectional support only went so far. Most northern Democrats, one supporter warned, wanted "a Northern man," and they preferred that the man be Douglas. Southern delegates might insist that it was their turn to choose the nominee, but Johnson expected Douglas delegates to resist compromise on this point. Not yet fifty-two, Johnson could afford to wait. Should Douglas secure the nomination, and Johnson thought that probable, the need to unite the party would require "the V. President [to be] from the South." Although five years Douglas's senior, the senator knew of Douglas's penchant for hard drinking, and he considered it likely that if "Tennessee Could Succeed now with the Second place"—he was of course thinking of himself—"it would place her in the field four years hence with much assurance of Success."[20]

Thanks to its egalitarian nature, the American political scene, even by this early date, also boasted a number of second-tier candidates whose most appealing quality was their charming confidence in their own electability. Georgia's Robert Toombs endorsed fellow senator Robert M.T. Hunter of Virginia, a bland but reliably proslavery attorney. Hunter, who would succeed Toombs as the second of three Confederate secretaries of state, was regarded as dependable enough that should he be given the nomination, one editor theorized, "the south [would] ask nothing but the [1856 popular sovereignty] Cincinnati platform, pure and simple." Virginia's delegates were split, however, with a minority backing Henry Wise, who had achieved regional fame as governor during John Brown's raid. Those who thought Wise "erratic and impulsive" planned to unite behind Hunter, and the Virginia delegation intended, if the convention failed to select Douglas, to "*demand*" a candidate from the upper South as Virginia's due.[21]

Georgians advanced the name of former congressman Alexander H. Stephens. Chronically ill, the diminutive, ninety-six-pound Stephens made his old friend Douglas appear robust by comparison; his belief that sipping teaspoons of whiskey throughout the day would keep him healthy had only turned him into an alcoholic. Yet Georgia newspapers routinely advanced the two as a winning ticket. Stephens was willing to accept the vice presidency, but as the most vocal southern supporter of Douglas, he refused to consider the top spot. The owner of several thousand acres and thirty-four slaves, Stephens could be expected to support slavery's westward movement. He had, in fact, been instrumental in pushing the Kansas-Nebraska Act through the House, which he later described as "the greatest glory of [his] life." Despite his fondness for Douglas, Stephens had also served as Buchanan's floor manager in the unsuccessful battle to approve the Lecompton constitution.[22]

As April arrived and delegates began to board trains and ships for Charleston, Douglas remained the man to beat. Four years before at the Cincinnati convention, Douglas had graciously withdrawn his name from contention after it had become clear that only Buchanan could achieve enough votes to be nominated. Since the Illinoisan remained the most powerful figure in the party, he and his backers regarded the top spot as his due. "The friends of Douglas are confident and uncompromising," reported Edwin M. Stanton of Ohio. But it was not merely a question of 1860 being Douglas's turn. Just as southern Democrats insisted that the nomination go to one of their own, northern politicians feared the destruction of their state organizations should the party adopt a proslavery platform. American voters paid great attention to platforms during this era, and a militant statement of party principles, even more than the nomination of a Davis or a Breckinridge, would cost the party seats, especially in New York. The fact that Douglas delegates could not safely compromise—rather than simply being *unwilling* to do so—was precisely what the fire-eaters were counting on. The destruction of the republic, Robert Barnwell Rhett Sr. argued in January, could only begin with the "demolition of the party." Unable to accept a repudiation of the popular sovereignty clauses in the Cincinnati platform, a majority of northern delegates would have no choice but to hold fast behind Douglas. "This is what our [two] Rhetts" and Yancey were "working for," a displeased James Henry Hammond admitted.[23]

Douglas had no plans to attend the convention; should any candidate have done so, the time-honored facade of his not desiring political position would have been shattered. But the senator encouraged many of his followers to go to Charleston, including those who had not been selected as delegates. Their sheer numbers and "outside pressure," he hoped, might persuade those inside the convention hall that he was the key to a Democratic triumph in the fall. Among those heading south was August Belmont, a New York banker who bore the title of Douglas's "National Chairman." The Empire State's Democrats had long been divided over a number of issues, among them antislavery and currency; "Hards" tilted toward free-soil candidates, while "Softs" like Belmont and railroad attorney Samuel J. Tilden (himself a future Democratic presidential nominee) perpetuated former president Martin Van Buren's policy of saying as little as possible about slavery. On April 18, Belmont, Tilden, and the entire New York delegation boarded the steamer *Nashville* for Charleston. A number of antislavery Hards arrived on Manhattan's docks to jeer, and some began to pelt the delegates with oranges. As a portent of trouble to come, one orange hit Belmont squarely in the groin, and he had to be helped to his cabin.[24]

Although the most elegant of southern ports and hailed by its boosters as the "Queen City of the South," Charleston proved to be the worst possible location for the convention. Four years previously, as a consolation prize to disappointed southern delegates over the nomination of yet another northern man, the Cincinnati convention had offered to hold the next Democratic National Committee convention in South Carolina. Ever since, party managers had rued their generosity. Rail connections to the port city existed but required endless transfers, so when possible, delegates who resided along the Atlantic, like the uncomfortable Belmont, chose to sail south. In 1859, representatives of various delegations had visited the city to secure lodgings, and they had been far from pleased with what they had discovered. The few hotels had clearly colluded in advance, since all demanded an extortion rate of five dollars per diem; one Illinoisan regarded that as a plot "on the part of Douglas' enemies to keep northern" delegates away. Charlestonians relied on cisterns and shallow wells for their drinking water, which even residents thought "undrinkable [and] hardly fit for washing." Squeamish northern representatives could not fail to notice the castlelike House of Correction, commonly known as the Workhouse, on the corner of Magazine Street. Built to punish "refractory slaves," the building featured a "whipping-room" constructed of double walls filled with sand to muffle the screams of inmates.[25]

One of those enduring the infinite rail transfers was thirty-year-old Ohioan Murat Halstead. A former teacher and attorney, Halstead had found his calling in journalism, and his position with the Cincinnati *Commercial* had allowed him to attend and cover the Republican and Democratic conventions in 1856, both staged locally. The popularity of those stories encouraged his publisher to send him to what would turn out to be four major (and several minor) conventions in 1860. Halstead arrived in Charleston three days before the conference was set to begin, on April 23. Situated on the corner of Broad and Meeting streets, Institute Hall was the site of the gathering. Built in 1854, the hall held three thousand people in its main auditorium. A stage faced hundreds of uncomfortable wooden chairs that were bolted to pine planks placed across the floor. The prudish Halstead disapproved of the "gaudy and uncouth" frescoes, particularly the one directly above the stage that featured three "highly colored but very improperly dressed females." Evidently local ladies did not object, since one third of the seats in the upstairs gallery were reserved for female observers.[26]

The genteel ladies, Douglas supporters soon discovered, had been perusing the pages of Rhett's *Mercury*. Although not a delegate, the elder Rhett was one of the more powerful voices in Charleston, and as April progressed, so had his newspaper's level of vitriol. Since Rhett was one of the first publishers to understand the importance of propaganda, the *Mercury*'s editorials goaded the city's white population into a collective rage. Any southerner willing to accept Douglas in the name of party unity was denounced as a "traitor" to the region. Even those delegates accustomed to the angry tone in Washington were shocked by the mood in Charleston. "I am surprized at the bitterness of some of our Southern opponents," observed one Illinois delegate. "They go so far as to call us abolitionists and say we had better stay home and attend the Chicago [Republican] convention where we legitimately belong."[27]

Belmont had rented Hibernian Hall as the official Douglas headquarters. Located on Meeting Street less than two blocks from the main convention, the elegant Greek-style structure normally housed the city's Irish American benevolent association. The first floor was given over to meeting space, with long tables littered with papers and boxes of James W. Sheahan's authorized *Life of Stephen A. Douglas*; kegs of whiskey were discreetly tucked below the desks. Belmont converted the second-floor hall into barracks, with several hundred cots covered "with white spreads and pillows." The hall's exterior columns and Ionic arches, however, masked growing unease within. As he passed the hall, Halstead spoke with a number of Illinois congressmen "seated mournfully on the steps." Already weary of the early "intense heat" and inhospitable tone of Charleston, the delegates assured the reporter that it would require "but a few ballots" to nominate Douglas "and all [was] over," and they could return home. (In fact, only the contentious 1924 Democratic convention would exceed the Charleston meeting in length.) Belmont, desperately trying to appease local residents, was counting the moments until the *Nashville* sailed. Obliged to attend one party, Belmont complained to his wife that it "was the most stupid of all stupid gatherings" he had ever attended. "There were about twelve ugly women with about sixty as ugly men."[28]

Monday, April 23, finally arrived. Just around eleven, an hour before the convention opened, a passing shower cooled off the city and washed the hot dust off its sidewalks. Halstead was just one of many reporters setting up alongside the stage; one young boy, hired to sprint to the telegraph office with dispatches, served the entire press corps. Each delegation had a number of tickets to dispense to family and supporters, who could sit upstairs in the gallery. On the main floor, delegates searched for their state's tables. Only a few minutes late, Judge David A. Smalley of Vermont, speaking on behalf of the Democratic National Committee, rose to call the convention to order. Seated nearby was party secretary and Ohio congressman Clement L. Vallandigham, a reluctant Douglas supporter who would later head the party's antiwar, pro-Confederate wing.[29]

As if the Democrats did not have headaches enough, they were burdened by a series of antiquated and contradictory rules. Since 1832, the party had required a two-thirds majority for the nomination. Complicating this requirement for a supermajority was the delegate selection process. Each state was granted as many votes in party conventions as it had in the Electoral College. But what had struck party founders as

The Democratic National Convention in Charleston's Institute Hall was only the first of many political gatherings held in 1860. Located on the corner of Meeting and Broad streets, the main auditorium could hold three thousand people, and the image here suggests the anger and chaos that typically reigned during the meeting. Renamed Secession Hall during the spring of 1861, the building burned down later that year. Courtesy Library of Congress.

equitable in the 1820s made little practical sense by 1860. Massachusetts, a state that the Democrats had never once carried, enjoyed thirteen votes in Charleston, giving its delegates roughly twice the clout of reliably Democratic Mississippi, which had just seven electoral votes. The more populous North rightfully controlled roughly sixty percent of the delegates, yet even a northern candidate (as Buchanan had demonstrated) would be hard-pressed to carry half the free states in the November election. And while Belmont had arrived in Charleston supported by a bare majority of delegates, southern delegates, who controlled forty percent of the seats in the hall, held seats enough to veto Douglas's chances.[30]

Complicating this was the fact that membership on the all-important Committee on Resolutions, which was in charge of the party platform, had nothing to do with population. Instead, each state received one vote on the committee, which guaranteed the less populous South parity when it came time to craft party policy. Douglas's backers could rely on no more than sixteen of the thirty-three delegates on Resolutions, so while his followers represented slightly more than a majority of the delegates in Charleston, they needed one more vote to block the creation of a proslavery, pro–Dred Scott platform. In short, the party's arcane rules were perfectly suited to Yancey and Rhett, as they allowed a disruptive minority to control the convention and fracture an already weakened Democracy.[31]

For the Douglas forces, events took another unfortunate turn when, on April 24, the second day of deliberations, the delegates selected Caleb Cushing as chairman of the convention. Although a lifelong resident of Massachusetts, the former diplomat, congressman, and attorney general had long been sympathetic to southern concerns. In a vote conducted by state rather than by delegates, Cushing received the support of every southern state, as well as Buchanan's Pennsylvania. As a vocal defender of the Dred Scott decision, Cushing had won the enmity of most northern Democrats, and Halstead reported that "the Douglas men dislike him intensely." But Cushing, who had graduated from Harvard University at the age of seventeen, was a formidable opponent. Now sixty, he was "in a remarkably fine state of preservation." Tanned and robust, his "clear, musical, and powerful" voice easily carried to "every part of the house." Dressed in a black satin vest, with his glasses hung about his neck on a black ribbon, the dapper New Englander was certain to rule against Douglas at every opportunity.[32]

As Cushing's selection indicated, it took party leaders less than twenty-four hours to begin serious backroom maneuvers. Although Cushing had initially backed Davis, his elevation into the chairmanship suddenly led him to hope that the role was but the first step toward his own nomination; one New Yorker assured him that there was an "unexpectedly strong current" running in his favor. A Virginia delegate supposed that Cushing's unsuccessful battle against his state's personal-liberty laws and his characterization of Boston's famously sober abolitionists as "drunken mutineers" might endear him to fire-eaters while holding conservative northern Democrats in line. Among those trying to engineer such a compromise were Louisiana delegates Richard Taylor and John Slidell. As Buchanan's "matchless wire-worker," Slidell hoped to deny Douglas the nomination yet hold the party together, a wish shared by state senator Taylor, the son of former president Zachary Taylor and a future Confederate general. Although the two were staunch proslavery men, they remained committed to the party. Taylor hoped that "an earnest appeal for peace and harmony" could yet carry the day in Charleston. Each believed that the party's best hope was to eschew prominent names from both sections in favor of a compromise candidate like Cushing, who could be persuaded to embrace a vaguely proslavery platform.[33]

Taylor was also willing to consider Kentucky's James Guthrie. A former treasury secretary under Pierce, the sixty-four-year-old planter was precisely the sort of dark horse who might unite the party. Guthrie also enjoyed the support of paunchy, cross-eyed Massachusetts delegate Benjamin F. Butler, whose long career was to carry him from southern sympathizer to antislavery Republican during the war. Support in Charleston for Guthrie hindered the prospects of Vice President Breckinridge, since the younger man would not allow his name to be advanced so long as his older colleague was in consideration. But as both Taylor and Slidell wished to pass over the party's celebrated lightning rods in favor of minor candidates with less political baggage, the fact that Guthrie blocked Breckinridge's path was all to the good. Their plan, however, hinged on keeping Yancey in the Democratic fold, and they knew it. Naively, Taylor hoped that the angry demands for the Alabama

Platform were merely designed to ensure the nomination of a sound proslavery man and were not intended to destroy the party.[34]

Despite the schemes and backroom stratagems of their opponents, journalists in Charleston thought the Douglas men "displayed the best tactics." They at least were united, while those who favored other candidates were bitterly divided. Douglas and Buchanan shared a birthday on April 23, and his delegates encouraged the convention to celebrate these twin anniversaries by wrapping up the younger man's nomination in short order. But the mood of the meeting continued to be contentious. Governor John S. Robinson of Vermont, although only fifty-five, died suddenly of "apoplexy" (probably a stroke). While dining at the Mills House, two members of the Ohio delegation fell into an argument and hurled plates at each other. One then drew a pistol, but other delegates separated the pair. Shortly after peace was restored, the same dining room witnessed another brawl, when delegate Andrew Craig of Missouri attacked a reporter for the *St. Louis Republican*. They too were parted by bystanders, but only after they swore to resolve the issue later with a duel.[35]

On April 25, the convention's third day, delegates finally began the critical business of crafting the party platform. Having correctly feared that the southern majority on the platform committee intended to amend the Cincinnati statement "so as to repudiate its Northern interpretation," Douglas delegates responded that any such changes violated the party's long-held beliefs. Insisting yet again that popular sovereignty bore the stamp of small-government Jacksonian democracy, they argued that southern demands for the protection of slavery in the territories was an "inadmissible" intrusion of federal authority into what should be a local matter. "Was this the doctrine of Old Hickory?" wondered Henry B. Payne of Ohio. Noting that both Thomas Jefferson and Andrew Jackson had denied the concept of judicial review on strict-construction grounds, Payne ridiculed attempts to praise the Dred Scott decision in the platform. If Seward won in November and was able to replace the eighty-three-year-old Roger B. Taney with a Republican chief justice, "would the south bow to its decisions" then? "Be on your guard," he added, "lest Jefferson in his angelic state come down with a sword" to smite southern apostates. Weary of endless southern threats, Payne threatened to lead the

Ohio delegation out in protest if the 1856 platform was substantially revised.[36]

Yancey, of course, was pleased to hear Payne's warning, and fire-eaters in a number of delegations held fast to the Alabama Platform. As Cushing called the convention together on the fourth day, Leroy P. Walker of Alabama rose to introduce his version of the Yancey-Davis resolutions. Although the federal government had "no power to interfere with slavery in the States," Walker insisted, it nonetheless remained Washington's duty "to afford adequate protection and equal advantage to all descriptions of property" both "within the Territories as upon the high seas." Startled delegates regarded the last clause as an implicit endorsement for reopening the Atlantic slave trade, but they were more alarmed yet by Walker's final resolution. If "this war upon the Constitutional rights of the South is persisted in," shouted the future Confederate secretary of war, "it must soon cease to be a war of words" and become "a conflict of arms."[37]

Although journalists who regarded the anti-Douglas forces as "divided" when it came to other possible nominees were correct, southern men *were* united in their opposition to the Illinoisan. Alabama's delegation stood firm on the demand for a territorial slave code, and few doubted that the state would withdraw from the convention if the platform committee upheld the Cincinnati document. Most of all, stubborn southern delegates understood that the party needed them more than they needed the party. Although Democratic rules provided Douglas delegates with a slight edge in Charleston, the party could not hope to capture the Electoral College without solid southern support. Ohio, New York, and Massachusetts delegates might threaten a walkout over a proslavery platform, but Buchanan had carried none of those states in 1856. By comparison, fire-eaters were content to abandon the party, ensure the defeat of Douglas, and secede from the Union. A "mere handful of fearless and patriotic Southern men," Rhett Jr. editorialized, had demanded war in 1812 "regardless of consequences." Some southern whites might be indifferent to the Alabama Platform, he added, but men of "nerve" must demand their rights in the convention, thus "controlling and compelling their inferior contemporaries" who cared more about a Democratic victory than they did about protecting slavery.[38]

Inside their headquarters at Hibernian Hall, the Douglas delegates, on the advice of Belmont and the senator, plotted a strategy that would prove to be yet another miscalculation. Traditionally, conventions first chose a nominee and then adopted the committee's platform. This time, Douglas's handlers intended to reverse the order. Although the majority faction on the platform committee intended to craft a fire-eating statement, Belmont reasoned that once the finished document came to the floor for ratification, the more numerous northern delegates could vote it down, proving to the convention (and the country as a whole) that Douglas dominated the party. "Douglas and his friends seem to act on the idea that our fear of Black Republican rule will make us submit to anything," groused Toombs from his home in Georgia. But he described the strategy as "a great mistake," and he was right. Since several southern delegations had been instructed to quit the convention only if the Alabama Platform was not accepted—and not merely if Douglas received the nomination—a good number of moderate southerners might have remained in Charleston following his nomination. Knowing that Douglas was unwilling to run at the head of a proslavery platform, calmer voices could have then argued for a more temperate platform. "If our little grog drinking, electioneering Demagogue can destroy our hopes," Davis worried, "it must be that we are doomed to destruction."[39]

Understanding that the two-thirds requirement for nomination (202 of 303 votes) provided southern states (who controlled 120 votes) with a veto over Douglas's chances, Belmont actually hoped for the secession of the Alabama and Mississippi contingents from the convention. No other state assemblies had instructed their delegation to walk out in protest, so part of Belmont's strategy was to push for adopting a platform first, with the idea that after the convention as a whole refused to ratify a fire-eating manifesto, the sixteen men from those two states would withdraw. C. P. Culver, one of the Douglas supporters in Charleston, wrote the senator that only "one or two of these states" might walk out, while the Georgia delegation would remain. Douglas still required southern votes to reach the necessary 202, but if he could achieve a simple majority, it would be easier to pressure the remaining delegates to give way with the gulf-state fire-eaters absent.[40]

April 27, the convention's fifth day, was the test of Douglas's strategy.

Cushing gaveled the proceedings to order at the early hour of eight A.M., after the platform committee indicated that its labors were complete. Confessing their inability to gloss over the yawning sectional divide that split the party as well as the republic, the committee members reported two documents, a Minority Report, reflecting the will of the panel's northern minority, and a Majority Report, which spoke for the planter class. Signed by fifteen delegates, including Ohio's Payne, the northern platform reaffirmed the Cincinnati declaration, declaring the belief "that Democratic principles are unchangeable in their nature." Although the six resolutions submitted by the Douglas men explicitly mentioned neither popular sovereignty nor the Dred Scott decision, by upholding the lengthy 1856 platform, they effectively endorsed Douglas's position. The group did concede, however, that "all questions in regard to the rights of property in States or Territories" were "judicial in their character," and so they pledged the party to abide by any decisions that had "been or [might] be made by the Supreme Court." Since Congress had twice endorsed popular sovereignty, Payne emphasized as he presented the document that any attempts to abandon that position would lead to the destruction "of the Democratic party of the free States."[41]

If the Minority Report spoke for northern Democrats, it also revealed the extent to which the Democrats had become a pro-southern party, as well as how far the Douglas men were willing to go to conciliate slave interests. The veiled reference to Taney's court and any decisions it might make in the future—and the allusion to "States" as well as territories—was not only a retreat from the party's strict-construction principles; it was an implicit endorsement of a possible proslavery decision in the Lemmon case. The report also denounced northern personal-liberty laws as "subversive to the Constitution, and revolutionary in their effect," and it promised to share the fruits of manifest destiny with the South by advocating a rail line from Atlanta to the Pacific and through the acquisition of the slave-powered sugar colony of Cuba, "on such terms as shall be honorable to ourselves and just to Spain."[42]

William Avery of North Carolina then rose to submit the Majority Report. Comprising six points, the platform began with a bold endorsement of the Alabama Platform. The party adhered to two "cardinal principles on the subject of slavery in the Territories." Congress had no constitutional right to abolish slavery in the West, just as no "Territorial Legislature" could legally "destroy or impair the right of property in the states by any legislation whatsoever." The rest of the report mirrored the points made in Payne's document, except that the southern demand for Cuba eschewed any meek talk of Spain's honor when it endorsed acquisition "at the earliest practicable period." As Avery took his seat, the convention floor exploded into chaos. Despite his impressive voice, Cushing could not restore order, and only after he bellowed that he would resign as chairman did something approaching calm descend on what one journalist drolly described as "a long and excited session."[43]

Timing is everything in politics, and it was at this volatile moment that Yancey decided to add to the anger and discord. So far, "the prince of the fire-eaters," as journalist Halstead dubbed him, had chosen to remain silent. But his extremist allies had tasked him with a major speech against Douglas, and as the sun began to set, Yancey strode toward the podium to defend the Majority Report. "The hall for several minutes rang with applause," Halstead reported. Speakers were typically granted no more than one hour, but as the crowd quieted, Yancey asked for and received additional time. He then began by addressing the question of why the Democrats were vanishing across the North. Their defeat at the polls, Yancey insisted, was due only "to the pandering by the party in the free States to anti-slavery sentiments; they had not come up to the high ground which must be taken on the subject," which was "that slavery was right." Typical of this cowardice, he sneered, was the refusal of "Douglas and his followers" to accept the Lecompton constitution. Yancey noted that the state representatives who had voted against the Majority Report in committee hailed from states that rarely went Democratic, whereas the proslavery platform was sure to be embraced by those states that could "be counted absolutely certain in the electoral college." Northern men might not wish to admit it, but the party had become a proslavery party, and it was better to lose "upon principle" than to win through "ambiguous issues." Although horrified by Yancey's rhetoric, Halstead marveled at his "intellect and captivating powers as a speaker."[44]

The southern delegates in the hall responded to each pause with applause and "rapturous enthusiasm." Having finished assailing Douglas, Yancey turned to southern grievances. As hall managers turned on the gaslights, Yancey focused on the "deep-seated conviction that the South, with her institutions, [was] unsafe in the Union." He assured the delegates that he was no "disruptionist," but he added that the only way to "reassure the Southern people of safety in the party" was to grant slaveholders their rights under the Constitution. Northern politicians might reject the Majority Report, but Yancey warned the convention that the document was "not all that Alabama want[ed], it [was] not even all that Alabama ask[ed]." What was required, Yancey insisted, was for the Democrats to denounce boldly "this great evil, this cancer" of abolitionism that was eating away at the "vast and magnificent Republic." By admitting "that slavery [was] wrong," popular sovereignty advocates "were in no position to defend it." It was not enough to recognize that the white South thought differently about organizing labor. Northern Democrats must join with them in announcing slavery to be a godly and moral institution.[45]

As if to force northern delegates to confront the most contentious aspect of unfree labor, toward the end of his ninety-minute oration Yancey took up the question of the Atlantic slave trade. Although Congress had banned the external traffic of humans in 1807 and declared it piracy (and hence a capital crime) in 1820, Yancey observed, the Constitution did not prohibit the trade, but simply allowed Congress to cease importing African captives after 1807. "If slavery is right *per se*, if it is right to raise slaves for sale," Yancey insisted, "does it not appear that it's right to import them?" Congressional interference with slavery proved a slippery slope. By passing laws against the importation of Africans, Congress had implicitly branded as "obnoxious" a labor system "founded upon high and immutable laws." To survive, the South had to expand westward, and to do so, it needed laborers less expensive than those sold by Chesapeake masters. "We want negroes cheap," Yancey concluded, "and we want a sufficiency of them, so as to supply the cotton demand of the whole world."[46]

The hour had grown late, and for fatigued northern delegates, Yancey's demands that they endorse the infamous slave trade were all too much. Some called to adjourn, but George E. Pugh of Ohio sprang to his feet. The elderly Pugh declared that although his career was nearly at an end, "he did not regret it." Like many northern Democrats, he had endured the animosity of many in his state in "battling for the doctrines of the South." He had watched while northern politicians lost their seats to Republicans, yet now Douglas men were "taunted by the South with weakness." Yancey was wrong, Pugh insisted. The "downfall of the Northern Democracy" was the result of them giving in to the insatiable demands of the planter class, and now they were ordered to embrace the Atlantic slave trade. They "were not children under the pupilage of the South," an enraged Pugh lectured the suddenly quiet chamber, to be ordered about "at the beck and bidding" of haughty slaveholders. "Gentlemen of the South," he shouted, "you mistake us—you mistake us—we will not do it!"[47]

The next morning was Sunday. The convention conducted no official business, and northern delegates slept off a long night's drinking. A few South Carolinians dressed and made their way to the numerous churches that lined Meeting and King streets. Others, like Richard Taylor, desperately searched for a way to keep the party intact. Still optimistic that moderate southerners could rally behind a compromise candidate and yet a third platform, Taylor visited Yancey in his hotel room, understanding that the Alabaman controlled those "of the ultra stripe." As had many mainstream Democrats before him, Taylor argued that only party unity could prevent a Republican triumph, but Yancey and former Alabama governor John A. Winston, among the other fire-eaters gathered there, would have none of it. Even a previously moderate Louisiana delegate told Taylor he welcomed disunion. Northerners were "all a set of cringing cowards," he swore. "If there was money in it, maybe they'd fight." A dejected Taylor returned to his quarters, finally aware that most fire-eaters agreed with Yancey that a Democratic victory in 1860 was not worth fighting for, and might even further damage southern interests.[48]

Elsewhere in the city, southern delegates met to decide on a course of action should the convention, as expected, adopt the Minority Report and should the Alabama and Mississippi contingents, as also expected, march out in protest. The Virginians caucused, and although many still hoped that the nomination of Davis, Guthrie, or Senator Joseph Lane of Oregon could hold the convention together, others argued that they had little choice but to "retire from the Convention" should it ratify "the

minority report or any thing like it." From Georgia, Toombs wired his
state's delegates instructing them to join the walkout unless they got a
"sound platform," and the Georgians finally voted twenty-two to twelve
to follow Alabama's lead. A desperate George N. Sanders sent a lengthy
telegram (with collect charges of $26.80) to the White House in hopes that
Buchanan would intervene, but the president declined to mediate if the
result would be a Douglas nomination.[49]

Despite the president's unwillingness to save his party, Slidell, widely
regarded as Buchanan's spokesman in Charleston, made one final attempt late Sunday night to hold the fire-eaters in line. Meeting with representatives from the Gulf South, Slidell proposed a compromise in which
northern delegates would be granted the Cincinnati platform (without
the 1860 additions found in the Minority Report) in exchange for the
nomination of Guthrie. Since Douglas enjoyed only a few votes beyond
a simple majority, when he failed to achieve the necessary two thirds, the
New York and Pennsylvania delegates would throw their weight behind
Guthrie. The proposal came to nothing, since compromise solutions require an interest in conciliation. "The seceding States came to the convention," reported Virginia journalist Robert Glass, "with the deliberate
purpose to break up the convention if they failed to get, as they knew
they would fail to get, their extreme ultimatum." Glass believed that if
Virginia had endorsed Slidell's plan, all of the North as well as the upper
South would have united behind it. A second journalist, also a witness to
Slidell's last, desperate attempt, agreed. The states that intended to bolt
the convention had no wish to compromise, he believed, because they
had arrived in Charleston with "a concerted plan for the dissolution of
the Union."[50]

The convention resumed its formal deliberations just after ten o'clock
on Monday morning. Northern delegates trooped into the chamber,
Halstead noted, "with a curious mixture of despair of accomplishing
anything and hope that something [would] turn up." The galleries had
thinned out as the week wore on, but on this morning they were full to
overflowing. Cushing announced that voting would commence on the platforms. John M. Krum of Missouri presented the Majority Report, but as
the few compromisers left in the chamber feared, the convention promptly
voted 165 to 138 to instead accept the Minority Report. As if on cue, Leroy

Walker of Alabama seized the floor. "This Convention has refused by the platform adopted," he read from a prepared statement, to settle the question of the territories "in favor of the South." As his delegation had been ordered by the state assembly "not to waive this issue," it was their "duty to withdraw from this Convention." As Alabama's contingent rose to withdraw, Mississippi's W. S. Barry, against the advice of Jefferson Davis, announced that his delegation too had to leave. Halstead glanced over to see Yancey departing with the rest of the Alabama delegation. Others were solemn, but Yancey was "smiling as a bridegroom."[51]

Twelve years before, when Yancey marched out of the Baltimore convention in protest of candidate Lewis Cass's popular sovereignty advocacy, only one delegate followed. This time, Yancey led a parade down the aisles of Institute Hall. Louisiana's Alexander Mouton denounced both Douglas and the platform and led his forces out of the chamber; a despondent Richard Taylor followed as Mouton pointed and cursed at the two Louisiana delegates who remained in their seats. As they had planned the previous afternoon, Charles W. Russell caught Cushing's eye and rose to announce that Virginians thought it "inconsistent with their convictions" to remain. As all or portions of the South Carolina, Florida, Texas, Delaware, Georgia, and Arkansas delegations joined the bolters, genteel women swept down from the gallery to place a single rose on the chair of each departed delegate. A few South Carolinians remained in their chairs, until taunts and hisses from the gallery drove them out. Had they remained, Robert Barnwell Rhett Jr. believed, "they would have been mobbed." The seceding delegates strode down Meeting Street toward the office of the *Mercury*, where they serenaded both father and son.[52]

Belmont and Douglas's other handlers were stunned by the magnitude of the withdrawal. They had hoped for "a little eruption" that would still allow their candidate to obtain the necessary two-thirds majority—and demonstrate to northern voters that their nominee was no fire-eater determined to carry slavery into the territories—but the departure of eight southern delegations forced Belmont to confront the hard fact that Douglas might ultimately capture a prize not worth having. The Alabamans had arrived in Charleston predetermined to create "a pretence for a quarrel and a secession," charged one Douglas supporter. The "designs of the seceders are so unveiled in all of their nakedness," insisted another, "that the people must choose between a cordial support for sound Democratic principles, or disunion." But as Yancey aimed for the latter, could a nomination built on the former carry the South in November?[53]

With eight delegations, including the moderate contingents of Virginia and Delaware, out in protest, the Douglas delegates faced two unhappy options. Since Douglas refused to be paired with the Majority Report—and discerning northerners understood that the bolt had as much to do with the candidate as with the platform—they could abandon Douglas for a doughface like Cushing. Or they could persevere in their course and pray that the protest was just one more planter attempt at political blackmail, and that responsible southern Democrats would later rally behind the nominee. In Washington, Douglas took the news hard, and as always, took to the bottle harder still. When California senator Milton S. Latham encountered him outside the Senate chamber, he was quite drunk and raving about enemies and "bloodhounds" who were trying to do him in. Still unwilling to recognize that the planter class stood united against him, Douglas blamed the walkout on Buchanan's allies. He was ghostly pale, Latham observed, and his hair had grayed considerably over the past months.[54]

On Tuesday, May 1, the seceding delegates reassembled in Military Hall, on Wentworth Street. Several delegates from the main convention, including New Yorkers hostile to Belmont, arrived at the hall in hopes of discussing a compromise candidate. But fearing that the entire Institute Hall meeting might simply follow, the southern delegates promptly voted to restrict membership to seceding states. Yancey rose to suggest that they call themselves the Constitutional Convention, and he laughed that those left behind were but the "Rump Convention." The group selected Senator James A. Bayard Jr. of Delaware as permanent chairman, and a platform committee began work on yet another proclamation. They declined, however, to discuss a nominee. Having decided that Military Hall was now the center of activity, most Charleston ladies abandoned the galleries at Institute Hall and directed their carriages toward Wentworth Street. There they gazed down at the dapper Bayard, who stood before a large stage backdrop depicting the bloody Palace of the Borgias.[55]

Four streets away at what was now essentially a northern convention, exhausted delegates prepared to make quick work of a Douglas nomination, and then flee the city. The departure of 51 delegates reduced overall attendance from the original 303 delegates to 252; the required two thirds now appeared to be 168. Since Belmont could count on the support of roughly 160 northern men, the prize appeared to be within his grasp, and the *Macon Daily Telegraph* pronounced Douglas's nomination "as certain." Complicating this simple scenario, however, was a resolution bequeathed several days before, which declared that nominees must obtain 202 votes. Illinois's William Richardson, a Douglas delegate, moved that the resolution "be laid on the table." The Tennessee delegation objected. As befitting the representatives of a border state that did considerable commerce with the North, Tennessee Democrats evidently hoped to deadlock the convention until cooler heads prevailed and the seceders could be persuaded to return. Equally desirous of slowing Douglas's momentum was chairman Cushing, who upheld Tennessee's position and ruled that a nominee must capture two thirds of the votes of the Democrats yet in Charleston, not merely those within the hall. A Michigan delegate appealed to the floor, but much to Belmont's dismay, the entire New York delegation voted to uphold Cushing's ruling, making the final tally 144 to 108.[56]

For the second time in as many days, bewildered Douglas backers watched helplessly as the convention took yet another unexpected twist. Richardson, Halstead scribbled, "looked as if at a funeral." Even so, Belmont was neither farther from nor closer to the requisite number than he had been one week before, and he yet hoped to win over the divided minority delegates as it became clear that their favorite sons could never match Douglas's numbers. On the first ballot, Douglas stood at 145½, with Guthrie at 35, Hunter at 42, and Johnson at 12. (Several states allowed delegates to split their votes.) Fifty-six more ballots followed that day and the next, but Douglas never rose above 152½. A furious Belmont blamed the deadlock on his fellow New Yorkers, who then returned to the Douglas fold and gave him their thirty-five votes. Yet Douglas never came within fifteen votes of capturing what would have been the two-thirds vote of 168 had Cushing ruled in his favor. Guthrie's and Hunter's numbers also held firm, and Johnson, still hoping to emerge as the

compromise nominee, lost his chance at the vice presidency when he refused to respond to a telegram urging him to endorse Douglas. A rumor
indicated that Douglas planned to withdraw his name, but his irate backers denied the report. "Douglas or nobody," bellowed Illinoisan Charles
Lanphier. "His friends will never yield."[57]

Having lost count of the endless ballots, Halstead walked up Meeting
Street to Military Hall. There he found the delegates quibbling over the
correct term for their actions. Leroy Walker was keeping a journal but disliked the word "seceding" to describe the walkout. One delegate suggested
"withdrawing," but most preferred the label "retiring delegates." Understanding who was in charge, Halstead sought out a smiling Yancey. The
convention had prepared a proper platform, Yancey informed the journalist, but that was all the group intended to do until "the rump Democracy"
selected its candidate. Depending on whom they chose, Yancey added, it
might then be their "privilege to endorse the nominee, or [their] duty to
proceed to make a nomination according to the will of this body." The
convention was leaning toward a geographically balanced ticket of Jefferson Davis and Douglas foe Mayor Fernando Wood of New York.[58]

Yancey, of course, desired no reunion with the northern majority. But
more mainstream southern delegates continued to believe that their protest
would force the main convention to recognize their importance in the
electoral count, abandon Douglas as a candidate, and invite them to return. God, or at least South Carolina's white clergy, encouraged them to
hold firm, and the minister at St. Michael's Episcopal Church offered up
daily prayers for a southern victory in the stalemate. Ever since the Missouri debates of 1820, planters had learned that their threats were effective in forcing the northern politicians to yield. But at long last they were
mistaken. The high cost of Charleston inns, weather that ranged from
"scorching" to "chilly," the inability to secure Douglas's nomination, and,
according to Halstead, the "great calamity" of empty whiskey barrels in
the Ohio and Kentucky headquarters began to drive delegates out of the
city. Stages rattled away from hotels, "loaded down with trunks and filled
with passengers." Each train and steamer ferried weary delegates away
from the city and toward home.[59]

By May 3, the convention's tenth day, so few delegates remained in
Institute Hall that a quorum barely existed. It was increasingly clear that

there was no solution to the impasse, at least so long as the party remained in Charleston. Several delegates discussed the possibility of ad-
journing for the time being and reuniting in Baltimore on June 18. Among
the virtues of the plan was that "those States whose delegates had withdrawn" would have an opportunity to replace the rebel delegations with
new members. Belmont hoped that more pragmatic legislators, faced
with the possible dissolution of their party, would replace fire-eating delegates with moderates "favorable to the Little Giant" and more willing
to compromise on the platform. A majority of those remaining in the hall
agreed, with only Kentucky and the distant states of California and Oregon
voting to continue. As the votes to adjourn were being counted, the aged
Josiah Randall of Pennsylvania climbed atop his chair and "screamed"
at Cushing to be recognized. Randall suggested that the Democrats instead meet on July 4 in Philadelphia's Independence Hall, as "a meeting
at that holy time and place would do them all a great deal of good." Sick
of the endless debate, other delegates shouted him down, and following
"three violent blows with his hammer," Cushing declared the convention adjourned.[60]

The news took the southern delegates in Military Hall by surprise.
Most had expected the Douglas forces to give way. But now they had to
return home and persuade their state assemblies to select them again as
delegates to the Baltimore gathering. As the delegates stared at one another in quiet confusion, Judge Alexander Meek of Alabama rose to
suggest that they remain in Charleston as the legitimate Democratic
convention. Any "Southern State that went into the Baltimore Convention," he argued, "did so as an approver of squatter sovereignty." Since
the northern delegates were withdrawing from the city, that left the
southerners as the sole representatives of the party. They should adopt a
platform and a ticket of Davis and Bayard. At this, Georgian Benjamin
Hill responded that they had become "a disunionist movement" and that
he too was leaving town. That earned a challenge from Yancey, who
archly "asked to know to whom [Hill] alluded." Hill declined to reply,
and Yancey again "demanded an answer." Amid the growing chaos,
William Whiteley of Delaware moved that they convene in Richmond,
Virginia, on June 11, and enough votes supported him for the motion to
carry.[61]

By sunset, both halls were nearly deserted. At Institute Hall, a small army of black porters swept up the debris—posters, handbills, newspapers, paper fans—left behind by departing conventioneers. Others scrubbed the steps of the hall that led down to Meeting Street. As delegates steamed north out of Charleston harbor, a few noticed stonemasons increasing the height of the sixty-foot walls that rose out of the water at still-unfinished Fort Sumter.[62]

CHAPTER THREE

Principles and the "Duty to Recognize" None

The Constitutional Union and Liberty Parties

A T THE AGE OF SEVENTY-THREE, John J. Crittenden was esteemed as the "*Pater Senatus*," the oldest member of the United States Senate. Born in Versailles, Kentucky, the son of a pioneer who fought beside George Rogers Clark during the American Revolution, Crittenden first entered the Senate chamber in March 1817, just as James Monroe began his first administration. His forty-three years in Washington had been interrupted by one term as governor and two nonconsecutive postings as attorney general, once briefly under Whig William Henry Harrison and later for a longer tour under Millard Fillmore. (His replacement in the office, following the election of Pierce, was Cushing.) Not unusual for a man his age and of that era, Crittenden had buried two wives and collected ten children and stepchildren. His third marriage, to the twice-widowed Elizabeth Moss, resulted in no further offspring, but it was a happy union, and Crittenden often thought it sad that his country was not as content as he.[1]

Nine years younger than Kentucky's Henry Clay, Crittenden came to regard the barely senior politician as a mentor and a beloved friend. So committed was Crittenden to Clay's career and program that in 1831 he stood aside to allow the Great Compromiser his seat in the Senate. "There was no *collusion*, no rivalry, between us," Crittenden assured his disappointed daughter. "All that was done was with my perfect accordance." Like Clay, Crittenden opposed the annexation of Texas in 1844 on the grounds that the admission of an enormous new slave state could reawaken long-slumbering sectional animosities. A decade later, he voted against the Kansas-Nebraska Act and then the Lecompton constitution for the same reason. He accepted the legality of Chief Justice Taney's Dred Scott decision, but as a Whig who believed in loose construction, he judged it wrongly decided and continued to believe that Congress possessed the power to ban slavery in the territories.[2]

Typical of their time, their border-South residence, and their political affiliation, Clay and Crittenden practiced slavery while claiming to lament its existence. Whereas Yancey and other fire-eaters defended unfree labor as a blessing to both whites and blacks, Clay denounced the practice as "indefensible" and "evil," although he thought "it better that Slaves should remain Slaves than be set loose as free men among us." Clay owned thirty-three black Americans at the time of his death in 1852; Crittenden was master to nine. Some were inherited from his father's estate, and the rest came as dowry with his first wife. He freed none of them. But in 1833, he joined an unsuccessful Senate minority in voting to restrict the further introduction of slaves into Kentucky. His life exemplified the divided mind of the upper South: Of his five sons, one, Thomas L. Crittenden, became a major general in the Union army. Another, George B. Crittenden, to his father's enormous sorrow, rose to the same rank in the Confederate military. Toward the end of his long life, Crittenden opposed Lincoln's Emancipation Proclamation.[3]

With the death of his mentor, the aged Crittenden took up the mantle of compromiser. He would spend the last three years of his life—his death on July 28, 1863, came one day before Yancey expired from kidney failure—desperately searching for a solution to the growing sectional divide. Like Clay before him, he thought it imperative that Kentucky take the lead in reconciliation, both because slavery was not as firmly entrenched in his state as in the lower South and because any conflict would likely place Kentucky on the military front. Quick to deplore abolitionists and Republican free soilers as dangerous to domestic peace, he was equally critical of southern fire-eaters. Crittenden denounced Davis's Senate resolutions as a dangerous abstraction. The genius of the Constitution,

Crittenden argued, had nothing to do with whether it was "made by people through the states or by the states for the people." As the lands between Texas and California might not be settled until the early days of the next century, Davis's resolutions made "a present evil out of an apprehension of a future one never likely to occur."[4]

In some ways, Crittenden's unsuccessful search for a political middle ground was more politically courageous than Douglas's disingenuous promotion of popular sovereignty as a compromise solution. The Kentuckian, at least, routinely branded slavery as "a great evil," and his vote against Kansas-Nebraska implicitly endorsed free-soil efforts to deny fresh lands to unfree labor. Yet his insistence that there were rhetorical "indiscretions on both sides" of the aisle was typical of self-professed moderates, who detested what they saw as the political extremes of anti- and proslavery forces. Crittenden's efforts, in the wake of the Charleston convention, to build a new party out of the ashes of the collapsed Whig organization—as well as his later attempts to devise a set of constitutional amendments in hopes of seducing a seceding South back into the Union—revealed the difficulties in trying to locate the political center of a national debate utterly unlike any previous one. For the past seventy years, politicians and voters had argued about tariffs or taxes. The antislavery critique of the South, however, was founded on moral considerations and not as easily negotiated away.[5]

Northern abolitionists faced a different sort of dilemma in the spring of 1860. As advocates of immediate emancipation and black social equality, militant abolitionists already held the moral high ground, as they saw it, and believed there was no virtue in sectional compromise. Many agreed with William Lloyd Garrison—who once famously burned a copy of the Constitution in protest of its clauses protecting slavery—that politics demanded the sort of concessions that no truly ethical person could countenance. Many declined to vote, and of course the white women and African Americans who populated the movement often could not vote. But with the dissolution of the Democrats in Charleston, it became clear that the outnumbered Republicans stood a chance of winning in November. Garrison's Massachusetts was safe for the Republicans, but New York had gone Democratic in 1852, and if Crittenden launched a third party that siphoned off moderate votes, it might do so again. Garrison was "indignant" that front-runner William Henry Seward had recently adopted a "cautious, calculating, retreating policy" in the wake of John Brown's raid, yet he conceded that Republicans might "not be in all respects as bad as another party." For abolitionists, that was the rub. Seward was no abolitionist, but neither was he Douglas, or worse yet, John C. Breckinridge or Jefferson Davis, both of whom remained viable candidates at the upcoming Baltimore and Richmond conventions. If abolitionists refused to vote, or threw their vote away to perennial protest candidate Gerrit Smith of New York, they risked helping to defeat an antislavery free soiler and electing a proslavery, expansionist president.[6]

Beyond the obvious fact that both abolitionists and former Whigs faced tough decisions in 1860, their differences were more profound than their similarities. Although white supremacy had never been as central to the Whig ideology as it remained to the Democrats, the Whigs had generally dealt with the issue by agreeing to disagree along sectional lines. (Their lack of coherence on the matter helps explain why the party collapsed between 1852 and 1856.) For every New England evangelical who abandoned the Whigs for the Republicans, there was a lower-North free soiler who feared that abolitionists, as Lincoln remarked in a eulogy for Henry Clay, would "tear to tatters [their] venerated constitution." Still, most Whigs, hailing from the party of capital, regarded unwaged labor as a clumsy and backward mode of production. If those in Kentucky and Virginia owned slaves, they also blamed the lack of southern prosperity on slavery. As a Whig congressman, Lincoln certainly believed that to be true, once observing that "a blind horse upon a treadmill" was the South's ideal "of what a laborer should be." Yet as late as 1856, Lincoln also worried that militant abolitionism would "shiver into fragments the Union of these states." Recognizing that a good many former Whigs along the border could support neither Republicans nor fire-eating Democrats, Crittenden, now essentially an independent, hoped to glue these fragments into a new political party.[7]

Whereas free soilers like Lincoln fretted over what he regarded as the ideological inflexibility of militant abolitionists, Crittenden worried about the dramatic rise of the Republican Party. In six short years, the party had gone from being a Kansas-Nebraska protest movement to being the republic's second-largest party, a truly remarkable achievement considering that it existed only in the North. New England was now solidly Republican, and in 1856 John C. Frémont had carried New York, Ohio, Iowa, Wisconsin, and Michigan. Crittenden doubted that the Democrats could unite in Baltimore, and their failure to do so would result in a Seward victory and southern secession. This ominous view was shared by numerous ex-Whigs along the border. Former congressman William C. Rives of Virginia insisted that slavery's expansion was "settled, once [and] for all, by the Constitution" and the Supreme Court, and nothing more need be said on the topic. A fellow Virginian agreed. The "theories" of both Democrats and Republicans were "equally defective and equally untenable in point of constitutional law." Attracted to the Whiggish economic policies of the Republicans but repelled by their intransigence regarding restriction, moderates like Rives and Crittenden were politicians without parties. Their job, as they saw it, was to silence "a few extremists" and speak for "the mass of right-thinking and right-feeling citizens."[8]

As it appeared increasingly likely that the two major parties would nominate sectional candidates who enjoyed little support outside their region, the question in the minds of many former Whigs was *whether the Union will endure.*" Southern Democrats habitually denigrated the Republicans as sectionalists, but Crittenden thought that equally true of Davis and Breckinridge supporters, "contingency Union men" whose loyalty to the nation depended upon who captured the White House in November. But if Crittenden was determined to be the architect of a new, centrist party, he was equally determined not to be that party's standard-bearer. September 10 would mark his seventy-fourth birthday, and America had not been kind to aged presidents. Crittenden was already five years older than Harrison had been at the time of his death in 1841 at age sixty-eight. Crittenden had served Harrison—then the oldest man to be elected president—as attorney general, and in 1859 his daughter Ann begged him not to consider a run. Crittenden assured her that he had never received *"wiser* or nobler advice." He wished only to complete his term in the Senate and help to launch a new party, after which he planned to "escape and get off smoothly."[9]

Aware of Crittenden's reluctance to serve, the editor of the *Republican Banner and Nashville Whig*, on January 9, 1860, instead floated the possibility of John Bell of Tennessee. Younger than Crittenden by eleven years, Bell had an equally impressive résumé. A member of Congress since 1827, he had briefly served in Harrison's cabinet as secretary of war, and from 1847 to 1859 he had represented his state in the Senate. Like Crittenden, Bell owned a large number of slaves but had cast his vote against Kansas-Nebraska. As a result, fire-eaters denounced him as "an Abolitionist, a traitor to the South, and an affiliator with the Republicans of the North." Southern moderates thought otherwise. "There is nothing of the demagogue about him," observed the New Orleans *Bulletin*. Similar endorsements quickly graced the pages of the New Orleans *Bee*, the Baltimore *Patriot*, and the Cincinnati *Gazette*. On January 11, former Whigs in the Tennessee legislature—calling themselves only "the Opposition" to the Democrats—held a caucus, which in turn advocated a state convention to be held on February 22 to elect delegates to a national convention. Bell, they added, was their candidate.[10]

The state convention, held in Frankfort, exceeded all expectations. Most counties sent at least one delegate, and the populous midstate counties appointed large delegations. Shortly after W. L. Martin was chosen as chairman, the delegates submitted a series of resolutions. Asserting that "the true test of devotion to the Union" was "obedience to the requirements of the Constitution," they condemned abolitionism as "fraught with infinite mischiefs," and as former Whigs, they advocated the return to a high tariff of protection. Martin read a statement signed by twenty-one former Whigs, including Crittenden, Rives, and former congressman and naval secretary John Pendleton Kennedy of Maryland, calling for a national convention to be held in Baltimore that May. The single-day Tennessee conference concluded with the recommendation of a Bell candidacy on the grounds of his "superior qualifications" and his "broad and expansive patriotism." Several days later, a gathering of "conservatives and patriotic men" met in Boston's Faneuil Hall to endorse the idea and select delegates for Baltimore. Self-described as "men of all parties," the Boston group actually consisted of followers of the late Daniel Webster, a leading Whig, so it is not surprising that Massachusetts's Edward Everett, who had replaced Webster in the State Department upon his death in 1852, was "prominently mentioned" as a potential candidate.[11]

At age sixty-three, Tennessee's John Bell was the oldest candidate in 1860.
Although a slaveholder and once a Democrat, Bell had become a Whig after
a falling out with President Andrew Jackson. Typical of both his state
and party, Bell had diverse holdings in agriculture and industry;
he both owned and leased slaves for his Cumberland Iron Works.
Courtesy Library of Congress.

Third parties rarely expect to win. As was the case with former congressman Gerrit Smith, who ran as either the Liberty Party or the Radical Abolition Party candidate in 1848, 1852, and 1856, third-party activists typically hoped to advance a single issue or prod one of the major parties into embracing their cause. Crittenden's movement, however, which increasingly adopted the name Constitutional Union Party, thought it likely they could name a president, if perhaps not in the general election. They assumed that Seward could secure the same eleven states captured in 1856 by Frémont, with the lower South rallying behind Davis or

Breckinridge. But with the Democrats in danger of collapse, they hoped to carry the border, which had gone to Buchanan in that election. Fillmore and his American Party (commonly dubbed the Know Nothings) had won 82,175 votes in Pennsylvania to Buchanan's 230,710 and Frémont's 147,510. If the Constitutional Unionists could win Pennsylvania and Ohio—especially if abolitionists in the latter states threw their votes to Smith—and add Crittenden's Kentucky, Bell's Tennessee, and Rives's Virginia, they might succeed in denying any candidate a majority in the Electoral College. The presidency would then be settled in Congress, with each state receiving a single vote. There, they hoped, moderation and compromise would prevail.[12]

As did every party in 1860, the Constitutional Unionists featured a number of potential candidates, or at least ambitious men who so regarded themselves. The *New York Herald*, always fascinated with counting candidates, put the number at ten. Notwithstanding the Nashville meeting's endorsement of Bell, and despite Crittenden's public demurrals, most former Whigs assumed that the Kentuckian would get the nod in Baltimore. (Traditional claims of indifference by leading candidates made it difficult for even seasoned political observers to tell how seriously to treat such protestations.) Even in Faneuil Hall, when a Bostonian mentioned Crittenden's name, "the severe decorum of the assembly completely broke down" with cheers and applause. A number of conservative newspapers, from the *Philadelphia Inquirer* and the St. Louis *News* to the Wilmington *Commonwealth* and the Louisville *Journal*, endorsed his candidacy.[13]

For those who took Crittenden at his word, Sam Houston of Texas appeared an attractive option. The Virginia-born, Tennessee-bred Houston boasted an eclectic résumé that included serving as a lieutenant in the War of 1812, governor of both Tennessee and Texas, president of the Republic of Texas, and senator from the state from 1846 to 1859. While in Washington, Houston joined Bell in voting against Kansas-Nebraska, correctly predicting that popular sovereignty would result in bloodshed on the frontier. Houston was then sixty-eight, but despite a long lifetime of dueling and heavy drinking, the giant Texan remained vigorous; his wife, Margaret, twenty-six years his junior, was then pregnant with their eighth child. But the proud Houston refused to have his "name submitted to any Convention." Although he was willing to serve, any movement to place him in the president's chair, he insisted, "must originate with the people themselves." And while voters disdained those who wanted office too badly—ever Henry Clay's fatal flaw—party activists were not much interested in haughty candidates who regarded conventions as subversive to the will of the American people.[14]

Constitutional Unionists from Missouri advanced the name of former congressman and Virginia native Edward Bates. Once offered the position of secretary of war in Fillmore's cabinet, Bates had nearly been tapped for the vice presidency by the Whigs in 1852. But the cagey Bates refused to flatly rule out accepting the Republican nomination if offered it, and fire-eater James De Bow regarded the man who in 1861 would become Lincoln's attorney general as a "Black-republican" in all but name. Some Virginians preferred Rives or former congressman John Minor Botts, although the latter, while a planter, was as publicly antagonistic to fire-eaters as any abolitionist. At least one Virginian thought General Winfield Scott the ideal candidate. Despite the fact that he shared Crittenden's birth year and had fared badly in the presidential contest of 1852—carrying only four states to Pierce's twenty-seven—Scott assured Crittenden that he remained "in the most vigorous of health." The increasingly obese old warrior, burdened by gout and rheumatism, admitted that he no longer "walk[ed] as well" as he once had. But he added that "once elected I fear I shall find it difficult to avoid a second term." Scott did, however, urge Crittenden to let him know if he believed that the general's day had passed. "I give you leave to retort," Scott informed the Kentuckian, "sufficient for the day is the evil thereof."[15]

Dedicated to a Bell candidacy, Crittenden declined to retort. Instead, he boarded a train for Baltimore to join what editor Horace Greeley dismissed as a "Great Gathering of Fossil Know Nothings and Southern Americans." Crittenden accepted an invitation to stay at John Pendleton Kennedy's home, while Houston's supporters established a headquarters at Barnum's Hotel. Rives, adopting the expected pose of apathy, begged off on business, but in a break with protocol Bell arrived in the city on May 7. He and his second wife, Jane, moved into the Eutaw House, as did several other Tennessee delegates. One ungenerously described Jane Bell as "ugly as ever," although he conceded that she was also "very shrewd" and deeply ambitious for her husband. Altogether, twenty-three of the thirty-three states sent delegates, and of those that did not, some, like California and Oregon, were too distant, while others, such as South Carolina, simply had no interest in the prospect of compromise.[16]

The convention was scheduled to begin on Wednesday, May 9. It had been just six days since the Democrats had put Charleston behind them, and the intrepid Murat Halstead, who was determined to cover all of that year's many conventions, arrived in Baltimore just before the gavel fell. Early that morning, the "National Central Executive Committee" met, incongruously, "in the saloon of [the] Temperance Temple." Stranger still, Crittenden announced that the committee "had no business" to transact and then herded the confused delegates toward the main convention, in a large Presbyterian church on the corner of Fayette Street and North Avenue. Hastily arranged patriotic imagery covered the religious furnishings. The side and rear walls were "festooned with tricolored drapery," and toward the front stood a full-sized painting of George Washington, "surmounted by an American Eagle" and two enormous flags. "The general appearance," Halstead noted with amusement, was as "patriotic as the *Times* office on Washington's birthday."[17]

As Crittenden entered the hall, delegates rose in ovation; some waved hats and handkerchiefs. Looking every day of his seven decades, Crittenden bowed "until he was tired" before finally taking his seat. The audience shouted for a speech, but Crittenden stood only long enough to remind the group that they represented "the party of the whole country" and to nominate former New York governor Washington Hunt as the convention's chairman. To more applause, Hunt took the podium and delivered a short speech, emphasizing the importance of goodwill and harmony. As the majority Democrats had been "wrecked on the mysteries of Territorial sovereignty," it was their "duty to recognize no principle," to see "no North, no South." The "slavery issue," he insisted, was "a miserable abstraction." Believing that the crisis in the West that had been sparked by the Mexican-American War could be solved by soothing tones, the delegates easily adopted the mood of "courtesy, and deferential deportment toward one another." One delegate reported that "there was not an angry word spoken throughout." A bored Halstead pronounced the assembly too filled with unanimity "to be interesting," but he also identified the new party's chief flaw. They believed "that political salvation so devoutly to be wished for" might simply be achieved "by ignoring all the rugged issues of the day."[18]

So determined were the Constitutional Unionists to take no position on the single most important issue of the decade that when Leslie Coombs of Kentucky, the chair of the platform committee, was called on to give a report, he provoked laughter by announcing that he considered preparing three. One, he declared, was for the Democrats, "who have lately agreed together so beautifully at Charleston," the second was for the "irrepressible conflict" Republicans preparing to meet in Chicago, and a third was for their own convention. But as experience suggested that platforms only caused "political divisions" and encouraged "geographical and sectional parties," Coombs proposed that their only platform be "the Constitution as it is, and the Union under it now and forever." This elicited not only "great applause" but also the approval of Washington's leading newspaper. Calling the gathering "the Whig National Convention," the *National Intelligencer* agreed that "platforms might be safely dispensed with, as at best superfluous appendages" that were "utterly powerless to secure consistency of political purpose."[19]

Halstead was less impressed, and rightly so. Constitutional Unionists might insist that only "abstract questions" divided the two major parties, but from the moment the Constitution had been ratified in 1788, Americans had squabbled over questions of constitutionality and loose versus strict construction. And for enslaved Americans who faced possible resale into the fresh lands of the New Mexico Territory, the fate of the west was far from a foolish abstraction. Unwilling to address this fundamental flaw in their philosophy, the delegates tried to paper over critical issues with raucous, patriotic oratory. Every speaker was received with tremendous applause, and key words—Constitution, law, Union, flag, conservative—inspired a general "stamping, clapping hands, [and] rattling canes." Halstead had been horrified by the vitriol and rage on display in Charleston, but in Baltimore he found only a rich source for ridicule. "When a speaker would put off something about the Constitution," he reported, the delegate "would be obligated to suspend his remarks until the tempest of approbation subsided." The unfortunate speaker would then start the sentence again, only to find that "the storm would break out again with redoubled fury."[20]

The forced good humor within the convention, however, did not stop New York's Daniel D. Barnard from publishing a hard-hitting pamphlet, *Truths for the Times*. A former Whig congressman, Barnard was clearly furious with those antislavery politicians who had abandoned his party for the Republicans, for his pamphlet barely deigned to mention the Democrats. While the publication was designed as an exposé of the Republican leadership, the "truths" revealed here surprised few readers, since his intent was to prove that Republican free soilers secretly desired the end of slavery. Barnard trotted out the usual references to Seward's "irrepressible conflict" speech and quoted Senator Charles Sumner's assertion that a ring of free communities in the West could serve as a "belt of fire" to prevent the expansion of slavery and force its eventual demise. Barnard reserved most of his venom for the "ultra abolitionist" Seward, and he warned that the New Yorker had promised to replace the aged Taney on the Supreme Court with an antislavery jurist. But Lincoln, who had toured the East following his senatorial campaign, earned at least a single rebuke, as Barnard mentioned Lincoln's hopes of restricting slavery as a prelude to its "ultimate extinction."[21]

That evening, moreover, all talk of party unity vanished as delegates began to lobby for their candidates—and dispute the electability of others—with as much grim determination as was ever evidenced in Charleston. Despite Houston's disdain for electioneering, one delegate counted his followers as "more numerous than the supporters of any other candidate," and a New York journalist regarded them as "the most zealous workers here." At least two thirds of the New Yorkers favored the flamboyant Texan, as did "a large majority" of the New Jersey men. Most of the Massachusetts contingent favored Crittenden, but Houston was their fallback should their man continue to refuse the position; Kentucky's delegation held much the same view. A few Virginians lobbied for Botts, but that attempt "utterly failed."[22]

For many delegates, the virtues of a Houston candidacy were abundant. Unlike Crittenden and Bell, Houston had spent most of his career as a Democrat, and David Porter, the former governor of Pennsylvania and an ardent Buchanan supporter, wrote to insist that Houston should run well among his state's "conservative democrats." As a resident of three southern states and the hero of two wars, Houston might appeal to enough southern Democrats to prevent the party from reuniting in Baltimore, "leaving Douglas only the free soil portions of the split democratic party." Although he owned a dozen slaves, Houston consistently denounced Kansas-Nebraska, so he might also appeal to moderately antislavery Whigs who believed that Seward was too radical. One New Jersey delegate claimed that Houston's nomination would toss "a thunderbolt [in]to the Chicago Convention."[23]

For their part, the former Whigs who dominated the convention refused to rally behind a man regarded as too friendly to the late Andrew Jackson, and they argued that a Houston candidacy would simply hand New York to Seward. As the Bell handlers spent a sleepless night in a room-to-room canvass, support for Houston began to melt away. Crittenden played his part by continuing to insist that he was "tired of public life" and "disgusted with the low party politics of the day." Given the political fluidity of the decade, as northern Whigs and Democrats became Republicans while border Whigs and Democrats found themselves without a political home, Bell's advocates thought it likely that leading Republicans, deciding that Seward was too polarizing a figure to win in November, might endorse Bell and pursue a fusion strategy. "We shall see how this billing and cooing will come out," quipped one reporter, "this *blackey* [Republican] and *whitey* [Constitutional Unionist] kissing in the dark." Since even Houston's backers knew him to be a rhetorical loose cannon—his friends called him "the Big Drunk" and referred to Texas as "the Big Drunk's Ranch"—there was always the danger that Houston might openly criticize slavery, where Bell could be counted on to maintain a discreet silence. As one New York journalist graphically observed of the party's slaveholding delegates, they "may sleep with the nigger, eat with the nigger, but [they] don't allow his woolly head to come into the convention [speeches]."[24]

Determined to maintain the image of a harmonious, united convention, the delegates "resolved almost unanimously" to proceed to balloting on May 10, the second morning of the gathering. As with the Democrats, each state was granted as many votes as it held in the Electoral College, but no two-thirds requirement burdened the process. Delegates responded "with loud applause" as each of ten names was placed in nomination. Of the ten, however, only four were regarded as serious candidates.

On the first ballot, Bell led with 68½ votes to Houston's 57, Crittenden's 28, and Everett's 25. For a party that claimed to disregard regionalism, the first ballot revealed the Constitutional Unionists to be badly divided along sectional lines. Fully half of Houston's strength came from New York, whereas Bell's scattered ballots represented Tennessee, Pennsylvania, and Maryland. Virginia and Kentucky men honored their favorite sons by casting all of their ballots for Rives or Crittenden.[25]

Multiple ballots were typical of the era, however, and the first round of voting was rarely much more than a test of strength, a way to honor local statesmen, and a method for winnowing out minor candidates. The second ballot would decide the nominee. With Rives and Crittenden off the ballot, Bell picked up Kentucky's vote. Massachusetts, which had cast its 13 votes for Everett, now gave 12 to Bell (despite the fact that Everett remained on the ballot). Texas, inexplicably, this time handed its 4 votes to Bell, who finished the count with 125 votes to Houston's 68. The announcement that Bell had won the majority set off "a tearing roar of cheers, [and] a violent stamping" that ceased only after a cracking noise in the gallery led to a mad rush for the stairs. The suddenly empty balcony remained standing, and embarrassed delegates below began the tedious job of changing their votes to make the selection unanimous. As Bell, on the advice of his managers, had finally departed for Philadelphia, Gustavus A. Henry of Tennessee accepted the nomination in his behalf. Whispers passed word of Henry's ancestry until somebody shouted that he was "a grandson of Patrick Henry," leading to yet another round of cheers. Chairman Hunt, "his eyes streaming tears," dashed down the aisle to shake Henry's hand. "We have presented [Bell] to the Union Party," Henry said, believing "that the country cannot, under any circumstances, do better than to elect him to the Presidential chair."[26]

The disgruntled Virginians had declined to cast a single vote in the second ballot, but one of their number now rose to recommend former secretary of state Edward Everett of Massachusetts for the vice presidency. The speaker, in a clumsy attempt at gallantry, added that he endorsed the handsome Everett "in behalf of the women of Virginia," which inspired former North Carolina governor John Morehead to second the nomination in behalf of his state's "wives and daughters." The ladies in the gallery applauded, but when telegraphed of the honor, Everett was privately mortified. Although supportive of the party and reluctantly prepared to accept the top position on the ticket, the idea of running behind the less accomplished Bell offended the celebrated orator. "It looks like favoring an officer with the command of a sloop-of-war," he complained to his daughter, "after he had magnanimously waived his claim to the flag of the Mediterranean Squadron, in favor of a junior officer." Many New Englanders agreed. One editor dubbed it the "kangaroo ticket," because its hind legs were longer.[27]

Exhausted and hoarse from shouting though they were, the delegates demanded still more speeches. Although lacking his celebrated grandfather's ability to shake the rafters, Henry was pleased to oblige, and he "ascended the platform amid great cheering." In a dreary speech broken every two sentences by applause, he assured the crowd that Bell's administration would be "pure, constitutional, economical, and patriotic." Henry hastened to add that Bell "was always ready" to endorse internal improvements, for that was a cause dear to every Whig's heart, but the crowd was too busy cheering to recall that most voters regarded federal spending on roads, canals, and railroads as anything but "economical." Henry briefly startled his audience by observing that the balding, grim-visaged Bell was "slow and cautious," but he recovered by dramatically pointing to the portrait of Washington. "That venerable man," he shouted, emotion trumping accuracy, "was always cautious."[28]

Ever since the election of 1840 and the cry of "Tippecanoe and Tyler, too," the Whigs had grasped the importance of political symbolism. Yet their platforms had always been clear as to policy. By comparison, the final speech of the convention revealed how utterly destitute of serious ideas the Constitutional Union Party was. In closing, Coombs, perhaps in an appeal to unhappy Houston supporters, insisted that the Bell and Everett ticket would "toll the [death] knell of the Democratic party." Most of the audience caught the pun and applauded. Pleased with the reaction, Coombs expanded upon it. The ticket furnished the "bell-metal necessary" to save the country, he roared, and voters were sure to rally to "the enormous National Bell which was to be sounded over the Union." And "so on for quantity," sighed Halstead. Finally satiated, the weary but pleased delegates spilled out into the night.[29]

In the coming days, party stalwarts returned to the imagery again and again. That Monday, Kennedy hosted a rally in Baltimore's Monument Square. One friendly journalist reported that the plaza was "densely thronged in all its parts, and that the greatest enthusiasm prevailed." A few of the delegates still lingered in town, and several spoke from the steps of Battle Monument, built to memorialize the soldiers who died in the Battle of North Point, during the War of 1812. The highlight was the appearance of a wagon carrying an enormous bell, which Kennedy rung "much to the merriment of the crowd." The party's motto, he added for those who had somehow failed to catch the symbolism, was "Our Bell rings to the sound of the Union; try it." One week later, a similar rally was staged in Everett's Boston, and once again party supporters marched behind a horse-drawn wagon pulling a giant bell. "It was too bad to laugh at," groaned one observer. "A more orderly and respectful funeral procession I have never seen, though the mourners were few."[30]

Bell and his family were in Philadelphia, staying at La Pierre House, on Broad Street, when news of his nomination arrived. On the Friday after the convention adjourned, supporters gathered outside the elegant, five-story hotel to serenade the candidate. The first to arrive were able to squeeze into the hotel's lobby and hallways, while as many as several thousand others illuminated several blocks of Broad with "flambeaux and torches." After a band played "a number of patriotic airs," Bell and Joseph R. Ingersoll stepped out onto the balcony. Ingersoll, a former Whig congressman and minister to Britain, introduced Bell "as *a* candidate for the Presidency." He then paused to play upon the sort of wishful thinking prevalent at the Baltimore meeting. "Perhaps he ought to say *the* candidate, for he trusted that other parties, convinced of the propriety and patriotism manifested in the choice, might concur in the wisdom of the nomination." The idea that partisan rivals in that angry, bitter year might embrace a party that willfully ignored the critical issues of the day inspired "enthusiastic applause," followed by a curious, implicit rebuke from the candidate himself. Leaning over the railing, Bell delivered a short speech indicating that while his party chose to ignore divisive political positions, that did not mean that he himself had none. "Not only are my sentiments known in regard to these questions" of slavery and the territories, he announced, "but in regard to every other question of domestic policy, as well as of foreign policy." Several other speakers hastily returned to bromides about "the flag," "principles of peace and harmony," and "fraternal brotherhood," but Bell's brief reference to "domestic policy" hinted that the bland Tennessean was not quite the hollow vessel his handlers wished him to be.[31]

Several days later, Bell returned to Nashville. Following the expected reception at the station platform and a procession to the City Hotel, on the Public Square, Bell shuttered himself in his room to draft the requisite letter of acceptance. Because candidates were not supposed to seek public office, part of this political theater required the candidate to appear surprised by the unexpected honor. On May 21, Bell notified Washington Hunt that, "diffident as [he] was of [his] worthiness," he did not hesitate to "accept the position assigned to [him] by that distinguished and patriotic body." The lengthy missive included the expected references to "the Union, harmony, and prosperity." But Bell also bluntly observed that the lack of a party platform "exact[ed] no pledge" from him as to what course he might pursue if elected, although a guide was "to be found in his past history connected with the public service." Since Bell had sided against the Kansas-Nebraska Act, his previous votes suggested he was no friend to slavery's extension. The Baltimore delegates emphasized that it was the prerogative of "the Judicial department to interpret" the Constitution, a veiled reference to the Dred Scott decision, but Bell would only promise "not to depart from the tenor and spirit of [his] past course," adding that "the obligation to keep this pledge derive[d] a double force from the consideration that none [was] required from [him]."[32]

Everett accepted in a letter to Hunt one week later, but the choice of the Bostonian proved to be unfortunate, and not merely because Everett's impressive résumé overshadowed Bell's political service. By selecting two prominent former Whigs, instead of choosing a disaffected northern Democrat for the second spot, the Constitutional Unionists revealed themselves, in the words of one San Antonio editor, to be little more than "the ghost of the old Whig party," whose "dead bones still rattle[d] to the breeze." The party had avoided a platform statement so as not to be divided along regional lines, and in the process they had also said nothing regarding economic policy. Henry's speech in Baltimore, however, reminded voters that Bell, like Crittenden and Clay before him, supported the pro-development programs despised by working-class

Democrats. It helped little that Bell's longtime friend James C. Welling, the publisher of the conservative *National Intelligencer*, hinted in his paper's endorsement of the ticket that the Baltimore convention had abandoned no Whig principle. As the pelting of August Belmont indicated, Douglas had critics enough among northern Democrats, but the selection of Everett allowed Democrats to brand the "old fogies" with "the condemned issues of a national bank [and] a high tariff."[33]

As a result, though, the Constitutional Unionists eventually injured the Douglas candidacy more than they did the Republican cause. Competitive only in the border South, the party ran well where Republicans could expect little support. Aptly characterized by Jefferson Davis as "the Whig candidate," Bell eroded potential nominee Douglas's popularity in Virginia. As a business-minded Democrat supportive of government assistance to the railroads, Douglas was anything but an old-style, strict-construction Jacksonian. But the presence of a purely Whig ticket in the contest allowed former Whigs in Virginia, Kentucky, and Tennessee to remain true to their old party. Especially since the Constitutional Unionists were none too secretive about their objective of throwing the election into the House, aged Whigs in the upper South regarded a vote for Bell as far from wasted.[34]

Hoping to expand their influence into the lower South, a small number of Constitutional Unionists in Alabama convened a statewide meeting in late June in Selma. Since the national body had declined to draft a platform, the Alabama minority decided to draw up one of their own. While pledging loyalty to the Union, the Selma faction made its position clear regarding the frontier. The "territories are the common property of all the States," they insisted, "and therefore, the people of all the States have the right to enter upon and occupy any Territory with their slaves." Neither "Congress, nor a Territorial Legislature" possessed the power to deny settlers their "enjoyment of their slave property." By adopting Yancey's and Davis's position, the Alabama members placed themselves in opposition to the national party, so much so that a few party leaders suspected the Selma meeting to consist of nothing more than Democratic disruptionists. But if this was an honest attempt to compete with Democratic fire-eaters in the lower South, it backfired. When northern members heard of the Selma platform, a good many opted to support the

Republicans. "I will vote the Republican ticket," decided one New Yorker who had initially favored Bell. "The only alternative is everlasting submission to the South," he concluded, and he wanted "to be able to remember that [he] voted right at this grave crisis."[35]

Historians have rarely been kind to the Constitutional Union Party and its candidate. Even Bell's modern biographer adopted the common assessment that his nomination "was probably an unwise move." Bell was "not a man of much stature," concluded another. The candidate, admittedly, was hampered by his cold, formal manner, as well as a lifelong habit of delivering bland, uninspiring speeches. His devotion to the Whig cause cost the party potential Democratic support, just as his ownership of slaves damaged his candidacy across the North. The fact that he appeared older than his sixty-four years reminded voters that his political cohort consisted of deceased giants like Clay and Webster; by comparison, the younger generation of candidates, men like Seward, Lincoln, Douglas, and Breckinridge, spoke to the future. Yet Bell did intimate that his future policies would not deviate from his past positions, and his lonely vote against Kansas-Nebraska had required political courage, even in Tennessee. Perhaps it was not that the party was hindered by Bell, but rather that Bell was held back by a party that stubbornly refused to debate the only issue American voters cared about.[36]

Whatever else he was, Bell was the first candidate to be nominated in 1860, and as the Democrats were repeatedly to demonstrate, that was no small accomplishment. Moreover, the fact that the venerable Whig Party was back under a new name indicated that there would be at least three candidates in the field that year, and perhaps four, if the Democrats failed to reunite in Baltimore. For antislavery radicals, though, 1860 would necessitate a hard choice, for all of their options appeared disagreeable.

The first was to maintain their moral purity by either casting a protest vote for Gerrit Smith or not involving themselves in any manner with a constitutional system that recognized the legitimacy of slavery. Garrison, for one, refused "co-operation with Mr. Smith and the Radical Abolitionists" on the grounds that antislavery legislators "fraternize politically with the existing [Buchanan] administration" and so "become partakers of its crimes." Another option was to vote Republican on the grounds that Seward, despite his recent "disappointing" shifts toward the center, was the closest thing to an antislavery president that America was likely to get. Yet while the Republicans claimed to be antislavery, they insisted they were not abolitionists, and there was nothing in their 1856 free-soil platform to contradict that claim. Secure in the rightness of their cause, militant abolitionists regarded the Republicans as rank politicians, too ready to compromise with the "Slave Power." Some charged that the anti-slavery movement might have accomplished more by 1860 had the moderate Republicans, as Abby Kelley Foster put it, not "stealthily suck[ed] the very blood from our veins." Parker Pillsbury agreed. In voting for the Republicans, he assured one antislavery audience, "you as effectively vote for slavery as you would in voting for Stephen A. Douglas." But rhetoric aside, popular sovereignty allowed for the possibility of slavery's expansion. Bell was on record as opposing Kansas-Nebraska, but only the Republicans were committed to overturning both the 1854 law and Taney's ruling.[37]

If white abolitionists were at best ambivalent regarding the Republicans, the northern black community was frequently hostile. Not only did the party refuse to commit to immediate emancipation, but prominent Republicans like Lincoln reluctantly admitted the constitutionality of the 1850 Fugitive Slave Act and continued to promote colonization despite the overwhelming repudiation of emigration by northern blacks. As Connecticut activist William Anderson wrote in response to a series of pro-colonization editorials in Greeley's *New York Tribune*, "there is no middle ground between Slavery and Freedom, [for] that time has gone by." Greeley "must either be the friend of the black man—or his enemy." The level of racial animus heard in Republican rallies rarely reached the lows found in a Stephen Douglas speech, but coming from men who professed to despise slavery, the insensitivity was all the more galling. Impatient with their refusal to endorse black voting rights or even citizenship—the latter having been denied them by Taney—the black journalist Thomas Hamilton charged that the "Republican party today" was "by far [a] more dangerous enemy" than the Democrats. In a March 1860 editorial in the *Weekly Anglo-African*, Hamilton admitted that under "the guise of humanity, they do and say many things." But Republican "opposition to slavery means opposition to the black man—nothing else. Where it is clearly in their power to do anything for the oppressed colored man, why then they are too nice, too conservative, to do it."[38]

When it came to social equality, the gulf between antislavery activists and most Republican politicians exposed the distinction between militants who answered only to their consciences and elected officials who answered to the voters. The vast majority of northern whites disapproved of slavery, but promoting civil rights for African Americans was something else entirely. African American men could vote in New England (with the exception of Connecticut), where they represented roughly 3 percent of the population, but Republicans could take those electoral votes for granted. Blacks constituted a larger percent of the population in the Empire State, but endorsing universal black voting rights there—in place of the $250 property qualification imposed on African Americans—could cost the Republicans moderate white votes, while newly enfranchised blacks might do as Rochester's Frederick Douglass did and vote for Smith. And political considerations aside, there was every reason to believe that most Republicans shared the attitudes of their white neighbors in 1860.[39]

Like all reform movements, the antislavery crusade was not a single, unified campaign. Many Massachusetts abolitionists shared Garrison's view that the Constitution was "a covenant with death" and refused to go to the polls. Others, like Smith, former Kentucky slaveholder James G. Birney, and merchants Arthur and Lewis Tappan, organized the Liberty Party in 1840 in hopes of working within the political system. In 1848, Senator Salmon P. Chase and Gamaliel Bailey, editor of the Washington antislavery newspaper *National Era*, sought to lead most Liberty members into the Free Soil Party, which advocated only the restriction of slavery in the lands taken from Mexico. Smith chose to remain with the Liberty remnants, and in that year he replaced Birney as the party's candidate, a role he performed twice more in 1852 and 1856. Smith, however, was nobody's idea of a chief executive. Although six feet tall and graced with elegant manners and a melodious voice (and enormous wealth due to his vast land holdings), Smith was given to sudden mood swings; even friends found him compulsive, childlike, and erratic. Garrison's *Liberator* ridiculed Smith's tiny but resolute party, calling them "a mere baker's dozen." Most Republicans preferred not to be identified with either faction of what Greeley characterized as a "little coterie of common scolds," and a January 1857 attempt to unify Liberty members with radical Republicans at a convention in Worcester, Massachusetts, came to nothing. Delegate Henry Wilson reported that all in attendance were "sick of the Southern gas on the subject," but beyond that, the Liberty and Republican delegates occupied little common ground.[40]

If Republicans rarely wished to be identified with abolitionists, neither did they desire their enmity. Black activists might not think them to be antislavery, but free soilers saw themselves as such, and if they did not expect to win many Liberty Party votes, they did hope that northern voters could distinguish between their policies and those of Douglas Democrats. In the spring of 1860, William H. Herndon, Lincoln's law partner, even traveled east to lobby Garrison. Although born in Kentucky, the short, dapper Herndon read widely and was enamored of transcendentalism. He was also a subscriber to the *Liberator*, which made Lincoln the only candidate whose office received Garrison's journal. "You hate Republicans," Herndon bluntly observed. "But never mind *that*; it is a midlink," a chain by which the abolitionists could "climb to heaven." For all of his contempt for politics, Garrison listened carefully. With the Democrats in disarray, Garrison understood that the Republicans had a real chance in 1860, and he thought it far preferable to have Seward or Sumner—he knew almost nothing about Herndon's partner—rather than Douglas in the White House. Herndon asked for nothing but consideration and departed with a copy of Garrison's *Selections* tucked under his arm. Checking up on Lincoln, Garrison was displeased with the Illinoisan's position on the Fugitive Slave Act. But Sumner sent word along that Lincoln was "a good antislavery man" and a "person of ability and real goodness."[41]

For all of their pious talk of being above squalid partisan politics, abolitionists of all stripes lived in the United States and were affected by decisions made in Washington. Pragmatists recalled the election of 1844, in which Liberty Party voters, according to furious Whigs, had cost Henry Clay the presidency. As a Kentucky planter and colonizationist, Clay was always suspect in the minds of abolitionists, and when his ever-shifting positions on Texas annexation began to tilt toward expansion,

Former congressman Gerrit Smith was the wealthiest of the many candidates,
and he used his considerable fortune to help finance a number of reform
movements, including temperance, education, and legal expenses for captured
runaway slaves. One of the Secret Six, the chief financial backers of
John Brown, Smith later joined with editor Horace Greeley to post bail
for Jefferson Davis. Courtesy Library of Congress.

irritated northern Whigs cast their vote for Birney. The Liberty Party
captured 2.3 percent of the national vote, and 8 percent in Massachusetts,
New Hampshire, and Vermont. New York and its 36 electoral votes went
to James K. Polk, although he drew only 2,106 more votes in the state

than Clay. Since Birney won nearly 16,000 votes in the Empire State, Greeley charged that by splitting the anti-Democratic vote, Liberty adherents "carried all these votes obliquely in favor of Annexation, War, and eternal slavery." Lincoln agreed. By refusing to stand by the Whigs, inflexible abolitionists had elevated a proslavery expansionist into the president's chair. "If the fruit of electing Mr. Clay would have been to prevent the extension of slavery," he fumed, "could the act of electing [him] have been *evil?*"[42]

Aware of the Constitutional Unionist strategy of attempting to throw the election into the House, editor Bailey worried that any coalition government could only damage the antislavery crusade through a lack of ideology. As Bell and Everett refused to issue an unambiguous declaration on the territories, the election of anybody but a Republican would surely lead to slavery's expansion. Even a few black abolitionists thought it wisest to support the Republicans in hopes of shoving the party into a more progressive stance after Inauguration Day. Republicans "talk of slaveholders' rights '*under the Constitution*' about as flippantly as the slaveholders do themselves," editorialized William J. Watkins. Yet they were also "the only political party in the land in a position, numerically speaking, to strike a deathblow to American slavery—such a blow as will send it staggering to hell." If most Republicans were not yet where militant abolitionists wished them to be, Watkins suggested, "let Abolitionists strive to make [them] right. More can be accomplished on the part of those who are right, by going into the party and renovating and revolutionizing it, than by standing outside harping upon beautiful theory." Dedicated Liberty voters might think little of the Republicans, but Garrison was correct in describing Smith's following as minuscule. By comparison to the 1,342,345 votes captured by Frémont in 1856, Smith's numbers were tiny. If "slavery is going to be voted down in this Republic," Watkins concluded, "it becomes a matter of arithmetic."[43]

The public criticism of Republican timidity, moreover, masked a series of friendly private relationships, especially between politicized abolitionists and radical Republicans. Smith and Chase maintained a lively correspondence, polite even in disagreement, as did Sumner and Theodore Parker, a Massachusetts abolitionist and Unitarian minister. If many Republicans sought to maintain a public distance from abolitionists, Chase actively sought the endorsement of Bailey's *National Era*, and like many antislavery Republicans, Chase understood that abolitionist protests helped to prepare the voters' minds for his more temperate party. "Our agitation," Boston abolitionist Wendell Phillips reminded Sumner, "helps keep yours alive in the rank and file." Northern Democrats and Constitutional Unionists, perusing critical editorials in the *Liberator*, assumed they could count on Liberty voters to again waste their ballots. But differences of opinion rarely reflected genuine dislike on either side, and in any case, the policy disagreements that separated Republicans from Liberty supporters were minute compared to the gulf that divided antislavery voters from even northern Democrats. Stephen Douglas routinely sneered at abolitionists, observed the Republican *Chicago Tribune*, yet "whatever may be their errors, [they] are still examples of that sublime fanaticism which dares and does for truth and right, [whereas] you are simply contemptible."[44]

Believing it necessary to maintain a formal distinction between themselves and the Republicans—as well as the Garrisonians, who many abolitionists thought had all but endorsed the party by moderating their criticisms of Seward—a small number of activists nominated Smith for what would be his fourth and final run at the presidency. Even by Liberty Party standards, the meeting was but a small affair. The party held a brief convention in Boston, endorsed Smith and Samuel McFarland of Pennsylvania, and collected only fifty dollars to finance the campaign. Candidates never openly campaigned for themselves, although in the past a few aspirants had found excuses to take lengthy vacations in critical states. The Sage of Peterboro, who had briefly checked himself into the Utica Asylum for the Insane after being implicated as one of John Brown's financial backers, was content to remain at home and accept by way of an open letter to Frederick Douglass. Announcing himself recovered from "dyspepsia, and over-working the brain," Smith was prepared for his last campaign. In a subtle attempt to suggest that there was little to distinguish Democrats from Republicans, Smith professed to admire "all the candidates for the presidency personally" but added that none had gone "far enough on the subject of abolition." Douglass, after briefly considering backing the Republicans, endorsed Smith.[45]

Fearing that the Constitutional Unionist strategy might prevail, a number of Liberty men quit the party. In a four- or five-candidate race, Smith's candidacy, gloated the Democratic *New York Herald*, could "spoil the calculations of the republicans in one, two, three or four very important Northern States." Seneca Falls, New York, abolitionist Henry B. Stanton joined the Republicans and even served as a Seward delegate in Chicago, despite the fact that his wife, feminist activist Elizabeth Cady Stanton, was Smith's cousin. Another to quit was Massachusetts abolitionist Thomas Wentworth Higginson, who later, as colonel of the South Carolina Volunteers, would lead black troops into battle. Syracuse minister Samuel J. May, a Garrisonian who had never voted and thought Seward "a heartless politician," assured his parishioners that by voting for the Republicans, the party "the slaveholder most fear[ed]," they were performing a godly chore.[46]

As the Democrats continued their internecine warfare and Constitutional Unionists gained momentum along the upper South, most abolitionists found a way to rationalize a vote for the Republicans. Garrison led the way with a spirited rebuke of Abby Kelley Foster and Parker Pillsbury. The Republicans, he editorialized, should be judged not by the standards of a reform movement but by comparison to other political parties. "The Republican party has certainly been consistent in its efforts to prevent the extension of slavery," he insisted. "Tell me that it is to be put in the same scale with the Democratic party." Wendell Phillips provided a somewhat more tepid endorsement. Seward, he thought, was a crass politician whose "two hands [were] filled with lies." But someday his presidential portrait would depict him "with one hand upon the American Eagle, and the other on the jugular of the slave system." Black abolitionists, especially, understood what was at stake. Weary of ideological purity, Douglass reminded voters in Geneva, New York, that they had helped to elect Polk in 1844. Although the Republicans were "far from an abolition party," he admitted that they promoted "the antislavery sentiment of the North" and added that their victory would mean only defeat for "the wickedly aggressive pro-slavery sentiments of the country." All but endorsing the Republicans, Douglass told his audience that while he was "resolved to cast [his] vote for an Abolitionist, [he] sincerely hope[d] for the triumph of that party over all the odds and ends of slavery combined against it."[47]

For both Constitutional Unionists and Liberty Party voters, much depended on who was to get the nod in Chicago. Just days after Bell received his nomination, Republicans began to converge on the Windy City for their convention, set to begin on May 16. For Constitutional Unionists, the nomination of Seward, perceived by many Americans to be a radical, would come as welcome news, as that was sure to add Pennsylvania, Indiana, and Illinois to the list of competitive states. For abolitionists, the selection of Chase or Seward could assuage troubled consciences, while a Bates candidacy would strengthen Smith. Phillips might regard Seward as dishonest, but that judgment was favorable compared to his low regard for Lincoln, whom he dismissed as a "huckster in politics" and a "country court advocate." In any case, like Yancey, Phillips expected the election to force the nation's hand with a likely Republican victory. Since the Republicans consented "to represent the antislavery idea," the election of any free soiler should cause a sectional explosion so severe that it would "force [slaveholders] into our position" of disunion, he predicted. Among those boarding a train for Chicago was the indefatigable Murat Halstead, anxious to discover if Phillips was correct, and to find out which of the minor parties would benefit from the convention's outcome, and who would lose.[48]

CHAPTER FOUR

"Moving Heaven and Earth"

The Republicans

PHYSICALLY, THE TWO ATTORNEYS who traveled Illinois's Eighth Judicial Circuit during the 1840s and '50s could not have been more dissimilar. In a century when childhood illnesses and poor nutrition robbed many young bodies of their ability to grow, Abraham Lincoln stood six feet four inches tall and weighed 180 pounds. His height was all in his legs, so when he rode the circuit, his size-fourteen boots skimmed atop the tall prairie grass. Never a graceful horseman, he resembled "a country farmer riding into town wearing his Sunday clothes." By comparison, David Davis broke the scales at three hundred pounds, and rival attorneys working the judicial "swing" laughed that each spring he had to be surveyed for a new pair of trousers. Too heavy for any mount, Davis rattled along beside Lincoln in a specially designed rig drawn by two horses. At night, the ill-matched pair found lodging in rural hostelries, where attorneys typically slept two to a bed and four to a room; Davis paid double for the luxury of a single bunk. Despite the poor conditions and poorer roads, both men enjoyed traveling the vast Eighth Circuit, which at twelve thousand square miles was roughly the size of Connecticut. The accumulated cases proved lucrative, and Lincoln enjoyed the nighttime political debates waged with colleagues. The lanky attorney was "as happy as *he* could be," Davis observed, "and happy no other place."[1]

Neither were their backgrounds similar. Lincoln was born into poverty in Kentucky, the son of a woman he feared was illegitimate and a man who, as the self-educated attorney regretted, "never did more in the way of writing than to bunglingly sign his name." Six years younger than his tall friend, Davis was born into wealth in Cecil County, Maryland, and he acquired even vaster sums speculating in Illinois real estate. Following an education at Ohio's Kenyon College, Davis read law in Massachusetts and then studied for a year at Connecticut's New Haven Law School. As his girth indicated, Davis loved rich food and fine wine, whereas Lincoln often forgot to eat and neither drank nor smoked. Alcohol, Lincoln complained, left him "flabby and undone." Perhaps because of this, Davis never really considered himself intimate with his melancholy companion. Lincoln "was not a sociable man by any means," he once complained, and "never confided to me anything."[2]

What the two shared was a love of politics and a devotion to Whig principles. Davis was elected to the Illinois legislature in 1845, just a year before Lincoln moved on to the national House of Representatives. An avid reader, Davis admired Lincoln's sharp legal mind. After becoming a judge, Davis frequently asked Lincoln to fill in as a substitute when he had to be absent. Like Lincoln, Davis regarded himself as an antislavery moderate, and after Kansas-Nebraska he followed Lincoln into the Republican camp. A deeply ambitious man himself, he recognized and admired the same trait in Lincoln. In the wake of Lincoln's unsuccessful 1858 Senate battle, a "mortified" Davis appointed himself campaign manager and began to plan for the upcoming Republican contest. "I have regretted for the past month that I had not early in the summer resigned my judgeship, & entered into the fight for you," the future Supreme Court justice wrote to the future president. Davis did not plan to make that mistake twice.[3]

The portly judge did not anticipate that his task would be a simple one, however. As the presidential campaign season opened, the one thing every seasoned political observer knew was that Senator William Henry

Seward would be the Republican nominee. After discussing the many Democratic candidates in the pages of his *Review*, James De Bow simply took it as a given that Seward owned the opposition's slot. "He is one of the most dangerous," De Bow observed, "and is by far the ablest of the Republicans, or what is much the same thing, abolition leaders." Only a handful of Charleston fire-eaters, among them Robert Barnwell Rhett and the Reverend John Bachman, suspected that Republicans might develop second thoughts about the New Yorker. Writing to Virginia's radical Edmund Ruffin, Bachman said he feared that when the Republicans met in Chicago, they might attempt to lull the South "asleep a little while longer" by tapping a dark horse who carried less political baggage. "They will probably get an ass into the presidential chair & get Seward to lead or drive him," the minister worried. "We will then see who will swallow black republicanism—nigger, tariff & all." Most observers thought Bachman's concerns absurd. Even before the Charleston disaster, Georgia's Howell Cobb believed that the mood of the North "fixe[d] the nomination of Seward as the Black Republican candidate." As for Democratic hopes that they could "beat Seward more easily than any other man," Cobb grimly added, "I doubt it."[4]

Bachman was right to be worried. Republican managers and editors had been pondering the race almost since the election of 1856. The party's impressive showing had immediately established the Republicans as the major rival to the majority Democrats, and John C. Frémont's 1,342,345 votes had surpassed everybody's expectations. Yet Horace Greeley attributed more than 100,000 of those votes to the northern outrage over South Carolina congressman Preston Brooks's savage caning of Massachusetts senator Charles Sumner in May 1856 on the floor of the Senate, as well as to the colorful Frémont's reputation as an explorer and adventurer. The race, party bosses knew, had been decided in the lower North. Buchanan had carried his home state of Pennsylvania as well as Douglas's Illinois. Although Frémont had captured New York and Ohio's heavy electoral count—thanks to the minor-party campaigns of New York natives Gerrit Smith and Millard Fillmore—the Republicans had won only 46 percent of the popular vote in the Empire State and 49 percent in Ohio. Frémont had secured but 29 percent of New Jersey's vote, and he had failed to best Buchanan in California, despite the fact that the Savannah-born officer had helped wrestle California out of Mexico's grasp and had briefly represented the new state in the U.S. Senate.[5]

Had the Republican convention been the first to meet in 1860, the nomination—and perhaps the fate of the Union—might have been far different. But as delegates boarded trains for Chicago, the events in Charleston and Baltimore forced them to reexamine their assumptions. One New York editor gloated that the Democratic Party had "bilged and bursted at Charleston" beyond salvation. "The work before the Republicans is, therefore, to rout a disabled enemy." Others were less sanguine. Not understanding the ultimate designs of the fire-eaters, many Republicans believed the southern Democrats to be, as always, merely rattling sabers. Faced with defeat in November, they reasoned, the Democrats would reunite in Baltimore. With John Bell and Edward Everett likely to appeal to the same border-state voters who had handed Maryland to Fillmore in 1856, Republicans needed to piece together a ticket and a platform that could hold the eleven states taken by Frémont (for a total of 114 electoral votes) while adding Pennsylvania and either Illinois or Indiana. Aware that they would surely lose if the election were thrown into the House, delegates pored over maps, anxious to discover the magic formula for the 152 electoral votes necessary to win. As Massachusetts delegate Fitz-Henry Warren explained, he was "for the man who [could] carry Pennsylvania, New Jersey, and Indiana." Beyond that, the candidate must only "be alive, and able to walk, at least from parlor to living room."[6]

Electoral considerations, together with the simple truth that survival in politics often requires more optimism than realism, allowed a surprisingly large number of Republicans to hope that they might be the one to fill Warren's prescription. The *Chicago Tribune* conceded that "a majority of the rank and file of the Republican party" favored Seward, but the editor proceeded to rattle off a list of viable candidates nonetheless. Pennsylvania senator Simon Cameron enjoyed the support of his critical state, and as a former Democrat and briefly a Know Nothing, Cameron could appeal to voters considering Douglas or Bell. The Chicago editor thought the same true for Salmon P. Chase, first elected to the Senate on a Free Soil–Democratic fusion ticket. The former senator and current

Ohio governor possessed "inflexible honesty and marked executive ability," attributes, the *Tribune* hinted, that political boss Cameron possibly lacked. Below these three stood a host of lesser-known candidates, including former Missouri congressman Edward Bates (briefly considered by the Constitutional Union delegates), Benjamin F. Wade of Ohio, William P. Fessenden of Maine, William Dayton of New Jersey, free-soil congressman Francis Preston Blair Jr. of Missouri, and aged Supreme Court justice John McLean, "whose life is without stain." Almost as an afterthought, the *Tribune* mentioned Illinois's own Abraham Lincoln, who lacked "the ripe experience of Seward, the age and maturity of Bates and McLean, or the fire of Fessenden and Wade."[7]

The 1856 nomination had been Seward's for the asking, but Thurlow Weed, his longtime manager, had kept him back until the new party grew more established. But now, editorialized one New York paper, the "coast is clear for Mr. Seward." Mail flowed into his Auburn, New York, home from supporters across the North, all reporting promising tidings for "the coming contest." One Concord politician assured the senator that "more than three quarters of all [in New Hampshire] preferred yourself," with the remainder divided between Bates, Chase, and Lincoln. Equally gratifying, if perhaps less politically useful, was the fact that black northerners appeared to favor Seward. Although African Americans could not vote in Illinois, William Bonner wrote on behalf of "the Colored people of Chicago" to say that "you do not alone belong to the Empire State [for] you are the acknowledged Champion and Leader of Freedom" in all "the States north of Slavery."[8]

Weed and Seward formed almost as curious a pair as Davis and Lincoln. The two had met years before in 1824 when young Seward's coach had lost a wheel in Rochester and the tall journalist had been among those who had helped drag it out of the mud. The dour Weed had never held political office; an incapacitating stutter denied him the oratorical skills required of antebellum statesmen. But he owned a series of successful newspapers, and since the formation of the Whig Party, Weed had championed Seward's career. Shorter than Weed at five feet six inches, Seward was of average height for men of his day. By 1860, his wavy red hair had grayed, but observers still commented on his strikingly blue eyes. For most of the previous year, Weed had laid the groundwork for Seward's nomination by bankrolling the candidacies of New York legislators loyal to the senator, and in the November elections, assemblymen financed by his machine won handily. "Allow me to congratulate you on the prospects of the Republican State Ticket," one assemblyman gushed to Weed. "What a glorious entering *Wedge* for the Presidency, will it be for our old & esteemed friend Gov. Seward."[9]

Curiously, Seward was not in the country to join in the celebration. After the Senate had adjourned in the spring of 1859, Seward had sailed for Europe following a brief visit to his family in Auburn. "All our discreet friends unite in sending me out of the country," he informed one supporter. With the election season under way, Weed believed that removing Seward from the increasingly turbulent political scene might enhance his chances of reaching the White House. Supporter Charles Sumner agreed, admitting that it was "hard for a person, who is in the Senate, exposed to bitter opposition & also to jealousies & rivalries, to rally for himself the whole party." A foreign sojourn also allowed Seward, who traveled alone, to escape his unhappy domestic life. His wife, Frances, had grown to dislike life in Washington, where manners were crude and moral compromises too frequent. A temperance advocate and a passionate abolitionist, Frances objected to her husband's serving alcohol to his cronies, and she often thought him insufficiently devoted to black rights. Shortly after guest John J. Crittenden spat tobacco juice on her dining room rug, Frances fled Washington for Auburn, and the prospect of serving as a president's wife gave her nightmares. She declined to see him off as he boarded the *Ariel*, so she did not hear the band bid him bon voyage by playing "Hail to the Chief."[10]

Seward did not return to New York until December 28, several weeks after the Senate had convened. He missed not only Weed's triumph in the state elections but also, and more important, John Brown's failed raid at Harpers Ferry. The adulation he had received in London and Paris initially blinded him to just how much Brown's actions had altered the political landscape, even within his own party. It was not merely that Democrats charged that Seward's "irrepressible conflict" rhetoric had inspired Brown, or that New Yorkers Gerrit Smith and Frederick

Hindered by a debilitating stutter in a time when politics demanded a big voice and oratorical skills, Thurlow Weed never sought office but instead devoted himself to advancing the career of fellow New Yorker William Henry Seward. Having first won election to the state assembly in 1830,

Douglass had been implicated in the raid. Rather, with even southern moderates openly discussing secession, party leaders previously nervous about Seward's chances in what were already being dubbed "battle-ground states" were forced to confront the possibility that he might actually carry fewer states than had Frémont. Writing to Lincoln from Washington, Josiah Lucas flatly predicted that Seward would "not be the

Seward served as the state's twelfth governor before moving to Washington and the Senate. Seward was to serve his rival as secretary of state and would be only one of two men to retain that position for a full eight years.
Courtesy Library of Congress.

nominee." With Democrats in Pennsylvania and Illinois blaming the Brown fiasco on Seward's rhetoric, Lucas thought it imperative to find a less controversial nominee. "Late developments have certainly damaged him," Lucas reported, and "our friends regard him as a dead weight and in doubtful districts he would lose instead of gaining us votes."[11]

Weed comprehended the danger, however, and urged Seward to deliver a major address in hopes of calming jittery Republicans and appeasing border-South moderates. Understanding the need for favorable press, Seward showed the lengthy speech to Henry Stanton, the upstate New York abolitionist turned Republican journalist, and urged Stanton to publish both the address and a description of its reception in the Senate. Delivered to a packed chamber on January 29, 1860, the three-hour speech revealed a far more conciliatory Seward than had been seen in years, and while party managers assumed his newfound restraint to be politically motivated, his centrist tone in fact presaged the moderate who was to guide the State Department for the next eight years. Gone was his inflammatory terminology of old. The slave states were now "the capital States," and the free states were rechristened "the labor States." He implored doubting southern members to "distinguish between [the] legitimate and constitutional resistance to the extension of slavery in the common Territories" practiced by his party and the "unconstitutional aggression against slavery established by local laws in the capital States" waged by militant abolitionist John Brown. Seward's daughter Fanny sat in the gallery, and she proudly informed her mother that the "whole house of Reps were there," while "ladies and gentlemen" crowded the doorway and spilled into the aisles.[12]

Frances Seward, far to the north in upstate New York, was less impressed. She informed Sumner—the one member of her husband's circle she had ever enjoyed talking to—that she "regretted" the portion of his speech that disclaimed any interest in black social equality. Other abolitionists felt the same. Upon reading the speech, Kentucky's Cassius Clay exploded that it *"killed Seward with me forever."* In Boston, Garrison insisted that "thousands" of New England Republicans were "mortified, disappointed, and privately indignant at [Seward's] cautious, calculating, retreating policy." But Seward and Weed were not hoping to appease Massachusetts abolitionists. They sought to win back uneasy Republican leaders, and so the tone of the speech, as one New Jersey editor observed, was designed to be "as distasteful to the radical fanatics of the North, as to the fire-eaters of the South." Most of Seward's New York supporters understood the ploy. George Ellis Baker admitted that he awaited the "speech with *anxiety*," but upon reading one of the half a million pamphlet copies circulating about the country, he thought it "as near perfect in all respects as [he] could desire."[13]

In the century before primaries became the method of delegate selection, state conventions chose the party activists who would attend the national conventions, a process that favored candidates from populous states. Immensely popular in his native New York, Seward faced no competition at home. Hostile editor Horace Greeley, who had turned on Seward years before when denied appointment to state office, advocated a more moderate candidate, but Weed's *Albany Evening Journal* praised Seward's conciliatory speech, and more to the point, Weed's Albany machine raised vast sums for Seward's campaign. When the state convention met in Syracuse on April 18, all seventy votes went for the senator. Since that tally represented nearly a third of the 233 votes necessary to nominate, the convention confirmed Seward's status as his party's front-runner. "I can see it becomes more and more evident that Seward will be our Candidate and next President," delegate Henricus Scholte assured Congressman Elbridge Spaulding.[14]

On May 11, five days before the national convention was to begin, Seward boarded a Washington train for Auburn. Like other candidates, Seward did not wish to appear too covetous of the prize, and he wanted to be among friends when word arrived of his nomination. So confident was Seward that he began to discuss potential running mates with Weed, an almost unheard-of practice in a time when conventions, rather than candidates, chose the second spot. Since Seward had openly criticized the anti-Catholic Know Nothings, Weed raised the possibility of his running with Maryland congressman Henry Winter Davis, a former Whig who had briefly joined the American Party before uniting with his cousin David Davis and the Republicans. That choice, Seward knew, would no more please Frances than had his conciliatory February speech, but more and more they lived separate lives, and in any case, the nomination was assured. Writing from far-off San Francisco on May 19, supporter Joseph Nunes hoped "to congratulate [Seward] upon having been selected by the Chicago Convention." Nunes took it "for granted that the nomination [had been] made on the 17th" and "that, in view of the disruption of the Charleston Convention," Seward was not just the Republican nominee but the country's next president.[15]

Sharing that assessment was Ohio's Salmon P. Chase, who enjoyed the dubious status of being generally regarded as a very distant second to the presumptive nominee. Even more ambitious than Seward, the New Hampshire–born Chase had served one term in the Senate, where he had won national fame as a vocal opponent of Kansas-Nebraska. In 1856, state voters had rewarded him with the governor's chair, where, as James De Bow drolly put it, he had become renowned "for his labors in behalf of the negro stealers and fugitive slaves." But if his absence from Washington meant his having relinquished the national stage to Seward, it had also kept some of his more inflammatory statements out of the eastern press. Although more radical than the New York senator, he was not as despised by southern planters as was Seward, and since Ohio lacked the large number of Irish Catholics found in Manhattan and along the Erie Canal, Chase was not on record as a critic of the Know Nothings. He enjoyed the backing of young men like James A. Garfield, then seeking a seat in the state assembly. Hoping that a Chase-led presidential ticket could carry the party to statewide victory, Garfield routinely ended his stump speech with the hope that "our worthy Governor" would soon hold a position "greater than a Governor."[16]

Especially in the West, Chase remained the candidate of radical Jacksonians, who regarded Seward's economic policies as Whiggishly spendthrift, and a number of Liberty Party activists continued as loyal supporters. The governor had been close to Kentucky's James G. Birney since 1836, when Chase, then a twenty-nine-year-old attorney, had defended a runaway slave named Matilda by adopting Birney's argument that slavery was protected by local statute only and could not exist outside that original jurisdiction. Most Republicans (and even Garrisonians) conceded that slavery was protected by the Constitution, but Chase had never abandoned Birney's theory and insisted that the Constitution was "a cooperative, evolutionary product" rather than the static document of 1787 that Chief Justice Taney claimed it to be. Consequently, Chase was favored by political abolitionists like editor Joshua Leavitt, one of the founders of the Liberty Party. Washington editor Gamaliel Bailey continued to champion his old friend in the pages of his *National Era*, although privately he regarded Seward as the stronger candidate.[17]

An astute politician, Chase was well aware of the odds against him. Not only did he lack Seward's fame in the nation's capital, but he also lacked Weed's well-financed organization. His few friends in New York reported that Weed's war chest contained at least fifty thousand dollars, cash designed to be spent on food and drink and less tangible forms of persuasion in Chicago. With limited financial resources, Chase instead hoped to rally western politicians behind him by again running for the Senate, a position to be selected by the legislature in early 1860. By announcing in 1859, he could use the contest to campaign for other Republicans across the state, which would provide him with a number of new assemblymen and congressmen indebted for his efforts. Chase campaigned vigorously, and when the new legislature met in February 1860, he handily defeated Democrat George Pugh by a vote of 76 to 53. The election earned him the attention of the eastern press and, according to one grateful congressman, "strengthen[ed] him for the Presidency." Chase thought so as well and boasted to Sumner that his chances "to infuse [the presidency] with the spirit of liberty, justice, and equality" had improved considerably.[18]

But like Seward, Chase was burdened by his radical politics at a time when party strategists were beginning to consider the need for a more moderate candidate. He had desired the nomination in 1856, but since losing the nod to Frémont, he had done nothing to build a national organization. Lacking a Davis or a Weed to orchestrate local support in other parts of the country, Chase simply hoped that his collection of celebrated supporters—Sumner, Birney, abolitionist Joshua Giddings, and Bailey—could overcome his organizational weakness in the eastern states. "Find out who concurs with us," he wrote to one, "and get them to act in concert." So little did Chase understand the necessity of building a following in the East that when William Cullen Bryant, the poet and editor of the New-York Evening Post, invited Chase to deliver a major address in the city, the Ohioan declined to make the lengthy trip, despite the fact that candidates often took advantage of such journeys to speak in each town and city they passed along the way to their destination.[19]

For those in search of a moderate alternative to Seward or Chase, and especially one who was also a relative unknown, Edward Bates of Missouri appeared increasingly attractive. A Virginia-born soldier and attorney, the sixty-seven-year-old veteran of the War of 1812 was the second-oldest potential Republican candidate. Bates had served a single term in Congress in the late 1820s and had remained a prominent-enough Whig to be offered the post of secretary of war by Fillmore. Bates had declined, and ironically, it was his very lack of national visibility, together with his public support for the hated Fugitive Slave Act, that caught the eye of Constitutional Unionists in Baltimore as well as Republican centrists. Greeley, a longtime critic of Weed's machine, began to run favorable stories about Bates in the *New York Tribune* early in 1859. On Greeley's recommendation, the powerful Blair family began talking up Bates's availability, despite the fact that many in Missouri preferred family member Francis Preston Blair Jr. As a former slaveholder who had liberated his bondmen, not only would Bates blunt the "black Republican" image in the lower North, but he might possibly give Bell a run in the upper South.[20]

Bates had remained secluded in Missouri, however, and his remoteness from the bitter political battles of Washington weakened his chances. Although his vote for Fillmore in 1856 had been based on loyalty to the only Whig in the race, the fact that the former president had officially led the nativist American Party ticket hurt Bates with German and Scandinavian voters in the critical state of Illinois. His views on slavery, moreover, better suited him to the Constitutional Unionists. In early 1859, he had denounced "the Negro question" as a "pestilent" issue dredged up by ambitious politicians determined only to "exasperate the unreasoning jealousy of sections." When warned by the Blairs that such statements placed him well outside the Republican mainstream, Bates published a letter on March 22, 1860, to the Missouri delegates to the Chicago convention assuring them that while he held "no new opinions on the subject," he was "opposed to the extension of slavery" and believed that the "Government ought to be against its extension." Greeley and the Blairs announced themselves satisfied, but the damage was done. "He is a dead cock in the pit," sneered one editor.[21]

Similar considerations plagued the candidacy of Pennsylvania senator Simon Cameron. A native of one of the key battleground states in 1860, the sixty-one-year-old Cameron had amassed a fortune in railroads and banking before entering politics in 1844 as a Democrat. He had abandoned his party midway through the 1850s, but his brief flirtation with the Know Nothings had less to do with opposition to immigrants than with a rivalry with Buchanan. The senator enjoyed the nearly unanimous backing of Pennsylvania delegates to Chicago, who insisted that Seward was "entirely too ultra" to carry their state or neighboring New Jersey. But Cameron's ever-shifting loyalties had won him few friends outside his state, and in discussing potential candidates, the *New York Herald* laughingly dubbed him a "Democratic Know Nothing Republican Conservative." His 1830s service as commissioner regarding Winnebago land claims had also led to whispers of financial impropriety that had not yet dissipated. "I expect to support the Candidate be he whom he may," one Republican informed Weed, "but the nomination of Sen. Cameron does not commend itself to my judgment."[22]

For western Republicans who found Bates too conservative, Cameron too untrustworthy, and Chase too ambitious, Ohio senator Benjamin F. Wade provided a possible alternative. A former Whig, Wade appealed to Ohioans who regarded Chase's economic policies as overly Jacksonian. But since becoming friends with abolitionist Joshua Giddings in 1831, Wade had proved himself every bit as devoted to women's rights, anti-slavery, and black social equality as any radical abolitionist. Although nicknamed "Bluff" Ben Wade, the senator could be as soft-spoken as he was blunt. One editor observed that his "frank, fearless and quaint way of saying what he [thought]" made him "quite a favorite in the Senate." Wade's standing was hampered by the fact that he honestly did not desire the presidency, but that did little to dissuade Robert F. Paine of Cleveland from appointing himself Wade's manager and organizing on his behalf. Paine contacted a number of eastern foes of Seward, and although Greeley remained committed to Bates, the *Tribune* began to mention Wade as "a candidate with a prospect of success should Seward be beaten."[23]

Ohio's John McLean, a former Democrat placed on the Supreme Court by Andrew Jackson in 1831, was the candidate of Pennsylvania congressman Thaddeus Stevens, who could not abide Cameron. But at the age of seventy-five, the elderly jurist offered nothing beyond a theoretical ability to carry Pennsylvania and New Jersey, and observers found it curious to see "the most radical Republican leader of the country" supporting "the most conservative candidate." Other moderates spoke of Congressman Francis P. Blair Jr., despite the fact that the Missouri attorney publicly backed Bates. Apart from his service in the Mexican-American War, there was little to recommend the free soiler aside from his distinguished family. Blair's father, known as Frank or "Senior," had served as an unofficial adviser to Andrew Jackson, and his brother, Montgomery Blair, had been one of Dred Scott's attorneys. But the thirty-nine-year-old "Junior" had accomplished little apart from being expelled from both Yale College and the University of North Carolina before barely graduating from Princeton, and his consumption of whiskey and tobacco was unparalleled, even in comparison to Douglas's drinking and Seward's love of cigars. Still, nominating the Kentucky-born Blair could allow the Republicans to boast of southern support, and in American politics dynasties often secure positions for otherwise unimpressive young candidates.[24]

And then there was Lincoln. His debates with Douglas, as one Washington publisher admitted, had given his name "a new celebrity beyond the bounds of his State," and ever since, a small group of Illinoisans had advanced the former congressman as a winning candidate. Like Seward, Lincoln was a former Whig, but he was also a native of Kentucky, and the hope was that he might not terrify the white South as much as a resident of the Burned-Over District. Also like Seward, Lincoln had been hostile to Know Nothings, but his denunciations of their intolerance had been limited to private correspondence rather than delivered in speeches in Manhattan. Compared to front-runners Seward and Chase, Lincoln could boast of little experience, but as a result he had gained fewer enemies along the way. What party activists *did* know about him, they liked. He was eloquent and resourceful, and his opposition to Kansas-Nebraska won him supporters in the East, as did his earlier criticism of President Polk's handling of the Mexican-American War. More important still, the Republicans desperately needed to add Illinois to their electoral map.[25]

One wonders whether Lincoln, for all of his ambition and oratorical gifts, could have survived in a modern, televised age. Visitors to Springfield were impressed by his height but often described his head as too small for his body. His voice was high and thin, and his manners betrayed his humble Kentucky origins. Lincoln greeted strangers with "Howdy" as he shook their hand with both of his. His coarse black hair, according to his partner William Herndon, "lay floating where the fingers or the wind left it." Bostonian Theodore Lyman thought him "the ugliest man [he had] ever put [his] eyes upon," and one southern woman agreed, writing, "His face is certainly ugly." Both observers quickly softened their opinions once he began to speak. For all of Lincoln's "plebeian vulgarity," Lyman found him "very honest" and "highly intellectual," and the young woman gushed that his "good humor, generosity and intellect" led guests to "almost find him good looking." Even so, young Lyman concluded his meeting with the curious remark: "I never wish to see him again."[26]

Even as he protested that he preferred to run for the Senate again in 1864, Lincoln quietly allowed Davis to keep his name before party activists. In December 1859, Lincoln responded to Joseph J. Lewis, the publisher of Pennsylvania's *Chester County Times*, who wrote to request biographical information for an essay he was preparing. Lincoln complied with a "little sketch" of 606 words, adding modestly that if "there was not much of it," that was because "there is not much of me." Lincoln also began to collect his 1858 speeches for publication, to be published by Follett, Foster & Company of Ohio as *Political Debates Between Hon. Abraham Lincoln and Hon. Stephen A. Douglas*. But perhaps the fledgling campaign's most adroit move came later that month when the Republican National Committee met at the Astor House in Manhattan. A subcommittee, chaired by Judge Norman Judd of Chicago, had to choose the site for the spring convention, and supporters of Seward, Chase, and Bates advocated Buffalo, Cleveland, and St. Louis, respectively. Judd was already leaning toward a western site to balance the presumed nomination of easterner Seward when a letter from Lincoln landed on his desk. Lincoln insisted that others attached "more consequence to getting the National Convention into our State" than he did, but he assured Judd that their "old whig friends" deemed "it important." When Judd promised the committee that a convention hall "should be furnished [for] free," Chicago bested St. Louis by a single vote.[27]

Lincoln also avoided Chase's missteps. Determined to deny Seward the nomination, Greeley had organized a series of lectures at Henry Ward Beecher's Plymouth Church, in Brooklyn. When editor Bryant,

The other odd political pairing of the Republican Party,
David Davis and Abraham Lincoln outwitted Weed and Seward at the
Chicago Republican National Convention and won the nomination for the
relatively obscure one-term Illinois congressman. In late October 1862,

who had previously extended invitations to Blair and Chase, invited
Lincoln to come east for a February 27 address, Lincoln leaped at the offer. Understanding the need to impress his sophisticated eastern audience, Lincoln purchased a new black suit for one hundred dollars from
Woods & Henckle. After a tiring two-day trip, Lincoln arrived in the
city, where he was met at the station by Carl Schurz. The Prussian-born

Lincoln would reward his manager by elevating the circuit court judge to the U.S. Supreme Court. In 1887, Davis stepped down to serve as senator from Illinois, a position he held for one term.
Courtesy Library of Congress.

Republican judged Lincoln's "store" coat short in the sleeves and his stovepipe hat "battered," but he had to "throw his head backward in order to look into [Lincoln's] eyes." The Young Men's Central Republican Union had relocated the speech across the river to Manhattan's more spacious Cooper Union. On the way to the Astor House, the two stopped at photographer Mathew Brady's Bleecker Street studio. To emphasize

Lincoln's great height and disguise his homely features, Brady moved his camera as far back as possible.[28]

Following a lavish dinner hosted by Greeley, the editor squired Lincoln to the hall. Although still formally a supporter of Bates, Greeley conspicuously took a chair on the speaker's platform. Despite inclement weather, at least fifteen hundred people packed the hall. The Illinois attorney, who had been riding circuit across the prairie only months before, gazed up in wonder at the twenty-seven crystal chandeliers that lit the auditorium. But when Lincoln stepped toward the wrought-iron podium, the audience fell silent. Following the requisite repudiation of John Brown's raid, Lincoln denounced the "nationalization of bondage" in the West but promised yet again to "leave [it] alone" where it already existed. That, he lamented, was not enough for planter-politicians. Adopting a phrase he was to use often in the coming year, Lincoln observed that slaveholders "want us to stop calling slavery wrong and join them, in acts as well as words, in calling slavery *right*." Southern whites' "thinking it right, and our thinking it wrong, is the precise fact upon which depends the whole controversy." As Lincoln concluded, the audience rose in a standing ovation, tossing their hats and waving handkerchiefs overhead. "No man," scribbled a reporter for the *Tribune*, "ever before made such an impression on his first appeal to a New York audience."[29]

Despite the overwhelmingly favorable press the speech received (which overshadowed Seward's Senate speech two days later), Lincoln remained pessimistic about his chances and worried about the May 9 Illinois state convention. But when the Republicans gathered in Decatur to select delegates for Chicago, Davis's organization easily outmaneuvered the few Seward backers in attendance. Since it was a state rather than national convention, Lincoln was on hand to watch. Much to his dismay, cheering delegates lifted him overhead and passed him toward the platform. For the candidate, who appeared "plagued" by the attention, worse was yet to come. Lincoln's cousin John Hanks arrived bearing two rotted fence rails and shouted that "Abraham Lincoln, the Rail Candidate" had split the timber in the 1830s. As the crowd gave three cheers "for Honest Abe," an uncomfortable Lincoln insisted that he could not "identify them." When the audience persisted, Lincoln admitted that they might be his but added that he had "split a great many better looking ones." The delegates then agreed to "vote as a unit" for Lincoln and named Davis and Judd to head the Illinois delegation. Even then, so little was the former congressman known outside his state that the *Albany Evening Journal* reported that the Decatur meeting had unanimously "declared Abram Lincoln" its choice for president.[30]

The candidate, who in reality was a prosperous and successful attorney, was embarrassed "most deeply" by his log-cabin origins and rarely spoke about his childhood. But Davis and others at the Decatur convention understood the power of political symbolism. As a self-made man who had raised himself out of frontier poverty and ignorance through industry and sobriety, Lincoln personified his party's free-labor ideals. Although luck and brilliance had also aided in Lincoln's rise, Hanks's fence-rail stunt conveyed the message that Republicans—unlike aristocratic southern Democrats who made their fortunes off the sweat of unpaid slaves—gloried in hard labor and promoted social advancement. Eloquent and wealthy though he might be in 1860, Lincoln had begun his life as the most disadvantaged candidate since Andrew Jackson, and while myth alone held that every poor boy could win the presidency, Lincoln's ill-fitting suit and prairie comportment reminded voters that he remained one of them. There was "something in his nature," editorialized one Republican newspaper, "in his personal appearance and manners [that] commend[ed] itself to the plain simplicity of the rural populations."[31]

Over the next few days, the delegates chosen in Decatur began to pack their carpetbags for the Republican National Convention, set to begin on May 16. In Chicago the conference's hosts hammered the final nails into the Wigwam, the specially built auditorium constructed over the past six weeks at a cost of five thousand dollars. Built of pine and sprawling along Market Street, the cavernous hall measured 180 by 100 feet. The Wigwam featured an enormous stage, inclined floor space for standing delegates—"which will allow short men every advantage," bragged one newspaper—galleries running around three sides for spectators, and, for the first time in American political history, a press box for reporters. The building was capped with a dome "surmounted by a large eagle and shield supporting a flag staff," while the inside was decorated with dried evergreen boughs and red, white, and blue streamers. Builders believed the hall, brilliantly illuminated by gas jets, could hold up to ten thousand people. It was, surely, the loveliest firetrap yet devised by American architects.[32]

Thrilled at the prospect of showing off their still rustic but rapidly growing city of one hundred thousand residents, Chicagoans lined the tracks outside the rail depot, greeting each arriving trainload of delegates with either the boom of two nine-pound brass cannons or the glare of rockets, depending on the time of day or night. Unlike the dispirited Democratic delegates who had fled Charleston just two weeks before, those arriving in Chicago were in high spirits and had, according to the intrepid Murat Halstead, enjoyed the large "quantity of whisky and other ardent beverages consumed on the train." A churlish Jefferson Davis later described "the so-called 'Republican' Convention" as a "purely sectional body," but if it is true that no delegate represented a state from the lower South, among the 466 men who held credentials were groups from the slave states of Virginia, Missouri, Maryland, Delaware, Kentucky, and Tennessee. Most had some political experience, usually as mayors or state assemblymen, and if many were new to the party, others had attended the Philadelphia convention of 1856.[33]

As was the case with the other major parties, the leading Republican contenders avoided the convention so as not to appear desirous of political office. But their handlers were well represented. Weed led the Seward men. Frank Blair and his son Montgomery served as delegates from Maryland, and Francis Jr., although himself somewhat a candidate, supported Bates while directing the Missouri delegation. Horace Greeley was in attendance, as was Massachusetts abolitionist Eli Thayer (both representing Oregon, a place neither had ever visited), and Carl Schurz, who had greeted Lincoln upon his arrival for the Cooper Union speech, held Wisconsin credentials. Davis had arrived the previous Saturday and been dismayed to discover that Judd had failed to establish a Lincoln headquarters. David Davis promptly rented two rooms at the Tremont House, paying the cost out of his own pocket. He was lucky to obtain the

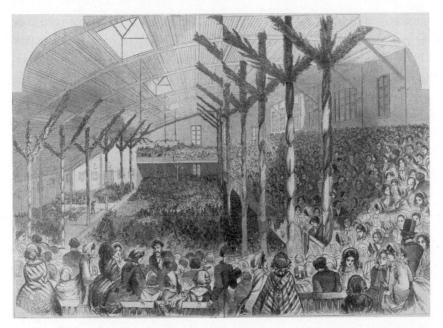

*Located at Lake and Market streets, the cavernous Wigwam was so-named
as it was specially constructed for the Republican "chiefs" to choose a nominee in
1860. Stephen A. Douglas gave his last speech there in May 1861, defending
Lincoln's decision to retain Fort Sumter before an audience of ten thousand
people. Courtesy Library of Congress.*

last rooms, however, as Halstead found the hotel "so crammed" that
guests could barely "get about in it from one room to the other." The
bulky judge commandeered a large table for one of the rooms and proceeded to delegate specific tasks to his more nimble subordinates. He and
they were "moving heaven & Earth," he telegraphed Lincoln the day
before the convention began. "Nothing will beat us but old fogy politicians [as] the heart of the delegates are with us."[34]

At eleven o'clock on the morning of Wednesday, May 16, managers
threw open the doors to the Wigwam. Within minutes, the floor was
"solidly packed with men," while the seats in the galleries "were equally
closely packed with ladies." As many as thirty thousand, Halstead
estimated, had arrived in hopes of admission, so the large front doors

were left open to allow the "crowds in the streets" to hear the speeches. At the stroke of noon, Governor Edwin D. Morgan of New York, the chairman of the party's Executive Committee and a staunch Seward advocate, pounded the heavy oak gavel (carved from a piece of Commodore Oliver Hazard Perry's 1813 Lake Erie flagship) and called the convention to order. "All the auguries are that we shall meet the enemy and they shall be ours," Morgan shouted in a paraphrase of Perry's famous report. In an important act of symbolism, Morgan then nominated former Pennsylvania congressman David Wilmot, the founding father of territorial restriction, for "temporary chairman."[35]

Determined to demonstrate that they were as united as the Democrats were in disarray, George Ashmun of Massachusetts, the convention's "presiding officer," rose to second Wilmot's nomination. The speaker's words bounced easily off the hard wooden surfaces of the hall, and even those in the far corners could hear every syllable. "I think we have a right here to-day," Ashmun shouted, "to impeach the administration of our General Government of the highest crimes that can be committed against a Constitutional Government; against a free people and against humanity." As Wilmot shoved his way to the stage, applause "grew and rolled from side to side and corner to corner of the immense building." Wilmot had lost a gubernatorial race three years before to a Buchanan loyalist. But now that the Charleston convention "had shown a great party in the ebb tide of disintegration," one delegate gloated, the scent of "victory was in the air."[36]

The speeches given in Chicago were primarily designed for national consumption, and those behind the podium spoke as much to the scribbling journalists squeezed into the press box as they did to the delegates on the floor. Reporters at the Wigwam telegraphed their stories to the papers that employed them, and smaller newspapers then cut and pasted the entire pieces onto their pages. Assured of quick and broad coverage, Wilmot had wisely prepared his speech well in advance, and he emphasized all the key points that the party leaders wished American voters to understand. In response to southern charges that Republicans represented only the North, Wilmot began by denouncing the "sectional and aristocratic [Democratic] party, or interest, [that] has for years dominated with a high hand over the political affairs of the country." Since 1854, Wilmot charged, "the one object" of the Democrats had been "the extension of slavery," and Republicans gathered in Chicago only to "resist this policy of sectional interest." Careful to insist that they posed no danger to slavery in the southern states, Wilmot avoided the smallest hint of concern for the welfare of African Americans and instead focused on southern threats against white liberty. "Whose rights are safe where slavery has the power to trample them underfoot?" he asked. "Who to-day is not more free to utter his opinions within the Empire of Russia, or under the shadow of despotism of Austria, than he is within the limits of the slave States of this Republic?"[37]

As the applause died, Ashmun then turned to business and took up the thorny question of slave-state delegates. Watching from the press box, Halstead was impressed. Ashmun was "cool, clear headed and executive, and will dispatch business." The lower South, of course, had sent no delegations, and "laughter and hissing" rose from the floor as Ashmun jokingly called for the credentials of Mississippi, Georgia, and South Carolina. But a handful of brave souls represented the upper South, and since state population determined delegation size, Virginia's contingent of twenty-three men was one person larger than Illinois's. No one in the hall actually expected the party to draw well in any southern state, but looking to the future, Weed promised patronage to Virginians who might otherwise support Bell over Seward. Wilmot, however, insisted that as the convention was composed of state delegations, and since there "never had [been] a Republican party in Maryland," it was absurd to allow its eleven men to vote. A visibly angry Charles Lee Armour, once burned in effigy in his native state, retorted that he had "dared more than [Wilmot had] ever dared" to serve the party. Republican leaders hoped to construct a viable party organization in Maryland, and to ban the delegates would play into southern allegations that they were nothing more than a sectional party. Wilmot was voted down; the delegates remained.[38]

With harmony restored, the convention adjourned until ten o'clock the next morning, when the delegates planned to vote on their platform. Thursday morning, sleepy delegates awoke to the sound of "three to four thousand" marchers, paid by Weed and led by the New York contingent, playing music and carrying a giant banner emblazoned with Seward's likeness. Inside the hall, a committee led by Pennsylvania judge William Jessup, Schurz, Greeley, and the elder Blair was already putting the finishing touches on the platform. Distant observers like *National Era* editor Bailey feared that the committee might weaken the antislavery clauses in the 1856 Philadelphia platform in hopes of winning over potential Bell voters, but such concerns proved unfounded. Following the example set by Wilmot, the committee emphasized the ways in which the "filibustering, Slavery-extending, sham Democracy" endangered the rights of white voters. Condemning the Dred Scott decision as "a dangerous political heresy, at variance with the explicit provisions of [the Constitution] itself," and denouncing popular sovereignty as "a deception and fraud," the platform dedicated the party to "abolish[ing] slavery in all of our national territory." It also denied territorial assemblies the authority "to give legal existence to slavery" and described efforts to reopen the Atlantic slave trade as "a burning shame to our country and age." Other sections demanded the immediate admission of Kansas as a free state and deplored "the threats of disunion so often made by democratic members" of Congress.[39]

If Jessup's group had no interest in watering down the party's core beliefs regarding the territories, it did broaden the platform in other areas to appeal to moderate voters. The nation's economy had declined sharply in 1857, a recession that almost nobody in Congress took notice of as they argued over Chief Justice Taney's ruling. John Wentworth, a former Democrat concerned with diminishing wages, advised Lincoln that the party required "some financial policy" to peel northern workers away from Douglas. As it had in 1856, the platform urged federal aid for a transcontinental railroad, but this time it also endorsed the old Jacksonian dream of a homestead act to provide free land in the West. Somewhat in contradiction, former Whigs on the committee had added language advocating a protective tariff to "encourage the development" of industry, while ex-Democrats like Blair had won support for a "policy of national [trade] exchanges which secures to the workingmen liberal wages, to agriculture remunerative prices, [and] to mechanics and manufacturers an adequate reward for their skill." The fact that the platform promised both "duties upon imports" and robust trade with foreign nations, while implying that northern industrialists shared their workers' demands for "liberal wages," revealed a party deeply divided on economic issues. So long as the main focus of the Republicans remained on the territories, however, such disagreements could be largely ignored.[40]

Understanding the need to appeal to foreign-born voters in Illinois and Pennsylvania, the platform committee had also included a promise to "oppose any change in our naturalization laws" and promote "full and efficient protections to the rights of all classes of citizens." Once again, Wilmot rose in objection, but Schurz, himself a refugee from Prussian militarism, spoke eloquently of the need for the "Republican party [to] be washed clean of the taint of Know-nothingism." Nobody in the hall seemed to think it curious that the committee sought to protect the political rights of "emigrants from foreign lands" while refusing to endorse voting rights for black Americans in Illinois or New York, but by embracing the term "citizens," Schurz was able to skirt that point. Taney's pronouncement that free blacks were not citizens in the country of their birth was the only section of his ruling that most Republicans chose not to contest.[41]

Apart from Wilmot's unfortunate tendency to introduce disharmony with his endless objections, the only drama on the second day came when Joshua R. Giddings, the sixty-five-year-old former Ohio congressman, asked to amend the platform so that it more explicitly embraced the natural-rights wording of the Declaration of Independence. Well aware of the chaos caused by the several Democratic platform statements in Charleston, Ohio's David Cartter insisted that the document be put to a vote without debate. Cartter, who like Weed suffered from a debilitating stutter, was finally able to explain that he wanted only to prevent any undue interference "with the dispatch of business." But the tall Giddings, "a look of distress on his face," slowly moved toward the Wigwam's doors. Young George William Curtis, a New York editor, climbed upon a chair and demanded to be heard. After repeatedly shouting, "Gentlemen!," Curtis finally won the floor. Were they not "the party of freedom?" he asked. "And would the representatives of that party dare to reject the doctrine of the Declaration of Independence affirming the equality of men's rights?" As the delegates shouted their approval, Giddings returned to the hall, "his white head towering above the crowd."[42]

So smoothly had the platform process gone that time enough remained to proceed to a first ballot before the announced adjournment hour of five o'clock. The Seward delegates, confident of their ability to obtain a nearly unheard-of first-ballot victory, called for an immediate vote. "The cheering of the thousands of spectators during the day," Halstead admitted, "indicated that a very large share of the outside pressure"— that is, the noncredentialed spectators in the galleries—"was for Seward." But the convention's clerks had not expected a vote on the second afternoon, and one embarrassed clerk admitted that they were unready to hand out the tally sheets. With that, the hall began to empty out. But as the Seward delegates strolled toward a champagne dinner at the Richmond House, one confided to Halstead that there was not the slightest "doubt of [Seward's] nomination in the morning." Delegate Elbridge Spaulding cabled the senator that he "felt confident of a favorable result." Perusing similar telegrams in Washington was Maine senator Hannibal Hamlin, who wrote to his wife on the following morning, "Today I presume Seward will be nominated at Chicago."[43]

That evening, the "exultant" New Yorkers began their celebration. A few wandered down to the McVickers Theater to attend the opening night of the comedy *Our American Cousin*. Most made merry at the Tremont. "Seward's success was certain," several more delegates assured Halstead. Weed hired a brass band, and on his floor at the Tremont, champagne continued to flow. A dejected Greeley sent a dispatch to his *Tribune* just before midnight. The "opposition to Gov. Seward cannot concentrate on any candidate," he conceded, and "he will be nominated." A far happier Edwin Morgan cabled Auburn, where the senator calmly waited, with the message "We have no doubt of a favorable result tomorrow."[44]

As the Seward delegates exchanged champagne for whiskey and the brass band for "bad songs," Halstead began to explore caucus rooms on other floors. Nobody was sleeping at the Tremont. In the Ohio chambers, delegates vacillated between Chase and Wade. Former Democrats in the contingent favored Chase, Wade having abandoned the Whigs in the early 1850s, and they argued that only the former governor stood any chance of wresting the nomination away from Seward, a former Whig who favored a protective tariff. But at least six of the Ohio delegates, including Cartter and Giddings, coveted Wade's Senate seat, and if they could elevate him into the White House, one of them was sure to get it. The Chase men also hoped to secure the last-second endorsement of Schurz, but the bespectacled Wisconsin delegate would only say that among "advanced antislavery" candidates, Chase stood second only to Seward.[45]

Chase had never understood the importance of a campaign organization, and in Chicago he left his affairs in the incompetent hands of his brother Edward. The younger Chase practiced law in Lockport, New York, and knew little of Ohio politics. Uncomfortable in the crowded corridors and smoke-filled caucus rooms of the Tremont, he made little headway in his effort to unite the fractured Ohio delegation. Salmon Chase understood that if his state remained divided, he stood little chance against a unified New York delegation, and on his advice Edward urged Giddings to insist on the "unit rule," which dictated that whoever enjoyed the support of an Ohio majority would win all of the state's delegate votes on Friday. But many in Chicago feared that Wade could benefit from such a vote and refused to accept Edward's proposal. Determined to "defeat the Wade movement at all hazards," even if it meant a Seward nomination, Chase's supporters passed on the unit rule. As a result, the forty-six Ohio delegates were free to scatter their ballots, and with that decision, Chase's candidacy, never strong, was utterly lost.[46]

Equally busy that night was a sleepless David Davis. Although "nearly dead with fatigue," Davis continued to manage the campaign from behind a desk in his Tremont suite. With the Illinois delegation safely united behind Lincoln, Davis wisely refused to waste time trying to pry other state deputations away from various favorite sons. Understanding that Seward probably lacked the simple majority necessary for a nomination only because a number of states were committed to first honoring regional candidates with a symbolic vote, Davis labored to secure pledges from states not committed to the New Yorker for the second ballot that they would support Lincoln at that point. It remains unclear whether this strategy originated with Davis or his candidate. Prior to the convention,

Lincoln admitted that he was "not the *first* choice of a very great many" Republicans. "Our policy, then, is to give no offence to others—leave them in a mood to come to us, [after] they shall be compelled to give up their first [choice]." But Davis certainly understood that many delegates preferred the nomination of a dark horse who might then owe them political favors over that of a powerful front-runner who regarded the position as his due. As one Illinois paper wondered in a reference to the unexpected Democratic nominee of 1844, "Why shouldn't [Lincoln] be the 'Polk of 1860'?"[47]

Although Lincoln hoped that Davis could make his case without disparaging others, the busy Illinois delegates routinely referenced the unelectability—Davis preferred the term "unavailability"—of Seward and the other prominent candidates. Around one o'clock on Friday morning, Halstead encountered one of Davis's allies, a "pale and haggard" Henry S. Lane of Indiana, who was working caucus after caucus. Lane insisted that both Seward and Chase were too radical to carry Pennsylvania or Illinois, while Bates was too conservative to win over antislavery New Yorkers and too nativist to please immigrant voters in the Northwest. Cameron, Lane hinted, was too unsavory to carry any state beyond his Pennsylvania. The moderate Lincoln, he argued, as a former Whig was sound on the tariff but could secure the lower North. Facing a long night, Lane left to lobby Caleb B. Smith, chairman of the Indiana delegation, to marshal his forces to vote as a unit for Lincoln.[48]

At the same moment, Pennsylvania delegates, painfully aware that Cameron enjoyed little support beyond their state's borders, began to consider other options. Delegate Andrew G. Curtin was also the party's nominee for governor, and he worried that a Seward-led ticket would hand the state to Douglas and cost him the election. Lane, also a candidate for governor, faced the same problem in Indiana, and the two surely colluded on the argument that a Democratic victory could cost the Republicans two Senate seats. Frémont had run badly in New Jersey, and that state's delegates voiced the same concerns. Lane and Curtin passed word that while "these prejudices" against Seward were possibly "unjust, [they] would endanger the success of the [entire] ticket in some States." Even delegates from Connecticut, a state that Frémont had carried by 10 percent, expressed similar worries.[49]

The Davis forces found an unofficial ally in Horace Greeley. Although the editor had arrived in Chicago hoping to see the party nominate Bates, his chief goal was to deny the nomination to Seward. Weed later denounced Greeley as "malignant" and charged that he had "misled many fair minded men." But in fact Greeley needed little help in raising doubts about Seward with the party's leadership. The delegates in Chicago stood ready to nominate the New Yorker, but the Lincoln forces simply stoked worries already being whispered in caucus rooms. Although Seward's reputation as a radical would be disproved during his tenure in the State Department, too many party bosses outside of New York regarded him as a foolish gamble in what could be a Republican year. One Indiana journalist later crowed that Greeley had "slaughtered Seward and saved the party," but while an avowed enemy of the senator, Greeley himself insisted that it was the availability question, rather than any single person's activities, that had denied Seward the honor. If a candidate from the lower North could be more easily elected without sacrificing the party's key position on the territories, why hazard a safe election—or a republic—on a longtime politician who had acquired far too many enemies over the years?[50]

After Lane secured Indiana's delegation, Davis himself went in search of Pennsylvania's forty-eight votes. Andrew Curtin had promised to back Cameron on the first ballot as a courtesy, but beyond that he was undecided, apart from his determination not to support Seward. Precisely what Davis did to obtain Pennsylvania's second-ballot support remains murky. Earlier that day, Edward L. Baker, the editor of the *Illinois State Journal*, had arrived in Chicago with a one-sentence note from Lincoln: "Make no contracts that will bind me." According to several sources, Davis snapped, "Lincoln ain't here and don't know what we have to meet." Judge Joseph Casey, who represented Cameron in Chicago, demanded that Cameron be named secretary of the treasury in a Lincoln administration, and Davis vaguely replied that Pennsylvania certainly deserved a spot in the cabinet and promised to recommend Cameron to Lincoln. That evidently satisfied Casey. Sometime after midnight, delegate Joseph Medill wedged past Davis on the hotel's stairs. "Damned if we haven't got them," Davis laughed. When asked how, Davis only replied, "By paying the price."[51]

The Seward forces, although cloth-headed and bleary-eyed, abounded in confidence on Friday morning, the third and final day of the convention. Rumors of deals made the previous night circulated as the delegates and several thousand observers descended on the Wigwam, but as even Halstead agreed, "the opposition of the doubtful States to Seward was an old story." By nine o'clock—one hour before the proceedings were to begin—the crowd outside the hall far exceeded the ten thousand allowed inside, so several thousand remained outside "anxiously awaiting intelligence" from the stage. "All right," Richard M. Blatchford cabled Seward. "Everything indicates your nomination today sure."[52]

Blatchford failed to account for the wily Davis. Hoping to give the impression of an irreversible groundswell building for Lincoln, Davis encouraged Ward Hill Lamon, a strapping Illinois lawyer who would later guard Lincoln during his travels to Washington, to round up leather-lunged Chicagoans who could shake the hall's rafters with cheers for their candidate. Allegations of counterfeit tickets carried by Lincoln supporters were probably true, but as Weed had employed professional boxer Tom Hyer to crash the hall with equally vocal Seward men, nobody wished to contest Lamon's many friends. Schurz, in any case, dismissed the importance of the "fierceness of shouting" as "mere reporters' talk." The "popular demonstrations for Lincoln in and around the Convention were," he remarked, "well planned and organized," but practical considerations remained the "decisive factor."[53]

Amid a din so loud that ladies in the galleries "stopped their ears in pain," Ashmun pounded his gavel and yelled for silence. Delegates would first have the right to nominate candidates, and then the convention was to move toward the first ballot. State leaders stood and advanced the names of Cameron, Chase, and Bates. But when William Evarts got up to present Seward's name, "tremendous applause" and a lengthy "shriek" arose from the floor. And when Judd nominated "the man who can split rails and maul Democrats," the building literally shook and creaked as the Lincoln men stamped and bellowed. "Imagine all the hogs ever slaughtered in Cincinnati giving their death squeals together, a score of big steam whistles going," Halstead marveled, "and you conceive something of the same nature." As the gasping audience finally quieted, one delegate cried, "Abe Lincoln has it, by the sound now. Let us ballot."[54]

The tense moment of balloting at last began. A candidate required 233 votes, or half the votes of the 466 delegates in attendance, for the nomination. States were called by region rather than by alphabetical order, and New England went first. Much to Weed's surprise and dismay, New York's neighbors scattered their votes. Maine handed Lincoln 6 votes to Seward's 10, and New Hampshire gave Lincoln 7 of its 10. As a first-ballot courtesy, Vermont thanked its senator Jacob Collamer with its 10 votes, a gift that posed no danger to Lincoln but helped to deny the front-runner his majority. Rhode Island and Connecticut, despite earlier promises to Weed, bestowed 1 or 2 votes on everybody but Seward. Only Massachusetts handed most of its 25 votes to Seward. The seventh state polled was New York, and finally Evarts had his chance to announce, "The State of *New York* casts her seventy votes for *William H. Seward*!" The senator now stood at 102, almost half of what he required, but New Jersey next gave its 14 votes to a favorite son, and Pennsylvania, as expected, cast 47 votes for Cameron. Maryland and Delaware went for Bates, but Virginia then split 14 to 8 for Lincoln over Seward, a move, Halstead noted, that produced worried stares among the New York delegation. Indiana and Illinois went solidly for Lincoln. When the secretary announced the vote, Seward led with 173½, but he was 60 delegates short of the goal. Lincoln ran second with 102, while Cameron, no longer a contender, took third with 50½ votes. Chase was a distant fourth at 49, and Bates was fifth at 48. Those in the hall understood that it was now a two-man race.[55]

The convention immediately began the second ballot. This time, New England shifted decisively for Lincoln, with Vermont, Rhode Island, and Connecticut voting unanimously and New Hampshire splitting 9 to 1 in his favor. "The New Yorkers," Halstead scribbled, "started as if an Orsini bomb had exploded." Only Massachusetts held firm. A worried Evarts again announced New York's 70 votes for Seward, but New Jersey again cast most of its votes for the favorite son, giving only 4 to Seward. With Cameron now all but off the ballot, Pennsylvania gave 48 of its 54 votes to Lincoln, while among Ohio delegates Chase's tally slid from 34 to 29 and Lincoln's count rose from 8 to 14. Amid "great confusion," the secretary shouted out the results. Seward still led with 184½ votes, but he had gained only 11. By comparison, Lincoln had gained 79 votes and was now just behind Seward at 181 votes. Chase had declined by 7 and was now a very distant third. "Tremendous applause [was] checked by the Speaker."[56]

After the second ballot, Weed and his closest advisers huddled in an anteroom of the Wigwam. One urged Weed to appeal to Wade's supporters, but since Wade had drawn only 3 votes on the second ballot, that could achieve little. Missouri's Charles Gibson hurried in with the curious request that Seward's forces band together with the Bates men in hopes of stopping Lincoln. A dejected Weed replied that Lincoln's nomination was now likely, but he proposed instead that if no candidate received the necessary 233 on the third ballot, Bates should then throw his 35 votes to the New Yorker. Gibson rushed off to confer with Greeley, who formally remained a Bates supporter. At the Chicago telegraph office, Elbridge Spaulding fired off another cable to Seward. "Your friends are firm & confident that you will be nominated after a few ballots."[57]

Weed was still frantically trying to make deals when the third ballot began. The hall fell into "breathless silence," but by the fourth state's vote, distraught New Yorkers realized it was over. Massachusetts shifted 4 votes to Lincoln, this time the Illinoisan carried 52 of Pennsylvania's 54 votes, and 14 Chase delegates abandoned their candidate for Lincoln, who now held 29 Ohio ballots. Seward actually declined to 180 ballots, while Lincoln nearly obtained the required majority with 231½. Weed's hope for a fourth ballot was not to be. Joseph Medill elbowed his way over to the Ohio contingent and whispered to David Cartter, "If you can throw the Ohio delegation to Lincoln, Chase can have anything he wants." Within seconds, Cartter was on his way toward the stage, and Halstead later cruelly described his stutter as he spoke: "I rise (eh), Mr. Chairman (eh), to announce the change of four votes of Ohio from Mr. Chase to Mr. Lincoln." For a moment, the hall was silent, and then thousands of voices cheered "with the energy of insanity." Although even those next to him could barely hear, Schurz certified the nomination, shouting defiance to "the whole slave power and the whole vassalage of hell."[58]

Almost as an afterthought, the convention nominated Senator Hanni-bal Hamlin of Maine for the vice presidency. Hamlin's only real compe-tition was Cassius Clay of Kentucky, and although the notion of a southern candidate was attractive to many, a ticket of two western men lacked bal-ance. Hamlin was regarded as a good friend of Seward's, so there was hope that his selection might unite the party. He was also a former Democrat from New England, which complemented a former Whig from the West. As Massachusetts delegate John Andrew explained, with "respect to locality, political antecedents, and manifest fitness for office," Hamlin was the consensus choice. "Not one Republican can be found from Maine to Oregon," he added, "who would desire any other result."[59]

High atop the Wigwam, a man waited with a small-bore cannon, ready to fire in honor of the nominee. Hearing the noise below, he peered through a glassless skylight. Somebody on the stage saw his gestures and shouted up, "Fire the salute—Old Abe is nominated." The cannon boomed, spewing hot ash across the roof of the wooden structure and filling the auditorium below with black powder smoke. More cannons exploded from atop the Tremont, and workers at the *Chicago Tribune* hurried to illuminate the building's windows. "There were bands of mu-sic playing, and joyous cries heard on every hand," Halstead reported. The entire city "could hardly contain itself," and utterly sober Lincoln delegates stumbled out into the streets "like drunkards, unable to man-age themselves."[60]

Cannons also sat ready six hundred miles to the east in an Auburn park adjacent to Seward's home. Certain that good news was soon to ar-rive, Seward and his neighbor, the Reverend John M. Austin, enjoyed the warm spring day beneath a shady tree. At length, Dr. Theodore Di-mon, who had volunteered to wait at the telegraph office, came running up the street, cable in hand. Signed by Edwin Morgan, it said only, "Lincoln nominated third ballot." Dimon later insisted there was no change in Seward's expression, only calm silence. "Well," Seward fi-nally remarked, "Lincoln will be elected and has some of the qualities to make a good president." The three sat in silence for some time, and then Austin and Dimon excused themselves and left Seward to his own thoughts. Nearby, sympathetic supporters quietly dragged away the unfired cannons.[61]

*Assured of "a favorable result" only the night before, Seward sat
with friends on his lawn, waiting to celebrate word from Chicago
of his nomination. Instead, at the cost of $1.15, Governor
Edwin D. Morgan cabled news of Lincoln's victory. Frances Adeline Seward,
who disliked politics and loathed Washington, thought it marvelous news
and hoped her husband would now retire from public life.
Courtesy Rush Rhees Library, University of Rochester.*

In Springfield, Lincoln also awaited word with a small group of
friends, first in the law office he shared with William Herndon and then
at the office of the *Illinois State Journal*. A series of telegrams told the
story of Seward's collapse, and when they learned the results of the second ballot, attorney Charles Zane saw a look of satisfaction pass quickly
across Lincoln's face. Shortly thereafter, a messenger boy burst into the
room and handed Lincoln a short cable. Lincoln sat staring at it for
"nearly three minutes" before passing it to the others. It read, "Mr. Lincoln, you are nominated on third ballot." Lincoln shook hands all
around and headed for home. "There is a lady over yonder who is deeply
interested in this news," he explained. "I will carry it to her." That evening, a torch-lit parade snaked past the Lincoln home on Eighth and

*Thanks to his thriving law practice, Lincoln was able to purchase a house and
a corner lot for twelve hundred dollars in January 1844. Later expanded to
include twelve rooms and two floors, the house on Eighth and Jackson streets
was an easy walk to Lincoln's law office. In early 1861, the Lincolns leased the
house to Lucian Tilton, a retired railroad president; Lincoln left Springfield
on April 11 and never returned. Courtesy Library of Congress.*

Jackson streets. Stepping outside, Lincoln apologized that his house was
not large enough to accommodate the well-wishers. "We will give you a
larger house on the fourth of March next," somebody shouted back.[62]

Hamlin received the news that evening in Washington. Telegrams
announced Lincoln's selection, and although the Republicans in Chicago
regarded Hamlin as an ally of fellow senator Seward, Hamlin had already concluded that the New Yorker was unelectable and so was pleased
by the news from the Wigwam. He had just finished dinner at his suite
in the Washington House when Congressman Schuyler Colfax of Indiana burst into the room, waving a telegram and saluting him as "Mr.
Vice-President." A stunned Hamlin responded that he had no wish to
be nominated, but Benjamin Wade, who followed Colfax into the room,
insisted that to decline the spot would only allow Democrats to claim

that he did not wish to join a losing ticket. When the news reached Bangor late that night, revelers awoke his brother and nephew, Elijah and Augustus Hamlin, by firing off the inevitable cannon. After donating his trousers for gun wadding, Elijah offered to be shot out of the cannon himself "if he could only kill the Democratic party." Augustus, who would later serve as a surgeon for the Second Maine Volunteer Infantry, would soon see war enough to regret his father's ghoulish joke.[63]

Elsewhere in Washington, the news reached Douglas. One of his supporters was "delighted" by the nomination, saying, "You have beaten him once and will beat him again." But having campaigned against Lincoln two years before, and having achieved reelection in 1858 by the narrowest of margins, Douglas thought otherwise. Still expecting his party's nomination when it met again in Baltimore, Douglas had anticipated and hoped for a Seward candidacy. Lincoln, he told an aide, would put up "a devil of a fight." Colfax saw Douglas later that evening, and he wrote to tell Lincoln that his old foe "surprised every one by the hearty & eulogistic manner in which he spoke of you." Douglas assured Colfax "that though he often met his fellow-Senators in debate none of them had ever proved so hard a match as you [and] that no stronger nomination than yours could have been made."[64]

Disappointed Seward supporters thought otherwise, and few in Chicago, including Weed, bothered to hide their anger. "They acquiesced in the nomination," Halstead observed, "but did not pretend to be pleased with it." Another journalist compared the "sad and sullen" Seward forces to the "Douglas or nobody" faction among the Democrats, noting that the *New York Times* had "not a word to say for Lincoln." Letters from furious supporters poured into Auburn. "Lincoln's nomination is a cause of so much regret to us here in Massachusetts," one correspondent reported, while another wrote to confess that he had "shed bitter tears" after hearing the news. "All our house mourns over the result of the Chicago Convention," raged an "utterly disgusted" Lewis Benedict. For the "last twenty years" Seward was "so connected with the cause of freedom," but now the party repaid the senator by "declar[ing] a divorce between you."[65]

Many of those writing from the Seward strongholds of New York and Massachusetts threatened to withhold their vote or throw it away to Gerrit Smith. A "grievously disappointed" Everett Banfield fretted that it was "in vain to expect that the highest place in our Government [would] ever be awarded to the wisest, most experienced & most competent Statesman." Another supporter cabled only, "Let those who nominated Lincoln *Elect Him*. We are against him *here*." Most such missives were posted on May 19 and 20, and Republican leaders hoped the party would unite around the candidate once passions faded and tempers cooled. The threat of yet another Democrat in the White House, the *Providence Journal* prayed, "will unite all our forces as harmoniously as any other [ticket] which could be suggested."[66]

More than hindsight suggests that the party leaders were correct. The nomination of Lincoln revealed just how much the party had matured in the six years since its birth as an anti-Kansas-Nebraska vehicle. Davis's "second choice" strategy was masterful, but in the end Lincoln secured the nomination because party managers understood the need to broaden the party's appeal in the North while conciliating the South (and preventing immediate secession). Lincoln's choice allowed the Chicago delegates to hold fast behind their party's core ideals while reaching out to northern moderates and winning over the states necessary to an electoral victory. Perhaps "honest old Abe," as one Seward correspondent conceded, was indeed the "rising sun of Republicanism."[67]

Davis understood the need to unite the party, but he was under no illusions regarding just how difficult a process he faced. Fearful that Lincoln's arrival in Chicago might be regarded by the Seward delegates as gloating, Davis warned his candidate not to "come here for God's sake." Charles Ray cabled with similar advice not to leave Springfield "till after New York has gone home." If Lincoln ever had any thoughts of doing so, he was finally dissuaded by a churlish letter from Chase. The defeated candidate congratulated Lincoln on his nomination but failed to hide his anger at his home-state delegation. "Doubtless the [unanimous] adhesion of the Illinois delegation affords a higher gratification to you than even the nomination itself," Chase fumed. "The only regret I feel connected with the Convention is excited by the failure of the delegates

of Ohio to exercise the same generous spirit." Lincoln promptly replied
that he was "very glad" to hear of Chase's support. No similar missive
arrived from Auburn, and understanding Seward's bitter disappointment, Lincoln chose to wait on posting a letter to the senator.[68]

CHAPTER FIVE

"Beyond the Power of Surgery"

The Democrats, Again

B Y MIDCENTURY, the venerable custom wherein candidates pre-
tended they cared little for public office was wearing thin in the
North. "I will be entirely frank," Lincoln admitted to Illinois senator Lyman
Trumbull in the months before the Chicago convention. "The taste *is* in
my mouth a little." And in later years, William H. Herndon famously
conceded that Lincoln's "ambition was a little engine that knew no rest."
But southern politicians had elevated the ritual into such an art form that
few could make an honest confession of ambition, perhaps even to themselves. Despite a lengthy résumé achieved at a young age, Vice President
John C. Breckinridge was no different. Not yet forty, candidate Breckinridge assured his fellow Kentuckians that he was unfairly "charged with
a premature ambition" and unjustly "charged with intriguing for the
nomination." Despite numerous offices held, the vice president promised
one audience that he had no desire "to thrust [himself] before them for
the highest office" in the land. Understanding their role in this set piece,
the audience cheered, and one person cried out, "That's so, John C."[1]

There was little reason for Breckinridge to be coy. Born near Lexington in January of 1821—five years after fellow Kentuckian John J. Crittenden first took his Senate seat—Breckinridge was the son of a Virginia
planter who had migrated west. Young John had money enough to study

at the College of New Jersey in Princeton and then pursue a degree in law at Transylvania University. Admitted to the state bar at nineteen, Breckinridge served as a major with the Kentucky Volunteers during the conflict with Mexico, and like many young veterans, he promptly parlayed his service into a spot in the state assembly. While in Lexington, he met a fellow legislator who was visiting his wife's Kentucky family. The lanky Illinoisan represented a district that lay just across the Ohio River from land Breckinridge owned near Jacksonville, Kentucky, and although he and Lincoln never became close, the two developed a mutual respect that lasted for years. Service as a two-term congressman followed in 1851, and in 1856 he was elected as Buchanan's vice president. The *New York Herald*, which otherwise accused him of representing the "seceding" branch of the Democratic Party, thought him "a young, fine looking, talented, cultivated and popular man." He would turn forty just two months before Inauguration Day of 1860.[2]

Even in the young republic, men did not become vice president at thirty-five through luck alone. After the debacle in Charleston, Breckinridge continued to publicly endorse James Guthrie, his senior in state politics but also a man whose sole national service had been as Pierce's secretary of the treasury. On May 5, two days after the Charleston convention adjourned, the vice president dined with several Pennsylvania delegates, and following what one described as a "little bender," a bleary Breckinridge admitted he was reassessing his position. Robert M.T. Hunter of Virginia and Oregon's Joseph Lane encouraged him to drop his public support for Guthrie. Although Breckinridge insisted he could not retreat honorably from previous pledges, he did inform several backers that if Guthrie could not obtain the nomination, delegates "should not refuse to recognize the greater strength of another Kentuckian." The vice president reasoned that Lincoln would not "run well east of the mountains," while it was "clear the party [could not] be united on D[ouglas]." If the Democrats had any hopes of winning in November, they would have to abandon both Douglas and Jefferson Davis. Although Breckinridge was every bit as dedicated to protecting slavery as the Mississippi senator, his role as presiding officer over the Senate allowed him to sit quietly while Davis assaulted Douglas and popular sovereignty. "I have some hope, but no great confidence in the general result at Baltimore," Breckinridge told a friend in late May. "If we can unite, *we will elect the nominees.*"[3]

Whether a single Democratic ticket of Breckinridge and New York's Horatio Seymour might have achieved a majority in the Electoral College—as several of the vice president's friends assured him it could—remains a historical mystery. Equally irresolvable is whether the election of a staunch proslavery southerner could have kept Yancey and other fire-eaters in the Democratic fold. As talk of his prospects grew in late May, the vice president came to believe—perhaps because he wished to—that his candidacy meant that southern ultras had abandoned their wish to secede in favor of a potential Breckinridge administration. Yancey would, in fact, cast his ballot for the Kentuckian in November, but he never ceased to argue that slavery remained endangered so long as southerners worked within the existing national framework. Southern Democrats like Breckinridge betrayed what was at best a conditional support for the Union. If not quite as ultra as Yancey, Breckinridge men required not merely Lincoln's defeat but also the success of a southern candidate. Throughout the coming months, Breckinridge was to insist that he was no "disunionist [or] traitor to [his] country." But within the year, after Kentucky refused to secede, the future general would gallop south to tender his sword to the Confederate government.[4]

Breckinridge's hopes, of course, required Douglas to give way, and neither the senator nor his chief supporters had the least intention of doing so. August Belmont, the senator's manager, regarded the vice president's electoral math as dead wrong, especially after the nomination of the allegedly more moderate Lincoln. "With you we can carry New York and the Northwest entire," he assured Douglas. A southern nominee would concede the North to the Republicans, "entire[ly] and forever." Northern editors echoed Belmont. The "sober, second thoughts of the people will be in favor" of Douglas, insisted one. A few argued this point with spectacular illogic. Douglas remained "stronger with the people in each of the cotton-growing States," insisted the *Wisconsin Patriot*, than even Senator Davis. "Were Jefferson Davis to run as President, Douglas would beat him in his own State of Mississippi by a sweeping majority."

The *New Albany Daily Ledger* agreed. "No Democrat can be elected President in 1860," it claimed, "without the aid of Stephen A. Douglas," the "heroic author and defender of the Kansas-Nebraska bill."[5]

Yet even a few observers who regarded Douglas as the candidate most likely to carry a handful of northern states assumed that the Baltimore convention would search for a compromise nominee. His air of inevitability gone, Douglas's prospects were "not as fair now" as they had been before Charleston, admitted one Connecticut editor. "The prevailing sentiment in the party" appeared to be "to let Douglas slide and take some man who [would] secure them a united south," even if that nominee appealed only to "the fire eaters of the Yancey stripe." Georgia's Howell Cobb also expected the Baltimore meeting to abandon Douglas in favor of Hunter. More prescient was the Republican vice presidential nominee, who believed that Douglas's slim majority of delegates planned to hold fast, even if it meant another southern walkout. "Douglas's friends may nominate him as an independent candidate and the South some other candidate," Hannibal Hamlin guessed. He little knew, of course, why ultras such as Yancey cherished the same hope.[6]

In hopes of ensuring Douglas's defeat, Davis once again took to the floor of the Senate. His February resolutions regarding a slave code for the West had never been brought to a vote—in large part because they had been designed as nothing more than a test of Democratic orthodoxy and a bludgeon to use against Douglas—so on May 7, just four days after the dissolution of the Charleston convention, Davis again presented them to the chamber. Unwell as he so often was, Davis struck observers as unusually pale, his hands thin and bloodless. But his voice was strong, and even more than in February, his attacks on Douglas and his threats of disunion were unambiguous. If "squatter sovereignty" failed to protect the southern species of "property" in the territories, the inconstant states' rights senator insisted, it fell to "the Federal Government [to perform] a duty which the Constitution require[d of] it." Although his fellow planters regarded the Democratic Party as "the best hope for the perpetuity of our institutions," should the party or the nation cease to protect slavery, Davis warned, "we look beyond the confines of the Union for the maintenance of our rights." With Douglas fuming just seats away, Davis concluded by expressing the hope that the upcoming Baltimore convention would "adopt a satisfactory platform of principles before proceeding to select its candidate," so that "the reason which [had] dictated the withdrawal of the delegates of the eight States [would] have ceased." To ensure that Douglas delegates recognized that he spoke for a unified South, Davis had the speech printed and invited fellow Democrats to affirm his position. Robert Toombs, Judah Benjamin, James M. Mason, and Hunter quickly became four of the nineteen men to endorse the speech.[7]

As he had three months before, Douglas understood himself to be Davis's target. He remained the party's front-runner, and hence "the most conspicuous man [in] the whole country." In a three-hour speech on May 15 and 16, he replied, but his rejoinder lacked fire and was almost conciliatory. Anticipating fireworks, a large number of diplomats and members of the House filled the galleries, but Douglas, ill and hungover, devoted most of his time to a standard defense of popular sovereignty. Hoping, perhaps, to win back at least some of the southern men who had admired him before his battle against Lecompton, Douglas made only one reference to Davis. "We have been actors for many years in the same scenes," he acknowledged, "involving the same issue that is now presented, he taking the one side and I the other." Noting that he had obtained more votes than any other man in Charleston, and that the convention had approved his platform, Douglas pleaded that he was "no longer a heretic [and] no longer an outlaw from the Democratic party." Before resuming his seat, however, Douglas asked two critical questions of his party. Could Democrats "preserve the party by allowing a minority to overrule and dictate to the majority?" His second query simply challenged party leaders to count electoral votes. So long as the Democrats had backed popular sovereignty, he observed, "the North [had been] Democratic." But after the party had openly championed the extension of slavery, it had lost elections in "New Hampshire, Rhode Island, Connecticut, New York, Pennsylvania, and Ohio." How many of those states might the Democrats carry should they "repudiate the Cincinnati platform" in favor of "this Yancey flag of intervention by Congress for slavery in the Territories in all cases where the people do not want it?"[8]

If Douglas expected to isolate the ultras with a single, pragmatic speech, he little understood just how much Yancey controlled the hearts, if not the minds, of southern Democrats. Even the choice of Baltimore was meant to heal the self-inflicted wound of Charleston, since the Maryland port had been the site of every Democratic convention from 1832 to 1852, and the party had lost few of those contests. Douglas's managers continued to hope that their southern brethren would eventually cool down enough to consider the electoral map. But, believing their candidate to have been unjustly treated in Charleston, on one question they refused to compromise. Belmont argued that the southern delegates had surrendered their credentials when they had stalked out of the South Carolina convention, and he called for new state elections to choose replacement slates. To welcome the rebellious contingents back at Baltimore would be folly, he insisted, as it would only give the fire-eaters a second chance to wreak havoc on the party. Senator George Pugh of Ohio spoke for many when he vowed to keep the Baltimore convention in session "until the fourth day of March, 1861"—that is, Inauguration Day—rather than allow a single ultra "to come back again." Douglas might address the Senate in soothing tones, but his handlers had grown weary of Davis's saber rattling. Northern Democrats were "stung by the taunts of their Republican neighbors that they were serfs of southern masters," one editor admitted, and they refused to concede to the endless "demands and arrogant intolerance of the South."[9]

Scholars routinely emphasize the refusal of southern fire-eaters to compromise when it came to slavery, and not without reason. But as the Baltimore convention approached, northern Democrats proved as adamant about holding fast. "At Baltimore, the secessionists will not be permitted to enlist and repeat their disorganizing farce," editorialized one Wisconsin paper. The majority delegates should "yield no further capital to the sectional demagogues intent on a dissolution of the Union." Douglas thought so as well, in part because he expected moderate southerners to rally to his candidacy in the wake of his reply to Davis. "All we have to do is to stand by the delegates appointed by the people in the seceding States in place of the disunionists," he counseled Belmont. Determined to campaign on a platform of popular sovereignty, Douglas recognized that ultras who had walked out of Institute Hall when denied the Alabama Platform would only "bolt again and break up" the Baltimore meeting.[10]

Ever capable of making a bad situation worse, President Buchanan, still the party's titular head, said nothing about electing new slates but simply urged "the seceders at Charleston" to "attend the Baltimore convention." In the Senate, Davis continued to express "admiration and approval" for the bolters as the only "faithful adherents of our party," men whose hands had been forced by northern delegates representing those "States that [would] certainly vote for republican candidates" in the fall. Far to the south, Yancey did his best to add to the disharmony. When a handful of southern congressmen, impressed by the conciliatory tone of Douglas's latest speech, proposed to cancel the Richmond convention or delay it until after the Baltimore meeting, Yancey, in an interview with the *Mobile Advertiser*, insisted that the Virginia conference, set to convene on June 11, represented "the only National Democratic party now in existence." If Douglas yet hoped to win back all but the most ultra southerners, Yancey and his followers, as one Washington editor noted, "meant dissolution of the Union and nothing else."[11]

In truth, almost nobody was interested in compromise. Georgia's Alexander Stephens, who was ill and could not attend the second statewide convention, hoped his state would choose an entirely new roster of men who had had nothing to do with the Charleston debacle. But when the same party leaders who had chosen the first slate of delegates reassembled, a majority of those attending not only reappointed the original slate but also formally instructed the delegates to bolt again if the Baltimore convention refused to adopt the Alabama Platform. In protest, a furious Governor Herschel V. Johnson quit the convention, taking a moderate minority of roughly 20 percent of the party leadership with him. Meeting the next day, Johnson's followers elected a rival delegation that planned to unite with the handful of Georgians who had not abandoned the Charleston meeting. Johnson believed that Stephens's absence left the moderates "almost without an advocate," but in fact his presence would have made little difference.[12]

The story was similar in most southern states. Florida and South Carolina—where Robert Barnwell Rhett dominated the meeting—even accredited delegates for Richmond alone, but they too selected the former slates. Writing from Washington, South Carolina senator James Henry Hammond urged the party to remain united against Douglas. With "our surplus productions of cotton, rice, sugar &c. and our substructure of black slaves," he counseled, *"we are safe."* Texans agreed; their party meeting reappointed the old delegates for service in Baltimore, and as with Georgia, the leadership instructed them to abandon that convention for Richmond if the party refused to protect slavery in the territories. By instructing delegates to prepare for Richmond if the Baltimore convention proved hostile to the expansion of slavery, southern Democrats served warning to the Douglas forces that they were ready again to split the party and rally behind a regional candidate.[13]

Stumping Alabama in preparation for the June 4 party meeting in Montgomery, Yancey encouraged his audiences to follow Rhett's lead and demand that the Democrats accredit delegates for Richmond alone. Baltimore would be little more than an "Abolitionism and squatter sovereignty" meeting of Douglas men, bent on placing "the constitutional rights of the slave States, and of the citizens thereof moving into a Territory, at the mercy of a numerical majority of anti-slavery men." Although Yancey controlled a majority of Alabama's delegates, John Forsyth argued that nothing could be lost by adopting Georgia's solution of sending the Charleston delegates to Baltimore, with strict instructions to quit the convention if not granted the Alabama Platform. Forsyth carried the vote, leading one of Yancey's enemies to gloat that "the fire-eaters [were] backing down in despair." But in losing his argument, Yancey, as a member of the original delegation, took pleasure in the fact that he could now wreak havoc in Baltimore.[14]

On his way to Baltimore, Yancey stopped in Washington to consult with Alabama congressman James Pugh. While there, Yancey was approached by George Sanders, a Douglas man from New York, who evidently spoke without authorization from Belmont. Sanders proposed that the party unite around the Illinois senator and that, in exchange for southern support and acceptance of the Cincinnati platform, the convention name Yancey as its vice presidential nominee. As a further inducement, Sanders bluntly added that the hard-drinking Douglas "must die within six months of his inauguration, and that then Mr. Yancey would have the whole matter in his power." Never having read Milton, Sanders failed to grasp that Yancey had no desire to serve in heaven, so he was surprised when the Alabaman responded to "the proposition with scorn" and instead boarded the train for Maryland.[15]

The refusal of southern Democrats to select new slates meant that their northern brethren could expect the Baltimore meeting to be yet another fiasco, unless they abandoned Douglas and turned the platform over to Yancey. But Belmont's demand for fresh delegations was based on the fantasy that southern voters would cast their ballots for Douglas over slaveholding Tennessean Bell come November. Nobody, in fact, expected Baltimore to turn out well. Riding east from Chicago was the intrepid Murat Halstead, who found himself on a train car with a Cincinnati delegate bound for Maryland. The delegate, whom Halstead declined to name in his account, was furious with southerners for their demands, especially after "all the battles" northern Democrats had waged on their behalf. He "wanted the South to sweat under an Abolition President," he told Halstead, and was pleased that "Seward was not the Republican candidate, for he would be too easy on the South. He hoped Lincoln would make them sweat." The Ohioan understood that his party could not now win, but it was past time to compromise, and as he warmed to his topic, the Democrat's class and racial resentments grew more obvious. "The Southerners had been ruling over niggers so long that they thought they could rule white men just the same," he swore. He "thought more of Black Republicans than of such fellows as they were," and "if there was to be a fight between sections, he was for his own side of the Ohio."[16]

As most of the delegates made their way toward Baltimore, the protest slates chosen by South Carolina and Florida, together with a handful of ultras from other southern states, settled into Richmond. Rhett had arrived on June 9, two days before the meeting was scheduled to begin, so that he might confer with Edmund Ruffin, the acknowledged leader of Virginia's small band of fire-eaters. Virginia's governor, John Letcher, endorsed the main convention in Maryland, and the eccentric Ruffin—who had briefly joined the cadets of the Virginia Military Institute in Charlestown the previous December so that he could watch John Brown die—had little standing with the state's Democratic establishment. When the conference convened at Richmond's Metropolitan Hall, it was but a small affair, and the Richmond press, with the exception of the ultra *Enquirer*, said little about the gathering. The conference organizers had booked the hall only two days before, and even those men expected the meeting to conduct no serious business. Most of the delegates accredited to both the Maryland and the Virginia conventions simply by-passed Richmond, and residents of the city paid no interest to the meeting. Halstead caught a train down from Maryland to watch the first day's events, and he was not much surprised to find few delegates and even fewer observers in attendance.[17]

At noon, Lieutenant Governor Francis Lubbock of Texas called the meeting to order. A short speech denouncing "compromises of the Constitution" earned Lubbock, a South Carolina native, polite applause, but as most of the Florida delegates had yet to arrive, the convention adjourned for the day. It met again at ten the following morning, and this time South Carolina's Andrew Pickens Calhoun, son of deceased sectionalist John C. Calhoun, rose to introduce two resolutions. The first proclaimed that the delegates remained loyal to the majority platform rejected at Charleston and thus thought it "unnecessary to take any further action in relation to the platform at the present time." The second proposed that they adjourn and demand their seats at the convention in Baltimore, despite the fact that South Carolina had instructed its delegates to attend only the Virginia meeting. Rhett spoke against the second resolution, but as it was clear that a majority of southern delegates planned to attend the Baltimore meeting first, remaining in session at the Metropolitan Hall was as pointless as it was embarrassing. Most of the "Seceders from the Charleston Convention," as one anti-Yancey Alabama editor dubbed them, voted to adjourn and apply for readmission in Baltimore. Only Rhett and the South Carolinians opted to remain in Richmond in preparation for what they expected to be another Democratic disaster.[18]

With that inauspicious prelude, the regular Democratic convention began six days later on Monday, June 18, in Baltimore's Front Street Theater, a favorite venue of actor John Wilkes Booth. A weary Halstead was present for what was—counting the two Charleston conferences and the Richmond protest meeting—his sixth convention of the political season. The crowd was greater than in Charleston, he noted, but not nearly what it had been in Chicago. As before, Douglas was the main topic of conversation, with his supporters resolved to nominate him "at any hazard or sacrifice," while southern activists "assumed an arrogance of tone that precluded any hope of amicable adjustment." Also as before, Caleb Cushing called to order the assemblage of 303 men, which promptly got off to an acrimonious start when he ruled that only those states present when the Charleston body adjourned could be formally recognized. Although sympathetic to southern demands, Cushing believed it not yet decided that the seceding delegations had been readmitted, so he refused to accept their credentials. Adding to the disorder, a majority of Connecticut's contingent burst into the hall while Cushing was attempting to explain his position, "there being some misunderstanding as to the hour of the meeting."[19]

Order was at least somewhat restored, and Cushing began again, this time in mollifying tones. He "congratulate[d]" the delegates for "being reassembled here for the discharge of [their] important duties." But similar to the Constitutional Union conventioneers who had met across town in the Presbyterian church, the Democrats pressing toward the front of the theater to better hear Cushing put too much weight on the boards covering the orchestra pit, and with a thunderous crash the panels collapsed into the hole, pulling the front of the stage down with them. Nobody was seriously injured, but as the delegates scrambled out of the pit, a new panic ensued when an umbrella mysteriously burst into flames. For those who put stock in such omens, it was clear that the Baltimore convention was doomed.[20]

Cushing might try to calm the rattled nerves of those in the theater, but there was no way to smooth over the three intractable, interlocking problems facing the convention. The first was the question of a nominee, and the Douglas men in the audience again made it clear that it would be "Douglas or nobody." Northern Democrats "have made up their minds," one delegate assured a Washington journalist, "and it cannot be helped." Convinced that the party could not win unless Douglas topped the ticket, delegates from Pennsylvania argued—as had their Republican counterparts in Chicago—that their constituents might well vote for Lincoln over Breckinridge or Davis. Ironically, Yancey often insisted that Douglas's adherents were little different from Republicans, and although no northern Democrat was willing to concede that point in Baltimore, Thurlow Weed was confident that if Douglas "should *not* be nominated we shall have many of his Friends with us."[21]

At this juncture, Douglas did a completely unexpected thing. Writing from Washington to Dean Richmond, the chairman of the Illinois delegation, the senator offered to withdraw his name from contention if it could prevent his "enemies" from "destroy[ing] the Democratic party, and perhaps the country." Always a staunch Unionist, if rarely a principled statesman, Douglas had finally begun to realize how determined some members of his party were to dismember the republic. Richmond shared those concerns, but the Douglas men had come too far to back down. For the northern delegates, the battle was not about one man but rather over the soul of the party. Richmond stuffed the letter into his pocket and even denied its existence, though word of the missive quickly circulated around the Douglas headquarters in the Gilmore House (which, unhappily, also quartered Yancey and the Alabama delegation). Even had Richmond been inclined to consider withdrawal, however, it would have been impossible to meet the terms that Douglas had set. The senator consented to give way in favor of "some other reliable Non-intervention and Union-loving Democrat." For fire-eaters who believed slavery to be endangered every day that the South remained within the Union, the exchange of one popular sovereignty candidate for another would be meaningless.[22]

Hoping that rumors of the Richmond letter might convince moderates to save the party, Cushing and Jefferson Davis continued to push for a compromise candidate. Letters arrived at Cushing's hotel endorsing New York's Horatio Seymour, but the once and future governor wrote to say that he could not, "under any circumstances, be a candidate." A brief attempt by Davis to lure Franklin Pierce back into public life came to nothing, leaving the Mississippian desperate to find a "sound" contender to put up against "our little grog-drinking, electioneering demagogue." Hearing of this backroom intrigue, Austin King of Missouri seized the convention floor and angrily urged the lower-South delegates to "go back to Richmond," where they would be free to nominate "some man who has neither heels nor bottom enough to get the nomination here." To the laughter and applause of Douglas supporters, King denounced Rhett and his newspaper. "Look at the tone of the Charleston *Mercury* since the Charleston Convention," he shouted. "Those delegates who come here from the seceding States are the associates of those men who say that while the Democratic party has kept its organization together nationally it was a stumbling block to disunion."[23]

Several of Douglas's handlers proved more willing to compromise on the platform, the second major problem facing the convention. Belmont still preferred the 1856 Cincinnati platform, but in hopes of winning over all but the most ultra southerners, John T. Howard of Tennessee crafted a consciously vague alternative, quickly dubbed the "Tennessee resolution." Howard's brief paragraph attempted to appease both popular sovereignty advocates and proslavery expansionists, as it guaranteed all citizens "an equal right to settle with their property in the Territories" and praised the unnamed Dred Scott decision as "the correct exposition of the United States Constitution." The final sentence averred that no rights regarding "property [could] be destroyed by congressional or territorial legislation," and although that contradicted Douglas's Freeport Doctrine, it was also true that no Democrat believed that Congress had the power to ban slavery in the territories. Even fire-eaters agreed with Douglas that once territories became states, however, they were free to outlaw slavery, so Howard's deliberately obscure prose provided a plausible solution for those willing to compromise. New York's delegation agreed to the resolution and informed Howard that it could support such a platform, provided no southern delegation withdrew over it or the possible nomination of Douglas. William Richardson of Illinois also indicated that his state could rally behind this "or the equivalent."[24]

Few southern delegates cared to gloss over the issue of slavery's expansion, but northern Democrats knew that Howard's ambiguous resolution was as far as they could go and still face voters in the fall. Delegates like W. B. Gaulden of Georgia, who gloried in "being a slave breeder" and loudly advocated the reopening of the African slave trade, made it virtually impossible to sell the Democratic Party to northern farmers, who desired the Great Plains to be clear of both slaves and free blacks. Proclaiming slavery a "blessing to all races," Gaulden hoped to see it spread across the continent, and as northern men grimaced, the Georgian added that the best vehicle for accomplishing this was "the great National Democratic party." Gaulden, Halstead marveled, was "in sober and resolute earnest," so all Douglas's handlers could do after such politically untenable speeches was make protests to the effect that proslavery expansionists exhibited "no difference in principle" from Republican "Interventionists."[25]

The real fight, of course, was over credentials. For four days, as conventioneers argued about candidates and platforms or just wandered Baltimore's streets, the credentials committee labored to resolve the issue of which delegates to seat. If that struggle was decided in Douglas's favor, the battle over his nomination and a suitable platform would be won as well. Since no southern state had complied with Belmont's demand for new delegations, there was never any doubt that most of the original Charleston slates would be seated in Baltimore. The question, rather, was what to do with states like Georgia, which had selected rival delegations, or Florida and South Carolina, which were accredited only to Richmond but now demanded admission to the main convention. Belmont and Richmond were reluctantly ready to seat most of the Charleston seceders, understanding that they had little choice if they wished to keep the convention intact. On one point, however, they refused all negotiation. Yancey and the Alabama delegation were not to regain accreditation. "Your friends steadfast and confident," one cabled Douglas.[26]

As Halstead observed, the very presence of the Charleston rebels at the Front Street Theater "produced extremely hostile feelings" among the Douglas supporters. Southern men, and not just fire-eaters, had the "power to control the Convention or destroy it," and everybody in Baltimore knew it. The hard feelings generated in Charleston had yet to dissipate, and for many northern delegates, a Douglas candidacy comprised only part of their demands. As Pennsylvania congressman William Montgomery insisted, they required an "honorable pledge" in advance from the bolters that they would "abide by the nominations that we may make" and promise not to "countenance a Seceders' Convention in another place." The fire-eaters, he added, had walked out in South Carolina after being outvoted, yet now they wished to return. "It is high time, if they ask to come back, that they shall declare that they have changed their minds." M. R. West of Connecticut agreed. Northern Democrats were "denounced from [New England] pulpits" because of popular sovereignty, but when they asked for a fair vote on a nominee or a platform, southerners "taunt[ed them] with being Black Republicans."[27]

Finally, on the morning of Thursday, June 21, Cushing announced that the committee had prepared two reports on credentials. As unable to forge a compromise behind closed doors as the leaders of the platform committee had been in Charleston, committee chairman John Krum of Missouri had finally given up and encouraged ten members to write a minority report. The "most intense anxiety prevailed," scribbled Halstead, as the meeting waited to see if the convention could survive yet another angry battle that revealed an insoluble sectional rift within the once-dominant Democratic Party.[28]

Isaac I. Stevens rose to read the minority report. It began with nine brief points, among them that the Alabama and Florida delegations were "invited to take their seats." The central dilemma, Stevens said, was not whether those remaining in Charleston had called for new elections to fill the vacancies created by the walkout. Rather, the heart of the matter was whether there were in fact vacancies in the southern delegations. "Their withdrawal was not a resignation," Stevens argued, since the latter must be "complete and final." By comparison, the delegates who had quit Institute Hall in April had merely "desired the instructions of their several constituencies." They had not formally resigned. In fact, the seceding Charleston delegations had insisted that they had been instructed to resign by state leaders. However, as Georgia delegate John A. Cobb observed bitterly, it little mattered that Stevens was rewriting history, since there was no chance that the minority report would be adopted by the northern majority.[29]

As expected, on June 22, the convention's fifth day, the gathering voted to adopt the pro-Douglas majority report on credentials, with 139 in favor and 113 against. Richard Glass of Virginia rose to announce that although he had "done everything in [his] power to preserve the nationality of the Democratic party," he had to stand by his state and region, and hence he "decline[d] any further participation with this body." Glass's announcement was met with mingled hisses and applause, and, evidently eager to give tempers time to cool, Cushing banged his gavel and ordered the galleries cleared. A second Virginia delegate shouted that Cushing should do no such thing and added that he hoped that as they "retire[d] from the grave of Democracy," they might be heard to [their] heart's content." Having made it clear that they would have their way or destroy the party, a majority of the Virginians marched out of the chamber, followed by delegates from North Carolina, Tennessee, Maryland, Texas, and Mississippi. "Men may bolt when they please," wrote an exasperated Alexander Stephens, "but they cannot escape the proper characterization of their actions." The credentials fight "was a pretext." The real issue, he thought, was Douglas.[30]

Long into the night, a handful of dispirited moderates tried to hammer out a compromise formula, but any such effort was too late by months, if not years. The next morning, with no resolution in sight, most of the Kentucky delegates withdrew, and they were followed by Arkansas and half of Missouri. In all, 105 delegates from twenty-two states quit the convention, leaving behind only 198 men, which meant that the convention was four votes short of the 202 necessary to nominate. It is suggestive, perhaps, that seven of the eight states that had seceded in Charleston were the seven that were to secede following the November election, while the first three states to quit the Baltimore convention—Virginia, North Carolina, and Tennessee—would also be the first three to secede following the attack on Fort Sumter. As they would be in the spring of 1861, Kentucky and Missouri were divided.[31]

Cushing had been part of the deliberations the previous evening, so he knew what the sixth day was to hold. In what his biographer describes as "a carefully orchestrated move," Cushing dramatically seized the moment to announce that as he no longer represented "the will of the majority" of those remaining in the convention—that is, the Douglas men—he thought it his "duty to resign [his] place as presiding officer." As Illinois and Ohio delegates loudly cheered his withdrawal, Cushing slowly walked to the Massachusetts delegation. When the jeers grew louder, Cushing rose again and departed the hall. Governor David Tod of Ohio, one of the convention's vice presidents, accepted the post of chairman, and this time the "thunders of applause from the Douglas men" carried no hints of sarcasm.[32]

With Cushing and the majority of the southern delegates absent, Belmont was ready to call for balloting. William S. Gittings, one of the remaining Maryland delegates, protested that the two-thirds rule adopted in Charleston was still in force, which meant that any candidate had to receive more votes than remained in the hall. But Gittings was shouted down by Sanford Church of New York and Paris C. Dunning, the former governor of Indiana. The two-thirds requirement was "outrageous, undemocratic, despotic, [and] wrong," Church insisted. New York had previously "submitted to it for the sake of harmony," but no longer. Dunning agreed. If the "will of the people was carried out by the democratic party," he added, "the little giant of Illinois would be the next president." Since very few men who were not Douglas supporters remained in the theater, and since nobody present apart from Gittings was anxious to adjourn in favor of yet another convention, the delegates quickly agreed that two thirds meant two thirds of those actually present and voting.[33]

The voting began, but any suspense had vanished with the southern delegations. A few southern men remained behind, and Maryland cast 2½ votes for Douglas. He received 3 each from Virginia and Tennessee and 1 from North Carolina. Ohio bestowed 23 on him, and New York gave another 35. Breckinridge received only 7½ votes, all from Connecticut and Pennsylvania, and Guthrie came in third with 5½. When the votes were tallied, Douglas had 181½ of the 194½ cast. J. B. Clarke of Missouri reflected his state's divided nature by taking the floor to confess that he had "never had any enmity to Douglas" and so moved to declare him "the democratic nominee for the presidency." The work of several months and two conventions at last finished, "cheer upon cheer now arose, every person in the theatre rising, waiving their hats, handkerchiefs and evincing great enthusiasm." Having anticipated this moment, "a band of the Keystone Club" rose in the gallery "and struck up a tune," which elicited more cheers from below.[34]

The convention agreed to reassemble that evening at seven o'clock to select a vice presidential nominee. Douglas had made it known that he preferred Alexander Stephens, but Belmont thought it prudent to allow the few remaining southern delegates in the hall to select the nominee. The handful of southern men caucused over dinner, and Louisiana's small contingent endorsed Stephens "with enthusiasm," as did the Arkansas delegation. Alabama, however, backed their senator, Benjamin Fitzpatrick. Since the few Alabama men who remained behind were hostile to Yancey, they reasoned that the popular Fitzpatrick, Georgia-born and a former governor (as well as the master to more than one hundred slaves), could isolate Yancey and carry the state for Douglas. Fitzpatrick's second and much younger wife, Aurelia Blassingame Fitzpatrick, was anxious for her husband's advancement and encouraged him to seek the spot.

Georgia's Robert Toombs, who had no interest in holding the party or the nation together, issued the final blow by discussing his diminutive friend's frail health shortly before quitting the convention. Other Georgians observed that Stephens, a former Whig, had opposed the Mexican-American War; the Democrats planned to make much of Lincoln's criticism of that conflict, and a Stephens candidacy would "spike that big gun."[35]

That evening, Tennessee's George W. Jones announced that the "Southern delegates [had] conferred together" and unanimously backed Fitzpatrick. Rising to second the nomination, J. B. Clarke avoided the faint praise he had heaped on Douglas earlier in the day and proclaimed Fitzpatrick to be "a tower of strength in the South." Since Fitzpatrick was a supporter of the Alabama Platform and had voted in support of the Davis resolutions in the Senate, one reporter thought the ticket "an incongruity [that was] quite inexplicable."[36]

The final task of the evening was to approve the platform. As Douglas had demanded for months, the final document retained the popular sovereignty clauses in the earlier Cincinnati statement. But with an eye toward attracting southern votes, the platform committee reworded the relevant paragraph in hopes of winning over all but the most dogmatic fire-eaters through sheer ambiguity. During the territorial stage of political development, the platform read, "the measure of restriction, whatever it may be, imposed by the Federal Constitution on the power of the Territorial Legislature over the subject of domestic relations" was to be decided by the Supreme Court. One southern delegate correctly complained that the obscure legalese "did not mean anything at all," but Samuel H. Moffat, one of the five (of thirty) Virginians who remained, announced himself satisfied. "I am an out-and-out pro-slavery man," he proclaimed. "I believe it is right morally, socially and politically. [But] have we not enough of higher law, revolutionary, abolition scoundrels in the North to fight, without fighting our friends? Must we fight the men who stood on the platform at Cincinnati in 1856, and kick them off and break up the Democratic party?"[37]

Across town, the seceding delegates set up yet another rival convention in the Market Hall, on Baltimore Street, the home of the Maryland Institute for Mechanical Arts. The cavernous auditorium featured elegant galleries running along all four sides; the room, which could seat nearly eight thousand people, had witnessed the nominations of Pierce and Fillmore. An exhausted Halstead spent June 23 racing back and forth between the two meetings, each claiming to be the regular "National Democratic Convention." Charles Russell, who took the podium of the breakaway gathering as temporary chairman, insisted that the main convention in the Front Street Theater had "lost all title to the designation of national." Although it was true that only one third of the delegates in Baltimore had reconvened at the Maryland Institute, Russell insisted, they represented "a majority of the people of the Democracy and of the Democratic States." His announcement was met with tremendous applause, and it was clear that, at least for 1860, the Democratic Party could not be stitched back together. "The case was beyond the power of medicine or surgery," Halstead reported.[38]

While Russell was talking, Caleb Cushing entered the chamber. His arrival was greeted "with immense cheering," the entire body "rising in a mass to their feet and giving cheer after cheer." Determined to prove that they owned the title of "the original *national* democratic Convention," Russell passed the gavel to Cushing, who now reigned as chairman of his third gathering of the year. Cushing began to call the roll, and although there was a smattering of northern delegates, the 105 men who presented their credentials were overwhelmingly southern. Seventeen Massachusetts delegates had followed Cushing across town, as had two from New York, one from Vermont, and one from Iowa, and there were also delegations from California and Oregon. But when Cushing called on Pennsylvania, though somebody from the floor shouted, "She is here," nobody was, in fact, nor had even single delegates arrived from eleven other northern states. (Nor was South Carolina represented, since Rhett and the rest of its delegates remained one state away in Richmond.) Still, Toombs, normally the dourest of men, was "lit up with good cheer," and Yancey "glowed with satisfaction." Most of the southern ultras "smiled radiantly," Halstead observed, adding, "I had not seen them look so happy during the sixteen weary days of the Convention, and the two days' episode at Richmond."[39]

Understanding that the northern delegates across town planned to nominate Douglas that afternoon, the southern men wasted little time in making their own selection. A few voices spoke in behalf of Treasury Secretary Howell Cobb, and the two New Yorkers pushed for former senator Daniel S. Dickinson. But everyone in the hall knew that the nomination was Breckinridge's for the taking, and in fact a delegation led by Benjamin Butler had already left for Washington to confer with the vice president. In later years, Butler (who was to run for Congress in 1866 as a Republican) claimed that his group pressed Breckinridge on his adherence to the Constitution and urged him to repudiate the widely held view "that if the Republican party came into power," he would urge his state to secede. The vice president, in keeping with the charade of disinterest, insisted that he made no promises and obtained the nomination "without any solicitation of my part, and against my expressed wishes," but several others later confirmed Butler's account of the meeting.[40]

It required only a single ballot. George Loring of Massachusetts (another future Republican) formally proposed Breckinridge, citing his devotion "to the Constitution and the Union." The few northern men there cast their votes for Dickinson, but as the count continued, most rose to shift their votes for the vice president. When it became clear that Breckinridge had the votes of a majority of those in attendance, Cushing declared him "unanimously nominated." (Since the convention was far short of the requisite two thirds of the 303 men who had originally arrived in Baltimore, the group first had to amend the rules "so as to make two-thirds of those present" enough to nominate candidates, and this time none of the strict constructionists in the hall filed a complaint. In fact, neither Douglas nor Breckinridge was properly nominated under party rules.) In even less time, the convention then selected Oregon senator Joseph Lane for the vice presidency. The North Carolina native, as James De Bow editorialized, possessed "sound Constitutional views" and had stood by his friend Congressman Preston Brooks after Brooks had beaten Sumner nearly to death, support that "endeared him to [De Bow's] heart, and to that of almost the entire South."[41]

That done, the convention swiftly adopted Charleston's majority platform, as one North Carolinian bragged, "without crossing a t or dotting an i." And then, as "the whole hall reverberated" with cries of "Yancey! Yancey!," the mastermind of the entire affair rose to provide closing remarks. Rather smugly, Yancey congratulated the body on finally reach-

Still the youngest vice president in American history, John C. Breckinridge
was only thirty-six when he took the oath of office in March 1857.
After quitting the country in 1861, Breckinridge rose to the rank of major
general in the Confederate army. His First Kentucky Brigade called
themselves the "orphan brigade," since they felt orphaned by a
state government that remained loyal to the United States.
Courtesy Library of Congress.

ing the conclusion he had come to "some nine or ten years ago" after
Congress had banned the slave trade in Washington, thus "initiating the
great policy of abolition." Yancey had then understood the need to "obtain a disruption of this Union," and at long last his party had joined him

in that endeavor. As his name was "connected with the movement carried out today," he thought it necessary to condemn "the great enemy of the democracy," Stephen Douglas, whose "rejection of democratic principles" had forced this second secession. "Breckinridge and Lane," he shouted, "that shall be our war-cry, but not for their sake as men," rather because they represented "the foundation principles of the democracy, Truth, Justice and the Constitution." To "loud and continued cheering and applause," Yancey left the stage, and the exhausted delegates drifted out into the night. The institute's director turned the gas jets off, and somebody noticed it was eleven in the evening; the Douglas men across town had finished just over an hour before.[42]

Two days later, on the evening of June 25, Breckinridge, Toombs, and Cushing dined at the Washington home of Jefferson Davis. As they ate, Davis raised the probability of a Lincoln victory with three major opponents in the race, and he advanced the curious suggestion that Bell, Douglas, and Breckinridge all withdraw from the contest so that the Democrats might again try to choose a compromise candidate, possibly even Pierce. Breckinridge was startled by the proposal, but Toombs played on his ambition by observing that when Douglas realized that Breckinridge would carry the solid South, he would withdraw within the month. Davis's motivation remains unclear, unless he yet hoped to win the nomination, and anybody who knew Douglas understood that he could not be driven from the race. Breckinridge, in any case, agreed to accept the Baltimore nomination with the understanding that he might withdraw later; with this caveat, his pretense of indifference remained intact. As the group strolled back to Breckinridge's home, they encountered a "very large and enthusiastic crowd of Democrats" who had come to serenade the candidate. Breckinridge stood on his front steps and delivered a brief speech, in which he again expressed "his devotion to the Constitution and the Union," and then Davis stepped up beside him to address the crowd. If Breckinridge had the smallest inclination to quit the contest, there was little evidence of that as the audience "extravagantly applauded" Davis's words.[43]

To the south, the South Carolinians yet waited in Richmond, and on Tuesday, June 26, the group convened in the Metropolitan Hall one final time to endorse Breckinridge and Lane. As had been the case two weeks before, few delegates were in the hall. But as rumor held that Yancey was to speak, the galleries were packed. After nearly a month of travel, however, Yancey was unwell and declined to leave his hotel. With that, "a large portion of the disappointed audience left," and the group made quick work of endorsing the southern ticket. Most of the Baltimore delegates, as one journalist observed, were simply "on their way home," and little wonder. The Richmond meeting was the fifth Democratic convention of the season, and the eighth national political convention if one counted the Constitutional Union, Republican, and Boston Liberty Party meetings. The indefatigable Halstead had attended seven of the eight gatherings, and he was more than content to board the Richmond train for home.[44]

If Davis thought it even remotely possible that the Richmond meeting's endorsement of the Breckinridge ticket might prod Douglas into quitting the race rather than handing the election to Lincoln, any final doubts on that score were erased by the Illinois senator's behavior over the next week. Northern delegates too descended on Washington, but with the intent of serenading their candidate. Douglas men waited at Union Station to escort the arriving delegates across town to the senator's home, and after a large group filled the street late on the night of June 23, Douglas stepped out onto his porch to deliver a brief speech. The republic was in peril, he warned his audience. "Secession from the Democratic party means secession from the federal Union." After the crowd left to serenade Senator Fitzpatrick—who, ominously, claimed to be indisposed and declined to acknowledge the well-wishers—Douglas returned inside to complete work on his formal letter of acceptance. Published on June 29, the letter contained the senator's pointed observation that he was the nominee of "the National Convention" and that he proudly embraced the popular sovereignty platforms upheld by the Democrats in "1848, 1852, and 1856." He condemned both Republican "Northern Interventionists demanding the Wilmot Proviso for the prohibition of slavery and the Southern Interventionists insisting upon Congressional Intervention for the protection of slavery." But he concluded with a warning that left little ambiguity as to his ultimate loyalties: "The Federal Union must be preserved."[45]

If Douglas's letter was more somber than celebratory, he had good reason to be so. The senator quickly discovered why his running mate had declined to greet their supporters. Having sought political advancement in part to appease his ambitious wife, Fitzpatrick immediately came under pressure from Aurelia to decline. Dozens of cables arrived at his door urging him not to accept, and Douglas's enemies, including Yancey himself, warned Aurelia that her husband would be "eternally ruined" if he ran on a northern-dominated ticket. Regular Democrats encouraged him to stand firm and played on his sense of honor. "To refuse now would be to cower before your enemies [and] disgrace your best friends," one Douglas man advised. But Fitzpatrick withdrew. Belmont and the national committee met and selected Herschel V. Johnson, the Georgia governor who had led the moderates' walkout in his state's second party convention. The choice made sense, as Johnson was a Stephens ally who in Baltimore had quietly urged the nomination of his friend over Douglas as a way to heal the party. In any case, Belmont had few options. As one New Orleans editor jeered, "it is hard for the Douglasite managers to think of any one in the South who would be likely" to serve "as the Squatterite candidate for Vice President."[46]

In previous years, sitting presidents typically kept their opinions private until after their convention met, and then they endorsed their party's selection (a tradition that has lasted into the present). But as R. B. Sloan, the Democratic editor of the *Washington Constitution*, admitted, after "unparalleled struggles and contentions and dissensions, and after two cases of secession from a so-called National Democratic Convention," the party had advanced two rival tickets, each claiming to be the rightful voice of the Democracy. For a time, therefore, President Buchanan chose to say nothing. Northern Democrats hoped the Pennsylvania-born Buchanan might save the party by endorsing Douglas, but Breckinridge served him as vice president, and his feud with the Illinois senator was nearly as old as his presidency. Buchanan was surely correct in believing that nothing he could say would motivate Douglas to quit. William Lloyd Garrison called it right when he rejoiced that the Democratic "breach [was] complete."[47]

Late in the month, Michigan Democrats met in a statewide convention in Detroit to endorse Douglas and popular sovereignty. Furious over the president's silence, the delegates refused, by a lopsided vote of 105 to 6, to approve a resolution commending the policies of Buchanan's administration. (Despite the fact that Secretary of State Lewis Cass was in the city, the party activists declined to invite him to attend.) The editor of Ohio's influential Columbus *Statesman* also endorsed the ticket, insisting that Douglas's nomination was "not the result of a blind and indiscriminate folly like that of Lincoln's." Ignoring the irascible Douglas's tendencies toward unpredictable and even erratic behavior, the newspaper recommended him as "the true representative of the sound, conservative, Democratic principles which should govern this country."[48]

Those southern Democrats who supported Breckinridge promptly fired back. Any voter who favored "the defeat of Lincoln," one Washington correspondent claimed, understood the need to rally behind the vice president. Should the Democrats continue to field two candidates, Douglas, the same reporter argued with what turned out to be amazing foresight, would "certainly fail to carry a single State, except, perhaps, Missouri." Had all but the most ultra southerners united behind Douglas in Charleston, the Illinoisan might have stood a chance, especially against Seward, but after the acrimony of the past several months, his chances of carrying a single southern state were remote, even if Breckinridge quit the contest. In the lower South especially, "Douglas has hardly an adherent," thought South Carolina's Thomas Palmer Jerman, "and throughout the state his chances are dwindling." The Charleston convention, Jerman believed, had "effected a change in the policy, not sentiment, of those who preferred him to others." By late June, most southern voters had bought the widely circulated charge that in practice little separated popular sovereignty from Republican free soilism, and Jerman was certain that South Carolina voters would "submit no longer to northern aggression."[49]

Admittedly, journalists who searched hard enough could find isolated voices that favored the other section's candidate. Yancey enjoyed the fact that former president Franklin Pierce of New Hampshire endorsed Breckinridge, while New York's Martin Van Buren gave Douglas but tepid backing. When New York Democrats met in two state conventions, one in Manhattan on June 28 and a second in Syracuse on July 3, both gatherings reluctantly chose Breckinridge as the candidate most likely to best Lincoln. In the South, the editor of the *New Orleans True Delta* ran a banner headline emblazed with DOUGLAS TRIUMPHANT, while a Richmond newspaper warned that their "seceding friends" in Baltimore were actually "in favor of a Southern Confederacy." But a few atypical cases could not disguise the essentially sectional character of the two Democratic factions. Although it was certainly true that not every southern voter was a secessionist, it was a fact, as Douglas claimed, that every secessionist was a Breckinridge supporter. When one of Douglas's supporters compiled a list of twenty-six southern politicians—congressmen, governors, and former governors—who supported Breckinridge but also argued that their states should secede if Lincoln won, nobody disputed the listing.[50]

The Republican leadership enjoyed the chaos across the aisle as much as Yancey did. The once-dominant majority party, noted the *New York Herald*, was rent as "neatly and completely as even 'Old Abe Lincoln,' with his axe, maul and wedges, split a chestnut log." Watching these events from Albany was Thurlow Weed, who gleefully wrote Lincoln that the "madness which precedes destruction has come at last upon our opponents." As a seasoned veteran of New York State politics, Weed was rarely one to predict victory five months in advance, but in the wake of Baltimore he saw little reason to be pessimistic. "I can see no reason to doubt our success in all the Free States," he informed the candidate on June 25.[51]

Similar sentiments arrived in Springfield from other quarters. Writing from Leavenworth, Kansas, just *before* the Maryland conventions adjourned, editor and judge Mark Delahay assured Lincoln that the "affairs at Baltimore rather please me." Douglas might win the nomination, Delahay predicted, "but the seceders will likely join in Richmond and present another candidate," which would hand the election to the Republicans. "Present my kind regards to the wife of the Next President of the United States," he jested. Edwin Morgan of New York agreed. Lincoln would "have no serious difficulty here," Morgan insisted, and the state would "be carried by a handsome majority." So many such missives arrived on his desk that even Lincoln, normally the gloomiest of candidates, grew increasingly confident. "I hesitate to say it," he admitted, "but it really appears now, as if the success of the Republican ticket is inevitable."[52]

"Inevitable" is a word embraced only by naive politicians, and Lincoln, who had lost more than his share of contests, was never that. As is the case today, experienced political observers of the period—editors, handlers, and elected officials—were incorrect in their predictions as often as they were right. What makes the predictions of late June of 1860 catch the eye, therefore, is how strangely accurate they turned out to be. The Washington journalist who believed Douglas would carry only Missouri was wrong only in the number of southern states he expected Breckinridge to capture, and when Lincoln, with three months to go before Election Day, named the states he expected to win, he was off only by California (which he narrowly carried but thought he might lose). As one supporter assured Lincoln on June 25, the "reflecting friends of neither [Democratic] candidate expect to Win," and any attempts by party leaders to force both Breckinridge and Douglas from the race "cannot succeed." Douglas was "resentful & not disposed to yield," and as "the South never surrenders, Breckinridge may be counted [as] certain." Even so, the Constitution demanded a November election, and that gave Americans—including a joyful Yancey—five months to prepare for the inevitable.[53]

CHAPTER SIX

"Lincoln Is the Next President.
I Will Go South"

The Campaigns

THANKS TO THE FACT that Lincoln's handlers had depicted him as a simple rustic given to splitting rails, reporters who descended on Springfield in the days after the Chicago convention half expected to find the candidate chopping firewood on his front porch. But those journalists who patronized "Honest Old Abe" as "always clean [if] never fashionable" were surprised to find his wife "a very graceful woman, with no such thing as awkwardness [*sic*] about her." Politicians' wives rarely played any public role beyond serving tea to their husbands' guests, but after the Chicago convention, Mary Todd Lincoln frequently served as hostess to as many as one hundred visitors each day. Reporters thought her comments on the numerous candidates insightful, and during a campaign season when newspapers devoted at best a few lines to Salmon P. Chase's daughter's beauty or Frances Seward's absence from Washington, the eastern press paid numerous compliments to Mary's poise and wisdom. "Whatever of awkwardness may be ascribed to her husband," admitted a writer for the *New York Evening Post*, "there is none of it in her. [Mary] converses with freedom and grace, and is thoroughly *au fait* in all the little amenities of society."[1]

The stressful White House years and the death of a son during the war would impose greater strains on what was rarely a perfect marriage, but all of that lay in the future. Guests who streamed through their Springfield home thought the two a curiously matched couple. Abraham, tall and thin and "careless" of dress, greeted visitors beside Mary, five feet two and fashionably plump. Abraham was self-taught, whereas young Mary had attended Kentucky's Shelby Female Academy, where she had studied history, geography, natural science, French, and theology, before receiving further education at Madame Mentelle's. Mary was supportive of Abraham's ambition, shared his devotion to Whig politics, and, as one Albany paper observed, took "manifest and honorable pride in the distinction which has fallen upon her husband." Few politicians' wives expressed opinions about public matters, and even fewer politicians desired their wives to do so. But Abraham, painfully aware of his lack of education and his humble origins, allowed Mary to order him new suits of "superior black cloth" and stop him "from using his knife in the butter rather instead of the silver-handled one." To the annoyance of his handlers, he also listened to her advice on party matters and personnel. (Rather more typically for her time, Mary had far less to say about political ideology or issues.)[2]

Although not yet voters in any state, women like Mary Lincoln played an increasingly visible role in electoral politics. Even in Virginia, a state in which Republicans made up roughly 1 percent of voters, elite women courageously supported the Lincoln-Hamlin ticket. Thirty-three young women of Wheeling—sixteen dressed in black, sixteen in white, and one in red to represent "Bleeding Kansas"—presented an American flag to the local Republican club. "Though not being allowed the privilege of being called voters," Louisa Griffith announced, "we represent to you our Union [and] We shout aloud the name of Lincoln." Most editors, however, hastened to assure male readers that Mary "eschew[ed] all politics" while they clumsily tried to appeal to wives (who often influenced their husbands' votes) by playing up the candidate's domestic values. Abraham Lincoln, editorialized one Vermont newspaper, "would be chosen from among a crowd as one who had in him the kindly sentiments which women love."[3]

Most of those who stopped by the parlor of the Lincoln home on Eighth and Jackson offered advice on the fall election, and with little wonder. On June 24, just after the Baltimore convention descended into chaos, the *New York Herald* marveled at the lengthy roster of national candidates. In terms revealing its Democratic allegiance, the paper listed the five contenders. Lincoln represented the "Black republican" party, Douglas spoke for the "Northern democracy," and Breckinridge headed the "Southern secession democracy." Bell ran for the "National Union" Party, while Gerrit Smith was the candidate of the "John Brown abolition" ticket. The *Herald* declined to mention the curious fact that Breckinridge, undeniably the candidate of fire-eaters, no longer owned an estate or slaves in Kentucky, while Bell, who refused to discuss the question of slavery in the territories, owned perhaps eighty bondpersons and Douglas, despised in the South for his battle against Lecompton and the Freeport Doctrine, continued to draw an annual income from his first wife's plantation. The *Herald* did add that only in a few states would more than two candidates face one another, and that since voters had to obtain paper tickets from party functionaries (rather than using modern ballots), there was no way for Lincoln supporters to vote for Lincoln in the lower South—not that any whites in the Gulf states wished to do so.[4]

As had previous candidates, Lincoln declined to campaign in his own behalf and spent the summer and fall at home in Springfield. Even given the custom, however, he remained surprisingly silent during the five months following his nomination. Aware that both Democratic candidates would twist his words and willfully misinterpret his speeches, both David Davis and Senator Lyman Trumbull warned Lincoln even against posting letters on the issues of the day. Editor William Cullen Bryant, who had invited him to speak at Cooper Union earlier that year, also urged the Illinoisan "to make no speeches [and] write no letters as a candidate." The Republican platform was in circulation, of course, as was Lincoln's publication of his 1858 debates with Douglas. The party thought those documents records enough. "I could say nothing which I have not already said," Lincoln complained to one persistent correspondent, "and which is in print and accessible to the public." Despite the fact that he was so little known outside his state that even friendly newspapers in neighboring Ohio consistently misspelled his first name as "Abram," Lincoln took his handlers' advice and rarely ventured beyond his parlor or law office. When pressed by reporters to comment on the other four candidates, he gently deflected the questions with humorous anecdotes.[5]

Reflecting the racist and ethnic stereotypes of the era, this cartoon features the
four major candidates dancing a quadrille—the precursor to square dancing—
to a tune played by Dred Scott. Breckinridge waltzes with a satanic Judas
goat, featuring the face of Andrew Jackson, while Lincoln engages
in a scandalous interracial dance. Bell, the former chairman
of the House Committee on Indian Affairs, dances with a
Native American, while Douglas takes the arm of an Irish voter.
Courtesy Library of Congress.

Lincoln nonetheless agreed to a short biography designed to supple-
ment the 606 words he had provided to editor Joseph J. Lewis in late
1859. Owing to the cut-and-paste newspaper style of the era, editors
routinely lifted stories—and inevitably also rumor and falsehood—from
other publications, and Horace Greeley wrote to suggest that a brief biography might be useful to Republican editors. At about the same time,
Lincoln was contacted by John Locke Scripps, the editor of the *Chicago
Tribune*, and with Greeley as publisher, the three agreed to craft a simple, pamphlet-length biography. Lincoln sent nine short paragraphs (in
which he referred to himself in the third person) to Scripps, with a plea

that the campaign biography be scrupulously accurate. He was surely exasperated, therefore, when Scripps wrote to say that he had taken "the liberty of adding Plutarch's Lives" to the list of books "you read in early life." Scripps added, "If you have not, then you must read it at once to make my statement good." Like any aggrieved author, Scripps complained about Greeley's editing and pronounced the conclusion "sadly botched." But the thirty-two-page biography, published by Greeley's *Tribune* for the price of $2.50 a pamphlet, sold more than one million copies.[6]

Not only journalists traveled to see Lincoln. On May 24, Thurlow Weed arrived in Springfield, having been invited by Davis and state assemblyman Leonard Swett, another of Lincoln's close advisers. Ever since the Chicago convention, Lincoln's handlers had been hoping for an overture from Seward's key supporters, and one finally arrived in a letter from Weed to Swett. The New York boss admitted he had wanted to write earlier, "but the hope of being able to say that our Friends in this State had got over their disappointment and buckled on their armour, has delayed me." However, Weed was careful to add that while Seward's backers (and obviously the senator himself) were saddened by the outcome, Lincoln enjoyed their "entire confidence." Swett promptly forwarded the missive to Lincoln, as Weed knew he would, and Davis swiftly dispatched an invitation to Albany. Although the resulting five-hour meeting in Lincoln's parlor was ostensibly designed for discussing campaign strategy, its actual purpose was to start the process of healing the potentially crippling intraparty wounds. Weed departed Illinois graciously praising Lincoln's sagacity, and Lincoln played his part by promptly writing to one of Weed's associates, complimenting the New Yorker's wisdom and insisting that he had never believed the rumors of Weed's corruption spread by his eastern enemies. The associate showed the letter to a pleased Weed, as Lincoln, in turn, expected him to do.[7]

At length, Seward swallowed his pride and made the pilgrimage to Springfield. Lincoln was anxious to mend fences, but recognizing that the New Yorker was unpopular in the southern portions of Illinois, the Republican State Committee was none too pleased by the visit. Accompanying the senator was twenty-five-year-old Charles Francis Adams Jr., grandson to John Quincy Adams and son of the 1848 Free Soil vice presidential nominee. Like most Massachusetts Republicans, Adams was a staunch Seward man, and he had nothing good to say about the local arrangements in Illinois. Seward's train carried him through Chicago, and as they transferred toward Springfield, both men expected a private car. None awaited them, and Adams churlishly noted that the carriage south overflowed with "ordinary passengers." But recognizing that Seward had journeyed far enough, Lincoln left his home and walked to the station with Trumbull. "There he was," Adams scribbled into his diary, "tall, shambling, plain and good natured." Lincoln was nervous about meeting the eminent New Yorker, "and very awkward in manner," but Seward too "appeared constrained." Trumbull handled the introductions, but as "ill-will and cold distrust" existed between the two senators, that did little to ease tensions in the carriage. Perhaps not wishing to publicly embarrass his defeated rival, Lincoln had organized no reception, so the small group simply stood "in the aisle of the car." Lincoln soon left the train, and Seward and Adams continued on their travels.[8]

Lincoln's sole speech during the campaign season was a brief one, delivered in Springfield. On August 8, the city hosted a grand rally and "ratification" meeting. Balancing the need of the press and public to see the candidate with the party's desire to limit and control its message, Davis decided to bring the campaign to Lincoln. Special trains carried as many as fifty thousand people to the capital. At ten o'clock, "the grand procession" began to snake its way past Lincoln's home toward the fairgrounds. As a veteran of Whig politics, Davis understood the importance of symbolism, and the parade included a series of log cabins on wheels, drawn by twenty-three oxen. By the time Lincoln arrived at two o'clock, the stage was surrounded by a "tumultuous populace," who lifted him out of his carriage and passed him above their heads to the podium. "It has been my purpose, since I have been placed in my present position, to make no speeches," Lincoln cautioned the crowd, but he urged them to stay and "hear this public discussion by other of our friends who are present." Lincoln finally escaped on horseback, but the masses lingered on into the evening to hear a series of orators, who, one Democratic editor sneered, "threw out an indescribable amount of gas on the nigger question."[9]

When not bringing the voters to Lincoln, Davis used a series of surrogates to bring Lincoln, or at least the Republican platform, to the voters. Although Seward had long been far more popular in New England than the unknown Lincoln, the party regarded that region as safe, as Frémont had carried every New England state in 1856. Even so, abolitionist Henry Stanton stumped for Lincoln in both New York and New England and penned pamphlets in the Republican cause, and Charles Sumner spoke "for the rail splitter" across Massachusetts. Davis also worked to secure voters in the lower North and the West. He was mindful to employ proxies with strong ties to the antislavery movement in hopes that they might contact their old allies even in safe regions and so depress Gerrit Smith's turnout. Carl Schurz wrote a series of editorials for German-language newspapers, including the Illinois *Staats-Anzeiger*. While Davis shrewdly portrayed Lincoln as a moderate free soiler and an advocate of a homestead act in the West, his eastern spokesmen emphasized Lincoln's antislavery credentials. Greeley's *Tribune* played its part and assured New York readers that Lincoln was "ahead of the Anti-Slavery sentiment of the Republican party, rather than behind it," a statement that had the virtue of being true.[10]

Greeley required no prodding from Springfield to sanction the ticket, but small-town editors and traveling speakers such as Stanton required funding. Davis coordinated fund-raising as well. Weed knew the sort of "prominent capitalist[s] most desirable for us to cultivate" in the East, and Davis, as a land baron and judge, was acquainted with their western counterparts. The two fired off requests for financial assistance to Republican governors and philanthropists. Davis then funneled the cash into closely contested states. Although some of the missives directed to Lincoln himself asked for money, the candidate passed them along to Davis, so Lincoln never saw budgets, expense vouchers, or even explanations of where the cash was going. When Caleb B. Smith of Indianapolis complained to Davis about the likelihood of illegal voting in Kentucky, the judge contacted an old friend and former Whig congressman, John Goodrich of Massachusetts, who responded with a grant of ten thousand dollars to combat the alleged fraud.[11]

Not requiring funding were the so-called Wide Awake clubs that had sprung up all across the North. The idea first emerged in the winter of 1860 when Lincoln spoke in New England following his Cooper Union address. Young Republicans braved the inclement weather wearing oil-cloth capes and bearing torches, and the image stuck. Encouraged by party leaders, young men adopted the costume, and party rallies were quickly accompanied by large numbers of Wide Awakes, whose "uniform" and tendency to march in formation gave the clubs a decidedly military appearance. One Chicago journalist described them as wearing "a black enameled circular cape, quite full and of good length, and a glazed military fatigue cap with a brass or silver eagle in front." When Hamlin spoke in Boston that October, he was met by more than one hundred Wide Awakes, and rather than take a carriage to a friend's home after his speech, Hamlin chose to march with "the boys." The paramilitary nature of the groups unnerved southern fire-eaters. Texas senator Louis T. Wigfall alleged that Wide Awake clubs intended "to sweep the country in which [he] live[d] with fire and sword," and Yancey denounced them as "a monster body" determined to inaugurate Lincoln by force if necessary. Even a few northern Democrats remarked that the thick smoke from one of their torchlight parades resembled nothing so much as burnt black powder after battle.[12]

College students in particular enjoyed the Wide Awakes' growing reputation in the South as "a vast army under the guise of political clubs." In New England, the groups took on an especially radical nature, since clubs in Massachusetts included a handful of black men. In late September, Elizabeth Cady Stanton presented a banner to the Seneca Falls club, and the following evening Wide Awakes returned the favor by holding a "drill" in her front yard. Both Elizabeth and Henry Stanton delivered brief speeches, as did guest Susan B. Anthony. The young women's rights activist encouraged them "not only to keep *Wide awake* to inaugurate Abram Lincoln, but also to go to the aid of the *Slaves*, in case of an insurrection, or another John Brown invasion in Virginia." Echoing those sentiments was Congressman Owen Lovejoy, who urged Wide Awakes to invade Virginia and arrest Governor Henry A. Wise. During the fall campaign, the clubs bore torches, Lovejoy shouted, but soon "they will shoulder their muskets."[13]

Among New Yorkers, Henry Stanton was unusual, since he quickly transferred his loyalty from Seward to Lincoln. Since other longtime

*To demonstrate their willingness to fight for party and country, young men
calling themselves Wide Awakes donned uniforms of black capes and shiny
caps. Although some of their rallies took place at daytime speeches, they
preferred to march by torchlight at night. The* New York Herald *estimated
that as many as four hundred thousand young men joined the clubs.
Courtesy Library of Congress.*

Seward backers remained alienated from the campaign, the most important surrogate was the senator himself. Although still angry and heart-
broken over his loss in Chicago, Seward understood that if he expected
to have any future in the party, he could not sit silently in Auburn during
the summer and fall. And disconsolate or not, Seward had no desire to
see Douglas win his state. Thanks in part to Davis's overtures to Weed,
by early July, Seward was beginning to hint that he would "take the stump
for Lincoln and Hamlin." One month later, the press formally announced
that Seward planned an extensive campaign across the North, starting in
New England and ending in Kansas. To accompany him, the senator
chose his fifteen-year-old daughter Fanny; George Baker, his friend and
official biographer; Charles Francis Adams Jr.; General James Nye of
New York City; and Nye's daughter, the latter as a companion for Fanny.

Young Adams, who would later see action at Gettysburg, was only recently graduated from Harvard, but he had been in ill health, and Seward invited him as a favor to his father, the free-soil pioneer who had been elected to Congress from Massachusetts's third district the year before.[14]

The swing began in Boston in early August, where Seward delivered his first speech of the campaign. Sensitive to his audience, the senator politely but firmly took Gerrit Smith and the Liberty Party to task for criticizing Lincoln as too moderate on race. "The Lincoln campaign is to inaugurate an anti-slavery policy in the government," Seward assured the gathering, and would "end the power of slavery under the government of the United States." Ever the clever politician, Seward tailored his stump speech to the needs and interests of each locale. In St. Paul, he promised his listeners that the ultimate center of American power would lie along the upper Mississippi, and as his train rolled westward, Seward emphasized the value of free labor in the territories and spoke in favor of railroad development. When the group neared Lansing, Michigan, they were met "by a cavalcade of mounted 'Wide Awakes'" and as many as ten thousand people who had arrived "in wagons and on horseback" to hear the senator.[15]

For young Adams, nearly fresh out of college, the venture was an introduction into the era's rough-and-tumble politics. Although he had been raised in a devoutly political household with a lengthy tradition of public service, campaigning never came naturally to any Adams. Seward, by comparison, delighted in the limelight, and Adams was impressed by the senator's ability to deliver a series of "really remarkable speeches" in "rapid succession." Most of all, the sheltered New Englander was astonished by Seward's ability to consume copious amounts of alcohol and cigars each evening. "When it came to drinking," Adams confided to his diary, "Seward was, for a man of sixty, a free liver." Seward favored brandy and water, but he also enjoyed champagne, "and when he was loaded, his tongue wagged." Adams simply "never could understand" how a small man might consume so much alcohol and then take to the stump the next morning. Seward also "smoked the whole time," Adams marveled.[16]

Quite possibly, Adams's perceptions were colored by the relatively temperate society of his youth, for he soon discovered that Seward's consumption paled by comparison to some. The group reached Toledo, Ohio, one evening just around midnight, and both Adams and Seward were slumbering in the train's sleeping cars. Adams heard a crash, and looking out into the aisle, he saw Douglas, "whiskey-bottle in hand" and "plainly drunk." The Illinois Democrat had given a speech in Toledo earlier in the day, and hearing that Seward was nearby, he and a crowd had rushed to the station hoping for a joint debate. "Come, Governor," Douglas shouted, "they want to see you; come out and speak to the boys." Seward mumbled that he was sleeping, but Douglas tried to drag him out of the berth. "Well, what of that?" Douglas persisted. "They get me out when I'm sleepy." Seward insisted that he "shouldn't go out," and Douglas finally gave up. As he left the sleeper, he "stopped to take a drink" from his bottle. The next morning, Seward blandly informed the stunned Adams that the strange episode was simply Douglas's "idea of political courtesy," and that despite their ideological differences, they had "always been on the most friendly terms."[17]

Although Seward and his traveling band of speakers were careful to highlight all aspects of their party's platform, prudently emphasizing support for a protective tariff in New England while stressing homestead issues and internal improvements when in the West, no Republican speech ever began or ended without a denunciation of slavery in the territories. Much to the annoyance of Democrats, who regardless of section underlined their loyalty to the Constitution while painting the Republicans as radicals intent on social innovation, Republican orators routinely compared themselves to those Founding Fathers who had voted to restrict slavery in the Old Northwest. The "Union which our fathers formed seventy years ago is not the Union of today," lamented Moses Davis of Wisconsin. Orville Hickman Browning agreed that his party's doctrines were "the same that were consecrated upon every battlefield of the Revolution," while David Wilmot assured one audience that Lincoln's election would "restore this government to its original policy, and place it again in that rank upon which our fathers organized and brought it into existence." Since Thomas Jefferson's 1784 draft legislation for the West had banned slavery in all territories, and not simply those above the Ohio River, how, Republican speakers wondered, could they be labeled as anything but traditionalists?[18]

Outside of New England, where Republicans competed with Liberty men for votes, Republican speakers rarely mentioned the impact of unfree labor on black Americans and instead played upon the threat posed to white pioneers by slaveholding planters. The upcoming contest, the *Illinois State Journal* warned, was between "conservative Republicanism [and] fire-eating, slave extending Democracy." In response, Douglas partisans insisted that if Lincoln was victorious, "hundreds of thousands" of runaway slaves would relocate into free states, which could place "them side by side in competition" with northern workers and allow for "African amalgamation with [their] fair daughters." Allegations of racial egalitarianism were especially prevalent in New York, where a coalition of Republicans and Liberty activists placed a proposed amendment to the state constitution enfranchising African Americans on the November ballot. Those who wanted to vote alongside "a large buck nigger," scoffed one Democratic orator, or believed "a nigger [was] better than an Irishman [should] vote for the Republican candidate." For decades, however, Irish Americans had voted solidly Democratic, and there was not much danger of their voting Republican in 1860. When the *New York Herald* denounced Lincoln as "exactly the same type as the traitor [John Brown] who was hung at Charlestown—an abolitionist of the reddest dye," it surely did less to keep immigrant voters in the Democratic fold than it did to push Liberty voters into casting their ballots for Lincoln.[19]

Anti-Republican rhetoric was far more heated in the South. No Breckinridge supporters expected Lincoln to earn many votes in their region; persistent allegations that Republicans intended to "get access to [their] Negroes to advise poison and the torch" were instead designed to prepare the ground for secession. Congressman Jabez L.M. Curry, always ready to inflame southern passions, advised his Alabama constituents that an army of abolitionists planned to invade the South just after the election, forcing "the poor man's daughters" to marry black men, and the Alabama press carried numerous stories reporting that Lincoln's advisers were already enticing enslaved blacks to murder their masters. Few outdid the Rhetts, who publicized the rumor that Hamlin was mixed-race. To "insult the South," the two Rhetts insisted in the pages of the *Mercury* and from the stump, the Republicans imposed "over the Southern States, [and] in the Senate, a man of negro origin." Claims that a man with black ancestry could soon be a heartbeat away from the presidency were designed to remind up-country voters that Republicans were not merely a threat to the planter class, as their "hatred and malignity" endangered the South's racially based class system of white privilege as well.[20]

Employing race as a weapon against the Republicans was the only tactic on which the increasingly antagonistic Breckinridge and Douglas camps could agree. As the summer wore on, it became ever more clear to leading Republicans what was to occur in the fall elections. "I do not doubt the result," Charles Sumner confided to a British correspondent. "Lincoln will be chosen." Despite a lifelong tendency toward pessimism, the candidate thought so too. "The prospect of Republican success now appears very flattering, so far as I can perceive," Lincoln assured Hamlin as early as July 18. Mary Lincoln, of course, never had any doubts as to her husband's success, and by midsummer she too felt "quite confident of [his] election."[21]

Election Day remained a distant three months away, however, and supporters of Bell and the Constitutional Union Party were hardly ready to concede. As was typical of the party's Whig forebears, Constitutional Unionists relied even more heavily on lively rallies and "grand ratification meetings" than did the other parties. Because the Unionists had declined to draft a platform, activists emphasized their candidate's credentials rather than any positions he might hold. Since Bell and Everett were neither antislavery men nor fire-eaters, their advocates were free to position them anywhere between those two extremes. John Minor Botts, a Virginia supporter (and unsuccessful candidate), declared himself opposed to any further extension of slavery and reminded voters that Bell had cast his vote against Kansas-Nebraska. As they had at the Baltimore gathering, party leaders typically accentuated their fealty to "the Union [and] the Constitution" while denouncing the "spirit of party [that] raised its serpent fangs above them all." At a ratification meeting held at Cooper Union on June 8, Gustavus A. Henry—the star of the May convention and a future Confederate congressman—delivered "an exceedingly effective speech" long on patriotic flourishes but short on specifics. Henry and other speakers discovered that each mention of General Winfield Scott, the Whig nominee in 1852, "was received with the wildest enthusiasm" and the "waiving of hats," so each orator found a reason to mention that "glorious veteran and peace-advocate."[22]

The Whigs, even in the border South, had always been more accepting of female activists than were Democrats, and that tradition continued under the Unionists. In part because the Whigs had been famous for their pageants and colorful demonstrations, in which they had encouraged women to participate, and because women could not vote, they in turn now found an outlet for their political energies in public exhibitions. Speaking in Petersburg, Virginia, Botts urged "the ladies present to use all their influence with husbands, brothers and sons, in behalf of the Union." Observing the large number of women at Virginia rallies, the sympathetic editor of the pro-Bell *Richmond Daily Whig* wrote, "Pity they are not allowed to vote." Perhaps aware of what a civil war would mean for their families, women in what was soon to become the Virginia battlefront organized Bell and Everett clubs, and as many of them were well-to-do urbanites, they raised funds and even penned campaign songs for the party. A few women adopted a more personal approach. Mary Virginia Terhune implored her husband to vote for Bell instead of Lincoln. "I have never interfered with your political opinions," she assured him, "but if I had a vote, I should be in no doubt where to cast it. Lovers of peace and concord should unite upon Bell and Everett."[23]

Yet the reliance on old Whig tactics hindered the party's ability to appeal to disaffected border-state Democrats. Party leaders hoped to win over southern voters who thought Breckinridge a disunionist but recognized that Douglas could not win. But owing to the selection of two prominent former Whigs instead of an ideologically balanced ticket of Sam Houston and Everett, "whiggery," as one disgruntled Texas editor put it, "hung like an incubus round its neck." A number of pro-Bell editors around the Chesapeake made no secret of the fact that they hoped the collapse of a national Democratic Party might "bring into the foreground a substantial, conservative Union party, somewhat resembling the old Whig party." For Unionist leaders who wished to downplay partisan sentiments, such editorials, or the fact that former President Millard Fillmore had published a letter announcing his intention to vote for Bell, simply drove prospective Democratic moderates away. Hostile newspapers derisively dubbed the group "the Whig Know Nothing American

Opposition" Party, and in a time when party attachments remained strong in the upper South, advertisements that Constitutional Unionists were merely Whigs under a new banner meant that in Maryland and northern Virginia, Bell won over former Whigs while capturing a handful of Republican voters in states that Lincoln could not possibly carry. Because their Whiggish tactics gave hope to former members who desired a rebirth of the old party, the Unionists eroded support for the moderate, pro-business Douglas in cities like Richmond and Baltimore.[24]

Like the Republicans, the Unionists relied on surrogates to speak for the silent candidate. Here too, the leading proxy overshadowed the nominee, as the aged John J. Crittenden traveled the border states on behalf of the less accomplished Bell. A number of northern activists begged Crittenden to speak in New York and Pennsylvania, but believing those states to be already in Lincoln's column, he instead stumped throughout Kentucky, Tennessee, Virginia, and Maryland. The supportive *Annapolis Gazette* applauded the party's lack of specificity. George Washington's "platform was the Constitution," it editorialized. "Is not this the platform for Maryland, Union-loving conservative Maryland?" Yet on the hustings, Crittenden was often forced to discuss policy, if only when criticizing the other parties' platforms. Popular sovereignty, he insisted again and again, was "a mere abstraction." Since no existing territory could support plantation agriculture, Crittenden argued (carefully failing to note that a handful of slaves had already been carried into the New Mexico Territory, or that both Democratic platforms advocated the acquisition of Cuba), why fight about slavery in the West at all? Crittenden conceded that Lincoln was no abolitionist, but thought that his party contained enough abolitionists to terrify the Deep South and that his election would thus be a "great calamity to the country." Breckinridge, he added, was the candidate of every disunionist in the South.[25]

For most voters, though, it was not enough to know what the Unionists were *against*. They demanded to know what policies Bell might pursue if successful in November. Crittenden could emphasize his party's loyalty to the Constitution at every train stop from Lexington to Baltimore, but Kansas remained a territory, Spanish Cuba was still coveted by Louisiana sugar planters, and eventually New Mexico would petition for statehood. Even potentially friendly voters peppered Bell with queries as to his positions on these and other pressing issues. John D. Woods was just one of many who pressed the nominee to state whether he was "in favor of restoring the Missouri Compromise of 1820," which would keep Kansas free and potentially the Utah Territory as well if expanded to include the Mexican Cession. "Are you opposed to Squatter Sovereignty as explained by Mr. Cass & Mr. Douglas?" Woods persisted. To all correspondents, Bell merely replied that he and Douglas were the only national candidates; the other three appealed to sectionalism. Most of Bell's handlers simply added that theirs was the candidate of experience. Republicans, they complained, described Lincoln as "honest Abe," as if "Abe was the only honest man in the Union. Mr. Bell is equally honest, and ten times as capable." Editors of every political persuasion lost patience with such appeals to blandness. Bell, the irritated Nashville *Union and American* snapped, "Stands on nobody's platform!! Fights nobody!!! Loves nobody!!!!"[26]

The fact that a man who owned as many as eighty slaves—Bell's diverse holdings in several states and his use of hired bondmen at the Cumberland Iron Works, which he co-owned, made precision on the number impossible—could refuse to take a firm position on slavery in the territories outraged southern fire-eaters. Correctly believing that Bell, and not Douglas, posed the greatest threat to Breckinridge in the South, southern Democrats pointed to his vote against Kansas-Nebraska as evidence of his "freesoil affinities." The *Montgomery Mail*, a pro-Yancey journal, denounced Bell and Everett's "abolition proclivities." Southern Unionists responded that Bell's record on slavery was "sound, constitutional, Southern, and natural." One friendly Georgia paper added that during Bell's tenure in Congress he had voted against receiving antislavery petitions, just as James Henry Hammond and Henry A. Wise had. With considerable justification, southern Unionists observed that if their peculiar institution and the fate of the republic were endangered, that was largely due to the separatist policies of fire-eating Democrats. Since Bell promised to defend both "the Union and the Constitution," which implied a defense of the Dred Scott decision, the ticket could "be accepted with honor, self-respect and safety by every citizen of the Republic not bent on mischief."[27]

Unlike other minor parties in American history, the Constitutional

Unionists were in it to win, and party leaders continued to believe that victory remained possible, if not, perhaps, on Election Day itself. As Bell's handlers pored over electoral maps, they regarded Virginia, Kentucky, and Tennessee as safe states. That, however, achieved only 39 electoral votes, and 152 were required to win. Few states featured all five candidates; most amounted to two-candidate contests. But a handful of states, and especially New York, listed all five, and as home to Gerrit Smith, the Empire State could complicate the electoral map for the Republicans. Ever since their Baltimore convention, Unionists had openly discussed the prospect of throwing the election into the House of Representatives. If no candidate earned a simple majority of electoral votes, the election (as had happened in 1824) passed to the House, with each state receiving a single vote and choosing from the top three candidates. Unionist editors correctly predicted that Douglas would finish fourth in the electoral count, and should this "lucky chapter of accidents" occur, editorialized the *Annapolis Gazette*, "the only compromise upon which the House will be able to agree for President will be John Bell."[28]

Working with Belmont, who incorrectly expected his man to best Bell, Unionist manager Washington Hunt hammered out an agreement in which a New York electoral ticket of ten Bell supporters and twenty-five Douglas men would run as a unit. Belmont raised the considerable sum of twenty-five hundred dollars to implement the plan, and after some negotiations with Breckinridge's camp, the final agreement was that if the joint ticket carried the state, Douglas would get 18 electoral votes to 10 for Bell and 7 for Breckinridge. Similar plans emerged in Rhode Island, New Jersey, and Pennsylvania, although Breckinridge's strong support in the latter earned him a majority of the potential electoral votes there. Douglas, however, was furious when told of the scheme and objected that "fusion with seceders merely added dishonor to defeat." Democrat Benjamin Hill attempted to craft a joint ticket in Georgia, as did Bell supporters in Virginia, but neither effort succeeded. All that the various managers could agree on was the necessity of denying Lincoln the election, and both Belmont and Hunt expected their respective candidates to emerge victorious in a House election. Weed assured Lincoln that the plan would come to nothing in New York and "fail to effect its object" in Pennsylvania.[29]

Although Constitutional Unionists prayed that antislavery voters would inadvertently aid their plans by casting their ballots for Smith instead of Lincoln, abolitionists, as ever, conducted an underfunded protest campaign. In mid-August, remnants of the Liberty Party met in Syracuse to ratify the earlier Boston convention's selection of Smith. The group invited "the men and women of this and the other States, who occupy radical positions on anti-slavery and temperance." Smith remained at home in Peterboro, and Frederick Douglass continued to openly endorse his old friend. But even as Smith publicly chided Republicans as free-soil moderates, he privately assured Joshua Giddings that Lincoln was "a very able man" and a candidate who was sure to "get a greater vote than Seward would have got." Smith was pleased to read that Lincoln regarded the egalitarian Declaration of Independence rather than the slavery-protecting Constitution as the nation's defining document. "I feel confident that [Lincoln] is in his heart an abolitionist," Smith told Giddings. Should he win in November, his election "will be regarded as an Abolition victory, not less so than if you yourself were elected President." Giddings required no assurances regarding Lincoln, yet candidate Smith's view of his Republican rival surely explains why he allotted so little of his own vast fortune to his party's coffers in 1860.[30]

Just to make sure, radical Republicans continued to emphasize the antislavery elements in their party's platform and warned abolitionists of the dangers posed by the fusion tickets in New York and Pennsylvania. Sumner, Giddings, and Chase all supplied abolitionist newspapers with documents and editorials recommending Lincoln. Garrison could not bring himself to formally endorse what he continued to describe in the *Liberator* as a "half-a-loaf party," yet he conceded that his "sympathies and best wishes" lay with the Republicans. After watching one Wide Awake march through Boston, Garrison admitted that it "was hard not to tap one's feet to the jaunty rhythms" of their song, "Ain't You Glad You Joined the Republicans." The editor had long been especially influenced by the views of his African American readers, and just before the election Garrison and his son, Willie, witnessed a procession of two hundred black Republican voters who marched behind a banner reading, GOD NEVER MADE A TYRANT OR A SLAVE. Glancing at his father, Willie said only, "Verily the world does move."[31]

A far less optimistic view of the fall elections could be heard in Washington, in what passed for Breckinridge's headquarters. Thanks to early efforts by Davis and Belmont, the Republican and northern Democratic parties emerged from their respective conventions with active organizations already in place. The same could not be said of the southern Democrats. When word reached Breckinridge that he was the choice of party rebels in Baltimore and Richmond, he realized that he had to build a campaign machine from scratch. On July 1, the candidate called on Caleb Cushing, who agreed to organize the operation. Cushing immediately suggested a sixteen-member Democratic National Executive Committee, to be chaired by Isaac I. Stevens, the governor of the Washington Territory. Cushing also recommended a series of campaign documents—mostly essays and speeches—and an official biography to be sent to friendly editors to familiarize northern voters with the candidate. Only Breckinridge, Cushing believed, could preserve the Union and prevent those who "in the blind zeal of stupid Negro worship, would thus drive the Southern States into revolution."[32]

Breckinridge devoted three days to crafting his letter of acceptance, which he posted on July 6 to Cushing as the chairman of the Maryland Institute convention. Predictably, he began his lengthy public missive by insisting that he neither "sought nor desired [to have] his name placed before the country." Like Douglas, he claimed the mantle of the "National Democracy," implying that he was the sole Democrat in the race, but unlike Bell, he admitted that it was "idle to attempt to smother [the] great issues" of slavery and the territories. For voters who expected presidential candidates to elucidate their platform positions unflinchingly, Breckinridge's assertion that there was "no evasive middle ground" on these questions had the virtue of honesty. While the "fanatical" Republicans denied the right of planters to carry "their negro slaves" into the West, the Democratic "friends of Constitutional equality" regarded it as "the plain duty of the Federal Government" to secure for all of its citizens "the enjoyment of their property in the common Territories." Breckinridge concluded by expressing the hope that the various campaigns could "be conducted without rancor, and that temperate arguments [would] take the place of hot words."[33]

Breckinridge also used the opportunity to answer the persistent allegations that he secretly wished for the dismemberment of the republic, and especially the charge that his southern followers actually hoped for a Republican victory. Both southern Unionists and northern Democrats repeated Douglas's accusation that while "all the Breckinridge men in the United States [were not] disunionists," there was "not a disunionist in America who [was] not a Breckinridge man." In response, the vice president noted that the Baltimore convention that had nominated him had contained more northern delegates than Douglas's convention had southern representatives. "I proudly challenge the bitterest enemy I may have on earth," he added, "to point out an act, to disclose an utterance, to reveal a thought of mine hostile to the Constitution and union of the States." The true disunionists, Breckinridge declared, were the Republicans who sought to restrict the spread of slavery and so deny to planters rights "affirmed by the highest judicial tribunal" in the nation.[34]

Northern voters were not alone in thinking Breckinridge disingenuous. His protestations of loyalty notwithstanding, his candidacy aided the cause of southern separatism by offering proslavery voters an ultra platform, by further inflaming the already overheated national discourse on the territories, and by perpetuating a crippling division within what had been the majority party. The fact that Yancey and the Rhetts were the vice president's staunchest advocates raised suspicions among southern Unionists. "Mr. Breckinridge claims that he isn't a disunionist," observed one disbelieving Texas editor. "Any animal not willing to pass for a pig shouldn't stay in the stye [sic]." Although the candidate could not control the many editors who advocated his election, it was no accident that pro-Breckinridge publishers printed the most inflammatory charges against Lincoln. If the mere prospect of an "Abolition ruler" led to slave restiveness during the summer months, wondered Athens, Georgia's *Southern Banner*, "what will be our condition when he is actually in power?"[35]

Breckinridge was honest enough to admit that he *wished* to be the sole Democrat in the contest, and his backers did everything they could to force Douglas out of the race. Especially in Manhattan, where conservative merchants and traders with ties to the South had long been solicitous of planter concerns, elevating the southern Democrat over Lincoln became a consistent theme. On July 6, Mayor Fernando Wood publicly urged Douglas to step aside. The *New York Herald* concurred that the "withdrawal of Douglas at this juncture, would assuredly give the whole South to Breckinridge," while a fusion ticket of Bell and Breckinridge "would as certainly defeat Lincoln" in the state. Speakers at rallies in Delaware and Iowa also proclaimed that "the majority of the democratic voters" in those states preferred Breckinridge, if only because they thought he was better positioned to "defeat the black Republican candidate." With no Douglas to draw votes in the North, they argued, Breckinridge was "bound to be elected by a combination of the conservative portion of the House of Representatives against the fanatical portion" of Republicans, and "peace and harmony [would] be restored to the country."[36]

Even in Lincoln's Springfield, Democrats organized a Breckinridge and Lane ticket, prompting Jefferson Davis to hope that the "political sky" was at long last "growing brighter, and permits us to look with increasing hope for the triumph of the National, that is, the Constitutional Democracy." Those Illinois residents who knew Douglas, however, understood that the senator was not a man to quit. "Like the Capulets and the Montagues," quipped one of Lincoln's backers, "they are 'biting their thumbs' at each other to provoke a mess." In Washington, Buchanan continued his lifelong habit of making bad situations worse. Having declined to intervene on the eve of the Baltimore convention, the president finally abandoned his official silence. In a speech delivered from the portico of the White House, he endorsed Breckinridge on the grounds that only the Kentuckian favored a federal slave code for the territories. For northern voters of both parties who had long suspected the presidency to be under the control of the planter class, Buchanan's remarks did nothing to alleviate such concerns, nor did they convince Douglas to concede control of his party to southern interests.[37]

One week after formally accepting his section's nomination, Breckinridge headed for Kentucky. Since candidates were not supposed to campaign, he assured his supporters that he was not doing so. But as his travels carried him north to Baltimore and then westward through Wheeling, he did consent to deliver speeches in both of those cities. Not much of an orator—one observer described him as "all ruffles and no shirt"—Breckinridge confined himself to reading aloud from his July 6 letter. On July 18, he reached Lexington, where a special state Democratic convention was under way. Like Douglas, the vice president had made Washington his home for the previous decade, and he no longer owned a home in Kentucky. So Breckinridge, the candidate of the planter class, instead checked himself into the Phoenix Hotel, on East Main Street, an establishment that employed free blacks as domestics. Bell supporters tried to turn the hotel into a story, alleging that Breckinridge was not a permanent resident of the state and did not pay taxes on any slaves. The charges were true enough, but the fact that they were hurled by Unionists who preferred a slaveholding Tennessean who had voted against Kansas-Nebraska to a nonslaveholding resident of Washington who championed slavery's westward expansion suggests just how angry and irrational America's political conversation had become.[38]

Since most candidates delivered at least one major address to their hometown supporters (and then to the nation by way of the press), Breckinridge accepted an offer tendered by James B. Clay to speak at a public barbecue at Ashland, the estate of his deceased father, Senator Henry Clay. Breckinridge arrived on September 5 to find a crowd of between eight thousand and fifteen thousand supporters spread across the lawn. Unwisely, he kept his listeners in the hot sun for more than three hours. His address began with the by-now-standard denials that he was "a disunionist or a traitor to his country" but quickly descended into an irrelevant recitation of the presidential candidates he had supported across the years. Instead of explaining what a Breckinridge administration might mean for the country, he devoted tedious passages to refuting widely disbelieved Unionist rumors that he had favored Whig nominee Zachary Taylor or had voted for statewide manumission in 1849. Rather than ignore allegations that he "does not keep house, and owns no slaves," he foolishly publicized the charges by declining to discuss his "private affairs." Only after several hours did Breckinridge finally take up the question of the territories. And even then, he chose to read lengthy "extracts" from his previous speeches and, stranger yet, from Douglas's speeches. "Oceans of ink have been shed, and thousands of speeches have been made" about slavery and the West, the candidate shouted, and rather than add to them, he instead finished by reciting four extended paragraphs from the Dred Scott decision. The pamphlet version published by Cushing mentioned "repeated applause," but few editors were as kind. "It [was] a very long speech," sighed the pro-Bell Washington *National Intelligencer*.[39]

And then there was Douglas. To coordinate his candidate's campaign, Belmont booked rooms in Washington's National Hotel, where an executive committee, chaired by Louisiana congressman Miles Taylor, kept in touch with regional Democratic organizations. Taylor entrusted the task of writing an official campaign biography to James W. Sheahan, although the candidate slowed its publication by rewriting the chapters that dealt with his childhood and early life. But a candidate who flattered himself an editor was the least of Taylor's problems. In the South, most party committees were committed to Breckinridge, so Taylor had to track down Douglas men and urge them to form rival committees. A few states had selected electoral tickets before the final eruption at Baltimore, and many of them included men loyal to both Democratic nominees. Taylor informed the southern tickets that electoral slates must pledge their "unequivocal support" to Douglas and Johnson, and that if they could not, the old tickets must be dissolved and new ones must be elected. Across the North, political machines constructed in advance by Davis and Weed raised money, funded speakers, and mailed out pamphlets and biographies of Lincoln. But as July dawned, the Douglas campaign found itself far in the rear, desperately trying to rebuild a national organization that should have existed for months.[40]

While Taylor tried to rebuild a campaign apparatus across the South, Belmont labored to fund the entire effort. In previous years, campaign chairmen had dunned congressional Democrats at least $100 each to finance the national campaign, but by late summer "not a single cent" had been collected. Most southern congressmen supported Breckinridge, and northern Democrats regarded the Douglas campaign as a lost cause. Belmont estimated that the coming contest would cost $23,700, and "unless we can give to our merchants and politicians some assurance of success," he wrote, the "selfish moneybags" in Manhattan would contribute nothing. A banker himself and the American representative of the Rothschild fortune, Belmont knew the city's great financiers, but they remained "lukewarm." When Belmont called an emergency meeting of the Democratic National Executive Committee—which bore the same name as Breckinridge's group—in early August, only two members attended.

The chairman tried to impress the city's business elite by contributing $1,000 of his own money, but no donor followed suit. In September, Taylor informed Belmont that the cause was hopeless without an influx of cash, and biographer Sheahan wrote to complain that he had not been paid for his efforts. "The Douglas men are making a desperate effort to raise money," Weed delighted in telling Lincoln.[41]

In hopes of overcoming Lincoln's funding advantage, Douglas made a decision that shattered precedent, and perhaps his health along with it. Defying seventy years of tradition, he would campaign in his own behalf. His dynamic stage presence, he believed, could excite voters and persuade reluctant financiers to open their ledger books to his cause. Initially, he planned only a brief campaign swing through New England. As it turned out, the ploy was so unusual that stunned journalists speculated as to his motivation. Since Douglas was only forty-seven, the *New York Times* presumed that he was again looking to the future and trying to rebuild his party in the wake of southern defections. "The Presidency in 1860 is not the prize for which he contends," guessed its editor. But Douglas's correspondence suggests otherwise. William A. Richardson, the Democratic governor of the Nebraska Territory, toured New England and assured Douglas that things were "much better than we had hoped for." With a little effort, the ticket could "carry Maine, New Hampshire, Rhode Island & Conn[ecticut]." Ever the optimist, Douglas believed his momentum was "gaining every day."[42]

The Little Giant boarded the train on July 14. In an attempt to disguise the fact that Douglas was taking to the stump, Belmont announced that the candidate simply intended to call on his mother in Clifton Springs, New York, attend his brother-in-law's Harvard graduation, and visit his father's grave in Vermont. Douglas's entourage planned to stop at each town and village along the way, where, much against his will, it was assumed that he could be "betrayed" by local audiences into delivering a political speech. Nobody was fooled. "No other man in the Union would have the audacity to stump the country as a candidate for the Presidency," remarked one editor. "In any other equally prominent politician, such a course would excite general disgust; but it is so thoroughly in keeping with his character and political habits, that no one thinks it worthwhile even to affect surprise." Republicans enjoyed the spectacle.

As Douglas's train meandered through New England, they posted hand-bills purporting to help "A Boy Lost!" The missing child, the critics gibed, "has not yet reached his mother, who is very anxious about him." The lost boy "is about five feet nothing in height and answers the same in diameter the other way," the handbill continued. "Has an idea that he is a candidate for President."[43]

After a lengthy address at Harvard University, "the candidate of the North democracy" moved on to Rhode Island, where Providence offi-cials had arranged a clambake for fifty thousand people. Since Belmont had sent out Douglas's itinerary in advance, town leaders had the oppor-tunity to organize celebrations, and rarely did his train enter a depot without "a salute of fifteen guns" fired in welcome. But even Douglas understood that many in the crowds attended out of curiosity, or simply

"TAKING THE STUMP"OR STEPHEN IN SEARCH OF HIS MOTHER.

Douglas's insistence that he was not campaigning but rather traveling to see his mother was widely ridiculed by Republicans. This cartoon also pokes fun at the fact that Douglas had to use a crutch after his accident aboard the Virginia. *Buchanan, in the background, urges his vice president (and preferred candidate) to campaign as well, while the confident and casually dressed rail-splitter leans against a fence. Courtesy Library of Congress.*

because of the free food and drink. Journalists accompanying the candidate complained that Douglas rarely varied his remarks, and since many of his speeches were published by the New England press, even supportive listeners began to grumble that he bored them "with the same old speech." Hearing of the size of the crowds, Hamlin fretted that a few Republican congressional seats could be lost in the fall, but George G. Fogg assured Lincoln that his "quiet and dignified retirement" in Springfield appeared statesmanlike in comparison to Douglas's search for "his 'father's grave,' and his 'anxious mother's' *pantry*." Everything was secure in New England, Fogg added. "The election is ours now."[44]

Understanding his audience, Douglas was careful to emphasize his support for the Pacific railroad bill, internal improvements, and tariffs of protection—yet another reminder that the Democrats of the 1850s were no longer a party that Andrew Jackson would have recognized, a point driven home by Douglas's clumsy effort to pander to Boston voters by praising the "godlike [Daniel] Webster." Yet his standard speech always concluded with a discussion of the territories and the virtues of popular sovereignty. "We must make the war boldly against the *Northern abolitionists* and the Southern *disunionists*, and give no quarter to either," he instructed one supporter. The handful of Republicans who turned out to jeer would have none of this. Since popular sovereignty in Kansas had allowed for the expansion of unfree labor, Douglas's platform "attempts to *cheat* the people into the support of slavery by every conceivable fraud," said one critic. Breckinridge and Lane, at least, "walk squarely up to the mark like bold men."[45]

On occasion, Douglas was kinder to his Republican opponents than they were to him. Like the other four candidates, he rarely mentioned his rivals by name, content instead to explain why popular sovereignty was preferable to either congressional restriction or a federal slave code. But at two stops, Douglas revealed a grudging admiration for his longtime Illinois foe. At Burlington, Vermont, he described life on the frontier, and he praised those industrious yeomen who cleared their own land— he paused here for effect—or split their own rails. The audience cheered and laughed, with Douglas joining in. A few days later, in Manchester, New Hampshire, he went further still and spoke of Lincoln by name. "He is a very clever fellow," he admitted, "a kindhearted, good natured, amiable man." The two had battled for "so long that [Douglas had] respect for him" and lacked "the heart to say anything against Abe Lincoln." When someone from the crowd shouted in response that Lincoln was good for little besides splitting rails, Douglas defended the Republican candidate, saying that as a young man he too had worked with wood, constructing "bureaus and secretaries."[46]

Douglas's confidence and good humor vanished in the early fall. On October 9, voters in the three battleground states of Ohio, Pennsylvania, and Indiana went to the polls to elect state officials and members of Congress. Democrats regarded Ohio as a lost cause, but Buchanan had carried the latter two by solid margins in 1856. This time, the Pennsylvania Republican gubernatorial candidate won by thirty thousand votes, and in Indiana, Republicans captured the governor's office by a margin of thirteen thousand. Less surprising was the fate of Maine, which had gone to Frémont four years before; it too elected a Republican governor by a near landslide. Douglas's headquarters in Washington cabled him with the grim news, and another of his advisers wrote to say that "the recent elections have knocked the Democracy of Illinois into spasms." Lincoln, of course, received far happier messages, apart from the one from his old circuit-riding friend Ward Hill Lamon, who thought it his "melancholy duty to inform" the candidate that the three-hundred-pound Davis had injured himself upon hearing the news. Davis "kicked over the clerk's desk [and] turned a double Somersault," Lamon joked.[47]

Having worried that Indiana was lost to the Democrats, Douglas now regarded "Lincoln's Election as being a fixed fact." He was not alone in that assessment. Cables and letters arriving in Springfield agreed that the November election was practically over. "All of the Douglas army are badly wounded," one Indiana organizer gleefully reported, and a Philadelphia activist agreed, saying that the "contest is altogether over in Penn[sylvania, which was] utterly abandoned by the Democracy." Indeed, among those who intended to abandon the North was Douglas, who understood that his election was doomed but feared that the Union was as well. Perhaps because of his experience with southern delegates at the Democratic conventions, Douglas was one of the few who began to realize that the fire-eaters' secession from the party was merely a prelude to state secession from the republic. "Mr. Lincoln is the next President," Douglas informed those traveling with him. "We must try to save the Union. I will go South."[48]

So began a new phase of Douglas's political career, one not previously distinguished by its selflessness or morality. The senator was long accustomed to winning, even when those victories—his battle against Lecompton or the doctrine announced at Freeport that saved his Senate seat—came at a high price. Only in defeat, perhaps, did Douglas find his reclamation. Even his running mate, Herschel Johnson, doubted that the candidate could "carry a single Southern State," but Douglas did not head south in hopes of saving his campaign. He instead hoped to prepare his southern audiences for the election of Lincoln, unite his fractured party, and persuade southern moderates not to follow the ultras into secession. Douglas's decision to "beard the lion of disunion in his own den" was uniformly greeted with high praise by the northern press, even by Republican editors. Illinois Democratic congressman (and future Republican) John Alexander Logan applauded Douglas for "bravely taking the field" in what he knew to be "a hopeless fight."[49]

The border states had long been politically contested territories, and just as Breckinridge enjoyed support in the lower North, Douglas had a following in Kentucky and northern Virginia. Even before his decision to turn his campaign southward, moderate Democrats in three Kentucky towns sponsored large and enthusiastic Douglas rallies, where "the seceders at Charleston" were "emphatically denounced, and resolutions endorsing Judge Douglas were unanimously adopted." His speeches in Baltimore and in Staunton, Harpers Ferry, Winchester, and Charlestown, Virginia, were also met by large audiences. In Frederick, Maryland, the weary candidate was greeted with a "display of banners" and the inevitable "roar of cannon." The "whole affair was very enthusiastic," reported one Washington newspaper normally supportive of Bell. But if Douglas began his southern "campaign in good earnest," he knew also that Maryland and Virginia's northern and western counties were hardly plantation societies. As his journey progressed, the crowds did not diminish in size, but their welcomes grew cooler.[50]

Douglas's speech in Norfolk, Virginia, delivered before "an immense crowed [*sic*]" of nearly six thousand people, became the most famous of the campaign. The senator had just begun to speak when William Lamb, the editor of the *Norfolk Argus*, handed him a slip of paper containing two questions. He was not normally "in the habit of answering questions propounded to [him] in the course of [his] address," Douglas noted, but he thought it imperative to "respond very frankly" to the two queries, which he read aloud to the audience. If "Abraham Lincoln be elected President of the United States," read the first question, "will the Southern States be justified in seceding from the Union?" To that, Douglas gave an "emphatic no." So long as the election was conducted "in conformity to the Constitution," no presidential contest by itself could "justify any attempt at dissolving this glorious confederacy."[51]

Douglas then turned to the second query. Despite his pretense of being interrupted by the editor, the senator was enough of a veteran warrior to understand political theater. Lamb was an ally of Governor Henry A. Wise, who had declined to denounce possible secession should the Republicans capture the White House, and since the inquiry went straight to the heart of why he was touring the South, Douglas decided the time had come to speak bluntly. "If they, the Southern States, secede from the Union upon the inauguration of Abraham Lincoln, before he commits an overt act against their constitutional rights," read the question, "will you advise or vindicate resistance by force to their secession." It was the simple duty of the president "to enforce the laws" passed by Congress, Douglas shouted, and as a member of the Senate he "would do all in [his] power to aid the government." The chief executive, "whoever he may be, should treat all attempts to break up the Union, by resistance to its laws, as Old Hickory treated the nullifiers in 1832." If the new president violated his oath, Douglas added, there was the remedy of impeachment, but the "mere inauguration of a President" could not "justify the revolution of secession." He concluded by challenging the editor to submit the same questions to Breckinridge.[52]

As if that direct response had failed to sufficiently infuriate fire-eaters, several days later Douglas expanded on the point. While he was speaking in Raleigh, North Carolina, a member of the audience dared him to repeat the words. Douglas did so and then paraphrased Andrew

Jackson's threat; were any American to attempt secession immediately upon the election of Lincoln, Douglas swore, the president should "hang him higher than Haman, according to the law." Douglas's straight talk won him no accolades in the South. In a society that bragged of its courage and honor, having to endure lessons in citizenship from "such a political mountebank as Stephen A. Douglas" was galling. One Georgia newspaper expressed "astonishment" that the Illinoisan retained any support, no matter how small, in states *where negroes are regarded as property.*" By saying that "he would support Mr. Lincoln *in hanging them as traitors,*" Douglas had finally revealed "his freesoil sentiments" and endorsed the "Black Republican programme." A Memphis journal agreed: "He comes in our midst with no worthier motives than the incendiary."[53]

The long days and stem-winding speeches took a toll on Douglas's always precarious health. His voice grew hoarse, and he medicated his throat each evening with yet heavier drinking. During a speech in Atlanta, one spectator noted "a stony glare about Douglas' eyes, particularly the left one." On another occasion, Douglas appeared confused and stammered throughout his oration. In Alabama, he was met with boos, eggs, and overripe tomatoes. And injury was added to insult soon after Douglas and Adele boarded the *Virginia* to sail from Montgomery to Selma. The two strolled to the top deck, but as they leaned over the railing, the fragile barrier gave way, and Douglas fell to the deck below. Adele "escaped injury by clinging to the railing." No bones were broken, but Adele was too bruised and frightened to continue the trip, and Douglas hurt his leg so badly that he had to hobble about on a crutch. Just to remind him that he was not the preferred candidate of the South, the doctor forwarded a bill for the crutch to his next stop.[54]

Among those in the Montgomery audience was Yancey. As he listened to the Illinois senator, an idea began to form. Instead of replying to Douglas in Alabama, which was hardly necessary, he would carry the argument to the border and even into northern states. A number of Breckinridge organizations in Tennessee and Ohio had invited Yancey to speak, and a lengthy tour on the eve of the election could invigorate southern ultras and revive his moribund League of United Southerners. Although not himself a candidate for political office, Yancey had already delivered thirty speeches since January, and he now planned at least twenty more, some of them as far away as New York. In the same way that Douglas had carried his fight into the heart of Breckinridge country to prepare the lower South for the election of Lincoln, Yancey wished to alert northern audiences that secession was all but inevitable.[55]

A nervous Washington press soon began to print rumors that Yancey was "coming North" and planned to speak "till the close of the Presidential contest." Even in distant California, his tour excited "considerable curiosity." The editor of the *San Francisco Bulletin* wondered how the words of the leading "Southern fire-eater" would be received, especially as Yancey had taken to arguing that there were "more disunion people" across the North "than in his own section." Buchanan had taken California's four electoral votes in 1856, and the *Bulletin* worried that Yancey's provocative orations would "do the Democratic (Breckinridge) cause little good." But as Yancey was no fool, he never expected to prod a single northern state into the Breckinridge camp; his purpose, rather, was to hasten the destruction of the Democratic Party.[56]

Beginning in Washington, Yancey zigzagged across the North, repeatedly charging that "the South would expect no protection from a Republican administration, and that John Brown raids would go unrestrained." In New York's Cooper Union, the same hall that had propelled Lincoln into his party's front ranks eight months before, Yancey warned that Republicans intended to "build up an abolition party in every Southern State." Always one to thrive on the distaste of others, the cheerful, unflappable Yancey gloried in taking his proslavery message into the hub of American antislavery. Speaking at Boston's Faneuil Hall, Yancey informed a shocked audience that the Founding Fathers had always intended for the republic to be governed by the "master race"; in Syracuse and again in Frederick Douglass's Rochester, the fire-eater assured listeners that Alabama slaves enjoyed softer lives than factory workers along the Erie Canal. Yancey even paid New York's senior senator the strange compliment that "either Seward or Lincoln [was] preferable to Douglas." The Republicans, Yancey admitted, were honest in their antislavery sentiments, while Douglas refused to admit that he was "an abolitionist."[57]

When not twisting the motives and willfully misreading the platforms of northern candidates, Yancey extolled the virtues of human bondage. In Boston, he explained that slavery was a moral system, since African Americans "sleep all day and prowl about all night [and] steal everything." He denounced the "Black Republicans" as the "negro party," while defending "the Breckinridge party [as] essentially the white man's party." White southerners, he added, opposed racial mixing—here he took care not to mention fire-eaters like Senator James Henry Hammond, who had fathered children with several slave women—and did "not want the negro introduced into either their blood, liberty, or rights." Giving the lie to later southern claims that secession resulted from tariffs or different interpretations of the Constitution, Yancey pronounced that the planter class could yield on those minor issues, but never on slavery, "the tool of our industry, the source of our prosperity." Although he was one year younger than Douglas, his health and voice were equally precarious, and by the end of his tirades only those closest to the podium could hear his standard conclusion. "We stand upon the dark platform of southern slavery, and all we ask is to be allowed to keep it to ourselves. Let us do that, and we will not let the negro insult you by coming here [to the North] and marrying your daughters."[58]

As election eve neared, Yancey returned home to Montgomery. In Virginia, his league ally Edmund Ruffin proudly cast his vote for Breckinridge and then boarded a train for Columbia, South Carolina, handing out secession literature to those who shared his coach. Far to the south, Election Day found Douglas in Mobile, carrying the fight to the bitter end. The night before the vote, he was still assuring his audience that their interests were far more secure within the Union than without, but the crowd was small and the applause weak. John Forsyth, one of Douglas's few supporters in the state, stopped at his hotel—appropriately named the Battle House—to get his opinion on an editorial that Forsyth had penned for the Mobile *Register*. Forsyth believed that a statewide convention to discuss secession was unavoidable, so the best course for southern unionists was to elect as many loyal delegates as possible and push for sectional compromise. Having seen too many conventions wrecked by fire-eaters, Douglas thought the effort futile. The senator looked "more hopeless than I had ever before seen him," worried his secretary.[59]

A very different scene took place in Springfield. November 6 dawned cool but sunny. Lincoln spent the morning receiving guests in his temporary office in the Statehouse. Around mid-morning, he strolled to the courthouse to vote, carefully clipping off the list of electors on the top of the ballot but still voting for state officials. Like all voters, Lincoln had to deposit his ballot in a large glass bowl designated for Republicans; the process was far from secret. Even Democrats handing out Douglas ballots cheered, and one laughed, "You ought to vote for Douglas, Uncle Abe, he has done all he could for you." At eleven thirty, a telegraph from New York arrived in the office. "We have made steady gains everywhere throughout the State," Lincoln read aloud, "but the city returns are not sufficiently forward to make us sure of the result." Lyman Trumbull arrived, bubbling with confidence. "You're the next President, and I know it." Those in the office cheered, but Lincoln continued to worry over possible Democratic surges in Manhattan. "Not too fast, my friends," he replied. "Not too fast, it may not be over yet."[60]

With no definitive word by late afternoon, Lincoln walked home to dine with Mary. At seven, he returned to the Statehouse in search of news, and two hours later he and Davis moved on to the telegraph office. Around one thirty in the morning, a telegram arrived from Philadelphia regarding Pennsylvania's twenty-seven electoral votes: "The city and the state for Lincoln by a decisive majority." Lincoln paused and then looked up. "I think that settles it," he said, adding that he needed to tell his wife. Walking with great strides down Eighth Street, he shouted out, "Mary, Mary, we are elected." Nobody in the town slept as church bells tolled and residents crowding the streets "cheered for Lincoln—cheered for Trumbull—cheered for New York—cheered for everybody." Somebody thought to fire the old cannon on Capitol Square, and the blast rattled "many a window in Springfield."[61]

Voters and antislavery activists were only slightly less enthusiastic elsewhere in the North. In Seneca Falls, Henry and Elizabeth Cady Stanton delighted in Lincoln's victory. Writing to her son just before a family Thanksgiving—then celebrated around mid-November—Elizabeth said she thought it a blessing that this would be "the last time we shall be compelled to insult the Good Father by thanking him that we are a slave holding Republic; I hope and look for dissolution." A few miles away in Rochester, Frederick Douglass, although bitter over the refusal of New York's electorate to abolish the $250 property qualification imposed on black voters, was enthusiastic about the new administration. "For fifty years the country has taken the law from the lips of an exacting, haughty and imperious slave oligarchy," he wrote. "Lincoln's election has vitiated their authority, and broken their power." Having voted for Gerrit Smith, Douglass nonetheless declared Lincoln "if not an Abolitionist, at least [a man with] an anti-slavery reputation."[62]

In Ohio, Abby Kelley Foster was no less fervent, if only because she expected the moderate Lincoln to disappoint militant abolitionists and force Garrison to "endorse resolutions strongly condemnatory of the Republicans." But Garrison was unrepentant. The "election of Abraham Lincoln will be a great and encouraging triumph," he wrote in the *Liberator*. "It will mark a hopeful epoch in the progress of our cause." Joshua Leavitt was equally jubilant. "Thank God! Lincoln is chosen," he rejoiced. "It is a joy to have lived to this day." One of Seward's correspondents expressed the same thoughts on the day after the election: "Glory to God in the Highest! I am so delighted, on this bright morning." Today "the political sky looks promising, yea splendid," added one of the elder Charles Francis Adams's constituents. "I trust it is the dawning of better days."[63]

In the popular vote, Lincoln gathered 1,865,908 ballots, or 39.8 percent. But the victory was impressive considering that almost all of the votes were cast in the North; only 1,887 Virginians and 1,364 Kentucky voters bravely obtained Republican tickets. Not only did Lincoln run 485,706 votes ahead of his nearest rival, but he also received half a million votes more than Frémont had four years previously. The Republicans captured 62.8 percent of the votes in Massachusetts and 75.7 percent of Rhode Island's tally. (In fact, Lincoln carried every single county in New England.) In Illinois, which Frémont had failed to carry, Lincoln picked up 14,600 more votes than the 1856 Republican nominee. Seward's New York went for Lincoln by 53.7 percent, and although his party lost Manhattan to Bell by 28,601 votes, even there Lincoln gained 17,700 on Frémont's total. In the electoral vote, Lincoln won every northern state except for New Jersey, which he split with Douglas. His total reached 180 electoral votes, far more than the 152 needed to win, and 57 votes more than his four rivals' combined count of 123.[64]

Lincoln's victory demonstrated that a sectional party could win in the Electoral College. In nine southern states, not a single voter requested a Republican ballot. Along the upper South, the highest percentage Lincoln achieved came in Delaware, where he captured 23.7 percent of the vote; in Maryland and Missouri, he earned a mere 2.5 and 10.2 percent, respectively. Although he carried those northern states with large metropolitan populations, Lincoln ran better in the countryside than in urban areas. Only in his home state of Illinois did he win a major city, Chicago, and then by 59 percent. As one New York Democrat put it, "we have been, as it were, driven to take refuge within the walls of our northern cities." Chicago, however, was Douglas's official residence in Cook County, and in turn, Douglas carried Lincoln's Sangamon County. Only Tennessee's Bell, curiously, carried his home county of Davidson, while also capturing Breckinridge's Fayette County. And in Springfield, twenty-one of twenty-four ministers cast their votes against Lincoln, regarding him as too much of a religious skeptic to occupy the nation's highest office.[65]

As Weed had predicted as early as September 7, the fusion efforts had been doomed to "end in *confusion*." Only in New York, Pennsylvania, and New Jersey had anything like a true four- or five-candidate race emerged, and in the Empire State, the fusion ticket derided by Greeley as "a hybrid, tessellated, three-legged anti-Republican ticket" lost by more than 50,000 votes. Belmont blamed the lack of funding for the effort's failure, while former governor Horatio Seymour thought that his state's voters had not wished to see the election decided by the House of Representatives. Since Breckinridge's southern advocates invariably hoped for a Lincoln victory, only Cushing, among his major advisers, had pushed for fusion cooperation. Indeed, Lincoln would most likely have won the electoral vote even had he faced a single opponent. Only in New Jersey, California, and Oregon did he run behind the combined votes of his many rivals, and those states gave him only 11 of his 180 electoral votes. (For complete election data and a discussion of possible nominee and election scenarios, see Appendix.)[66]

Voters in 1860 did not yet use paper ballots or vote behind curtains.
Voters had to obtain a ticket, which included all state party candidates,
from a party functionary and then deposit the ticket into a bowl or box
marked by party affiliation. Only 1,887 courageous Virginians,
or 1.1 percent of the state's voters, obtained a Republican ticket.
Because Republicans fielded no candidates for governor or Congress,
the Virginia ticket was shorter than in northern states.
Courtesy Abraham Lincoln Presidential Library, Springfield.

As is ever the case, many voters surely cast their ballots *against* one candidate as much as they did *for* another. After eight years of Democratic blunders, scandals, and mismanagement, Douglas was badly tainted by his party affiliation despite his public break with the unpopular Buchanan.

Although Douglas endorsed many of the legislative items important to northern voters—a railroad to the Pacific, a homestead act, and federal support for internal improvements—his party did not, while the Republican platform embraced all three. Douglas might be the enemy of his party's fire-eating southern wing, but they remained members of the Democracy, and the northern candidate paid the price for their disloyalty. In the popular vote, Douglas ran second with 1,380,201, but that was a meager 29.4 percent of the ballots cast. He won only 3 electoral votes in the free states, by taking half of New Jersey's count; the only state he carried outright was Missouri, and there his tally of 58,801 votes inched ahead of Bell's count by a mere 429 ballots. With 12 electoral votes, Douglas, once so sanguine of victory, finished fourth in the College; only Gerrit Smith, who never expected to carry any state, did worse.[67]

Most of the upper South stood behind Bell, who carried Virginia, Tennessee, and Breckinridge's Kentucky for a total of 38 electoral votes. Although he came in third in the Electoral College, his popular count of 590,901 placed him fourth among voters, with only 12.6 percent of the ballots cast. In the three states Bell captured, he carried those counties once loyal to the Whigs. But in the free states, former Whigs rallied to Lincoln, himself a former Whig. In Massachusetts, once a reliable Whig stronghold, Bell gathered only 13.1 percent of the votes, while in Pennsylvania, a state carried by Whig candidate Zachary Taylor in 1848, only 2.6 percent of the votes went to the Constitutional Unionists. "The 'old line Whigs,'" as William Herndon had confidently predicted, were "almost unanimously and wildly for Lincoln." In Indiana, one of the states Frémont had failed to carry in 1856, Lincoln won at least 40 percent of the votes once cast for Millard Fillmore, while Bell garnered only 1.3 percent of that state's votes.[68]

As late as July 4, Douglas had been confident that Breckinridge could not "carry a single State, except South Carolina, and perhaps Miss[issippi]." In fact, the vice president won eleven states, from Maryland and Delaware along the border to Texas in the Southwest. Breckinridge's electoral vote of 72 put him in second place and was greater than the combined electoral count of Bell and Douglas. But his popular vote reached only 18.1 percent, and even in the South his 44 percent of the popular vote ran only slightly ahead of Bell's 40 percent. In the states that would soon comprise the Confederacy, Breckinridge won 416,000 votes to a combined tally of 394,000 for the other candidates. Voters in the upper South, by comparison, preferred Bell to the man widely regarded as the "secession candidate." In Maryland, which Breckinridge won, he barely edged Bell, 45.9 percent to 45.4 percent (and there, Douglas's and Lincoln's combined 8.9 percent of the vote probably cost Bell the state).[69]

Despite Lincoln's impressive victory, the election did nothing immediately to alter the composition of the Supreme Court, which, Chief Justice Taney's advanced age notwithstanding, remained controlled by Democrats and southern jurists. And even with striking gains in Senate races, Republicans would hold only 29 seats in the upper chamber compared to 37 Democrats and Unionists, while in the upcoming Thirty-sixth Congress, 120 Republicans would barely outnumber the 108 members from other parties. For months, candidate Lincoln had routinely denied that he was an abolitionist, but even if he was, Democrats in the Senate and on the Court enjoyed the power to kill any antislavery legislation that might emerge from Republican-dominated House committees.[70]

Among those not celebrating, however, was Georgia's Alexander Stephens, who sourly remarked on the morning of November 8 that Lincoln's election did "not surprise [him] in the least." He had expected this news "ever since the bust up at Baltimore." But just up the coast in Charleston, the mood was as festive as it was in Springfield. City residents declared an informal holiday and took to the streets, and as enslaved South Carolinians watched quietly, joyous Breckinridge voters erected a tall liberty pole near the battery, much as their ancestors had done eighty-four years before. Booming cannons saluted the Palmetto flag, and the *Mercury* editorialized, "The tea has been thrown overboard— the revolution of 1860 has been initiated." The foreman of a grand jury sitting in a federal court rose and suggested that they adjourn, since Washington no longer wielded any authority over the state. Judge Andrew G. Magrath banged his gavel in agreement. "In the political history of the United States," he remarked, "an event has happened of ominous import to fifteen Slave-holding States." That evening, in a portentous foreshadowing of events to come, fireworks lit the sky above Fort Sumter, and Robert Barnwell Rhett addressed the cheering crowd. "The long weary night of our humiliation, oppression and danger is passing away," he shouted, "and the glorious dawn of a Southern Confederacy breaks on our view."[71]

CHAPTER SEVEN

"The Union Is Dissolved"

The Lower South Secedes

BORN IN PRINCE GEORGE COUNTY, Virginia, in 1794, Edmund Ruffin was the elder statesman of secession. As a descendant of the eighteenth-century planter William Randolph, Ruffin was kinsman to both Thomas Jefferson and Chief Justice John Marshall, but unlike those distant cousins, Ruffin always defined himself as a southerner and slaveholder, rarely as a Virginian and never as an American. An eager member of Yancey's League of United Southerners, Ruffin was also an agronomist and writer, and for a time he edited the *Farmers' Register*, a journal dedicated to improving agricultural productivity. A longtime "hater of the North," as his granddaughter put it, he reached the peak of his animosity in 1859 with John Brown's raid at Harpers Ferry. So furious was he that he traveled to Charlestown to watch Brown hang. To get close to the gallows, he had to join the cadets of the Virginia Military Institute, which placed him, he conceded, in the "ludicrous position of being the youngest member [of the] company of boyish soldiers." While in Charlestown, Ruffin obtained fifteen of the deadly pikes that Brown's men had forged. He sent one to each of the southern states, with a note reading, "Sample of the favors designed for us by our Northern brethren."[1]

During the summer of 1860, Ruffin penned a curious novel, *Anticipations of the Future, to Serve as Lessons for the Present Time*, in which "the obscure and coarse" Lincoln won the election but was replaced by Seward as the Republican nominee in 1864. Narrated by an unnamed southerner through a series of letters mailed to the London *Times*, the novel has South Carolina finally deciding to secede on December 24, 1868, when it becomes clear that Seward will be reelected. Five other lower-South states follow; in *Anticipations*, distant Texas remains with the Union. The fighting between the North and the revolutionary South begins in Charleston, but in Ruffin's telling, U.S. troops stationed at Fort Moultrie unsuccessfully attempt to dislodge soldiers from Fort Sumter, now in the hands of the "new confederacy." A provisional government, organized in Atlanta, selects "Mr. Y, of Alabama" for the vice presidency. After Moultrie surrenders, a larger conflict ensues, and Ruffin's Virginia is drawn into the war. A riot in Manhattan weakens the Union war effort, and France and Britain eventually sign commercial treaties with the Confederacy. California separates as an independent republic, and a second wave of secession hands Washington to the southern president, who promptly banishes all free blacks from the city. Virtually unreadable, the 342-page novel contains not a single line of dialogue. As Ruffin himself admitted, the book's "very existence seems to be ignored by the public."[2]

Having voted for Breckinridge in Virginia and then boarded the train for Columbia, South Carolina, by election night Ruffin was in the state capital. On the evening of November 8, Ruffin, the "Old Virginia Nestor of States Rights"—as one Georgia newspaper dubbed him in reference to the aged, mythical Greek king who dispensed advice to younger warriors—delivered a public address. "Southern independence had been [his] lifelong study," he promised the "rapturously applaud[ing]" crowd, but it "could only be secured by the secession of South Carolina." Ruffin lamented the fact that his native Virginia was "not as ready as South Carolina" to leave the Union, but, perhaps thinking of his novel, he assured his audience that the "first drop of blood spilled on the soil of South Carolina would bring Virginia, and every Southern State, with them." Bonfires along the street lit the scene and gave an eerie glow to Ruffin's long, white hair, which fell far below his shoulders. "Old as he was," he promised, "he had come [to Columbia] to join them in that lead."[3]

Hoping to transform his fiction into fact, Ruffin would be in Charleston the following April, when shore batteries opened fire on Fort Sumter. In recompense for his service to the southern cause, he was allowed to yank the lanyard on the cannon that fired the first shot, just as he was permitted to fire the first salute when word arrived in Charleston that Virginia had seceded. That summer, the sixty-seven-year-old took part in the Battle of Manassas, where he displayed "all the spirit and energy of a young soldier." But the conflict would take its toll on Ruffin. A grandson was killed at Seven Pines in 1862, his daughter died of unknown causes, his son Julian was killed in 1864, and much to Ruffin's horror, his son Charles deserted. Ten weeks after the surrender at Appomattox Court House, he draped a Confederate flag about his shoulders and scribbled out a final oath of "hatred" toward "the perfidious, malignant, & vile Yankee race." Bracing his rifle against a trunk on the floor, Ruffin positioned the muzzle in his mouth and, using a forked stick to pull the trigger, blew off the top of his head.[4]

The ultimate failure of Ruffin's fictional predictions lay well in the future, of course, and throughout the fall of 1860, white South Carolinians faced the coming months with enormous optimism. As early as September, as it became clear that the two Democratic candidates could not unite, Charleston attorneys Edward McCrady and Robert Gourdin, together with low-country planter and pamphleteer John Townsend, organized the 1860 Association. Designed to coordinate statewide efforts toward secession and raise money for anti-Republican publications, the association had an executive committee of fifteen that met every Thursday night to sip wine and plot separation. Within two months, the group produced two hundred thousand copies of ten pamphlets, including James De Bow's *The Interest in Slavery of the Southern Non-slaveholder*, Townsend's own *The Doom of Slavery in the Union: Its Safety out of It*, and reprints of his earlier *The South Alone Should Govern the South*. Townsend was especially exasperated with Senator James Henry Hammond's argument that Lincoln's election, if constitutional, was not itself provocation for secession. Why wait for Lincoln "to commit some overt act,"

Townsend fumed, as if "the Black Republicans would not do what they had threatened?"[5]

The association also encouraged militia companies to form and parade, although more in the name of visible propaganda than in actual defense. According to Congressman John D. Ashmore, young men marched the city's streets wearing the blue cockades of secession and promising "the slaughter of an hundred Waterloos" if necessary. "*Three hundred thousand swords are now ready* to leap from their scabbards in support of a Southern Confederacy," Ashmore gushed. Hoping to spread their disunionist fervor, former governor James Adams and attorney Maxcy Gregg began to correspond with secessionists in Georgia in imitation of the Revolutionary era's committees of correspondence. Gregg, who would be killed in December 1862 at the Battle of Fredericksburg, thought it unlikely that Republicans could put up any fight. But prudence required them to "accomplish something towards putting the South in a state of preparation for the issue that is almost upon us."[6]

When South Carolina governor William H. Gist read of the October elections in Ohio, Pennsylvania, and Indiana, he too embraced immediate action. A devout Methodist who advocated restrictions on the manufacture of strong drink, Gist was also a planter and slaveholder, and on October 5 he drafted letters to his fellow lower-South governors. The Republicans were going to win, Gist insisted, and he urged a "concert of action, which is so essential to success." Not wishing to place his explosive missives in the federal mails, the governor entrusted the letters to his kinsman, the aptly named States Rights Gist. The young militiaman, like his forenamed cause, was to perish in the war, but in the fall of 1860 he galloped for the Gulf. Louisiana and Georgia leaders replied that they planned to "wait for an overt act" on Lincoln's part, but Alabama promised to secede "if two or more States will cooperate with her," and Mississippi's John J. Pettus agreed to push for disunion the moment the November results were in. With those responses in hand, Governor Gist met with his state's congressional delegation on October 25 in North Augusta. There he began to prepare a special message to the legislature, in which he "earnestly recommend[ed] that, in the event of Abraham Lincoln's election to the Presidency, a Convention of the people of this

State be immediately called, to consider and determine for themselves the mode and measure of redress."[7]

Gist's view that collective secession provided protection to the cotton South enjoyed the virtue of logic, but it ran counter to three decades of states' rights theory. Since the Constitution did not flatly state that sovereign legislatures could *not* quit the Union, southerners had long argued that individual states implicitly possessed the right to do so. In the late 1820s, South Carolina's John C. Calhoun had articulated the so-called compact theory of Union, which held that since special state conventions had ratified each state's participation in the republic between 1787 and 1790, states similarly enjoyed the authority to call second special conventions and deratify the process, or secede, as individual and sovereign states. As Virginia's Henry A. Wise explained, "the Union was made by the States, and the States were not *unmade* by the Union." A few fire-eaters gazed back farther still and observed that while the Continental Congress had declared national independence in 1776, each colony had seceded from the British Empire through its individual assembly. "I am a secessionist and not a revolutionist," Yancey insisted, and De Bow agreed. "*We* are not revolutionists." They were merely reaffirming an ancient right to withdraw their consent to be ruled by a distant government.[8]

How secession operated had little to do with *why* white southerners planned to leave the Union. Despite much later claims that the war was due to every possible cause but slavery, in 1860 southern ultras made no attempt to obscure the fact that it was for the purpose of protecting unfree labor that they sought independence. As William Boyce editorialized in the Charleston *Daily Courier*, the "need" for disunion stemmed from alleged Republican support for "negro equality, the only logical *finale* of which is emancipation." Boyce's assertion that Lincoln's party stood for black social equality might have come as a surprise to northern audiences familiar with David Wilmot's openly racist twist on free-labor ideology, but he was right enough in charging that Republicans planned to build a following in the border South, and that within a few years the Supreme Court would start to fill with Republican appointees. "If the South acquiesces in a Republican administration," Boyce worried, "emancipation is only a question of time." During the campaign, Robert Barnwell Rhett argued that the election of Breckinridge would "serve to protract for a few years a feverish and therefore dangerous existence." But as slave property was imperiled by further contact with the northern states, he saw "the election of Lincoln as the best thing that can happen to the Southern States."[9]

During the Nullification Crisis of 1832–1833, when South Carolina had threatened secession, the state had found itself isolated and alone, and Senator Hammond feared that history might repeat itself. But while Gist preferred coordination with other states, most white South Carolinians were determined to quit the Union even if they were the sole state to do so. For so long the only state with a white minority—Mississippi had finally caught up—South Carolina was accustomed to being in the forefront of sectional issues. Far from regarding themselves as radicals, most state leaders believed they were simply more perceptive than neighboring southern moderates. "Should a Black Republican President be elected," Thomas Y. Simons insisted, that would conclusively prove "that a majority of the people of the country have endorsed his principles and raised a banner on which is inscribed—death to the institutions of the South." Republican orators (and disgruntled Gerrit Smith supporters) might insist that Lincoln was no abolitionist, but a determined free soiler in the White House would mean an early end to an expansionist slave South. Unable to migrate into the territories or seize Cuba, planters along the southern frontier, one nervous South Carolinian noted, would have to sell their surplus laborers at low cost, driving down slave prices in the East and liquidating "four hundred and thirty millions of dollars" in capital investment. Faced with containment, planter-politicians could accept the outcome of the election and its attendant consequences. Or they could secede, defend their way of life, and run the risk of civil conflict.[10]

Apart from their firm conviction that delay only strengthened the North, fire-eaters in South Carolina wished to secede as soon as possible so as to fortify ultras in nearby states. Realizing that the upper South would never secede unless provoked by the incoming administration, the Rhetts expected to force the hand of Virginians and Maryland slaveholders by pursuing the same strategy that they had in the Charleston

Democratic convention. If the lower South seceded, they argued, that might force the non-cotton states "to choose between the North and South." The Rhetts believed that Yancey could prod Mississippi and his Alabama out of the republic, but even so, South Carolina should "secede first" as a point of honor. Who could doubt "that the other Slaveholding States, when once the Union is broken," would fail to "rally together to save their institutions, from Abolition rule at Washington?" South Carolina was destined to lead "in the formation of a Slave Republic," the *Mercury* editorialized, for as a "matter of policy it has been considered best for the South to strike out for herself and establish an independence of her own."[11]

If the cotton South did not have to secede as a bloc, class unity within the states of the lower South nonetheless was critical. Since a majority of southern whites owned not a single slave, planters desperately wished to keep the yeomen on their side, even if they little cared to hear their political voices regarding secession. As they had for most of the previous year, slaveholding politicians emphasized the alleged dangers that future abolition posed for white families. The South Carolina farmer, insisted Congressman Ashmore, "knows the honor of his wife and daughter would hardly be safe an hour if these slaves, totally unfit for self-government, were turned loose upon his community." The determination of low-country planters to win nonslaveholders over to the idea of creating what the Rhetts aptly described as a "Slave Republic" suggests that some politicians feared that secession might not be peaceful. Yet publicly, fire-eaters pounded away at the notion that Yankees were a greedy and cowardly people too consumed by business to wage a bloody war. When Senator James Chesnut promised to drink all of the blood spilled as a result of disunion, the elder Rhett bested that by swearing to eat all of the bodies of those slain, so sure was he that the Union could be peacefully disbanded. Those farmers who did not support their cause were "slaves and cowards," and for a time the yeomen endorsed secession as a method of sustaining their unstated rights. South Carolina should take "a bold and noble stand," one farmer agreed, and he did "not fear the consequences."[12]

On November 5, the day before the election, South Carolina's legislators convened for the sole purpose of casting the state's electoral votes,

Born Robert Barnwell Smith, Rhett early on abandoned what he regarded as a
dull surname in favor of that of his colonial ancestor William Rhett.
Although a U.S. senator for the first two years of the 1850s, Rhett preferred to
publish the Mercury *and agitate for secession. He was elected to the*
Confederate Congress but found the policies of Jefferson Davis too moderate
for his tastes. Courtesy Library of Congress.

which they unanimously gave to Breckinridge. Governor Gist urged
them to remain in Columbia, however, so that they could call a special
convention to deratify their participation in the Union should Lincoln
win. Rhett arrived from Charleston to urge the chamber to support
immediate and unilateral secession. As they waited for news of the

election, the state senate passed a resolution authorizing Gist "to use one hundred thousand dollars already appropriated to purchase arms," while the House debated a bill "compelling free negroes to leave the State or select masters." Since South Carolina's free people of color—most of whom were mixed-race—constituted only 2.4 percent of the state's African American population, the bill, which was referred to committee for further deliberation, suggests just how determined white Carolinians were to put their internal house in order. Toward that end, Rhett delivered yet another speech that evening, assuring his audience that Yankees were too spineless to fight should it come to that. Among those listening was Congressman Milledge L. Bonham, who fretted that Rhett was wrong. "I have seen them fight in Mexico," Bonham confided to one bystander, and, like John Brown, they were hardly cowards.[13]

When word of the election results reached the state, Judge Andrew Magrath set the legislature's course: He promptly resigned his position on the federal district court following his sudden adjournment. James Connor, the U.S. attorney for the district of South Carolina, and William F. Colcock, Charleston's port collector, also resigned "in consequence of Lincoln's success." Three days later, James Chesnut became the first southerner to quit his seat in the Senate. His wife, diarist Mary Boykin Chesnut, was stunned that he might do so without consulting her first, as she regarded herself as his chief adviser. But she "thought him right" to quit. The following morning, twenty minutes after hearing that Chesnut had resigned, South Carolina's other senator withdrew as well. Hammond did so with less confidence than Chesnut, but with so many South Carolina officials resigning, the senator thought it his only option. "You know the Japanese have an *ancient* custom, which therefore must have its uses," he told a friend, "of ripping up their own bowels to revenge an insult." The South Carolina delegation, he added, had "pretty much done that" by resigning, and his usefulness in Washington was at an end.[14]

Confident though they were that the lame-duck Buchanan administration would do nothing to keep them in the Union, South Carolina's white minority were less sanguine about the state's enslaved majority. Speaking to the South Carolina Agricultural Society on November 13, Andrew Pickens Calhoun, son of the deceased nullifier, warned his audience that Republican rhetoric, combined with the temporary disarray attendant on disunion, could incite slave rebellions. Calhoun urged his listeners to arm themselves, and within days already existing slave patrols found support from thousands of young men who purchased uniforms and organized themselves into minutemen units. Aware that previous slave uprisings and plots had matured during periods when white elites were divided against themselves, fire-eaters desperately wished to keep the process of withdrawal peaceful. In late November, the elder Rhett mailed a blunt missive to Buchanan, informing him that South Carolina would undoubtedly leave the Union within the next month, and that it was in the president's hands "to make the event peaceful or bloody." Should any of the federal forts around Charleston's harbor receive fresh troops, Rhett warned, "*it will be bloody.*"[15]

Buchanan was rarely one to act decisively. And compounding the problem was the four-month interval between the November elections and the March 4 inaugural. Lincoln was president-elect but as yet exercised no actual power, while the aged Buchanan, having seen American voters repudiate his party, nominally possessed legal authority but was hardly in a position to resolve the escalating crisis. Writing from Albany, Weed assured Lincoln that the "President and his cabinet, too, will first be called upon to rebuke Treason," but if Weed expected bold action from Buchanan, that revealed how little he knew of the president's character. The situation in South Carolina permitted no easy resolution, and as the *New York Herald* observed, Buchanan wished "to avoid this first bloody collision." Were he to try to coerce the South into remaining in the republic, he could trigger "a war of extermination" that might result "in a peace enforced by a military despot, or by a treaty and a partition of States and Territories between several military chieftains."[16]

The president chose to address South Carolina's impending secession in his annual message to Congress. As he toiled over his draft, Buchanan showed versions to his cabinet, giving Attorney General Jeremiah S. Black's opinion special attention. As strict constructionists, Black and Buchanan doubted that any president held the power, even as commander in chief, to send an army into a sovereign state or even to fill the void left by the resignation of federal officials there, such as the many who had relinquished their positions in Charleston and Columbia. After reading the draft, Secretary of State Lewis Cass urged the president to explicitly disclaim the power to compel South Carolina to remain in the Union. Like Buchanan, Cass blamed antislavery activists in the North for the crisis, and he hoped that by openly siding with the planter class—even more than he had in the past—Buchanan might slow the march toward secession.[17]

In keeping with a tradition established by Thomas Jefferson, Buchanan sent his communication of December 3 to Capitol Hill rather than delivering the speech himself. (Clerks typically droned out the address to the separate chambers.) Buchanan was well known for believing it wise to appease the vocal slaveholding minority on the grounds that the prosperous, free-labor North could afford to be magnanimous. But his message nonplussed even those in Congress who had assumed that the president would again take the side of the South. What, he asked rhetorically, was the source of the present emergency? The crisis, he argued, did "not proceed solely from the claim on the part of Congress or the territorial legislatures to exclude slavery from the Territories, nor from the efforts of different States to defeat the execution of the fugitive slave law." The South had long endured these assaults, Buchanan insisted, carefully ignoring the fact that the Alabama Platform was the cause of his party's dissolution. Instead, the "immediate peril" arose from "the incessant and violent agitation of the slavery question throughout the North for the last quarter of a century," which "produced its malign influence on the slaves, and inspired them with vague notions of freedom." Talk of liberty and equality, the president argued, and not human bondage itself, sparked "servile insurrections" and terrified the plantation mistress "throughout the South [who] retire at night in dread of what may befall herself and her children before the morning." Secession was unconstitutional, Buchanan added, yet neither could he legally force any state to remain in the republic. The solution to the crisis, he concluded, was to acquire "Cuba from Spain," approve the Lecompton constitution, and permit the slave states "to manage their domestic institutions in their own way."[18]

The northern response was swift and predictable. "Never was there a condition of public affairs so disgusting as under President Buchanan's administration," charged the *Philadelphia Inquirer*. "He is not only detested, but held in contempt, having done all in his power to deliver [the nation] to her enemies." Senator Seward mocked Buchanan's claim that although secession was unconstitutional, he had no authority to halt it. The message "shows conclusively that it is the duty of the President to execute the laws—unless somebody opposes him," Seward marveled, "and that no State has the right to go out of the Union—unless it wants to." The recently elected Congressman Charles Francis Adams thought the address much like its author, "timid and vacillating in the face of slaveholding rebellion, bold and insulting toward his countrymen whom he does not fear." Buchanan would "have to be impeached," Adams concluded. Not surprisingly, Garrison's *Liberator* gave the message short shrift: "Mr. Buchanan is about to retire from office, and the Southern dynasty at Washington is drawing to an end."[19]

Nor was the derision over Buchanan's message limited to antislavery voices. Douglas Democrats were especially outraged over what they regarded as the president's feeble response to southern sectionalists, with several unfavorably comparing Buchanan's speech to Andrew Jackson's stern response when South Carolina attempted to nullify federal law in 1832. Instead of "treating Secession from the Jacksonian standpoint," complained Illinois congressman John Alexander Logan, "President Buchanan feebly wailed over the threatened destruction of the Union [and] garrulously scolded the North as being to blame for it." One pro-Douglas editor urged his readers to "contrast the past with the present." Decades before, "in a season of trial and peril," Jackson had threatened to crush "rampant rebellion," but now a lesser Democratic president denied that "there is any sagacity in sustaining a government according to supreme law." In California, a state that Buchanan had carried in 1856, editors charged that the president "connive[d] at the success of the seceding States." The fact that northern Democrats denounced Buchanan's inaction with the same fury as Republicans should have served as a warning that secessionists faced not a minority president but a nearly unified northern population determined to maintain the Union.[20]

Although northern audiences found the president lacking in reason and vigor, lower-South politicians objected to Buchanan's characterization of secession as unconstitutional. Jefferson Davis promptly visited the White House to register his protests. But for Buchanan, the greatest blow was losing Treasury Secretary Howell Cobb, who decided that he could not serve an executive who believed secession to be illegal. On December 8—six long weeks before his state of Georgia was to secede—Cobb informed Buchanan that he could "no longer continue to be a member of [the] cabinet." While the two disagreed on some of the "theoretical doctrines" outlined in the president's address, Cobb observed, the key factor in his resignation was "the late Presidential election," which forced Georgia into "a struggle where the issue is life or death." Cobb's friends in Milledgeville, the state capital, required his "views and counsel," so the future Confederate congressman and general believed the time had arrived to return home.[21]

One week later, Secretary of State Cass followed, but for far different reasons. Fort Moultrie, situated on the edge of the Charleston harbor, was held by too few men should Gist attempt to seize it, so Cass and General Winfield Scott encouraged the president either to send reinforcements or urge the fort's commander, Major Robert Anderson, to abandon the coastal garrison for the more defensible walls of Sumter, in the middle of the harbor. When Buchanan declined to do so, saying that he could "not sanction a movement which might lead to collision and bloodshed," Cass resigned, pointedly observing that Jackson had ordered troops to Moultrie during the Nullification Crisis. Cass and Buchanan had never been close, and the seventy-eight-year-old Cass had been given the spot in recompense for his long service to the party. But the fact that the originator of popular sovereignty had "surrendered his portfolio" allowed the northern press to renew its censure of the "traitor" Buchanan.[22]

The resignations were little mourned across the North. Critics charged that Cobb had "wrecked the nation's finances" by presiding over the recession of 1857 and now quit only "to preach secession in the noble State which has been dishonored by his birth." But the two departures allowed the president to reorganize his cabinet, providing his last few months in office with much-needed efficiency and resolution. Buchanan asked the incompetent and partisan secretary of war, John B. Floyd of Virginia, to resign as well. He replaced Cass with Attorney General Black, whose portfolio went to Edwin M. Stanton, an antislavery Democrat and future secretary of war under Lincoln. Northern journalists knew almost nothing about Stanton—one Philadelphia reporter misnamed him "Edward"—but they cheered the departure of Floyd, whom they accused of placing "the whole military resources of the country" in the hands of southern secessionists.[23]

On December 17, two days after Cass's resignation, the convention called to decide South Carolina's destiny met in Columbia. According to "the formal steps for secession" (which Charles Sumner dubbed "the mild phrase for treason"), the state assembly called upon the electoral districts in the state to elect delegates to the conference. Among the large group of 169 men was former governor Gist (who had just been replaced by Francis W. Pickens), Maxcy Gregg, former senator Chesnut, former judge Magrath, and the elder Rhett. Since the convention was called by the legislature but was supposed to retain the appearance of legal autonomy, the gathering met not in a government building but at Columbia's First Baptist Church. Watching in dismay was attorney and politician James Louis Petigru, who in 1832 had led the anti-nullifier forces. When a stranger to Columbia stopped to ask Petigru for directions to the state insane asylum, the lonely unionist replied that it stood "upon the outskirts of the town," then added, pointing at the church, "but I think you will find the inmates yonder."[24]

Although a majority of South Carolina whites owned no slaves, that was hardly true of the convention delegates, 90.5 percent of whom were slaveholders. Potential unionists lived in the upcountry on scattered farms, so they were handicapped politically by apportionment laws and inequitable districting that favored lowcountry planters. Of the convention delegates who owned African Americans, 41.4 percent owned fifty or more, and twenty-seven were among the largest planters in the South, as they each owned more than one hundred enslaved South Carolinians. By comparison, the few who did not own slaves urged delay until the president-elect engaged in an act that they deemed clearly provocative. Slaveholding delegates might insist that "the poor white laborer" was their equal, as he belonged "to the only true aristocracy, the race of *white men*." But in truth, the men who chose to sweep their state out of the Union represented a small segment of the state's population.[25]

The yeomanry would later be among the first to abandon the Confederate cause, but in the frenzy of the moment, South Carolina's non-elites largely rallied behind the state's planters. To remain part of Lincoln's republic, Chesnut warned the convention, was to risk race war in which whites must "*slay the Negro, or ourselves be slain.*" Two young women who listened to the convention's speeches agreed. When asked by an English visitor what they would do if slaves rose in revolt, one replied that she "should kill them like so many snakes." Also swearing their fealty to secession were eighty-two members of Charleston's exclusive Brown Fellowship Society, composed of mixed-race freemen. Aware, surely, of discussions about re-enslaving or exiling free African Americans, the Browns hurried a message along to the mayor. "We are by birth citizens of South Carolina," they claimed, "in our veins is the blood of the white race in some half, in others much more, [and] our attachments are with you."[26]

The convention's pursuit of disunion was briefly stalled by the outbreak of smallpox in the city. Nervous delegates fled Columbia for Charleston, where they planned to reconvene on December 20 in the Institute Hall, the same building that had played host to the first Democratic convention the previous spring. Upon arriving, the enthusiastic participants renamed the building Secession Hall. Like many of those within, the hall would not survive the war. It burned down in late 1861, a fitting symbol for the conflagration that by then consumed the South.[27]

The delegates then made quick work of quitting the United States. The actual Ordinance of Secession consisted of one brief paragraph, which simply repealed the act of May 23, 1788, in which an earlier special convention had ratified the Constitution. The vote came at one fifteen in the afternoon and was unanimous, 169 to 0. After the ordinance passed, David F. Jamison, the convention's president, announced that the "Union now existing between South Carolina and other states, under the name of the United States, is hereby dissolved." Never again, Jamison added, should South Carolina "be reunited with any of the non-slaveholding States." As the news spilled into the streets, "a crowd collected, which did some immense cheering." Sitting in the gallery was Mary Boykin Chesnut, who recorded that the ladies around her "breathed fire & defiance." One delegate thought to mail Stephen Douglas a copy of the *Mercury*'s special edition, which bore the banner headline THE UNION IS DISSOLVED.[28]

That evening, as bonfires illuminated every street corner, the delegates hosted a ceremony that they hoped might rival the grand signing of the Declaration of Independence in 1776. Nearly three thousand spectators filled the hall and poured out into the streets, and thunderous applause greeted Jamison and the delegates as they paraded back into the building. Over the course of the afternoon, the Ordinance of Secession had been embossed onto a sheet of thick linen parchment more than two feet high. Jamison stamped the great seal of South Carolina onto the document, the first time the 1776 silver stamp had been used since it had imprinted the Nullification Ordinance of 1832. Seventy-year-old Reverend John Bachman rose to pray for peace and the wisdom to "protect and bless the humble race that has been entrusted to our care." A clerk then called out the name of each delegate, who mounted the stage and signed the parchment. When Rhett's turn came, he dramatically sank to his knees in thanks that his labors of thirty years had finally come to pass. At nine fifteen, the ceremony concluded as Jamison proclaimed the "State of South Carolina an Independent Commonwealth." The state, a despondent Petigru sighed, was "too small to be a nation and too large for an insane asylum."[29]

On December 21, the convention started at noon. A different minister began with a prayer, which praised God for "unit[ing] the people of the South in the forming of a Southern confederacy," before the convention turned to two lengthier tasks. Secession required a Declaration of Immediate Causes for its justification, just as Jefferson's Declaration of Independence had explained why the colonies were seceding from the British Empire. Also necessary was an Address to the Slaveholding States, designed to encourage the formation of a southern republic. Christopher G. Memminger, a German-born legislator (and the future Confederate treasury secretary), introduced a resolution calling for a committee of nine to draft the former. The convention approved the move, provided that Memminger would chair the committee. Matthew Mayes seconded the motion and added the proposal that commissioners bearing the Ordinance of Secession, together with the two documents, "be sent to each of the slaveholding states." The causes that forced South Carolina to separate, Mayes claimed, "emanated from the states north of Mason and Dixon's Line, which [use] hireling labor only," so other southern states should wish to join "in the formation of a new confederacy."[30]

By Christmas Eve, both documents were ready for approval, and the gathering, now calling itself "the State Sovereignty Convention," debated both during the evening session. The Declaration of Immediate Causes, which Memminger largely composed himself, began with a tedious discussion of the means by which South Carolina had ratified the Articles of Confederation and then the Constitution. "Thus was established," it read, "by compact between the States, a Government with definite objects and powers, limited to the express words of the grant." Yet "fourteen of the States have deliberately refused, for years past, to fulfill their constitutional obligations," especially when it came to returning runaway slaves. Northern activists had also tried to incite "servile insurrection in the State of Virginia," the document charged, and hence "the constituted compact has been deliberately broken and disregarded by the non-slaveholding States, and the consequence follows that South Carolina is released from her obligation." Within a few short months, "a sectional party" would "take possession of the Government," it continued. "It has announced that the South shall be excluded from the common territory, that the judicial tribunals shall be made sectional, and that a war must be waged against slavery until it shall cease throughout the United States." Under Lincoln, the "slaveholding States will no longer have the power of self-government, or self-protection, and the Federal Government will have become their enemy." As a result, the document concluded, "the Union heretofore existing between this State and the other States of North America, is dissolved." After two hours of discussion, the declaration was adopted "with a few dissenting voices."[31]

That same evening, the convention also approved the Address to the Slaveholding States. Drafted in a committee chaired by the elder Rhett, the address, not surprisingly, read like an angry editorial in the *Mercury*. Eschewing constitutional presumptions regarding the compact theory of government, Rhett instead sought to explain why the federal government had turned to "despotism." When the Constitution was framed in 1787, Rhett correctly noted, there was "no negro fanaticism," for "African Slavery existed in all the States but one." Thus, the "Union of the Constitution was a Union of slaveholding States." But as time passed, northern states began to denounce "as sinful the institution of slavery," and they "permitted an open establishment of societies whose avowal and objects are" to encourage "thousands of our slaves to leave their homes." Republicans now wished to restrict planters' access to the new territories of the West, "the most fertile regions of the world where the Caucasian cannot labor" but can be "brought into usefulness by the labor of the African." White South Carolinians asked only "to be let alone," Rhett concluded. "We ask you to join us in forming a confederacy of Slaveholding States."[32]

Both Memminger's declaration and Rhett's address, like Yancey's speeches, had the virtue of candor. They ignored any issues but those that pertained to slavery and the need to expand westward. Secure in the justness of their cause, white South Carolinians saw no reason to disguise their message; it would only be in later years, after the Confederacy had collapsed under northern guns, that statesmen writing their memoirs would think it necessary to point to more morally acceptable causes, such as economic grievances. Even Caleb Cushing, long regarded as a staunch defender of southern rights, was utterly ignored when he arrived in Charleston to counsel patience. Governor Pickens bluntly informed Cushing that secession was inevitable, and following a sleepless night spent in a hotel room listening to fireworks and ringing church bells, Cushing departed for Washington. Regarding all those who came to "advise the postponement of secession," the *Mercury* gleefully suggested, "feed them—drench them in champagne, and let them go."[33]

For the merry delegates, Christmas was a day spent in one of Charleston's many churches, all of them erected with funds earned from the unpaid toil of African Americans. But on December 26, the convention resumed. Having previously explained to other southern states why they should unite with South Carolina, Rhett now proposed that a convention of "all of the slaveholding states" meet in Yancey's hometown of Montgomery, Alabama, "to frame a constitution for a southern confederacy." No other state had yet seceded, but Pickens thought there would "be no difficulty" in uniting "the slave holding race" from "Deleware" to Texas. At length, the convention agreed and selected six delegates to the proposed convention, including Rhett and Memminger.[34]

At the same time, the convention also selected three commissioners to deliver a copy of the Ordinance of Secession to Buchanan. Since the president had already denounced secession as unconstitutional, the decision to hand Buchanan "an authentic copy" of the decree was far more confrontational than the polite wording of the convention's order implied. The commissioners were also empowered to "treat for the delivery of the forts, magazines and lighthouses" in what was now a foreign nation. Complicating matters was the fact that Major Anderson, having decided that Fort Moultrie could not be defended against a determined state militia, quietly spiked the fort's cannons on the night of December 26 and transferred the men under his command across the harbor to Fort Sumter. Anderson's move was undertaken without orders from the president; vengeful South Carolinians raised the Palmetto Flag above Moultrie. But when a furious Jefferson Davis stormed into the White House and demanded that Anderson be ordered to vacate Sumter, the president, his courage bolstered by Secretaries Black and Stanton, declined to do so until he possessed "official information from Major Anderson himself."[35]

When the three delegates arrived in Washington, they argued that Anderson had violated the status quo by taking up a new position against Charleston. Had they simply asked Buchanan to order Anderson's return to Moultrie, he might have done so. But the demand that federal troops remove themselves beyond the borders of South Carolina, together with news that South Carolinians had also occupied Castle Pinckney and seized the customs house, the post office, and the arsenal, forced the often irresolute Buchanan's hand. Even failed, lame-duck presidents worry about their future reputations, and after being attacked by the Democratic press following his December 3 address, the president could ill afford to back down. Republicans, of course, counseled firmness. Congressman Adams concluded that Buchanan was "guilty of treason," and when Lincoln was informed that Buchanan might surrender the forts, he exploded, "If that is true, they ought to hang him." After recovering his famous composure, the president-elect sent General Scott a confidential message, commanding him "to make arrangements at once to hold the forts, or if they have been taken" before he could be sworn in, "to take them back again."[36]

Hoping to buy time, Buchanan again declined to order Anderson to retreat, but his draft reply to the commissioners was so conciliatory that Black threatened to resign. At length, the president chose to return "their note without comment," which prompted the furious South Carolinians to tell the press that they considered "their treatment to be a declaration of war." Governor Pickens ordered that five thousand copies of their correspondence with Buchanan be printed as pamphlets and mailed to the other southern states. In response, the president sent Congress all of the documents regarding Charleston. In an explanation largely ghost-written by the secretary of state, Buchanan explained that while he had no authority to coerce a state, it was his "duty to use military force defensively against those who resist federal officers in the execution of their legal functions." Then, maintaining his strict-constructionist posture, he pointedly observed that Congress alone was empowered "to declare war, or to authorize the employment of military force."[37]

That was January 8; one day before, Mississippi had met in its special convention. Governor John Pettus had been one of the first to assure then-governor Gist that his state would follow South Carolina, and as early as November 13 he had called on the legislature to meet in thirteen days' time. The Republican victory, he wrote, proved that reformers anxious to "destroy the peace, property, and prosperity of the Southern section" had gained control of the executive branch, and only secession could save Mississippi "from Black Republican oaths." But having summoned the assembly, Pettus promptly suffered second thoughts. If Alabama and Georgia did not secede, Mississippi would be geographically isolated from South Carolina. Pettus dispatched emissaries to Alabama and Louisiana, and he began to wonder if it was not wiser to wait until March 4. The influential Jackson *Mississippian*, however, argued that it was prudent to withdraw while the weak Buchanan remained in the White House. "The planting states have a common interest of such magnitude, that their union, sooner or later, for the protection of that interest is certain," Jefferson Davis assured the younger Rhett. "United they will have ample power for their own protection."[38]

When the convention met, there was little sentiment for delay. Senator Albert Gallatin Brown denounced "submissionists" and announced that even if disunion came at the cost of "our fortunes, our lives," it was better to lose both than to accept Lincoln's election, "a disgrace so deep and damning." That Mississippi planters believed an electoral loss to be disgraceful revealed much about the mentality of slaveholders. As men who demanded the constant submission of human chattel, they defined themselves by what they were *not*. The "domination of Black Republicanism is wholly inconsistent with every idea of a free or beneficent government," observed another Mississippian. To submit "to Lincolnism would betray the spirit of a slave." There was even scanter talk of abstract motives related to state sovereignty than there had been in South Carolina, with delegates largely voicing only blunt concerns about the future of slavery under a series of Republican administrations. If their state did not secede, militants argued, that failure could mean "the loss of property worth four billion dollars of money."[39]

After just two days of deliberation, the convention put secession to a vote. The tally was a lopsided 84 to 15 in favor, and after the vote was taken, the dissenting minority promised to sign the ordinance the following day so as to make the decision unanimous. A number of visitors from South Carolina and Alabama were in attendance, and they were invited to occupy seats on the conference floor. That night, "a grand display of fireworks" saluted the delegates' handiwork. Pettus telegraphed the news to the state's delegation in Washington, and Jefferson Davis immediately responded: "Judge what Mississippi requires of me and place me accordingly."[40]

In later years, the former Confederate president would insist that Mississippi's actions were only designed to "arouse the sober thought and better feelings of the Northern people," who might then "agree to a Convention of [all] the States" that would achieve a compromise solution to save the republic. But the rhetoric heard in Mississippi's state convention left little doubt that planters firmly believed slavery to be endangered by their existence in the United States. Their Ordinance of Secession had nothing to do with gaining leverage and everything to do with permanent disunion. As early as the previous August, Davis had confided to Cass that he felt himself to be "a pretty good secessionist," and although he advised Pettus to delay secession until March 4, it was not in hopes of providing the president-elect with time for conciliation, but rather because he thought that a withdrawal conducted on Inauguration Day would "present in a palpable form the fact of our resistance to Black republican domination." Certainly Davis made his position clear, both on the floor of the Senate and in remarks on South Carolina's secession that were published in pamphlet form. "It is the right of a State to withdraw from the Union," he argued, and the "Constitution gave no power to the Federal Government to coerce a State."[41]

The Florida state convention met on January 2. For several days, the Tallahassee conference did little more than elect John Charles McGehee chairman and listen to prayers by the Reverend Rutledge. Still awaiting the arrival of some delegates, the meeting then adjourned for several more days, giving hope, as one northern editor put it, "to Union-loving minds at the North." But on January 7, the gathering approved a resolution "declaring it the right and duty of Florida to secede" by a vote of 62 to 5, and three days later the conference formally signed the ordinance. Since Florida had been a state only since 1845 and was home to just 78,679 whites, giving it the smallest population in the lower South, its withdrawal provided little clout to the future Confederacy. Yet the state's population was also 44 percent enslaved, and its departure maintained critical momentum for secessionist drives elsewhere in the South.[42]

Alabama's departure was already under way. As early as February 24, 1860, long before the Democrats convened in Charleston, the Alabama legislature passed a joint resolution requiring Governor Andrew Moore to hold special elections for a state convention should a Republican win in November. When Lincoln was victorious, Moore lost his nerve and somewhat disingenuously declared that no gathering could be held until the electoral vote was counted, just in case some electors chose to switch their votes. Under pressure from state fire-eaters, Moore relented on December 6 when cables from Washington reported that Lincoln had secured 180 electoral votes. A special election was set to take place on December 24, he announced, to elect delegates for a convention in Montgomery on January 7.[43]

As ever, the state's leading ultra was driving events. On November 10, Yancey and Moore addressed a large crowd in Montgomery. Somebody yelled from the floor that only "a Southern Confederacy" could protect "the religious institution of slavery," and the governor agreed that there was little alternative to secession. Seizing the rostrum, Yancey shouted that Alabama should not wait for other states to act. Even if the outcome was war, that was preferable to remaining in a country that relegated him to "a position inferior to the Northern free negro." Before the meeting ended, a Central Committee of Safety was named to coordinate disunion with other lower-South states. Yancey was one of the thirteen men selected. The committee drafted an Ordinance of Secession to be used by the expected state convention, and it also formalized Rhett's invitation summoning other slaveholding states to meet in Montgomery on February 4 for possible reunion as a sectional nation. "We all feel confident that we will soon have a glorious South[er]n Confederacy," Charles Pelham taunted his aunt, feminist and abolitionist Martha Coffin Wright, "with our own gallant & brave William L. Yanc[e]y for our Pres[iden]t."[44]

When the Alabama convention met, nobody spoke for remaining in the Union, but a sizable minority of moderates representing the state's yeomen-dominated northern counties urged patience and cooperation with other states. A few even questioned the legality of the process, since the convention was also considering a number of amendments to the state constitution, which moderates argued was not within the purview of the gathering. On January 8, the meeting's second day, Yancey lost his temper and nearly derailed the proceedings, bellowing that those "who shall dare oppose the action of Alabama, when she assumes her independence out of the Union, will become traitors—rebels against its authority, and will be dealt with as such." The bedlam that followed forced William Brooks, the convention's chairman, to adjourn for the day. In the end, however, it would be the actions of Mississippi and Florida, more than Yancey's bullying tactics, that secured the secession of Alabama.[45]

Yancey was especially affable the next morning as the convention resumed the march toward secession. The final vote was conducted behind closed doors, but at least 39 delegates voted against the ordinance as drafted. A majority of 61 endorsed the document, which stated that the rise of "a sectional party, avowedly hostile to the domestic institutions" of the state, constituted "a political wrong of so insulting and menacing a character as to justify" disunion. As a clerk announced the vote, a group of Montgomery women unfurled a banner nearly the width of the chamber. Yancey accepted the flag, emblazoned with the words NOLI ME TANGERE, Latin for "touch me not," as cannon fire shook the building's walls. A southern nation, Yancey assured the cheering crowd, with its "homogeneous people, accustomed to slavery, holding it in reverence for its origin and its effects," was sure to be "prosperous and powerful, for the purposes of peace or war."[46]

Even the editor of the pro-Douglas *Macon Daily Telegraph* was swept up by the fervor. Alabama had said, "Good by[e] Abram," and would Georgia "go and do likewise?" As the most populous state in the lower South, Georgia enjoyed the ability to slow the secession movement, even with four states already gone. But upon hearing of Lincoln's election, Governor Joseph E. Brown had instructed the assembly to call a special convention and recommended the appropriation of one million dollars to shore up the state's defenses. The governor's message did not explicitly advocate disunion, although he did detail what he regarded as a long history of abuse on the part of the North, focusing particular attention on the passage of personal liberty laws in some northern states. Howell Cobb resigned soon after, and the secretary's younger brother, Thomas R. R. Cobb, publicly called for immediate secession. Edmund Ruffin and the elder Robert Barnwell Rhett both arrived in Milledgeville in hopes of spurring Georgia forward. As early as December 13, Senator Robert Toombs supported the calling of a convention. The "Republicans had long been sowing the dragon's teeth," Toombs remarked in the Senate, "and now were reaping a crop of armed men."[47]

The lonely voice against what he described as a wild "passion and frenzy" was that of former congressman Alexander Stephens, who had quit the House in the spring of 1859. A former Whig, Stephens had served his last two terms in Congress as a Democrat, and as a supporter of Douglas, he had denounced his state's bolt from the Charleston convention. In mid-November, Stephens addressed the Georgia legislature and urged patience. "Revolutions are much easier started than controlled," he cautioned, and "the men who begin them, even for the best purposes and objects, seldom end them." The assembly listened politely to the small, frail planter, but his old friend Toombs informed him that the political tides ran toward secession. The fact that Stephens remembered Lincoln from their days as Whig congressmen and praised him, faintly, as "not a bad man" who "will make as good a President as Fillmore did and better too" did him little good among Georgia ultras. Even before the state convention could meet, Brown ordered the preemptive seizure of Forts Pulaski and Jackson, which protected Savannah, in the process capturing two howitzers, two cannons, and twenty-two thousand muskets and rifles.[48]

Because fewer than one third of Georgia's 132,317 adult white men were slaveholders, the yeoman majority was courted with the by-now-typical tactic of preying on white pride and fear. Slavery created "the poor man's best Government," Brown insisted, so the incoming administration meant particular hardship for Georgia's farmers, and not simply because many of them bartered their cereal crops to their planter neighbors. Eugenius A. Nisbet charged that Republicans planned "to free [the slaves] and leave them in our midst, upon a footing of social and political equality with the whites." Another secessionist editorialized that "in a government ruled by Lincoln and his crew," within "TEN years or less our CHILDREN will be the *slaves* of negroes." Ignoring the fact that nothing in the Chicago platform called for abolition or black rights, as well as the fact that Lincoln remained stubbornly, if naively, wedded to colonization for freed African Americans, a writer in the *Macon Daily Telegraph* mocked Stephens's desire to remain in the Union. Why "wait to be bound hand and foot by the Black Republicans before we resist?" Since the Republicans were openly hostile to slavery, immediate secession meant "never to submit to Lincoln for an hour."[49]

On January 2, Georgia voters braved winds and torrential rain to return to the polls, this time to elect delegates to the state convention. "The elements of nature seemed to be in accordance with the distemper of the times," a chilled Stephens complained. Fire-eaters encouraged "all advocates of secession [to] rally to the polls," but Brown feared that the upcountry districts might support cooperation-minded candidates. Early returns indicated that voters were "largely for secession," but the governor did not reveal the official count until late in April, well after Georgia's course was secured. Brown claimed that 50,243 voters had preferred secessionists, while 37,123 had cast their ballots for cooperationists. Stephens later contested those numbers, as have some later historians, and he long believed that bad weather had cost the convention "at least twenty Union members." But the 87,000 Georgians who reached the polls comprised 80 percent of those who had voted the previous November, and in any case, those candidates who had run as cooperationists refused to disavow secession under any circumstances. They instead wished to wait for a provocative act on Lincoln's part. The voting did reveal, however, that in Georgia, as elsewhere in the South,

secessionist sentiment was highest in those counties with heavy percent-
ages of slaves and weakest in the upcountry, where bondpersons were
few in number and whites more impoverished.[50]

The vote in the convention came on January 19, the result expected
by all. Stephens and his brother Linton were among the minority to
cast their lot with the Union. The inevitable cannon boomed across
Milledgeville's Capitol Square, firing "fifteen rounds in honor of the fifteen southern states," with "nearly every house in town" illuminated.
Watching the celebration was Mary Jones, an ardent secessionist who
nonetheless fretted about the future. "Thankfully would I wake up," she
assured her husband, "and find it all a dream, and Black Republicanism
a horrible nightmare." The formal signing of the state's ordinance came
two days later on Monday, January 21. Following that, the convention
agreed to a resolution introduced by Toombs, calling for the selection of
delegates to the upcoming slaveholder-states meeting in Montgomery.[51]

The pattern continued in Louisiana, where the election of delegates
for a state convention demonstrated the usual correlation between slaveholding and demands for disunion. Those parishes that had supported
Bell or Douglas chose delegates who favored delay, while twenty-two of
the thirty-six Breckinridge parishes selected immediate secessionists.
The final tally was surprisingly close, with 20,214 ballots for pro-secession
candidates and 18,451 for cooperation candidates. But Senators John
Slidell and Judah Benjamin both openly endorsed prompt withdrawal, as
did the mayor of New Orleans and the wealthy sugar planters along the
lower Mississippi River. "Give me the right to own [and] protect *my
property*," declared one flamboyant ultra, "or give me death." Even before
the convention met, such sentiments were bolstered by the knowledge
that the entire lower South, with the exception of Texas, had already quit
the republic. Editors once loyal to Douglas switched allegiances as their
neighbors seceded, and the publisher of the New Orleans *Bee*, which had
met Lincoln's election with the advice that the state should "stand by the
Union as long as it respects our rights," soon came to wonder how
Louisiana could remain in the country "if other cotton states secede."[52]

The delegates convened in Baton Rouge on January 23, two days after Georgia's master class signed its ordinance. Confident that secession
was unavoidable and anxious to avoid a situation like that with Major

Anderson at Sumter, Governor Thomas O. Moore had already ordered the seizure of Forts Jackson and St. Phillip, as well as the federal arsenal at Baton Rouge. Wasting little time, the convention approved an Ordinance of Secession by a vote of 113 to 17, as well as a resolution endorsing Moore's actions by 118 to 5. Two weeks later, Benjamin and Slidell resigned their seats in the Senate. Douglas, who had campaigned across the state, was furious, and he pointed out that the Louisiana region had been purchased in 1803 "with the national treasure, for the common benefit of the whole Union." With Mississippi and Alabama gone, Illinois boatmen reached foreign soil just below Memphis, and this fact more than any other fueled Douglas's growing rage at those who had denied him a unified nomination. But the senator's anger was no match for that of William T. Sherman, then watching events as superintendent of the Louisiana Military Academy, in Pineville. "You don't know what you are doing," Sherman lectured one secessionist. "This country will be drenched in blood."[53]

Texas, the last of the seven states to secede before Inauguration Day, proved to be a unique and difficult case for the ultras, if only because its governor was the staunchest of unionists and one of the most formidable persons in the state. The eccentric Sam Houston, who could have had the Constitutional Union nomination had he indicated any desire for it, announced that although he regarded Lincoln's election as regrettable, it provided "no cause" for secession. But the old warrior was out of touch with his state's wishes. So opposed was he to disunion that he refused to call the legislature into session or to sanction a state convention. When a handful of influential members of the assembly announced that they would meet regardless, Houston tried to outflank them by calling a special session of the legislature for January 21 in hopes that a majority of its members would stand with him. They did not. Led by Senator Louis T. Wigfall, whom Houston denounced as one of the "transplants from the South Carolina nursery of disunion," the legislature called for a secession convention to meet in Austin. In response to the governor's warnings of potential civil war, Wigfall gave the customary assurances. "Not only are our non-Slaveholders loyal," he maintained, "but even our Negroes are." A series of fires west of Dallas the previous July had been attributed to enslaved arsonists and Republicans, who sympathized with "such things," so Wigfall felt the need to insist that legislators had "no apprehensions whatever of insurrection—not the slightest."[54]

When the convention met on January 28, the group of 177 delegates included one former and four future governors, as well as Congressman John H. Reagan, soon to serve the Confederacy as postmaster general. Slightly more than 90 percent of the delegates had been born in slaveholding states. Still hoping to find a way to stem the tide, Houston demanded that Texas voters ratify whatever course the gathering chose, and once more the governor miscalculated. After voting 171 to 6 on the proposition that "Texas should separately secede from the Union," the convention scheduled a referendum for February 23. Voters upheld the convention's decision in a landslide of 46,129 votes to 14,697, nearly the same margin of victory that Breckinridge had earned against Bell in Texas the previous November. Houston reluctantly confirmed the voters' decision on March 4 but insisted that the referendum returned Texas to its previous status as a republic, rather than making it a part of the already forming Confederate States of America. When called on to declare his loyalty to the Confederacy, Houston refused to answer the roll. The legislature declared the governorship vacant and fired the hero of San Jacinto.[55]

Of the seven states that had seceded thus far, only Texas had an African American population of less than 43 percent, and it was far from coincidental that the first two states to quit the republic, South Carolina and Mississippi, enslaved a majority of their residents, 59 and 55 percent, respectively. By comparison, the upper-South states of Kentucky and Delaware were 20 and 19 percent black, and although Lincoln's election was hardly met with cheers along the border, neither was the region prepared to withdraw from the Union. Fire-eaters in the lower South had boasted that by March 4 their new nation would consist of fifteen slaveholding states, but the drive for disunion stalled after Texas. In hopes of prying their upper-South brethren out of the republic, seceded states dispatched commissioners to address neighboring legislatures. One Alabama commissioner, speaking before the Kentucky assembly, resorted to customary racial appeals, but this time with less success. "What Southern man, be he slave-holder or non-slave-holder, can without indignation and horror contemplate the triumph of negro equality," he shouted, "and see his own sons and daughters in the not distant future associate with free negroes upon terms of political and social equality?" Mississippi's commissioner to Delaware attempted the same tactics, but his speech was "received with mingled applause and hisses." After granting the envoy every "courtesy due him," the legislature passed a resolution stating Delaware's "unqualified disapproval" of Mississippi's course and rejecting its invitation "to join the Southern confederacy, about to be formed."[56]

Ultra commissioners fared little better in Tennessee and North Carolina, where the black populations stood at 25 and 36 percent. Approximately 37 percent of whites in the seceded states owned slaves, compared to only 20 percent of whites in the upper South. Governor Pettus and the Mississippi legislature also sent commissioners to Raleigh, but although the North Carolina assembly appropriated three hundred thousand dollars to buy arms, the legislature went out of session without calling a special convention. Governor John Willis Ellis was content to leave the issue in the hands of voters, but whites in North Carolina and Tennessee chose to remain in the Union. "*Nine-tenths of the community are opposed*" to secession, editorialized the *Wilmington Herald*. Shortly thereafter, conventions in Arkansas and Missouri, the latter only 10 percent African American, voted to reject secession. "The question of secession is a new one in Arkansas," one commissioner admitted. "It has never yet been debated or considered there," unlike in Mississippi, "where it has been discussed for many years."[57]

Virginia, of course, was the prize most coveted by the lower South. Although the state was only 34 percent black, its population was an impressive 1,596,318, almost half a million residents more than Georgia. It was also the birthplace to numerous presidents and closely identified in the public mind with the nation's founding era; should Virginia secede, the fire-eaters' claims to a revolutionary right of disunion would gain considerable credibility. But the state had a long record of unionism, and during the previous November, Breckinridge had captured only 44.5 percent of the state's votes. Virginia was home to Edmund Ruffin, but also to John Minor Botts, one of the many potential Constitutional Union candidates, who compared lower-South fire-eaters to New England's discredited Hartford Convention delegates of 1815, men now held "in terms of scorn and ignominy." In early January, outgoing governor Henry A.

Wise urged the immediate calling of a special convention, but Congressmen John T. Harris, William Smith, and T. S. Bocock all recommended delay until Congress had a chance to devise a compromise package. Many editors agreed with the publisher of the Charlottesville *Review*, who claimed that he "hated South Carolina for precipitating secession."[58]

To a large extent, Virginia's future course was to be determined by outside forces. Beyond the state's borders, the political situation was far from stable. Former president John Tyler, an ardent expansionist, mourned the election of Lincoln, saying, "I fear we have fallen on evil times." If Virginia planters could not gain access to the West, they must "sooner or later look to Mexico, the West India Islands, and Central America as the ultimate reservations of the African race." When the state legislature met, it passed a resolution denouncing possible federal "coercion" of the seceded states, and with John Letcher, the new governor, the assembly approved legislation calling for a February 4 election of delegates to a special convention. The legislature also asked the state's residents to vote on whether the convention's ultimate response would have to be put to a statewide referendum. Requesting the will of the voters was "all wrong," complained Louisiana's Robert Grinnan, who had arrived in Richmond to urge immediate secession. "It gives delay and will prevent decided action."[59]

The February vote was a major setback for potential Confederates, if not, perhaps, the stunning defeat for secessionists often depicted by modern historians. Of the 152 delegates selected for the convention, only 40 proposed immediate secession, and the question of whether the gathering's decision should then face a statewide referendum passed by an impressive margin of 100,536 to 45,161. Ruffin remained in South Carolina, disgusted with his native state. But many of the 70 self-professed "moderates" not committed to either union or disunion were prepared to secede if events outside Virginia forced their hand. And the gathering, which ultimately decided to delay pending congressional action in Washington, provided Virginia fire-eaters with the opportunity to confer and to listen to the advice of lower-South commissioners. Christopher Memminger arrived from Columbia in mid-January, and as the convention opened, he was followed by Fulton Anderson of Mississippi and Henry Lewis Benning of Georgia. When allowed to speak, Benning launched into a point-by-point explication of the alleged dangers of a Lincoln administration, which concluded with a passionate appeal for slaveholders' solidarity. "We will be overpowered and our men will be compelled to wander like vagabonds all over the earth," Benning swore, "and as for our women, the horrors of their state we cannot contemplate in imagination." Where Senator Wigfall had expressed the greatest confidence in the loyalty of Texas slaves, Benning held out the threat that "the white race" would soon be "completely exterminated." The land, he warned, "will be left in the possession of the blacks, and then it will go back to a wilderness and become another Africa or St. Doming[ue]."[60]

It was not only border-state moderates who watched these proceedings with dismay. New England industrialists conducted all manner of business with the seceding states, and between Election Day and the end of January 1861 the average share price of stock in New England cotton mills plummeted from $518.34 to $304.22. Nor was the economic anxiety over secession limited to mill owners. Carriage makers in New Haven, Connecticut, sold a majority of their products to southern planters, as did many Philadelphia boot makers. "Boston streets to-day are full of discharged workmen," reported the Boston *Courier*. Bankers fretted about the "bad fix of the Federal Treasury" as secession carried seven states' worth of crop-exporting revenue out of the national economy. From Wall Street to its docks, Manhattan was so wedded to the southern economy that Mayor Fernando Wood recommended to his city council that they secede from New York State and become an independent city-state. Since most of Illinois's commerce flowed south toward New Orleans, a few Chicago businessmen expressed interest in the same idea. But Douglas, increasingly radicalized by what he saw as the faithless behavior of southern Democrats, began to repeat what the press quickly dubbed his "Norfolk Doctrine," that secession was not justified, to which he now added that the mouth of the Mississippi River was too critical to the North to be turned over to a foreign government.[61]

Few other public officials in the North shared Wood's views, although many favored some concessions to the South. New York governor Edwin D. Morgan urged "the repeal of all laws conflicting with federal laws, on the subject of slavery." Although a Republican, Morgan singled out the 1841 statute that protected his state's sizable free black population by granting jury trials to alleged runaways, a course also endorsed by Ohio governor William Dennison Jr., a fellow Republican. Less surprisingly, Caleb Cushing delivered a series of speeches across the north, insisting that states that declined to repeal their personal-liberty laws were equally guilty of "secession from the Union," at least in spirit."[62]

John Andrew, the newly elected governor of Massachusetts, thought otherwise. Andrew observed that minor protections accorded to black defendants hardly prevented "the execution of the fugitive slave law," which had been enforced in his state by President Franklin Pierce in 1854 when federal marshals returned runaway slave Anthony Burns. Massachusetts residents, he added, were "against all concessions involving a surrender of fundamental principle[s]." Even Morgan was unequivocal on the right of secession. "To permit or to acquiesce in a treasonable conspiracy against the national authorities," he lectured the New York assembly, "is to confess that our government is an absolute failure." Dennison agreed. In his address to the Ohio legislature, the governor denounced any right to secession and called, ominously, for "a reorganization of the [state] militia."[63]

Most residents of the northern states thought any talk of military preparedness absurdly premature. Older Americans with long memories had grown weary of southern saber rattling, and to many observers the secession movement was yet one more act of political blackmail in a long, tiresome drama stretching back to the Missouri debates of 1819–20. The sooner it became clear that northerners would no longer play the slaveholders' "game," insisted one Springfield editor, "the sooner shall we be delivered from these periodical soundings of the Disunion gang." Historians now understand that militant secessionists were deadly serious, and that no concessions could have won them back. But after several decades of fiery rhetoric warning of the grim consequences of the federal government's failure to secure southern expansionists Nebraska, or Cuba, or New Mexico, northern voters had ceased to be impressed by the threats of "slave propagandists." In any case, Republican candidates who had taken their case to the voters in November were little inclined to regard a fairly won victory as cause for disunion. Nineteen times before, Congressman Charles Francis Adams noted, Americans had gone to the polls to elect a president, but now the South "suddenly broke out into violent

remonstrance, and dashed into immediate efforts to annul their obligation to the Constitution." Even had they understood the seriousness of
the crisis, Republicans could not have done anything to allay southern
fears, apart from renouncing the basic principles that had elevated them
into the White House. The very "election of the candidate of the Black
Republican party," admitted North Carolina senator Thomas L. Cling-
man, "demand[s] resistance on our part."[64]

The one whose opinion mattered most lived in Springfield. Like so
many of his neighbors, the president-elect "could not be made to believe,
that the South meant secession and war," complained one frustrated Ohio
politician. Counsel poured in from all quarters, some visitors and letters
reaching Lincoln directly, while others peppered leading Republicans
with advice. "Freedom & Slavery are incompatible and ought not to exist
under the same government," New Yorker George Ford informed
Seward. Let the "southern or slave states" secede in peace, while those
"who voted for Lincoln and freedom, constitute an independent and free
Confederacy by ourselves." In Rochester, Frederick Douglass feared the
opposite outcome. He assumed that the Republican leadership would
give way on slavery's extension in the name of peace, making Lincoln
the abolitionists' "most powerful enemy." Neither Ford nor Douglass was
privy to the president-elect's correspondence, of course, and had the latter seen a private missive sent to Alexander Stephens in late December,
his fears might have vanished. "You think slavery is *right* and ought to be
extended; while we think it is *wrong* and ought to be restricted," Lincoln
told his old friend. "That I suppose is the rub." As Lincoln pieced his cabinet together, that was to prove the one policy on which there would be no
compromise.[65]

CHAPTER EIGHT

"Others to Share the Burden"

Two Governments Prepare

NEXT TO FIRE-EATERS in Charleston and Wide Awakes in Springfield, perhaps the person most pleased with the November elections could be found at 33 South Street in Auburn, New York. Frances Seward had always despised Washington and years before had refused to again leave her home in upstate New York for the swampy, unfinished capital. The day William Seward learned of Lincoln's nomination was the hardest day in his life since the death of his daughter Cornelia, but possibly "the happiest" that Frances had seen in quite some time. Henry J. Raymond, the editor of the *New York Times*, spoke to the disappointed candidate on May 22, 1860, and reported that the senator regarded "his public life as definitely closed." Seward would "serve out the remainder of his term in that body, but will not, in any event or under any circumstances, be a candidate for reelection." Decades before, in 1830, after only six years of marriage, Frances had watched as her husband had left for Albany to take his seat in the state assembly. At long last, he was returning home for good. "Let those who are disposed to cavil go and do as well as you have done," she told him. "You have earned the right to a peaceful old age."[1]

Unhappily for Frances, peace was further off than she supposed. Late on election night, as bleary celebrants stumbled for bed and Springfield returned to "its usual quietness," a sleepless president-elect began to scratch names onto a list. "I began at once to feel that I needed support," Lincoln later admitted, "others to share with me the burden." Before sunset on the following day, Lincoln had nearly "made up [his] Cabinet." Although unsanctioned by the Constitution, the president's circle of advisers had come to be of critical importance in the early republic. Originally designed to provide the executive with specialized information, presidential cabinets had become vehicles for unity, with geography and patronage playing decisive roles in their composition. For Lincoln, heading a party only six years old, cabinet selections would be a way to wed radical former Democrats with free-soil Whigs and New England abolitionists with lower-North moderates. Cabinet portfolios also expressed gratitude to party leaders for past service, and for a president-elect who was an outsider in Washington, it was a way to honor—and watch—his closest rivals. Lincoln's list included those who had been the leading competitors for the nomination—Seward, Salmon P. Chase, and Edward Bates—as well as former Democrats Montgomery Blair, Gideon Welles, and Norman Judd and former Whig senator William L. Dayton of New Jersey. And because a similar process was soon under way in Montgomery, Alabama, Lincoln's list was the first hint that when it came to politics and human psychology, the one-term Illinois congressman possessed a native shrewdness lacking in his accomplished Confederate counterpart.[2]

Just before the election, Lincoln had moved into the governor's office in the Illinois capitol, but as the legislature was soon to convene, he rented a large room in the nearby Johnson Building. As demands on his time grew and random papers began to cascade off his desk, the president-elect realized he needed secretarial assistance. He first hired John G. Nicolay, a serious, systematic, German-born journalist and clerk to the Illinois secretary of state. Still buried by the rising volume of mail, Nicolay turned to John Hay, a nephew of one of Lincoln's former legal apprentices and a recent graduate of Brown University. Although born in Indiana, Hay thought Springfield "a miserable sprawling village" by comparison to Providence, but the future secretary of state quickly grew devoted to his boss. Nicolay, then twenty-eight, and Hay, twenty-two, were to faithfully serve Lincoln until his death. The former retained the title of chief secretary, while Hay, although detailed to special service at the White House, drew his salary as a clerk in the Department of the Interior.[3]

His Springfield office in good hands, Lincoln next contacted Hannibal Hamlin. The overture was unexpected, since vice presidents then played little if any role in administrative matters; their job was to carry their state in the Electoral College and weld their ideological or geographic following to the new president. Hamlin, as a former Democrat from Maine, had performed his expected function. Apart from one brief hiatus as governor, however, he had served in the House or Senate since 1843, whereas Lincoln had not set foot in the nation's capital in more than a decade. On November 8, two days after his election, Lincoln posted a confidential letter to Hamlin. "I am anxious for a personal interview with you at as early a day as possible," he informed the vice-president-elect. "Can you, without much inconvenience, meet me at Chicago?" Understanding the delicacy of the nearly unprecedented meeting, Hamlin urged his son to "let this be *strictly confidential* [and to] say to no one I am going." When he boarded the train in Bangor on November 19, he allowed his neighbors to assume that he was heading for Washington, so he was amazed when the ever-intuitive Thurlow Weed intercepted his car somewhere in New York State. Guessing that Hamlin had been summoned to discuss the cabinet, Weed insisted that Seward would not accept a position in the administration, although he added that as a courtesy Lincoln should offer the New Yorker the job of secretary of state.[4]

As his train continued westward, Hamlin discovered that the southern press continued to claim he was mixed-race, and that several fire-eaters had snidely offered to buy "the mulatto" if offered a fair price. But he carried no pistol, insisting that he needed only his fists as defense against potential assassins. The tall, slump-shouldered Hamlin finally arrived in Chicago on November 22 and took a carriage to the Tremont House. When Hamlin encountered the president-elect in the hotel lobby, he was impressed by Lincoln's even greater height but puzzled by the beginnings of a beard on the formerly clean-shaven Illinoisan. As was his custom, Lincoln grasped Hamlin's hand in both of his and promptly set his visitor at ease by claiming to remember that one of his speeches in

Congress had been "filled 'chock-up' with the very best kind of anti-slavery doctrine." The two spent the remainder of the day sightseeing about Chicago. They visited the cavernous Wigwam, which the city was already considering demolishing in favor of a more permanent (and possibly less flammable) conventional hall.[5]

The next day, Lincoln and Hamlin, together with Senator Lyman Trumbull, rode out to Judge Ebenezer Peck's home in nearby Lake View in search of privacy. The central question, everybody knew, was Seward. Hamlin personally liked the New Yorker and understood why having him within the cabinet, where his advice (and criticism) could be private, was imperative, but he also suspected that Seward was temperamentally unfit to guide foreign affairs. With Seward, moreover, came his handler, Weed, a longtime state "boss" whose alleged dishonesty was infamous far beyond New York. Trumbull advised Lincoln "that it would be disastrous to us as a party if the men implicated in the Albany corruptions should receive the favor of your administration." Writing from Maryland, seventy-year-old Frank Blair, once a member of Jackson's informal "Kitchen Cabinet," advanced the same argument. National confidence in Lincoln's "honesty & patriotism," Blair insisted, might be damaged by the inclusion of Seward or the reputedly corrupt Simon Cameron in the cabinet. But despite Seward's recent shift toward the center, he continued to enjoy the backing of New England abolitionists. Since 1856, he had been the presumptive Republican nominee, and even Blair conceded that Seward's "many and strong friends" had let it be known that the relatively unknown president-elect could leave Seward outside of his executive family only at great political cost.[6]

The three spent another long day discussing lesser cabinet positions. Lincoln was so impressed by Hamlin's political acumen that he gave him a list of names—including Charles Francis Adams and Gideon Welles—and instructed the vice-president-elect to select one as New England's representative in the cabinet. Hamlin recognized, of course, that this limited his freedom to choose *any* man he wished, but no previous executive had ever granted this sort of privilege to a vice president. "I shall accept and shall always be willing to accept," Lincoln assured Hamlin, "any advice" that he wished to impart. Most important of all, Lincoln placed Hamlin in charge of negotiating with fellow senator

Seward. The "sentiment" in New York, "which [had] sent a united delegation to Chicago in favor of Gov. S. ought not, and must not be snubbed,"
Lincoln explained to a dissatisfied Trumbull, "as it would be by the omission to offer Gov. S. a place in the cabinet."[7]

Because so few politicians or journalists in the East were even aware
of the meeting in Chicago, rumors began to circulate in Manhattan and
Washington that Seward would not be offered a position in the cabinet.
William Cullen Bryant, editor of the influential *New York Evening Post*,
let it be known that only "honest men with clean hands" should serve in
the new administration. Other gossip held that Lincoln would offer
Seward the post of secretary of state, but only as a courtesy. Lincoln
continued to be serious about the posting, however, and he encouraged
Hamlin to raise the question with Preston King, New York's junior senator. King replied that he possessed no special insight into Seward's
plans, and he encouraged Hamlin to speak to Seward directly about the
position. When informed of this, Lincoln promptly sent Hamlin two letters for Seward, which he instructed the vice-president-elect to first
read. "Consult with Judge Trumbull," Lincoln told Hamlin, "and if you
and he see no reason to the contrary, deliver the letter[s] to Governor
Seward at once."[8]

Within a few days, Hamlin found his opportunity. After the afternoon's Senate business was finished, Hamlin and Seward walked along
Pennsylvania Avenue toward their respective rooms. Hamlin invited
Seward in for a private discussion. The New Yorker agreed but moodily
began to talk of his impending retirement. If Hamlin intended to offer
him a position in the cabinet, he added, both men were wasting their
time. Instead of arguing the point, Hamlin simply handed Seward the
two letters. The first missive was brief and formal. "With your permis-
sion," it read, "I shall, at the proper time, nominate you to the Senate, for
confirmation, as Secretary of State." The second, longer letter was
marked "Private & Confidential." He was aware of rumors in the press,
Lincoln began, that the post would be tendered only "as a compliment,
and with the expectation that you would decline it." Lincoln hastened to
add that not only had he said nothing to justify such gossip, but that it
had been his "purpose, from the day of the nomination at Chicago, to as-
sign you, by your leave, this place in the administration." Playing upon

the New Yorker's vanity and conviction that only he could save his country from the current crisis, Lincoln urged Seward to accept the job in "the belief that your position in the public eye, your integrity, ability, learning, and great experience, all combine to render it an appointment pre-eminently fit to be made." Visibly moved, Seward grasped Hamlin's hand and muttered that the letter was remarkable. He promised a formal reply as soon as possible.[9]

Lincoln's offer was far more gracious and sincere than Seward had ever expected, and suddenly the morose Senator was excited about the prospect of holding the top position in the cabinet. Meeting first with King, Seward hinted that given the precarious state of the nation, he could hardly decline the invitation. The senator next posted letters to Weed in Albany, asking his advice. As Lincoln had already invited Weed to return to Springfield, Seward decided to wait for the results of that conference. On December 13, he replied to Lincoln, asking for "a little more time to consider whether I possess the qualifications and temper of a minister and whether it is in such a capacity that my friends would prefer that I should act if I am going to continue at all in public service." In the meantime, letters arrived from supporters and allies urging him to accept. Hamlin had already written to assure the New Yorker that he had "full faith in Lincoln, and that he *will be true to principle*." Simon Cameron, who expected to receive a similar missive from the president-elect shortly thanks to promises made in Chicago by David Davis, wrote to Seward as early as November 13. "You will be offered the State Dept. within a few days and you *must not* refuse it."[10]

Weed arrived back in Springfield on December 20 and met with Lincoln, Davis, and state assemblyman Leonard Swett. After a long campaign season of serving as hostess, Mary had left to rest and visit relatives. Although Lincoln welcomed her advice on appointments, Davis did not and was pleased by her absence. (Being away from Springfield did not, however, hinder Mary from sending unflattering gossip regarding Norman Judd along to Davis.) The four men discussed patronage in New York, as Seward had sent along suggestions for the cabinet. The senator recommended Charles Francis Adams for treasury secretary, John C. Frémont for war, and Congressman John A. Gilmer of North Carolina for an unnamed position. Both Weed and Seward hoped for a cabinet dominated by former Whigs, especially since former Whigs and former Democrats disagreed on economic policy. When Lincoln raised the possibility of giving posts to Cameron and Welles and placing Chase in the Treasury Department and Montgomery Blair in the War Department, Weed objected that the seven-member cabinet would be controlled by ex-Democrats. "You seem to forget that I expect to be there," Lincoln laughed, adding that the ever-vacillating Cameron was "not Democrat enough to hurt him."[11]

Weed pushed hard on placing a southerner in the cabinet, and like Seward he suggested Gilmer, a slaveholder and former Whig, or James Guthrie of Kentucky. Lincoln thought the appointment could lead to complications should either state secede, which would force Gilmer or Guthrie to either quit the cabinet publicly and embarrass the new president or remain in Washington while being powerless at home. Davis and Swett sided with Weed. In fact, Lincoln had already entered into an exchange with Gilmer, since the congressman had written on December 10 with a series of queries he hoped the president-elect might address. An annoyed Lincoln wrote back five days later, saying he was "disinclined" to publish his thoughts on the growing national crisis. "May I be pardoned if I ask whether even *you* have ever attempted to procure the reading of the Republican platform, or my speeches by the Southern people?" Lincoln wondered. "On the territorial question," he added, he was "inflexible." But the president-elect did write Seward that he would urge Gilmer to visit Springfield, and if, "on full understanding of my position, he would accept a place in the cabinet," Lincoln would "give it to him."[12]

As Weed's train puffed for home, Seward intercepted him in Syracuse, and the two discussed the Springfield conference on the ride to Albany. By this time, South Carolina had seceded, increasing the likelihood of some kind of dangerous clash over Sumter or Moultrie. Seward yet hoped to achieve some sort of negotiated solution in the Senate, but Weed warned him that Lincoln was resolute on the question of the territories. Yet if the New Yorkers now had a better grasp of Lincoln's determination, both when it came to constructing a cabinet and in the realm of not compromising away key Republican platform issues, they continued to believe that the prairie lawyer required a wise counselor in

Washington. If Seward remained in the Senate or retired, as Frances hoped, he would have no influence whatsoever on the new administration. On December 28, he picked up his pen and informed Lincoln that "after due reflection, and with much self distress," he had concluded that it was his "duty to accept the appointment."[13]

Word of Seward's acceptance leaked out immediately. The appointment was a bitter defeat for the anti-Weed men in New York and especially for Horace Greeley, who thought it poor recompense for his early support for Lincoln. But the selection of Seward was an early indication that Lincoln regarded political loyalty as less important than competence, and most eastern journalists, ignoring the calculation involved in healing old convention wounds, welcomed the choice. The pro-Democratic *Washington Constitution* speculated as to whether "Seward's appointment to the first place in the new Cabinet is to be regarded as a surrender on his part to Mr. Lincoln, or of the surrender of Lincoln to Seward." Weed and Seward perhaps wondered the same thing, but given the degree to which Seward had shifted both his tone and his position regarding the South over the previous year, moderates took the announcement as "a sign from Springfield." Seward's position in the cabinet, agreed the *New York Herald*, "is equivalent almost to the proclamation of a compromise from the President elect and the republican party to the American people."[14]

A less welcome sort of legacy from the Chicago convention was found in the case of Simon Cameron. In early December, Lincoln wrote to David Wilmot requesting his thoughts about Pennsylvania's place in the cabinet, and on Christmas Eve the former congressman arrived in Springfield. Wilmot told the president-elect that he was "rather inclined to Gen. Cameron," although he admitted that Cameron's shady business dealings made him "very objectionable to a large portion of the Republicans of [his] State." Neither man believed that Pennsylvania, a state carried by the Democrats in 1856, could be denied a seat. The only alternative appeared to be Congressman Thaddeus Stevens, and many Republicans doubted that the mercurial, sarcastic Stevens possessed the proper temperament for the cabinet. Several of Cameron's handlers had hurried to Springfield, evidently hoping to remind Davis of pledges made in Chicago. Whether Lincoln's manager had made specific promises or

vague assurances of consideration in exchange for Pennsylvania's delegate support, the fact remains that Cameron had met with Davis at least
once during the previous summer. On December 30, the senator himself
appeared in Springfield, and Lincoln was impressed by his commanding
presence and piercing gray eyes. The next morning, the president-elect
officially notified Cameron that he was to be nominated for "Secretary
of the Treasury, or as Secretary of War—which of the two, [he] had not
yet definitely decided."[15]

Lincoln almost immediately regretted the offer. As he had with Seward, Frank Blair promptly condemned the choice, as did former Ohio
congressman Samuel Galloway. Pennsylvania state senator Alexander
McClure was so troubled that he boarded the train for Illinois as soon as
he heard rumors of a Cameron posting. Meeting with Lincoln on January 2, McClure raised the issue of Cameron's alleged dishonesty. The irritated president-elect interrupted to insist that McClure either prove the
old charges or cease repeating them. Expecting this response, McClure
replied that if it was his "disagreeable duty of establishing [Cameron's]
personal & political integrity, it [would] be done with fearful fidelity."
McClure showed Lincoln a series of documents, and while no record of
what they contained now exists, they were clearly persuasive. The following morning, a shaken Lincoln mailed Cameron a second letter, re-
tracting the offer. "Since seeing you things have developed which make
it impossible for me to take you into the cabinet," Lincoln bluntly noted.
"And now I suggest that you write me declining the appointment, in which
case I do not object to its being known that it was tendered you."[16]

Cameron opted to do nothing, evidently believing that the untested
president-elect could not afford to publicly disavow an appointment after only two days. Cameron also expected Seward to take his side, which
the New Yorker soon did. "I regret to say that Mr Cameron is very much
grieved, by the result of the proposition to him of a cabinet place," Seward
wrote, adding that he was "willing to be the mediator of conversation
between you and Mr Cameron as a mutual friend." Henry Simons also
wrote to object to charges made against Cameron "by the abolition &
ultra portion of the republican party," a reference, undoubtedly, to the
Blairs. Unwilling to risk a rupture with Seward at this juncture, Lincoln
wrote to the unresponsive Cameron again on January 21, asking "if you

will visit me again." Once more, Cameron simply declined to answer, and so for a time the issues remained unresolved. "This matter of Cameron's has got into an awkward fix," Swett admitted. It certainly did nothing to ease tensions between Seward and the Blairs. "Cameron was brought into the cabinet by Seward," Montgomery Blair groused.[17]

As for the Blairs, there was never any doubt in Lincoln's mind that one of them deserved a seat. The dynasty had long been influential in the critical border states; the elder Blair was born in Virginia, had lived in Kentucky (where Montgomery and 1860 presidential candidate Francis Jr. were born), and currently resided in Maryland, where Montgomery practiced law after first having established a practice in Missouri. Frank Blair adopted a hard line against southern "conspirators against the union," and Lincoln hoped that Montgomery Blair could be an invaluable counterweight to Seward and Cameron. Frank thought the attorney generalship appropriate for Montgomery, a former U.S. solicitor and co-counsel to Dred Scott, while press speculation placed him in the War or Navy department. Lincoln, however, had others in mind for those posts and urged Montgomery to accept the postmaster generalship, recognizing the position's considerable patronage powers. As the party hoped to build a Republican base in Maryland, using what the *Baltimore Sun* called the "potent Blair element" to do so was sound logic. Blair accepted.[18]

From Washington, Seward continued to push for the inclusion of North Carolina's Gilmer as a signal to upper-South unionists. The New Yorker doubted that Montgomery Blair, renowned for his antislavery activities, could do as much good among southern moderates as the slaveholding North Carolinian. Speculation over Gilmer being given the Navy Department appeared in the *Albany Evening Journal*—information surely leaked by Weed—and the *Washington Constitution* published rumors that Robert E. Scott, an obscure former member of the Virginia legislature, was among Lincoln's "probable Southern advisors." In early January, Gilmer promised Seward that he would discuss the proposition with home-state advisers and provide "an answer in a few days." Late in the month, however, Gilmer responded to Lincoln, and although he did not flatly decline an offer, he complicated the issue by instead recommending Schuyler Colfax as a "faithful & excellent P. M. Genl." That position had already gone to Blair, and as the New York–born Colfax was then an Indiana congressman, such an appointment would have had little appeal in the upper South. When Gilmer wrote in February to again "beg & entreat" Lincoln to publicly respond to his December queries on slavery, the president-elect simply ceased any further correspondence with the congressman.[19]

Since he had determined to include Missouri's Edward Bates as early as election night, Lincoln believed he could safely abandon Gilmer and still appeal to southern moderates. Ten years before, Bates had declined Fillmore's offer of the War Department, and although he expected to receive an offer again, he confided to his diary that his "pecuniary circumstances (barely competent) and [his] settled domestic habits" made it "very undesirable" to accept a "high office with low pay." But Francis Blair Jr. urged Bates to visit the president-elect in Springfield, which he did on December 15. With his nation "in trouble and danger," Bates "felt it his duty to sacrifice his personal inclinations," and he assured Lincoln that this time he would accept any position tendered. He also thought "a good effect might be produced on the public mind—especially in the border slave States—by letting the people know" in advance of his appointment. Lincoln agreed and suggested that Bates quietly inform the editor of the Missouri *Democrat* that he "will be offered, and will accept, a place in the new Cabinet." Lincoln had not yet decided where to place Bates, and should Seward decline the State Department post, Bates would most likely get the top spot. Press speculation, incorrect as usual, guessed that the Missourian "will be Secretary of the Interior." When Seward accepted on December 28, Lincoln decided on Bates as attorney general, with Blair as postmaster.[20]

Four days prior to Seward's acceptance, Lincoln again wrote to Hamlin, asking the former Democrat to recommend a fellow "man of Democratic antecedents from New England." With Pennsylvania, New York, and the border South represented by Cameron, Seward, Bates, and Blair, respectively, the president-elect required a New Englander for balance. Lincoln had included Gideon Welles—a Connecticut journalist, attorney, and state assemblyman—on his election night list, but out of courtesy he wished the seat to be Hamlin's choice. As Lincoln-hoped, Hamlin expressed "no hesitation in saying" that Welles, whose name he misspelled, was "the better man for New England." Rumors of a Welles appointment reached the press, but as the winter of 1861 dragged along, Welles remained "in an agony of suspense." Finally, on March 1, Hamlin telegraphed Welles, urging him to head for Washington "forthwith." Impressed by Welles's former service as chief of the Bureau of Provision for the navy, if perhaps less so by his enormous, ill-fitting wig, Lincoln gave the Navy Department to the man he soon dubbed "Father Neptune."[21]

That left the Midwest without cabinet representation, apart from the president himself. For interior secretary, the least important of the seven-member body, Davis recommended Caleb B. Smith. Indiana deserved a slot, Davis argued, and Smith struck him as "the ablest man in the state." He also enjoyed a reputation for honesty, something believed to be lacking in Colfax (who in fact would later be caught up in the Crédit Mobilier scandal as Ulysses S. Grant's first vice president). The selection, Davis admitted, was also political. Not only had Smith campaigned hard for Lincoln during the previous fall, but his willingness to hand Davis the entire Indiana delegation at the Wigwam had been critical to Lincoln's nomination. "No one rendered more efficient service from Indiana at the Chicago Convention than he did," Davis reminded Lincoln. "He was the Chairman of the delegation, and without his active aid & co-operation, the Indiana delegation could not have been got as a unit to go for you." Lincoln conceded the point, and Smith became the sixth member to join Lincoln's official family.[22]

Anxious to maintain good relations with all wings of his squabbling party, Lincoln welcomed a visit from Greeley, still distraught over Seward's elevation, when the journalist traveled west in late January on a lecture tour. Realizing that it was too late to do anything about his rival's appointment, Greeley instead spent the visit condemning Cameron and pushing for the inclusion of Colfax and Salmon Chase. The former Ohio governor and senator-elect, of course, had appeared on Lincoln's original November 7 list, and next to Seward, Chase had been the nearest thing to a Republican front-runner in 1860. Although irate with his own state's delegation, Chase had written to Lincoln on May 19, pledging his support, which Lincoln had interpreted as a willingness to "stand ready" for service. Initially elected to office on a Democratic–Free Soil fusion ticket, Chase provided the cabinet with geographic and political balance.

"It seems to me not only highly proper, but a *necessity*, that Gov. Chase" should be "offered the Treasury," Lincoln explained to Trumbull. "His ability, firmness, and purity of character, produce the propriety." As for political considerations, nothing less than Chase's selection could appease Greeley and fellow editor Bryant regarding "the appointment of Gov. S. to the State Department."[23]

Chase and Seward also represented the new party's broad spectrum of opinion regarding slavery and secession. Despite his reputation among southern whites as an abolitionist, Seward continued the shift toward moderation that had characterized his course since his January 29, 1860, speech. Chase, as one journalist put it, was "the representative of the ultra wing of his party." Not much inclined to compromise with secessionists himself, Lincoln needed "two such radicals as Chase and Blair" to help hold the line against concessions that might surrender critical parts of the Chicago platform. Most of all, as much as he desired to maintain peace among the various factions of his party, Lincoln required a certain level of tension within his cabinet if he wished to maintain control of his administration. As soon as Seward's appointment was announced, newspapers controlled by Weed boasted of "his selection as [Lincoln's] 'prime minister.'" One of Lincoln's correspondents warned that "Seward would insist on being *master* of the administration, and would utterly scorn the idea of playing a subordinate part. He has no more doubt of his measureless *superiority to you*, than of his existence." In a cabinet packed with former Whigs and Seward allies, Lincoln would be relegated to the role of helpless spectator. And so it was no accident that the president-elect's final band of advisers closely resembled his original list, or that it contained none of the names Seward and Weed had submitted at the December 20 meeting.[24]

On New Year's Eve, the same day that he informed Cameron of his intention to bring him into the cabinet, Lincoln wrote to Chase: "In these troubled times, I would much like a conference with you. Please visit me here at once." Chase arrived in Springfield on January 4, after two days' travel on four railroads. He had just checked in to the Chenery House when Lincoln appeared in the lobby, asking for him. The two returned to Lincoln's office and spent a long afternoon discussing political affairs. Tall and clean-shaven, Chase struck many observers as sanctimonious and arrogant. But there was also a sadness about the thrice-widowed Chase that resonated with the melancholy, private Lincoln. Because Chase had defended so many runaway slaves in court, he remained popular with New England abolitionists, even as they began to express doubts about Seward. "Governor Chase in the Cabinet would be an omen of good," one activist wrote Lincoln from Boston. Oddly, Lincoln and Chase had never met, but as the day's conversations continued, each impressed the other.[25]

Even before Chase arrived in Springfield, rumor and speculation were rife that he was about to be offered a position. Pennsylvanians who worried that the former Democrat and free trader opposed "the cherished principle of protection to [their] industry" peppered Lincoln with complaints. One anonymous critic thought it an *"outrage"* that "such an Ultra Abolitionist should anywhere be so considered." Once burned by the Cameron debacle, Lincoln was now overly cautious. The president-elect explained to Chase that he "had felt bound" to offer secretary of state to Seward, as the New Yorker was "the generally recognized leader of the Republican party." Then, after telling Chase that he wanted him for the Treasury Department and hoped he would "accept the appointment," he added awkwardly that he was not "exactly prepared to make that offer." The problem was Pennsylvania, Lincoln admitted. The situation with the War Department remained unresolved, and Pennsylvania deserved a seat in the cabinet, but its Whiggish support for tariffs made Chase unpopular there. Chase was stunned by the non-offer and replied that he "was not prepared to say that [he] would accept that place if offered." Chase had just gained election to the Senate and indicated that he was reluctant to quit that body. But Lincoln pressed him again the next morning, and before the insulted Ohioan returned to Columbus, he hinted that he might accept the treasury secretary offer if tendered.[26]

When it became clear that Cameron had no intention of withdrawing, Lincoln concluded that Pennsylvania would have to be content with a single appointment. Chase was to get the treasury post. The news came as a blow to Seward and his supporters, who saw their hopes for a moderate, Whig-dominated cabinet with Seward as premier rapidly vanishing. "There are many busy-bodies making up Mr Lincoln's Cabinet," one New Yorker warned. Since Seward agreed so rarely with Chase and

Blair, the cabinet could never act harmoniously. Failing to grasp that Lincoln demanded a diversity of opinion from his advisers, with the president to act as the group's head and deciding voice, Seward finally wrote to complain "that he had not been consulted as was usual in the formation of the Cabinet." He "insist[ed] on the exclusion of Mr. Chase" if he were to remain in the administration. An exasperated Lincoln replied that he was "surprise[d] after all that had taken place and with the great trouble on his hands, that he should be met with such a demand on this late day." As Lincoln clearly had no intention of giving way, Seward wrote again on March 2, just two days before the inauguration. "Circumstances which have occurred since I expressed to you in December last my willingness to accept the office of Secretary of State seem to me to render it my duty to ask leave to withdraw that consent," he insisted. "Tendering to you my best wishes for the success of your administration with my sincere and grateful acknowledgements of all your acts of kindness and confidence, towards me."[27]

Believing that his carefully constructed, ideologically and geographically balanced cabinet was finally in place, Lincoln was in no mood to reshuffle his official family. "I can't afford to let Seward take the first trick," he told John Nicolay. Picking up his pen, the president-elect tried again, once more appealing to Seward's egotism. The attempted resignation was "the subject of most painful solicitude with me," Lincoln wrote. He felt "constrained to beg that you will countermand the withdrawal." The perilous times, he added, and "the public interest" demanded that he do so. The next day, Seward retracted his withdrawal. Lincoln won the hand, and remained premier of his own cabinet.[28]

There was considerable wisdom in Lincoln's strategy of placing his chief rivals within his administration, tying their careers to his and keeping them close where he could watch them. The president-elect's choices also said much about the prairie attorney's enormous self-confidence, as the group contained seven accomplished, strong-willed individuals. The cabinet never truly became the team of adversaries that Lincoln intended, however, for Chase and Seward never grew to like or respect each other. Nor did Chase ever cease to aspire to higher office, and at length Lincoln grew weary of his presidential dreams. Chase quit the cabinet in June 1864, and when the aged Roger Taney died that October, Lincoln removed this persistent thorn by naming Chase the new chief justice, a position he retained until his death in 1873. Still, if the cabinet contained more than its share of difficult personalities, the only mediocrity was Cameron. As the *Philadelphia Inquirer* gushed, Lincoln's choices "present a tower of strength in fitness, ability, and character." The editor's "one anxiety" was over "the position which General Cameron should occupy." When the war proved the *Inquirer's* concerns valid, Lincoln removed Cameron, in January 1862, and replaced him with the exceedingly competent Edwin Stanton.[29]

Five hundred and fifty miles to the south, in Montgomery, Alabama, an entirely new government, and not merely a cabinet, was in the process of coming together. When Andrew Pickens Calhoun arrived at the Alabama secession convention as a commissioner from South Carolina, he carried with him his state's formal invitation to Alabama to meet in a

President-elect Lincoln filled his cabinet with political rivals and sought both sectional and ideological balance. This image from July 1861, left to right, depicts Montgomery Blair, Interior Secretary Caleb B. Smith, Salmon P. Chase, Lincoln, William Henry Seward, Simon Cameron, Edward Bates, and Gideon Welles. Courtesy Library of Congress.

regional convention to create a slaveholding confederacy. As an incentive, the South Carolina legislature had instructed Calhoun to recommend Montgomery as the meeting place. The suggestion had logic. The market town was located in the heart of what was expected to be the southern republic, and it enjoyed good railroad and river transportation. The city council had recently invested $5,271 in a string of lampposts and gas lines to illuminate Main Street, and one visitor described it as "a nice, tidy little Southern town." At the heart of the South's rich-soiled black belt, Montgomery was surrounded by cotton fields valued at roughly $51 million; more than 130,000 bales of cotton shipped across its docks each year. On a per capita basis, the town was in one of the wealthiest regions in the South. It was also home to the prince of the fire-eaters.[30]

In other ways, though, the choice was an inauspicious beginning for the new nation. The ornate gas lamps could not disguise the fact that Main Street, which stretched from the state capitol down to the Alabama River, was less a grand boulevard than a sandy, rutted sewer. Less than two decades before, a team of oxen had drowned on Main when a sudden storm had transformed the street into a muddy river. In 1860, the population of Manhattan and the Bronx stood at 805,658; by comparison, Montgomery was home to but 8,843, a majority of whom were enslaved. One critic sneered that the young town had been "laid out before the surveyor's compass was in use," and though it intended to host a major regional convention, it could boast only two hotels, Montgomery Hall and the Exchange House, which visitors found as expensive as they were filthy. Not surprisingly, given the experience that Democratic delegates had with Charleston hoteliers, the Confederate Congress would debate members' pay in secret session to keep Montgomery's proprietors from gouging them.[31]

The Montgomery conference formally got under way on February 4, although many delegates had been in town for several days. As representatives from the six states that had thus far seceded settled into their seats in the capitol, William Parish Chilton, Yancey's law partner and a member of the state senate, gaveled the proceedings to order. The delegates then graced Robert Barnwell Rhett with the honorific title of convention president before selecting Howell Cobb as the permanent president. Although the original invitations sent by South Carolina had only proposed creating a new regional government, the Georgia delegates suggested that they also assume the functions of a legislative body, which was approved. Even for Alabama, the day was sunny and warm, and the enthusiastic delegates took that as a good omen. After Cobb was called to the chair, he delivered a brief speech of acceptance. Of "the causes" that led to secession, he need say little, but their course was "now a fixed and irrevocable fact," and secession was "perfect, complete, and perpetual." Their revolution, he hoped, was to be a nonviolent one. "With a consciousness of the justice of our cause, and with confidence in the guidance and blessings of a kind Providence," Cobb concluded, "we will this day inaugurate for the South a new era of peace, security, and prosperity."[32]

As had the founders in Philadelphia eighty-five years before, the architects of this very different sort of republic then divided into committees. Rhett and James Chesnut lobbied to serve on the committee to devise a Confederate Constitution. (Chesnut also served on the Committee on Territories, an indication of Confederate plans for westward expansion.) For the two South Carolinians, this was the chance to revisit American foundations and forge a purely slaveholding republic, and Rhett especially was determined to purge their document of potential limits on the slave trade with Africa, repeal the three-fifths clause, and explicitly exclude free states from their union. As a strict constructionist, Chesnut also wished an explicit right of secession to be written into the document, and Mary Chesnut, who joined her husband in Montgomery, "could hear scratch scratch go the pen" late into the night. The three veiled references to slavery in the 1787 Constitution had all resulted from regional compromises, but free of northern states, lower-South ultras now dreamed of a republic perfectly suited to the planter class. As the younger Rhett editorialized in the *Mercury*; "it now remains to be seen whether, with slave institutions, the master race can establish and perpetuate free government."[33]

Rhett's dreams began to dissipate when moderates, particularly Robert Toombs and Alexander Stephens, informed him that some of his more extreme ideas could never survive a floor fight. Thomas R. R. Cobb agreed with Rhett that entire free states should never be allowed to join the Confederacy, but others suggested that portions of some, such as the

Little Egypt section of Illinois, might wish to join for commercial reasons. And counting each slave as a full person for legislative apportionment, rather than counting only three out of five, would boost South Carolina's representation but inhibit secession in the upper South, where whites greatly outnumbered blacks. Most southerners, in any case, did not object to most of the original Constitution; they simply disagreed with the loose interpretation increasingly embraced by the North. Most changes were thus small. The preamble was adapted to read, "We, the people of the Confederate States," and to ensure that no president could amass too much power, the executive was limited to a single, six-year term. Where the original Constitution made vague references to "person[s] held to service or labor," Rhett's document was explicit. Representation was to be based on "three-fifths of all slaves," and the Constitution banned any "law denying or impairing the right of property in negro slaves." It allowed for the acquisition of "new territory" and protected "the institution of negro slavery, as it now exists in the Confederate States," on the frontier as well. "No slave or other person held to service or labor" in any state would become free by "escaping" into another. And much to Rhett's dismay, the "importation of negroes of the African race from any foreign country other than the slaveholding States or Territories of the United States of America [was] forbidden."[34]

For South Carolina radicals, the convention's refusal to reopen the transatlantic traffic in humans was worrisome evidence that moderates were methodically seizing control of their revolution. "Either Negro slavery is a beneficent, merciful, God-chartered institution, or it is not," fumed William Gilmore Simms. "If beneficent, why limit it?" The *Mercury* agreed. The entire "world" was determined "to assert that slavery itself is wrong," the younger Rhett editorialized, "and if we forgo the slave trade in consideration of the moral feelings of the world, then why not slavery also?" But the lopsided convention vote of 66 to 13 to ban the trade had nothing to do with moral qualms. Since most ships that had brought Africans to Charleston and Savannah had hailed from New England ports, a return to African shores would mean a reliance on northern merchants. Most slaves sold into the Southwest were born in the Chesapeake, and lifting the congressional prohibition of 1807 would do little to pull Virginia and Maryland into the Confederacy. "If Texas shall want labor," John Perkins of Louisiana conceded, "she must be content with that *only* which comes from other States on this continent." Even if the upper South decided to remain in the Union, Virginia was "at least assured of a market for her slaves at undiminished prices," and the Confederacy retained a key ally within the United States.[35]

Rhett and Simms were not wrong in suspecting that the small cadre of hotspurs that had labored for this moment for over a year was being quietly shoved aside. Popular revolutions, of course, always required charismatic orators and determined dreams to launch the revolts, but once under way, new nations needed stolid builders, and those whose tendencies ran toward destruction were no longer useful. For disgruntled fire-eaters, Montgomery suddenly seemed too much like the old capital, a town filled with moderate men of elastic principles. As Mary Chesnut complained, "political intrigue is as rife as in Washington." But their infant republic, she conceded, "must be supported now by calm determination and cool brains." Rhett chaired several important committees, including Foreign Affairs, but he dominated and controlled none of them. As committees often met in secret session, admiring Montgomery women were unable to hear Yancey's radical eloquence, which in any case was no longer essential to the movement. For ultra delegates, the only promising note in the convention's first week was word that Texas had finally seceded and was sending representatives.[36]

As agonizing as the compromises over the Constitution might have been, the Convention had done the easy work first, and its members knew it. The most momentous question facing the assembly was who would lead the new nation. As the most populous of the lower-South states, Georgia, one editor argued, "ought to be called upon to furnish the first president." Georgia, however, had three possible contenders—Stephens, Howell Cobb, and Toombs—all of whom were present in Montgomery. All had impressive résumés that easily surpassed those of any other delegates. Stephens had served in Congress since 1843, the same year that Cobb had arrived in Washington; following his service in the House, Cobb had been elected governor and, until his recent resignation, had been Buchanan's treasury secretary. Cobb's younger brother, Thomas, was also present in Montgomery and was active on behalf of his sibling, whose influential position as convention president was another factor in his favor. Toombs, a tall, broad-shouldered man, had served in Congress almost as long as Stephens and Cobb and in 1852 had been elevated into the Senate, a position he had retained until just a few days before the convention had met.[37]

Despite his visibility at the convention, Cobb refused to lobby for the position (which the convention intended to bestow on a provisional basis). He assured his wife that "the presidency of the Confederacy is an office I cannot seek and shall feel no disappointment in not getting." Early American politicians were always forced to walk the fine line between ambition and indifference, and as Sam Houston had discovered, the danger in tilting too far toward the latter was that observers could never decide how seriously to take such claims. "So far from making an effort to obtain" the presidency, Cobb insisted in a second letter to his wife, "I have frankly said to my friends that I greatly prefer not to be put there." He evidently neglected to pass that sentiment along to his brother, who frantically continued to argue his case. But enough delegates were convinced that Cobb honestly regarded the presidency as "a most undesirable position" that he was dropped from consideration. He would have to settle for the position of speaker in the Confederate Congress; later he served in the field as brigadier general. His brother Thomas was to die at Fredericksburg.[38]

The enormous Toombs and the diminutive Stephens carried even greater baggage. Both were former Whigs in a convention dominated by Democrats, and Stephens's vote against secession in the Georgia convention had won him few friends even among moderates. Despite the disarray among the Georgia representatives, however, Toombs might still have gotten the nod had he ever learned the virtue of self-discipline. Unlike Stephens, who sipped whiskey from a teaspoon almost from the time he rose in the morning, Toombs was no alcoholic. But despite his robust size, he could not hold his liquor. "When he measured himself with others, glass for glass," one friend admitted, "the result was distressing, disastrous." Two nights before the convention chose a president, Toombs made the mistake of his life. He wandered back and forth from his table to the sideboard, continuously refilling his champagne glass. Even by the standards of an era that deemed excess no vice, Toombs lost all control, launching into a wild tale of how South Carolina governor Francis Pickens had sent him a telegraph saying that shore batteries had opened fire on Sumter. Stephens was forced to explain to the startled delegates that when Toombs drank, he became "a monomaniac." The "fits wear off very soon," Stephens promised, "and tomorrow he will have no recollection of what has occurred." For men facing the prospect of war with their industrializing neighbor, Toombs's bizarre "exhibition," Stephens later remarked, "settled the Presidency."[39]

For southern firebrands, only Cobb was appropriately radical, and he just barely. The "fire-eaters per se wanted [Robert] Barnwell Rhett" for the presidency, Mary Chesnut reported, and the South Carolinian thought the position his due. Yancey was also ready to accept the post if offered it. But only a handful of dogmatic supporters could imagine either man as chief executive, and not simply because their beliefs marked the fringes of the southern political spectrum. Neither possessed the temperament to govern. Rhett had resigned his Senate seat in 1852 when South Carolina had responded to the Compromise of 1850 by meekly passing an ordinance upholding a state's right to secede, and Yancey's brief tenure in the House of Representatives had been as stormy as it had been devoid of actual legislative accomplishment. As with the Atlantic slave trade, delegates hoped to seduce the upper South into their Confederacy, and a President Rhett or Yancey would all but guarantee Virginia's loyalty to the Union.[40]

And then there was Jefferson Davis. Although the Mississippi senator had remained in Washington until the withdrawal of his state, he had maintained almost daily contact with allies in both Jackson, Mississippi, and Montgomery. Even while still drawing a salary as senator in December, Davis quietly began to advise Governor John Pettus on the purchase of weapons for the state militia, and when Mississippi seceded in early January, Davis resigned his seat and telegraphed Pettus to secure him a position. The governor did just that by appointing the Mexican-American War veteran as a major general in the state's forces. In Montgomery, many delegates assumed he would play a similar role for the Confederacy, and Mary Chesnut recorded that "everybody wanted Mr. Davis to be general in chief." But when Toombs proceeded to drink himself out of the presidency, delegates increasingly began to consider Davis for a higher post. In later years, Robert E. Lee described his former commander in chief as "one of the extremist politicians." But despite his frequent adoption of ultra positions, Davis's calm, even aloof demeanor kept most observers from perceiving him as such. Davis was "not by any means the *fire eater* which many Northern presses have represented him," proclaimed the *Macon Daily Telegraph.*[41]

Compounding these deliberations was the fact that had Virginia already seceded, its population, wealth, and prestige would surely have guaranteed it the presidency. Rumor had it that Senator Robert M.T. Hunter was being discussed for the position, with Senator James M. Mason as secretary of state and Davis in the War Department. But with the drive for secession stalled in Virginia, the Montgomery delegates had to choose from the materials available to them, especially since they wished to have their government functioning by March 4, when Lincoln would take office. For those yet undecided, news from Virginia that Hunter and Mason favored Davis proved decisive. Mississippi backed its senator, as did Florida and Alabama; the former had no candidate, and the latter understood that Yancey's fanaticism prevented his selection. Stephens continued to endorse Toombs, but when Cobb announced "his wish that Davis should be unanimously elected," even his brother Thomas abandoned his campaign. Toombs, who, true to form, had completely forgotten his drunken performance of two nights before, was stunned by the sudden stampede toward Davis. Meeting behind closed doors, the convention chose the Mississippi senator around eleven o'clock on the morning of Saturday, February 9.[42]

Despite the unanimous vote, not all of the delegates were pleased. A disappointed Thomas R.R. Cobb continued to protest that Davis was "a reconstructionist" who would use the presidency to reunite with the United States. Unless the new president clarified his goals in his inaugural address, Cobb hinted, "we shall have an explosion here." Others admitted that Davis could be stiff, humorless, and difficult to get along with. Even Varina Howell Davis once conceded that her husband "did not know the arts of the politician and would not practise them if understood." But as they believed the convention was running out of time and options, most delegates thought his choice the lesser of several evils. A few observers actually regarded his icy aloofness as an admirable trait for a chief executive. The selection of this "statesman of great power,"

A West Point graduate and veteran of the Mexican War, Davis boasted an impressive résumé that also included secretary of war under Pierce and chairman of the Senate Committee on Military Affairs. Southerners were certain that when it came to commanders in chief, they had the better of the two. Courtesy Library of Congress.

insisted one Georgia editor, demonstrated "the wisdom and good sense of the Southern Congress."[43]

With a Mississippian in the executive's chair, a Georgian was sure to win the consolation prize of the vice presidency. Cobb and Toombs were out. Neither desired the second spot, and Toombs continued to drink until "mellow" every evening, as Stephens delicately put it. That left Stephens himself. Although he too protested that he had no desire to serve, his candidacy could come as no surprise, since James Chesnut had first raised the possibility as the two had traveled toward Montgomery. Once the convention began, two Mississippi delegates pressed Stephens to accept the presidency if it was tendered, and when he finally agreed after two hours of argument, they took that to mean that he would assent to the second spot as well. Ironically, the fact that Stephens had opposed his state's secession cost him the presidency but won him the vice presidency. Pragmatic representatives understood that they now had to unify their new nation, and a high-visibility post for a former Whig and a Unionist could do so. Even the radical Louis Wigfall, whose Texas delegation had yet to reach Alabama, telegraphed ahead in support of Stephens. The United States had witnessed the death of two presidents in the previous twenty years, but Davis appeared healthy, while the sickly, alcoholic vice president, according to one delegate, was "so feeble [in] frame yet [with] such spirit and intellect."[44]

As was the case with Hannibal Hamlin, the choice of Stephens was designed to appease an important region and pull the broad southern Democratic Party together. Yet even in a century when vice presidents rarely attended cabinet meetings, the selection proved to be unfortunate. If his political positions were more moderate than Davis's, his personality was even more rigid and intractable. Given to curious hatreds—he despised the waltz, railing against the "follies of man" who had invented the sinful dance—and wont to hold grudges, Stephens was to devote the next four years to feuding with Davis. Fire-eaters such as Thomas R.R. Cobb opposed his selection as "a bitter pill," although they conceded the logic behind it. Even his inaugural on February 11—his forty-ninth birthday—got off to an inauspicious start when he declined to say more than a few words. Despite the large crowd gathered outside the Exchange House, Stephens disappointed the throng by merely pledging to support whatever policies Davis's "superior wisdom and statesmanship" might reveal. If they desired a lengthier speech, Stephens churlishly added, they should return in a few days to hear Davis.[45]

Two days before, Davis had received word of his appointment. It fell to Toombs to telegraph the news to Vicksburg, a mere twenty miles above the Davis Bend plantations (adjacent estates owned by Jefferson and his brother Joseph). Recognizing the importance of the telegram, the Vicksburg operator hired a "discreet messenger" to gallop down the river road. When the rider reached the plantation, Jefferson and Varina were trimming rosebushes. "We are directed to inform You that You were this day unanimously elected President of the provisional Government of the Confederate States of America," Davis read. Varina later recorded that the look on her husband's face was so grim that she "feared some evil had befallen our family." After twenty-five years in politics, Davis understood what was expected of him, and in a brief note of acceptance that he scribbled out for the weary rider to carry back to Vicksburg, he insisted that the office was "much more than [he] deserved" and "far more of official honors than [he] desired." But, he added, "whatever circumstances demand shall be met as a duty."[46]

After five exhausting days of travel, Davis arrived in Montgomery around ten o'clock in the evening on February 16. A crowd had gathered at the depot, and Davis stepped off the train to the strains of "Dixie" and the inevitable booming of cannons. Weary from his trip, Davis shouted but a few words—"Our separation from the old Union is complete. No compromise; no reconstruction can now be entertained"—before heading for the Exchange House and bed. But at the hotel a far larger throng awaited, led by a beaming Yancey. After briefly promising to devote "all I have of heart, of head and of hand" to the cause, Davis begged off from fatigue and hoarseness. Standing on the hotel balcony, Yancey was more than happy to take over. "The man and the hour have met," he roared. "Prosperity, honor and victory await his administration." Davis shook a few more hands and met Mary Lincoln's pro-secession sisters, who informed an amused Davis that they were not responsible for their sibling's poor choice in a husband.[47]

Following a quiet Sunday devoted to rest and the preparation of his inaugural address, Davis, somewhat refreshed, awoke early on February

18. As the men of Montgomery wished to depict themselves as the revolutionary heirs of the nation's founders, they had planned the day's festivities in imitation of George Washington's 1789 inaugural event. As had the earlier president in Manhattan, Davis and Stephens rode in an open barouche drawn by six gray horses. Led by a brass band, the procession crept slowly up Market Street toward the capitol. The day was cloudy and cold, but the "audience was large and brilliant upon my weary heart," Davis confided to his wife, and they "showered smiles plaudits and flowers." Those close enough to see the carriage were impressed by the fifty-two-year-old Davis's dignified, military bearing. Although his blind eye was covered with a thin film, the other, according to one witness, blazed with "fire and intelligence." Howell Cobb guessed that the crowd numbered ten thousand, but Montgomery was home to just 4,341 whites, and nobody bothered to record how many of the city's enslaved majority turned out to celebrate a government, as the *Montgomery Advertiser* bragged, founded "on the basis of *liberty, equality and independency for white men, and slavery for negroes.*"[48]

When the pageant reached the capitol, Davis pushed his way through the throng and into the building; a number of admiring women handed him flowers, and one draped a wreath over one of his arms. At one o'clock, Cobb introduced Davis, and "one universal shout rent the air." Always too stiff and formal to be a dynamic speaker, Davis spent several long minutes explaining the legal basis for secession and how the separate states had "merely asserted the right which the Declaration of Independence of 1776 defined to be inalienable." Their actions, he insisted, were "a necessity, not a choice." Unlike other orators in the various secession conventions and in Montgomery, Davis said almost nothing as to *why* the lower South had seceded, only that "a re-union with the States from which we have separated is neither practicable nor desirable." The new country he was asked to lead, Davis observed, desired "peaceably to pursue our separate political career," but if that was "denied us, and the integrity and jurisdiction of our territory be assailed, it will but remain for us with a firm resolve to appeal to arms and invoke the blessings of Providence upon a just cause." Since there was no Confederate chief justice, Cobb then administered the oath of office, to which Davis added, "So help me God," and kissed the Bible on which his hand rested.[49]

Almost concealed by the ceremonial, legalistic tone of the brief address of 1,848 words were two significant points. Davis argued that since the original intent of the Union had "been perverted from the purposes for which it was ordained," the South was justified in its "peaceful appeal to the ballot box." In reality, it was Lincoln, with his 1,865,908 votes, who was the product of popular democracy. With the exception of Texas, no seceded state had put the momentous question of disunion to anything approaching a statewide referendum. The withdrawal of seven states had been the work of 854 convention delegates, 157 of whom had voted against secession and most of whom had been chosen by state legislatures. Davis himself had been selected president by approximately 80 delegates; by comparison, the despised Stephen A. Douglas had received 1,380,201 votes, 3,282 of them in Davis's Mississippi. By referring to a vote that had never taken place, Davis attempted to disguise the harsh truth that his was a planters' rebellion. Not until too late did the region's yeoman majority begin to curse the resulting carnage as "a rich man's war and a poor man's fight."[50]

The second significant point in the address was the one left unstated. By repudiating any hopes of reunion, Davis appeased most of Montgomery's firebrands. But those fire-eaters who hoped the wealthy Mississippi planter would also explain the nature of their new republic were disappointed spectators. Never once in the speech did Davis even hint at the institution he once defended as of "Divine decree," a topic that others at the convention were hardly reluctant to identify as the root of this irrepressible conflict. Perhaps Davis took that reality for granted, but many observers expected the new president to mark the birth of his republic with a statement of his profound beliefs. Aware that his inaugural was being covered by journalists from both sides of the Atlantic, however, the pragmatic Davis chose to soften his remarks. Not until his April 29 address to the Confederate Congress, in fact, did the president attribute secession to "a persistent and organized system of hostile measures" waged by northern politicians "for the purpose of rendering insecure the tenure of property in slaves." As the owner of more than two hundred black Americans, President Davis regarded slave labor as "indispensable" to southern prosperity, and after the Republicans had earned an electoral majority, he claimed, the planter class had been driven "to the adoption of some course of action to avert the danger with which they were openly menaced."[51]

Lacking an office, Davis settled into his hotel suite, where he began to piece together his cabinet. On February 22, the Confederate Congress appropriated five thousand dollars for the annual leasing of an executive mansion, located two blocks from the Exchange House. Varina joined Jefferson there on March 1 and pronounced the two-story clapboard house "roomy enough for our purposes." Eighteen years younger than her husband—whose first wife, Sarah Taylor, the daughter of former president Zachary Taylor, had died in 1835 after just three months of marriage—Varina struck one observer as "a comely, sprightly woman, verging on matronhood, of good figure and manners, well-dressed, lady-like and clever." Although born in Natchez, Mississippi, she had attended school in Philadelphia and privately considered Montgomery "a strange community." Mary Chesnut thought it obvious that Varina missed Washington, and her tendency to gush about her former friends made her "somewhat unpopular" among politicians' wives in attendance. But the women of Montgomery, thrilled to have so much excitement visit their hamlet, sent her flowers and, as a way of personalizing their affection, a white satin case, inscribed "C.S.A., 1861" and containing a bouquet woven from strands of their hair.[52]

On February 20, the Confederate Congress passed the requisite legislation to create six cabinet positions (declining to authorize an Interior Department). Unlike his northern counterpart, Davis gave no thought to sounding out potential members in advance, since he assumed that appointees would simply regard it as their duty to serve the new nation if asked. Like Lincoln, however, the Confederate president paid close attention to geography. As there were now seven seceded states but only six seats at the cabinet table, Davis concluded that he should represent Mississippi, with each of the other states earning one slot. Stephens had boasted that he "intended to use his influence on Davis to persuade him toward the best possible cabinet appointments," but if he knew about the unusual courtesy that Lincoln had afforded Hamlin by asking his advice, Stephens was to be very disappointed. Davis cared nothing about the former Whig's opinions, and Cobb complained that the president "consults no one out of his own State." Not expecting to be offered a position, Cobb coolly informed Davis that he "positively refused to go into the cabinet."[53]

In part because Davis stubbornly refused to take anybody into his confidence, guesses as to who was to fill the various cabinet posts surpassed even the speculation that had swirled around Springfield. One newspaper, which reported that Herschel Johnson of Georgia had been offered secretary of state, managed to get only one name correct: Stephen Mallory of Florida, who was appointed secretary of the navy. Another journal speculated that Yancey was to get secretary of state, and that Thomas R.R. Cobb would "take the part of Chief Justice of the Supreme Court." (Since the Confederate Congress never found time to pass the legislation necessary to create one, there never was a Confederate Supreme Court.) For the State Department, Davis wanted Robert W. Barnwell, an obscure South Carolina planter. He had known the South Carolinian, he later wrote, "during a trying period of our joint service in the United States Senate." But Rhett opposed his distant kinsman as too moderate, and when Barnwell declined on the grounds that he knew nothing about foreign affairs, Davis offered the job to Toombs, who also begged to be excused, for the same reason. Davis persisted and, perhaps in unconscious imitation of his Illinois rival, submitted the name of his closest presidential contender to the Senate for confirmation.[54]

With Barnwell out of the equation, and with Georgia and Florida settled, Davis needed to find another South Carolinian for treasury secretary, the second-most prestigious appointment. As the principal author of South Carolina's Declaration of Immediate Causes, Christopher Memminger was perhaps the most famous man in the state next to Rhett. In the early 1840s, Memminger had served, between stints in the state assembly, as director of Charleston's Planters and Mechanics Bank. Few could claim, as they did of Toombs (who lasted but six months in the State Department), that Davis had chosen the "right man for the wrong job." But the brilliant Memminger, who had finished second in his class at the South Carolina College at the age of sixteen, was brighter than most of his colleagues and was never shy about saying so. One Confederate bureaucrat was to later complain that Memminger "treats others with rudeness, and is, besides, dogmatical [and] narrow-minded." The devout Christian also refused to work on Sundays, and he frequently if unsuccessfully urged other cabinet members to follow his example. Few liked him personally, and Wigfall later scoffed that Memminger proposed to finance the government by leaving collection bags in church.[55]

Alabama required a seat, and as Yancey had almost single-handedly destroyed the Democratic Party, Davis knew that he had to make an elaborate show of offering him a position. The two met in Davis's suite on the afternoon following the inauguration. Having once dreamed of the presidency, Yancey had no interest in a minor cabinet post, and when Davis offered him the attorney generalship, the Alabaman bluntly replied that he could not retain his radical supporters at home while working within an administration that was already being praised for its moderation. Adept at placing people in positions that ill suited their talents, Davis then offered Yancey the diplomatic mission to Britain, evidently unconcerned that his infamous impatience and quick temper might be handicaps in delicate foreign diplomacy. Yancey accepted, but would quit London within the year, returning home to die at age forty-eight of bladder and kidney disease.[56]

Alabama's seat instead went to Leroy P. Walker, who received the War Department. A native of Huntsville and an attorney rather than a soldier, Walker was the one undeniable fire-eater in Davis's official family. He at least looked the part. One reporter described him as "tall, lean, straighthaired, angular, with fiery impulsive eyes and manner." But chronic tobacco chewing had left him in ill health, and a discerning Mary Chesnut thought him a "slow coach." Never having served in even the state assembly, Walker substituted confidence for administrative ability. He so admired the sanguinary metaphors used by Rhett and James Chesnut that he boasted he would be able to wipe up all of the blood shed in a conflict with his pocket handkerchief. When pressed to explain how he intended to translate that boast into policy, he simply added that if war began, the Confederate flag would soon be waving over the capitol in Washington, and perhaps Boston's Faneuil Hall as well. When the fighting actually began, Davis, himself a former secretary of war, treated Walker like a clerk. The Alabaman resigned after seven months' service.[57]

With now-former-governor Houston continuing to loudly oppose his state's secession, the Texas seat, that of postmaster general, went to John

H. Reagan, a congressman before his state's departure from the Union. But the surprise appointment was that of Attorney General Judah P. Benjamin. Born in the Danish colony of St. Thomas during a period of British occupation, Benjamin immigrated to the South as a boy and grew up in both Carolinas before entering Yale College at the age of fourteen. Finally settling in Louisiana, where he purchased a plantation and 150 slaves, Benjamin won a seat in the U.S. Senate as only its second Jewish member. His religion remained an issue, and Republican senator Benjamin Wade once denounced the slaveholder as "an Israelite with Egyptian principles." But despite a near duel with Davis in 1853 over a perceived slight, the two men had grown close, and the president correctly regarded Benjamin as a

Like Lincoln, Davis was also concerned about regional balance in his official family. His original cabinet, left to right, included Attorney General Judah P. Benjamin, Stephen Mallory, Christopher Memminger, Vice President Alexander Stephens, Leroy Pope Walker, Davis, Postmaster General John Reagan, and Robert Toombs. Toombs would not finish out the year in his post, and after briefly serving in the War Department, Benjamin became Davis's third and final Secretary of State.
Courtesy Library of Congress.

person of "systematic habits and capacity for labor." Over the next four years, Benjamin would briefly serve as Davis's second secretary of war before becoming his third and final secretary of state.[58]

Then as now, journalists and historians emphasized the fact that apart from Walker, Davis barred radicals from his cabinet. Even the *New York Herald* admired how "much wisdom" was displayed in the Confederate president's choices, "the extremists and fire-eaters having been carefully excluded." Modern scholars also observe that for a region generally regarded as aristocratic, most of those who earned a seat in the cabinet were of humble origins. Reagan's father was a tanner, and he himself began his career as a plantation overseer for hire. Memminger briefly lived in an orphanage following his arrival in Charleston. Mallory's father was a Connecticut mariner, and his mother ran a boardinghouse in Key West. Benjamin, the son of a Portuguese mother, was the ultimate outsider; one friendly home-state newspaper joked that he "was born nowhere in particular," and poet Stephen Vincent Benét dubbed him "the dapper Jew" and "dark prince" of the Confederacy.[59]

In no century and in no country, of course, were claims to aristocracy ever based as much on etiquette as they were on class power. Edmund Ruffin might snicker that yeomen could not achieve sophistication above the level of "boors who reap rich harvests from the fat soil of Belgium." Yet what supported the planters' pretensions to southern nobility was not their gentle births, but their ownership of hundreds of black Americans and the fortunes they amassed from the toil of unpaid workers. Toombs owned 102 slaves, and the value of his real and personal estate was $232,000. Memminger owned 35 bondpersons, Benjamin 140, and together with his brother Joseph, Davis owned roughly 500 slaves. Almost as unnoticed is the fact that most of Davis's selections, with the exception of Benjamin, were either ill suited for their particular post or, as in the case of Walker, simply incompetent. Among Lincoln's choices, only Cameron—and that unfortunate secretary was essentially forced upon the president-elect by Seward and David Davis—proved inept. Over the course of the next four years, no fewer than seventeen men rotated through the six seats in the Confederate cabinet; only Reagan would begin and end the war with the same title. Lincoln desperately wanted competent advisers "to share the burden," but Davis had little inclination to delegate authority. As one Confederate congressman quipped while his colleagues speculated on possible appointments, "for Secretary of State, [it would be] Hon. Jeff. Davis of Miss.; War and Navy, Jeff. Davis of Miss.; Interior, ex-Senator Davis, of Miss.; Treasury, Col. Davis, of Miss.; Attorney General, Mr. Davis, of Miss."[60]

If the Confederate president was unexpectedly coy about discussing the fundamental nature of the government he led, the same did not hold true for his vice president. In late March, Stephens returned to Georgia, where a state convention met to ratify the Confederate Constitution. When the gathering invited him to address the assembly, meeting in Savannah's Athenaeum, he was pleased to do so. Although Stephens spoke without preparation, the talk, which would come to be known as the "Cornerstone Speech," provided the vice president with the opportunity to defend the new Constitution, explain the necessity of secession, and elucidate why this new government was preferable to the old Union. Thrilled that their state had won the second position in the Confederacy, the people in the audience were in good humor, and as Stephens approached the stage, they spent several minutes whistling and stamping their feet in applause.[61]

When the audience at last fell silent, the vice president began. He started by discussing several unique features of the new Constitution; cabinet heads, for example, could sit with members of the House, and the president was restricted to a single term of office. Most significant of all, however, was the fact that the "new constitution has put at rest, *forever*, all the agitating questions relating to our peculiar institution." The "proper *status* of the negro in our form of civilization," Stephens observed, "was the immediate cause of the late rupture." Thomas Jefferson had long predicted that slavery would divide the nation, but the Virginian "and most of the leading statesmen at the time" were wrong in believing "that the enslavement of the African was in violation of the laws of nature; that it was wrong in *principle*, socially, morally, and politically." That view explained why the word "slavery" never appeared in the original Constitution, Stephens insisted, as the founders "rested upon the assumption of the equality of races. This was an error."[62]

As the spectators howled in support, Stephens warmed to his topic. "Our new government is founded upon exactly the opposite idea," he shouted, "its foundations are laid, its corner-stone rests upon the great truth, that the negro is not equal to the white man; that slavery—subordination to the superior race—is his natural and normal condition." The founders had spoken of an inherent right to liberty, but this "new government, [was] the first, in the history of the world, based upon this great physical, philosophical, and moral truth." Now that the South was freed from "the anti-slavery fanatics" and their "species of insanity," it could again turn its attention to the West and be secure in the knowledge that slavery would be protected in the territories it expected to acquire. "With us, all of the white race, however high or low, rich or poor, are equal in the eyes of the law," Stephens explained. "Not so with the negro. Subordination is his place. He, by nature, or by the curse of Canaan, is fitted for that condition which he occupies in our system."[63]

The speech was widely reprinted, and for fire-eaters who had suspected Stephens of unionist tendencies, the ringing defense of human bondage erased any lingering doubts. Proslavery expansionists especially found much to applaud, but the editor of the Georgia *Sun* thought that the vice president's allusions "to the probable expansion of the Confederate States" into the West did not go far enough. "The South must [also] occupy Mexico, to prevent the Abolitionists getting on the southern border," he argued. "Surely it is no greater wrong to carry negroes to Mexico," which had abolished slavery in 1829, "than it was to carry them here; and it is no greater wrong to carry negroes to Mexico than it is to hold the negroes now here in bondage." Employing the same logic used by Rhett and other advocates of reopening the transatlantic slave trade, the editor insisted that "the motto of 'might makes right' must often be adopted," since "a 'cordon of Free States' must never surround the God-given institution of slavery."[64]

The reception across the North was considerably less enthusiastic. Several Democratic-leaning newspapers, including the *New York Herald* and the *Crisis*, a rabidly anti-Lincoln journal from Columbus, Ohio, thought the address "bold, manly, and to the purpose." Most Republicans found Stephens's honesty bracing, even though they were appalled by his message. "Mr. Stephens's extreme ideas on the slavery question," reflected one Massachusetts editor, should "convince many doubting minds of the folly of endeavoring to propitiate or satisfy the rebel states by concessions." Those who backed Seward's shift toward moderation, as well as almost all northern Democrats, continued to believe that if the president-elect would only give way on the territories, the course of secession could yet be reversed. But Stephens's assault on cherished American ideals of equality, the *Lowell Daily Citizen and News* maintained, "show[ed] quite clearly the precise character of those concessions which will be required of the people of the free states." White southerners could talk all they wished about potential Republican belligerence, but the vice president's words revealed "the real reasons for revolution to be something far different from northern aggression or infidelity to the constitution."[65]

Several weeks earlier, in Springfield, a very different sort of speech was heard. The president-elect had been engaged in final arrangements prior to his departure for Washington. He and Mary rented out their home to Lucian Tilton, a retired railroad president, for $350 a year. Lincoln paid a final call on William Herndon, his law partner of sixteen years. Glancing up at the shingle of "Lincoln & Herndon" hanging above the door, Lincoln urged his old friend to leave the sign in place. "If I live I'm coming back some time," he added quietly, "and then we'll go right on practising law as if nothing ever happened." The next morning, February 11, Lincoln and his large entourage left the Chenery House at seven thirty and boarded an omnibus for the Great Western Railroad depot. Mary and their two youngest sons would travel separately to St. Louis to buy clothes, but accompanying the president-elect was his eldest son, Robert Todd Lincoln, secretaries John Nicolay and John Hay, David Davis, and Ward Hill Lamon, Lincoln's associate from his circuit-riding days, who had appointed himself as guard. Lincoln had roped up the family trunks himself, tacking handwritten cards to the boxes reading, "A. Lincoln, White House, Washington, D.C." Jameson Jenkins, a black porter, loaded them into the baggage car as Lincoln climbed the steps to his private coach.[66]

When he reached the platform, Lincoln turned to gaze at the city he was never again to see. Although the morning was cold, with a persistent drizzle, "nearly 1000 citizens had already collected" to see him off. Despite the light rain, Lincoln doffed his hat, prompting those around the train to do the same, and he began to speak.[67]

"My Friends—No one not in my position can appreciate the sadness

I feel at this parting. To this people I owe all that I am. For more than a quarter of a century I have lived among you, and during all that time I have received nothing but kindness at your hands. Here I have lived from my youth until now I am an old man. Here the most sacred ties of earth were assumed; here my children were born, and here one of them lies buried. I know not how soon I shall see you all again. A duty devolves upon me which is perhaps greater than that which has devolved upon any other man since the days of Washington. He never would have succeeded except for the aid of Divine Providence, upon which he at all times relied. I feel that I cannot succeed without the same Divine aid which sustained him, and on the same Almighty Being I place my reliance for support. I hope you, my friends, will all pray that I may receive that Divine assistance without which I cannot succeed, but with which success is certain. Again I bid you an affectionate farewell."[68]

As the train began to slowly pull out of the station, the audience responded with three cheers, "loud applause and cries of 'We will pray for you.'" The normally controlled president-elect, one newspaper reported, "betrayed much emotion and the crowd was affected to tears." John Hay later confirmed that the farewell address "left hardly a dry eye in the assemblage." Among those who braved the weather that frosty morning was James C. Conkling. "He is now fairly on his way for weal or woe of the nation," Conkling wrote the next day. "God bless him and preserve him and nerve him for the terrible struggle and dangers which he may be called upon to meet and endure."[69]

CHAPTER NINE

"All Our Labor Is Lost"

Compromise Committees and the Washington Peace Conference

JUST TWO YEARS OLDER than the president-elect, Charles Francis Adams had become the Free Soil Party's 1848 vice presidential nominee at the young age of thirty-nine. Apart from several terms in the Massachusetts statehouse, Adams had done little to deserve that honor. But he was an Adams, son and grandson to presidents, and his nomination was a posthumous way to pay tribute to his father, John Quincy Adams, who, while serving as a congressman, had died the previous February in the Capitol's Speaker's Room while speaking against the Mexican-American War. As staid New Englanders, the Adams family prided themselves on their moderation, and even when attacking the Gag Rule or defending captured Africans before the Supreme Court in the *Amistad* case, John Quincy stubbornly refused to embrace the term "abolitionist." But the Adams men and women were ever sound antislavery Christians, and old John Adams had lectured his sometime friend Thomas Jefferson that unfree labor was a sinful "black cloud" upon the country. In March 1859, Charles Francis began his first term in the House, representing Massachusetts's third district, but he did not expect to remain long in Congress; he supported Seward's candidacy and hoped to play a role in his administration.[1]

Charles Francis was in fact destined to serve Seward, but under the auspices of the State Department rather than in a Seward cabinet. For the next seven years, Adams would act as his nation's ambassador to Great Britain. From London he remained in contact with his son Charles Francis Adams Jr., the former campaign companion to Senator Seward, who fought at Gettysburg before taking command of the all-black Fifth Massachusetts Cavalry. But if Lieutenant Adams opposed slavery on the grounds that it ran counter to "the spirit of modern progress and civilization," he thought that black soldiers made poor cavalrymen. "A sick nigger," he informed his father, "at once gives up and lies down to die, the personification of humanity reduced to a wet rag." To the extent that the Adams men—antislavery Republicans all—believed in their cause without endorsing the uncompromising methods of American abolitionists, they exemplified the willingness of moderate northerners to consider concessions during what the younger Charles's brother Henry called "the secession winter." As upper-South politicians and northern Democrats frantically called for assurances to keep the border loyal and perhaps win back the seceded states, Republicans would have to weigh the cost of conciliation, both to their party and to the nation they had won the right to govern.[2]

When President Buchanan sent his annual message to Congress on December 3, 1860, the executive's "absolute abnegation of the powers of the general government," as a furious Congressman John Sherman of Ohio described the "feeble wail of despair," made it clear that if compromise was going to come, it would have to originate with Congress. In asserting that, while secession was unlawful, he lacked the executive power to hold the republic together, Buchanan indicated that he intended to do little besides criticize northern states for their "unconstitutional and obnoxious" personal-liberty laws. Until noon of March 4, however, the lame-duck president wielded legal authority—whether or not he wished to exercise it—while the president-elect remained far off in Springfield, as yet a private citizen. Northern voters watched helplessly as South Carolina prepared to secede, as did newly elected Republican congressmen and senators who had yet to take their seats. Republican opinion, with no clear leader in Washington, drifted uncertainly, leaving control of the crisis to the Thirty-sixth Congress, many of whom had lost their seats during the previous fall's elections.[3]

With the president all but abdicating his authority, House leaders decided they had to act. The day after Buchanan's message was read to the chamber, Virginia congressman Alexander R. Boteler moved that the address "be referred to a special committee of one from each state." Sherman objected on the grounds that there was no precedent for a committee chosen along regional lines, and Jonathan D. Morris, an Illinois Republican, attempted to amend the motion by adding that "nothing in the election of Abraham Lincoln to the Presidency" justified dissolution. Boteler, a former Whig turned Constitutional Unionist (and future Confederate congressman), protested that he desired to make his motion "as simple as possible." Anxious to resolve the crisis, the House agreed by a vote of 145 to 38. Adams sided with the majority, although his vote, rather to his surprise, "seemed to disturb" his supporters in Massachusetts. Most of the negative votes were cast by Republicans who feared that the committee might demand that their party abrogate its platform; the few remaining South Carolinians also voted no before packing their trunks for home.[4]

In hopes of avoiding the sectional and partisan wrangling that had paralyzed Washington for much of the previous decade, House Speaker William Pennington, a New Jersey Republican, carefully packed what came to be known as the Committee of Thirty-Three. Although he selected a numerically equitable group of sixteen Republicans (including Adams and Sherman), fourteen Democrats, and three Unionists, with a respected chairman in Ohio Republican Thomas Corwin, many of the Democrats were border-South representatives with secessionist tendencies. None of them were Douglas supporters. Reading of this development in Illinois, Lincoln feared that the committee was too large and unwieldy to accomplish much good. His suspicions that its Democratic members essentially hoped to overturn the election's results proved well-founded when one of them, Albert Rust of Arkansas, introduced a resolution claiming that "the existing discontents among the Southern people, and the growing hostility among them to the Federal Government, are not without cause." After northern members attempted to amend Rust's words to say that the only legitimate responses to political grievances were "constitutional remedies," the committee began to argue over a series of dueling resolutions, revealing not only the problematic composition of the group but also the possibly irresolvable nature of the crisis facing the nation.[5]

One day later, on December 5, the Senate followed suit with the creation of a Select Committee of Thirteen. Although Washington insiders expected the smaller group to prove more manageable than its House counterpart, the Senate committee included not merely some of the nation's leading figures but also some of its most irreconcilable voices. Among the original thirteen were former presidential hopefuls Seward, Douglas, Robert M. T. Hunter, and Jefferson Davis. Crittenden served, as did Robert Toombs and the radical Benjamin Wade. Seward and Douglas were honestly desirous of finding some solution to stop secession in its tracks, but the committee's "Southrons," a bitter John Alexander Logan groused, "would accept nothing less than a total repudiation by the Republicans of the very principles upon which the recent Presidential contest had by them been fought and won." In reality, most of the southern members on the committee, and especially Toombs, were just marking time until their states withdrew. Typical was Senator James M. Mason, who voted in favor of creating the committee but desired his Virginia to follow South Carolina out of the Union. His vote, Mason informed the chamber, was taken "without an idea that it is possible for anything that Congress can do to reach the dangers with which we are threatened."[6]

The future Confederate president had no interest in compromise, and when told he had been appointed to the committee, Davis begged to be excused. When other senators implored the Mississippian to remain, he did so, but on the condition that the committee accept a procedural rule that all but doomed the group's already limited chances of success. Rather than their voting on the basis of a simple majority, Davis demanded that no recommendation be sent to the Senate floor unless supported by a majority of the group's Republicans and Democrats alike. Any amendments to the Constitution, he observed, would require bipartisan and bisectional support. Although this was true, no compromise package could secure the endorsement of both Wade and Toombs, as Davis well knew. So sure was he that "the so-called 'Republican' Senators of the North," as he later described them, would refuse to abandon their party's platform that on December 14 he affixed his signature to a declaration authored by Senator Louis Wigfall of Texas and Congressman James Pugh of Alabama declaring that "the primary object of each slaveholding State ought to be its speedy and absolute separation" from the Union. Toombs, of course, agreed, and in a circular letter he warned his constituents to abandon any hope of compromise, as secession "will be your best guarantee for liberty, security, tranquility, and glory." The committee on which he had agreed to serve, Toombs added, was "controlled by Black Republicans, your enemies, who only seek to amuse you with delusive hope."[7]

Within the week, two thirds of the congressmen and senators from the lower South had signed Wigfall and Pugh's declaration. As early as December 6—two days before his resignation—Secretary Howell Cobb condemned compromise in an address to the people of Georgia, swearing that every hour that the state remained part of the United States was "an hour of degradation." One day later, future postmaster John Reagan assured a correspondent in Texas that congressional efforts to resolve the crisis were in vain. The moderate Republicans and northern Democrats on the two committees who thought otherwise committed several critical errors. Although the notion that politics was "the art of compromise" was already an old maxim by 1860, that dictum assumed that a common ground existed upon which compromise could be forged. Even as it became clear that South Carolina planned to secede before the year's end, politicians enamored of negotiation continued to pray that Wigfall did not speak for all the southerners when he informed Congress that he believed Alabama planned to withdraw no matter what concessions were offered by the committees. Too many slaveholders, he thought, devoutly believed that their livelihood was endangered by remaining in a country led by a President Lincoln to allow for any possible conciliation.[8]

For those who would listen, southern ultras made their determination to withdraw from Lincoln's republic all too plain. "We spit on every plan to compromise," admitted one plainspoken secessionist. Having nearly reached his goal, Yancey was in no mood to countenance anything short of total independence. "No new guarantees," he counseled, "no amendments to the Constitution" should induce the lower South to quit its drive for secession. The problem with the Union, Yancey believed, was not the nature of the Constitution, but rather the "disease" that had infected northerners with the belief that slavery was "a religious as well as a political wrong." Since nothing could heal this "deep-rooted cancer," the only cure was disunion, and desperate moderates who clung to the hope that the repeal of personal-liberty laws might win back southern fire-eaters naively chose to ignore their words. Andrew Johnson, for one, learned early on that southern extremists had no interest in compromise, as he watched Judah Benjamin sit quietly while the Senate voted to create the Committee of Thirteen. "It is not guara[n]tees in reference to slavery they want," an increasingly perceptive Johnson complained, "it is a go[vern]ment South so they Can have the absolute Control of it in their own hands."[9]

Across the North, militant abolitionists and a surprising number of Republicans also opposed any concessions. Evangelicals had long thought themselves tainted by living in the same nation as slaveholders, but mainstream politicians, having just won a hard-fought victory at the polls, were almost as anxious to rid themselves of the southern master class. Horace Greeley's *New York Tribune* had argued for some time that the slave states should be allowed to secede in peace, and the Philadelphia *Public Ledger*, the Springfield *Republican*, and the *Chicago Tribune* all echoed Greeley's sentiments. Terrified that Seward, as a member of the Committee of Thirteen, was about to retreat on his party's core platform of free territories, dozens of New Yorkers peppered the senator with calls to stand firm. "Let me beg of you to do nothing which can be tortured by enemies even into the slightest surrender of the high ground you have always occupied," urged the editor of the Albion *Daily American*. "To abandon a principle," wrote another, "to which some of us have devoted life-times, and built a dominant party, is degrading." A third writer urged "that there may be *no* concessions by the North to Southern Insolence & threats." Ironically, as Seward began to consider accepting Lincoln's offer of the State Department, his actions were no longer restricted by the will of his New York constituents. His thoughts now turned to saving the nation. But as far as the majority of Seward's constituents were concerned, they had won the election fairly, and if they "yield[ed] a *hair*, & the Cotton States *remain[ed]* *in* consequence," it would result in "an inglorious adm[inistratio]n by Lincoln."[10]

For the better part of the 1850s, antislavery politicians had battled southern expansionists, so the determination of Republican voters to hold fast to the Wilmot Proviso was understandable. But with secession, Republican concerns over concessions took on a deeper meaning. As southern states withdrew from the Union, the central question was no longer slavery in the territories, but rather the survival of democracy and the country itself. Republican policies had prevailed in November, but with the candidate not yet in office, fire-eaters indicated a refusal to accept their loss by seceding. "Should we yield now—& any offer is concession," Charles Sumner fretted, "every Presidential election will be conducted with the menace of secession by the defeated party." Decades before, in the early 1830s, South Carolinians had sought to nullify federal law, and now they wished to nullify the legitimate results of a presidential contest. By emphasizing the constitutional right of the victor to take office on March 4, Republicans elevated the discourse from slavery's western restriction to preserving majority rule, a cause that even northern Democrats could support. "The day of compromises has passed," snapped sixty-year-old Wade, "and a Government which is moved to compromise by the threats of traitors is not worth preserving."[11]

The person whose opinion counted most, of course, remained in Springfield, far from the corridors of power. The exigencies of the modern nuclear age, in which successful candidates are briefed about national-security concerns almost on election night, were far distant from the lethargic transition envisioned by the founders. For four long months following his election, Lincoln was a remote observer of affairs in Washington. Understandably, he was frustrated by what many Americans were already coming to regard as a flaw in the Constitution, although some advocates of compromise welcomed the president-elect's absence from the nation's capital. If as yet legally powerless, Lincoln understood that he did enjoy the power to influence wavering members of his own party who were prepared to abandon key platform policies in hopes of preserving the republic. "He was a terrible man when he put his foot down," Mary Lincoln later remarked, and "no man nor woman could rule him after he made up his mind."[12]

Lincoln was especially worried about the fate of the Wilmot Proviso, and rightly so. Within two weeks of his election, the *New York Times* reported that "leading men" in Washington were discussing the possibility of extending the 36° 30' Missouri Compromise line—which had applied only to the Louisiana Purchase lands prior to its repeal by the Kansas-Nebraska Act—to the Pacific Ocean. For Lincoln, that was worrisome enough, but two days after Seward joined the Committee of Thirteen, Thurlow Weed's *Albany Evening Journal* endorsed the scheme. For six years, Republicans had unequivocally denounced the idea of a single new acre of slave soil, and to use the vast New Mexico Territory and southern California as bait to reel back seceders violated the tenets of the new party. Lincoln was concerned enough to post Weed a "Private & confidential" missive on December 17, knowing that it would remain neither. "You judge from my speeches that I will be inflexible on the territorial question," Lincoln bluntly observed. Extending "the Missouri line" or embracing Douglas's "popular sovereignty would lose us every thing we gained by the election." If the party gave in to southern demands on the West, that might lead to "filibustering for all South of us, and making slave states of it." Lincoln reluctantly supported the repeal of personal liberty laws. Beyond that, he refused to go.[13]

Although Lincoln's party contained its share of strong-willed individuals, Sumner and Wade among them, less-established congressmen in particular awaited a signal from the president-elect. Unlike Seward, Lincoln took lower-South ultras at their word and suspected that nothing Congress might do could stem the tide of secession. Had he endorsed the extension of the Missouri Compromise line, however, he probably could have influenced enough junior congressmen to follow his lead. But for Lincoln, conciliation was worse than fruitless, for it led not to peace but toward conquest and war, if only with the republic's southern neighbors. Either secessionists were "attempting to play upon us," he counseled one congressman, "or they are in dead earnest." If the party offered concessions now, a "year will not pass, till we shall have to take Cuba as a condition upon which they will stay in the Union." Believing it necessary to disseminate his views as widely as possible, Lincoln posted a number of brief missives to Republican congressmen and senators, all of them containing a variation of the arguments he had used with Weed. "Let there be no compromise on the question of *extending* slavery," Lincoln urged Senator Lyman Trumbull and Congressmen William Kellogg and Elihu B. Washburne, taking care to underline "extending" in each of the three letters. If the Republicans agreed to open the Southwest to slavery, "all our labor is lost, and, ere long, must be done again." On this point, he urged Washburne, "hold firm, as with a chain of steel." To Kellogg and Trumbull, he added, "The tug has to come, & better now, than any time hereafter."[14]

In hopes of forcing the resolute prairie lawyer to bend on the West, President Buchanan dispatched a personal emissary to Springfield just after Christmas. Sixty-nine-year-old Duff Green was a Kentuckian, but never a fire-eater, and as a younger man he had served in Jackson's informal Kitchen Cabinet. Lincoln repeated his worries that any temporary territorial adjustment could only result in further demands for Mexico or Cuba and "put us again on the highroad to a slave empire." As did Sumner, Lincoln worried that as he had not yet set foot in Washington or taken any actions against slavery where it existed, any offer of concessions to secure the right to hold office would hold every future president-elect hostage to the will of a dissatisfied minority. "We have just carried an election on principles fairly stated to the people," Lincoln warned Congressman James T. Hale, a Pennsylvania member of the Committee of Thirty-Three. "Now we are told in advance, the government shall be broken up, unless we surrender to those we have beaten, before we take office." If Lincoln had to bargain away his platform—and flout the will of the voters—in exchange for being sworn in on March 4, no subsequent president or voter could ever assume that a party's policies carried any weight.[15]

Judging from his incoming mail, Lincoln's supporters approved of his refusal to give way on the party's position on the territories. Most Republican editors also endorsed his statements against slavery's extension; Greeley was just one of many publishers who returned to Springfield to bestow "any amount of backbone needed." Lincoln's resolve was further bolstered by some of those he was then selecting to serve in his cabinet, just as *his* determination surely strengthened theirs in return. "If we must have civil war," announced future attorney general Edward Bates, "perhaps it is better now than at a future date." Whether Lincoln led or mirrored public opinion remains unclear. But there can be little doubt that the president-elect, Republican voters, and the party's editors demonstrated far greater resolve than the nervous politicians who served on the House and Senate committees. "We are heartily tired of having this threat [of disunion] stare us in the face evermore," wrote one Republican editor. "We never have been better prepared for such a crisis than now."[16]

Moderates in the Senate found such sentiments appalling, and none more so than Crittenden. While not formally the chair of the Committee of Thirteen, the determined Kentuckian quickly seized control of the group. Although chosen by the Senate leadership on December 5, the committee did not officially meet until December 22, and the intervening days provided Crittenden with time to piece together what he hoped would become known as the Compromise of 1860. When the group met, absent Seward, who was still on his way down from Albany, Crittenden suggested a package of six constitutional amendments. The most important component of his grand design was an amendment pertaining to "all the territory of the United States now held, or hereafter acquired, situated north of latitude 36° 30', [where] slavery or involuntary servitude, except as a punishment for crime, is prohibited." South of that line, however, "slavery of the African race is hereby recognized as existing, and shall not be interfered with by Congress." Two additional amendments stated that the federal government was also forbidden to abolish slavery in places under its jurisdiction within a slave state, such as a military post, and in the District of Columbia without the consent of Virginia, Maryland, and the district's white residents. Fourth and fifth, Congress could not prohibit or interfere with the interstate slave trade, and in the case of successful runaways, the federal government was to compensate masters and then sue "the wrong doers or rescuers" who assisted fugitives to cover reimbursements. And finally, a sixth proposed amendment banned a future Congress from altering these amendments or interfering with slavery where it existed. With "these provisions," Crittenden believed, "we have a solid foundation upon which we may rest our hopes for the restoration of peace and good-will among all the States of this Union."[17]

Crittenden preferred to call his plan a "compromise of the slavery question," but as critics observed, there was no give-and-take involved in his amendments, merely capitulation. Previous sectional adjustments had provided something for North and South alike. In the Compromise of 1850, California had entered the republic as a free state, and the slave trade had been banned in Washington, D.C., in exchange for concessions to the slaveholders. In Crittenden's arrangement, however, all six proposed amendments aimed to conciliate the South. Republicans were expected to abandon the central feature of their party's platform, despite the fact that voters had endorsed that plank only one month before. For the first time, the word "slavery" was to replace the polite euphemisms preferred by the founders, and the phrase "or hereafter acquired" appeared to endorse expansionists' demands for Cuba and Mexico. Crittenden's plan even violated Douglas's theories of popular sovereignty, as its restoration and extension of the Missouri Compromise line did not merely allow for slavery's possible expansion into New Mexico, but instead "recognized [it] as existing" and "protected [it] as property." Crittenden might hope that his amendments could "settle the controverted questions which now so much agitate our country." But they would do so by fulfilling the wildest dreams of even the most rabid fire-eaters.[18]

In spite of the fact that Crittenden's plan provided slaveholders with the sort of guarantees that popular sovereignty lacked, Douglas promptly agreed to support the package. Early on in the session, he began to confer almost daily with the aged Kentuckian. "I am ready to make any reasonable sacrifice of party tenets to save the country," he confided to August Belmont. Since southern Democrats had denied him the nomination, Douglas felt free to reach across the aisle, not merely with former Whigs like Crittenden but with moderate Republicans as well. "No adjustment will restore & preserve peace *which does not banish the slavery question from Congress*," Douglas assured a number of correspondents. Crittenden's amendment extending "the Missouri line accomplishes this object, and hence I can accept it now," the senator decided. He continued to prefer his former position "of Non Intervention & popular sovereignty," but as the South had rejected that platform at the Charleston and Baltimore conventions, he believed that nothing less than Crittenden's six amendments could keep the nation intact.[19]

Despite assuring Crittenden that he supported his proposals, however, on December 24, Douglas unveiled his own plan to the Senate. In hopes of retaining some aspect of popular sovereignty, he suggested that Congress revise the 1787 blueprint for how territories become states outlined in the Northwest Ordinance. Under the original plan, territories required sixty thousand free settlers to apply for statehood, but in Douglas's design, once a region had fifty thousand white residents, it was to enter into an intermediate phase—which Douglas confusingly dubbed its "new State" period—during which a territorial assembly could pass any legislation it saw fit regarding slavery. Finally, when the territory had another ten thousand residents, it could write a constitution and apply for statehood. Since Congress was forbidden to legislate on slavery during any stage of this process, Douglas's plan was not likely to appeal to Republicans. And unlike Crittenden's plan, it did not protect the Southwest for slavery's expansion. In hopes of winning over moderate Republicans, however, Douglas suggested that the government acquire no further land without a two-thirds majority in both chambers, and he revived the old Whig idea of purchasing land outside the United States for the colonization of freed blacks. As a sop to Democrats, he added that "persons of the African race" should never be allowed to vote in the new states of the West—a position that ran counter to both his states' rights and his popular sovereignty principles.[20]

Whatever its failings, Douglas's proposal, unlike Crittenden's six amendments, approached the spirit of compromise in that it made a few nods at northern concerns. Some of the upper-South politicians in Washington expressed the hope that either the Crittenden concessions or the Douglas variation "would be satisfactory to Moderate Southern States." But while still a member of the Committee of Thirteen, Toombs made it clear that the lower South could accept nothing but the Alabama Platform—federal protection of enslaved property in the West—for *all* of the territories, including those in the Pacific Northwest. He also demanded that accused runaways be turned over without a writ of habeas corpus or a jury trial, which most personal liberty laws provided for in violation of the Fugitive Slave Act. And in a clear reference to the Lemmon case, Toombs insisted that slaveholders be granted the right to carry their human chattel through free states for purposes of transit, and that any future constitutional provisions regarding slavery be approved by every slaveholding state. In his response to Douglas, Toombs deliv-

ered what one Massachusetts newspaper described as "a decided secession speech." Should the northern members of the committee deny the
white South "its rights," he added, "he would invoke the God of battles,
and trust to him for security and peace."[21]

The Georgia senator's extreme demands only strengthened many Republicans' determination to support the president-elect, and if they had
been displeased by earlier, vague talk of conciliation, now that the Crittenden plan was formalized, they were especially determined to resist
slavery's expansion. The pro-Democratic *New York Herald* complained
that the "incoming administration" had "no intention to make a compromise," but the *New York Times* fired back, pointing out that Crittenden's
amendments were nothing but concessions. In previous years, its editor remarked, compromises "have been tried over and over again and in each instance the controversy has been broadened and sharpened and made
worse." As fire-eaters had responded to earlier compromises with escalating demands for new territory, the *Times* charged, northern voters had
given up hope that congressional solutions could paper over fundamental
differences regarding labor systems. Radical Republicans, moreover, understood the human cost of appeasement. Turning over the Southwest and
obtaining Cuba for the planter class might spare white men from combat,
but only at a cost to black lives and shattered black families. Lengthening
the Missouri line, Iowa senator James W. Grimes charged, "convert[ed] the
Government into a great slave-breeding, slavery-extending empire."
Sumner agreed. "To sanction the enslavement of a single human being is
an act which can not be called small," he replied when informed that
only twenty-four slaves then resided in the New Mexico Territory, "unless the whole moral law which it overturns or ignores is small."[22]

On December 22, even before Seward reached Washington, the Senate committee put Crittenden's proposals to a test vote. The Republicans
requested a delay until Seward could join them, but Crittenden, expecting the New Yorker to vote against his amendments, threw "the weight
of his mighty intellect into the scales of concord," as one admiring journalist phrased it. The Republicans unanimously voted against extending
the Missouri line, and the southern Democrats on the committee—
Toombs, Hunter, and Davis—voted no as well, charging that Republican bad faith had destroyed hopes of compromise. "Northern Senators

seem disposed neither to harmonize old quarrels nor to prevent new ones," complained a conservative Philadelphia editor.[23]

Much to Crittenden's surprise, when Seward finally arrived in the capital, he appeared ready to make concessions. Despite Lincoln's earlier warnings to Weed, which Seward learned of on the train from Syracuse to Albany, the New Yorker continued to believe that he would have to guide the untested president-elect. Although he had accepted the post in the State Department, Seward was yet a member of the Senate, while Lincoln was a private citizen. Seward believed that if a compromise was achieved now, Lincoln would have no choice but to agree to its provisions after being sworn in on March 4. Seizing control of events in Washington, he believed, had the virtue of saving the nation while making it clear to all that he reigned as the administration's premier. After conferring with Congressman Adams, Seward advanced the idea of immediately admitting the vast New Mexico Territory, presumably as a slave state. Since the Chicago platform grudgingly allowed sovereign states to maintain slavery, Seward hinted that his plan did not violate Republican doctrine. Others on the committee responded that it ran counter to the spirit of free soilism, while some observed that the region lacked the requisite population to apply for statehood. On December 31, a dejected Crittenden informed the Senate that the committee could agree on no solution. Having decided that secession was the only option for his state several weeks before, Davis now announced that his "hope of an honorable peaceable settlement" was effectively abandoned.[24]

Crittenden was far from beaten. Several days before he reported their deadlock to the full Senate, he and Douglas had fired off a telegram to Georgia voters, insisting that they remained optimistic "that the rights of the South and of every state and section may be protected within the Union." On January 3, Crittenden took to the floor to introduce a resolution containing his original six amendments and Douglas's additions regarding black voting rights in the West and funded colonization. Admitting that his proposals had failed in committee and stood an equally slim chance of success with the entire Senate, the aged Kentuckian called for a national plebiscite on his amendments. Nothing existed in the Constitution or within American political theory to sustain the idea of a referendum, but that hardly failed to stop Douglas from promptly rising in endorse-

ment. "Why not give the people a chance?" Douglas wondered. Even Lincoln voters were likely, he thought, to "ratify the proposed amendments to
the Constitution, in order to take this slavery agitation out of Congress,
and restore peace to the country." Greeley, for one, feared that Douglas
was right, and that in the name of saving the republic, American voters
would back Crittenden's plan by "an overwhelming majority."[25]

Douglas was particularly annoyed by what he regarded as the naive
Republican view that secession, being unconstitutional and unjustified,
could be wished away. "In my opinion South Carolina had no right to
secede," he huffed, "*but she has done it.*" Since he could not countenance
either the breakup of the country or a "war with our own brethren and
kindred," the only remaining option was some sort of compromise
package. By late December, Douglas had come to doubt that the Senate
could "carry Mr Crittenden's proposition to run the Missouri line" westward, and that left a plebiscite as the final hope. "The prospects for saving the Union are indeed gloomy," Douglas wrote Alexander Stephens.
But he continued to believe that his two anti-black additions to Crittenden's amendments were "all the South can wish."[26]

Late in the afternoon on January 3, after Crittenden finished speaking,
Douglas stood to deliver what he regarded as the most important speech of
his career. Most members of the House hurried down the hall to hear the
oration, as did a number of foreign diplomats. Those spectators who
hoped that the senator could perform miracles were sadly disappointed.
His health ever more damaged, Douglas had nothing new to add to the debate, and his lengthy speech was disorganized, repetitive, and contradictory. He assured the South that Lincoln's election was no cause for
secession, but paradoxically he then quoted his victorious opponent as
claiming that restriction would place slavery "on the course of ultimate extinction," before wondering whether it was "surprising that the people of
the South should suppose that [Lincoln] was in earnest." Having depicted
Republicans as dangerous radicals bent on attacking southern "firesides,
their family altars, and their domestic institutions," Douglas nonetheless
"indulged the fond hope" that planters might be "content to remain in the
Union and defend their rights under the Constitution." When he attacked
unnamed senators who refused "to listen to compromise," Benjamin
Wade and a number of other Republicans began to interrupt his tirade.

Concluding with the hope that northern voters would abandon the platform they had just voted to support, Douglas renewed his call for a referendum on Crittenden's amendments and slumped into his chair.[27]

A handful of pro-Democratic papers endorsed Douglas's plan and
urged "ultra Republican leaders" to "follow his standard." But neither free
soilers nor southern firebrands found much to admire in the oration.
Lower-South planters had long opposed federal offers to colonize free
blacks in Liberia or elsewhere on the grounds that such funding was a dangerous first step toward compensated emancipation, and in any case,
Yanceyites wanted more enslaved workers, not fewer. "It would not be
very safe for the South," one critic of Douglas's speech thought, "to have
the government clothed with such power." Having read the oration in
advance, Stephens warned his old friend that his idea regarding "the colonization of the blacks would never [be] agreed to by the South." Republicans were contemptuous. Young Henry Adams, serving as secretary to his
congressman father, noticed Adele Douglas in the gallery as her husband
spoke. "Poor girl! What the deuce does she look forward to!" he wrote.
"Her husband is a brute, gross, vulgar, demagogic; a drunkard; ruined as a
politician; ruined as a private man; over head and ears."[28]

With the nation's leading Democrat publicly behind the Crittenden
plan and the president-elect warning against it, the question for most
Washington observers was what position the country's second leading
Republican would take. Seward announced that he would follow Douglas
onto the Senate floor on January 12. Despite Lincoln's numerous con-
demnations of concessions, rumor had it that the future secretary was
leaning toward endorsing much of the Crittenden plan. Where Lincoln
feared that any signs of weakness could only embolden southern hotspurs, Seward was quietly circulating the idea of dividing the South by
conciliating the border states. Once the lower South realized that the
Lincoln administration was not filled with abolitionists, it would abandon secession and return to the Union. Even Charles Francis Adams Jr.,
normally so admiring of the New Yorker, thought that Seward's policy
was "based on an entire misapprehension of the facts, and fore-doomed
to failure." But if Seward had begun to shift toward the center in early
1860 in hopes of winning the nomination, his post-election moderation
was founded upon a naive faith in human progress. Despite the fact that

American freedom had actually *regressed* over the course of the 1850s, Seward remained confident of the ultimate victory of antislavery, and thus believed that any adjustments made now in the territories would merely slow the march of freedom. As he pledged in a bold toast offered at a dinner hosted by Douglas for the French minister; "Away with all parties, all platforms of previous committals and whatever else will stand in the way of a restoration of the American Union."[29]

With the nation facing the prospect of war and disunion, Seward was not without supporters. The Democratic *New York Herald*, of course, was pleased to hear the senator's name "among [the] advocates [of] a common sense understanding" regarding "liberal concessions." A few Republicans also wrote to endorse his newfound conservatism. "Let me implore you by all you hold most sacred to advocate Mr. Crittenden's Amendment[s]," begged one. A Baltimore resident insisted that "a Compromise will quiet the States of Maryland [and] Virginia," adding that the Kentuckian's package "will prevent Bloodshed anarchy & Civil War." Even the Republican-controlled New York legislature passed a series of "very strong conciliatory Union resolutions," which provided the senator with the political cover necessary to abandon the Chicago platform. Armed with the resolutions, Weed hurried to Washington to provide support. But Congressman Adams was not alone in thinking that the time had arrived for Seward to abandon his mentor. When Weed called on Sumner, the senator bluntly told him that he was "not welcome here." Despite the long-standing alliance between Seward and the Adams family, Henry admitted that Seward "puzzles me more and more," adding, "I can't see how he works at all."[30]

Congressman Adams dined with Seward just before his speech and found him "very low-spirited." But the New Yorker remained certain that he could hold the upper South in place, though he confided to Adams that bringing the seceded states back into the fold might be the work of several years. He conceded as much when he finally rose in the Senate on January 12. Like Douglas, Seward believed that attempting to prove "that secession [was] illegal or unconstitutional" was a waste of valuable time. Even "Congressional compromises [were] not likely to save the Union." What did the South want, and what might the government offer? Although Seward did not endorse Crittenden's notion of extending the

Missouri Compromise line to the Pacific, he continued to push for the immediate admission of New Mexico as a state, a position he had embraced the previous month in the Committee of Thirteen. On runaway slaves, he tried to find a middle ground by promising the more efficient enforcement of the Fugitive Slave Act, but with safeguards to "protect freedmen being, by abuse of the laws, carried into slavery." As did Lincoln, Seward also agreed to an amendment permanently exempting already existing slavery from congressional meddling, and he hoped to somehow craft federal legislation making raids like the one at Harpers Ferry impossible to conduct. "I feel sure that the hour is not come for this great nation to fall," he concluded. "It shall continue to endure; and men, in after times, shall declare that this generation, which saved the Union from such sudden and unlooked for dangers, surpassed in magnanimity even that one which laid its foundation."[31]

By the time Seward took his seat, a number of northern men were in tears. Seward himself thought the speech a great success, and a few of his backers wrote in agreement. "Your sentiments will find a cordial reception among the true hearted Republicans of Wisconsin," one wrote. Another argued that the "noblest revenge" against "the disunion plotters" was to give them what they wanted, on the curious grounds that spreading slavery into the territories might bury planters in "disgrace." But if the oration was designed to placate upper-South moderates, Seward's efforts were not completely successful. He called for a "free debate" on Crittenden's package, but as one departing Texas politician scoffed, "*a great many of these free debaters were hanging from the trees of [his] country.*" Nor were a majority of the Republicans in Washington convinced that Seward's course was morally sound. Should the president-elect seek "to purchase peace by concession, and ignoring platforms, *à la mode* Seward," Congressman Thaddeus Stevens snapped, "I shall give up the fight." A disappointed Carl Schurz agreed. "What do you think of Seward?" he asked his wife. "He bows before the slave power." As somebody who once was "so affectionately attached to him," Schurz thought it "hard" to see how the "mighty is fallen."[32]

Within days, Seward's euphoria vanished as he realized how many of his former supporters, both within and outside of Washington, despised his position. Unimpressed by the tears of northern moderates, Benjamin Wade barked out, "What a downfall," as Seward finished his oration. One missive from Ithaca, New York, urged the senator instead to take steps "to prevent the rebel seceeders from coming back to Congress." Not surprisingly, the Blairs were appalled by the speech. Montgomery Blair was just one of many Republicans who feared that Crittenden's concessions would only inspire southern politicians to demand Cuba. So long as planters believed that "one Southern man is equal to half a dozen Yankees," he suspected, they might never submit to any election results that did not go their way. Sumner's equally hostile response at least came as no surprise, since Seward had read him the address on January 8. After listening silently, Sumner first begged Seward "to abandon every proposition of concession" and then bluntly told the New Yorker that he "deplore[d]" the speech. Others were harsher still. "God damn you, Seward," snarled one senator, "you've betrayed your principles and your party; we've followed your lead long enough." But surely the hardest words for Seward to read arrived from his wife in Auburn. "Eloquent as your speech was it fails to meet the approbation of those who love you best," Frances chided him. "You are in danger of taking the path which led Daniel Webster to an unhonored grave."[33]

By that date, the Committee of Thirty-Three, the House counterpart to Crittenden's committee, had nearly concluded its deliberations. Following its initial acrimony over how to best phrase a resolution justifying its existence, the House group had finally begun to hold daily sessions on December 11. After the committee dispensed with Albert Rust's incendiary resolution blaming the crisis on Republicans, the group agreed to accept as a starting point six resolutions drafted by Thomas R. Nelson, a Tennessee Whig turned Unionist. Nelson's plan was a variation of the proposals then being floated by Crittenden, Seward, and Douglas, as he too advocated an extension of the Missouri line, the repeal of all personal liberty laws, and a promise not to abolish slavery in the District of Columbia. One resolution was new, however, and went even beyond Douglas's idea of restricting voting rights in the territories to white men. "No person shall vote in any State, under the Constitution of the United States," read the fifth resolve, "unless he is of the Caucasian race, and of pure and unmixed blood." Since this proposal violated the principle of states' rights, it was unlikely to win over many northern Democrats, and as if to ensure that Republicans would find his entire package repugnant, Nelson condemned the "howl of famished free labor" that had "brought destitution and misery." The North must "recede from its false position" on the virtues of capitalism, he announced while introducing his resolutions, or "the streets of your cities [will] run with bloody gore."[34]

Despite Nelson's incendiary rhetoric, some Republicans on the committee were inclined to side with Democrats in supporting his call for the repeal of personal liberty laws. As Seward's delicate balancing act on this matter revealed, northern moderates were reluctantly willing to bend on this point, especially as it was of particular concern to the upper South. But even those free soilers who were open to compromise wished to protect the security of free-born or manumitted African Americans, while southern politicians regarded jury trials for runaways as unconstitutional interference in their property rights. Committee members also understood that any package they endorsed would have to be approved by the Senate as well, where Massachusetts's Sumner was trumpeting his state's protections as "one of the glories of our Commonwealth." Yet Adams was inclined to be guided on this by Seward. As always, however, southern firebrands overplayed their hand. Shortly before his state seceded, Mississippi congressman and committee member Reuben Davis insisted that the group first approve southern demands regarding fugitive slaves. When the committee declined to put aside other business, Davis and his supporters stalked out of the chamber in protest. "They only seceded into the next room," marveled Henry Adams, "where they sat in dignity, smoking and watching the remaining members through the folding doors."[35]

The behavior of the lower-South members emboldened moderates like Congressman Adams, who was so weary of such antics that he secretly hoped southern Democrats would "kick us out and refuse everything" and thus end all compromise efforts. Although he remained open to debating some of Nelson's propositions, in late December, Adams rose to offer his own constitutional amendment, which would ban "any interference within the States with the relation between their citizens" on the matter of voting. Since the founders had left voting rights up to the states, Massachusetts and its New England neighbors permitted their small African American populations the right of ballot. Adams demanded that Nelson's national ban on black voting rights require "the assent of every one of the States composing the Union." His resolution passed by a margin of 22 to 3, with Congressmen Rust and Davis and six other indifferent lower-South members listed as "absent or not voting."[36]

Still following Seward's lead, Adams was more amenable to the immediate admission of the New Mexico Territory, seemingly as one enormous slave state that would stretch from Texas to California. The lawyerly congressman believed that by simply admitting the region without adopting Crittenden's troublesome language on the protection of slavery, Republicans could not be accused of violating the letter of the Chicago platform. The Massachusetts representative—who evidently knew little about canals or irrigation—also accepted the common wisdom that cotton slavery could not survive in the arid Southwest. The committee's southern members knew better, so they too saw the political wisdom in simply bypassing New Mexico's territorial stage. But as ever, southern planters wanted more. Andrew Hamilton of Texas complained that the House plan, unlike Crittenden's Senate version, failed to mention the status of *future* territories. A few Republicans also criticized the plan on the grounds that it violated the spirit of the Republican platform, and from across the hall, Sumner thundered that the admission of New Mexico as anything but a free state constituted "*a fatal dismal mistake*." Never close to the Adams family, Sumner posted dozens of letters to his friends in the Bay State, urging them to warn their congressmen that "weak-kneed" politicians should not expect to "get a corporal's guard to vote for [them]" in the future.[37]

Compromises are especially difficult to forge when even those willing to do so wish to obscure their objectives in vague, legalistic language. When free soilers protested that admitting New Mexico under a tacit agreement that it was to become a slave state was a violation of the core principle of the party, they were undoubtedly right. But Democrats and border-South men on the committee desired Crittenden's guarantees as well. Essentially, they demanded the Alabama Platform or nothing, and if Adams could support an unstated expansion of unfree labor into the Southwest, he could not vote for a package that explicitly protected slavery and still face his constituents. Maryland's Henry Winter Davis assured Adams that lower-South congressmen would accept nothing less than protection for slave property in the West—an absurd demand that Davis hoped might strengthen the hand of border-South unionists— just as Adams could not endorse the extension of the Missouri Compromise line. When Adams and a majority of the Republicans on the committee voted to include admitting New Mexico to statehood but only without guarantees, Crittenden publicly accused Adams of betrayal. That even the Kentucky unionist failed to understand Adams's need for political cover suggests the difficulty of crafting acceptable compromise *language*, let alone an actual package, during the increasingly polarized winter.[38]

The fact that southern members rejected Adams's willingness to quietly sanction the spread of slavery past Texas only served to convince ever more Republicans that compromise was futile. Never enthusiastic about the committee's chances, Ohio's John Sherman decided late in December that nothing "less than the protection of slavery in the territories" could satisfy southern Democrats. "All who voted for Mr. Lincoln or Mr. Douglas," Sherman argued, "over three million three hundred thousand citizens— voted against this claim." Young Henry Adams observed that Lincoln, writing from Springfield, continued to exercise "a strong influence through several sources on the committee," and Henry judged the president-elect's positions "always right." As southern states continued to secede, the Republican majority in Congress grew almost daily, and southern members complained that any compromise packages that might finally emerge from the committee would be "exclusively the work of Republicans." Yet one old ally of Congressman Adams was right in thinking that even southern unionists—as apart from die-hard secessionists—had no interest in negotiation. Their position was to state their demands and force the North "to grant them, or take the consequences." Republican moderates sincerely hoped to discover some miracle solution to halt secession, but not at the price of giving up the newly won White House.[39]

The one item that most Republicans on the House committee could unite on was what Adams sourly dubbed the southern "ultimatum," the "protection to Slavery nailed on to the constitution." Kentucky's Francis M. Bristow crafted a simple paragraph that acknowledged slavery as existing in fifteen states and "recognise[d] no authority, legally or otherwise, outside of a State where it so exists, to interfere with slaves or slavery in such States, in disregard of the rights of their owners." An alarmed Joshua Giddings, who had retired from Congress the previous year, prayed that neither Adams "nor any other Republican" would agree to the proposed amendment. But with the president-elect signaling that he could endorse any scheme that did not violate the party platform—and nothing in the Chicago platform demanded the emancipation of bondpersons where slavery already existed—committee members felt secure in voting for the amendment. Chairman Thomas Corwin reported to Lincoln that although "Southern men are theoretically crazy," this amendment and the repeal of personal liberty laws might spare the nation from "a long & bloody civil war." Corwin warned that "Treason is in the air around us *every* where," but, he added, in a not terribly comforting aside, "I think if you live, you may take the oath."[40]

Corwin scheduled a final meeting of the committee on January 14, two days after Seward's speech endorsed many of the same proposals raised by the House group. But as had been the case with Crittenden's Senate body, the House committee failed to agree on a concise package to bring to the floor. Although four of the original thirty-three members had left Washington, the committee wrapped up its work by engaging in yet another acrimonious debate. Southern congressmen demanded nothing less than federal guarantees for slavery in the Southwest, while Adams and others remained committed to admitting New Mexico without any reference to unfree labor. Most northern members continued to endorse Bristow's language on what would have become the Thirteenth Amendment, protecting slavery in the southern states, but southern congressmen, Adams concluded, desired not merely safeguards but the extension of their labor system. The committee finally voted to report on whatever measures the chairman might "think proper to submit." Corwin sent four bills and one amendment to the floor, but Adams suspected that the "results [we]re pushed forward without any guarantee of support in any quarter." In addition to Bristow's amendment, Corwin submitted a plan to repeal personal liberty laws, but also a bill giving accused fugitives the right to a jury trial—the only compromise measure that attempted to appease the North. A third bill authorized the admission of New Mexico on a popular sovereignty basis, and the last streamlined the process of extradition for persons fleeing indictment in one state (as if John Brown had not been captured and hanged).[41]

At this juncture, with two interlocking sets of proposals before the House and Senate, the state of Virginia decided to throw its considerable weight into the drive for reconciliation. On January 19, five days after the final meeting of the Committee of Thirty-Three, Governor John Letcher and the Virginia legislature endorsed resolutions calling for a "peace convention" to meet in Washington on February 4. The assembly recommended that Crittenden's package serve as the foundation for "some suitable adjustment" and invited each state to select delegates for the meeting. With 490,865 bondpersons—making it the largest slave state in the Union—Virginia was in a precarious position. As one nervous advocate of peace admitted, the Old Dominion sat "midway between the bristling bayonets of the belligerents, her territory and people easily accessible to invasion from either north or south." White residents in the northern and western counties wished to remain with the Union, while planters along the Tidewater and North Carolina border favored secession. As soon as the Virginia resolutions reached Buchanan's desk, he passed them along to Congress with an enthusiastic endorsement, giving the proposal the appearance of federal recognition.[42]

The legislatures of the other border states, also painfully aware of their positions along what was sure to be the front lines should fighting commence, promptly agreed to send delegates. Kentucky, Maryland, and Delaware joined Virginia in agreeing to attend, as did the lower-North states of Pennsylvania, Ohio, and Indiana. The rest of the North, with the exception of Michigan, Wisconsin, and Minnesota, soon fell into line, although California and Oregon remained too remote to select delegates. Ominously, the "six States which had already seceded were of course not of the number represented," Jefferson Davis scoffed, "nor were Texas and Arkansas." Seeking the most famous names possible, New Hampshire encouraged Franklin Pierce to attend, but the former president, whose earlier addiction to alcohol had reappeared in retirement, begged off on the grounds "of Mrs. Pierce's health," although not before advocating the "overthrow [of] political Abolitionism." In New York, former president Martin Van Buren also declined, as nobody associated with the convention had thought to contact the president-elect to receive "satisfactory assurances of [his] acquiescence." Thurlow Weed supported the plan and was asked to serve as a delegate, but he too passed, handing his seat to Francis Granger, a Bell supporter who might have greater influence with the border states. Pennsylvania selected free-soil pioneer David Wilmot. Much to his embarrassment, for he had not yet formally accepted the offer of treasury secretary, Salmon Chase was selected as an Ohio delegate. Not much happier about being invited was Charles Francis Adams, if only because the offer provided Sumner with yet another opportunity to denounce the congressman and any other Republican inclined to make concessions to slaveholders.[43]

The one former president who felt he could not refuse the call was Virginia's own John Tyler. Then on the eve of his seventy-first birthday, the executive dubbed His Accidency after becoming the first vice president elevated into the White House by the death of his predecessor doubted that the convention could achieve lasting results. But Tyler missed the attention that had come with the presidency, and he was flattered by letters from Boston praising his "spirit of reconciliation & of patriotism." He left for Washington on January 29, but only after drawing up a final will, leaving his plantation and roughly seventy slaves to his considerably younger second wife, Julia, who had given birth to seven children (to add to the eight born to his first wife). None of his slaves were to be freed upon his death; rather, his wife was to "select for each [of his sons] a Negro boy as his own separate property [upon his] attaining the age of twenty-one years," an agreement that would bestow a black American on his youngest son in 1877. As Tyler rode for Washington, he hoped to achieve a solution that might preserve the Union while protecting his family's investment in other humans for at least another generation, a wish shared by his nineteen-year-old granddaughter, Letitia, who raised the new Confederate flag over dedication ceremonies in Montgomery.[44]

The commissioners, eventually to number 133 and represent twenty-one of the thirty-three states, began to gather at Washington's Willard Hotel on the morning of February 4. Although only half of the delegates had arrived, former Kentucky governor Charles S. Morehead gaveled the meeting to order promptly at noon. The group then selected Tyler as presiding officer, and the Virginian rose to thank the convention with a brief speech promising "glory and immortality" to those who were able to "snatch from ruin a great and glorious confederation." Only those in the hall, however, were able to hear Tyler's words. Virginia's James Seddon (a future Confederate secretary of war) urged the group to close its deliberations to the press and public since, given "the present excited condition of the country," considerable "harm might result from that publicity." That evening, Tyler and Illinois delegate John M. Palmer, who had quit the Democratic Party after Kansas-Nebraska, dined with Douglas, who alarmed the former but pleased the latter by describing secession as a "rebellion" and predicting that if Congress and the convention failed in their endeavors, the "continent will tremble under the tread of a million armed men before the Rebellion is ended."[45]

If nothing else, the very existence of the Peace Convention gave hope to those who believed it bought the republic time. Like Weed, Seward endorsed the conference because it slowed the drive for secession in the upper South, and as the early-February elections for delegates to special state conventions in Virginia and Tennessee had revealed, Seward was undoubtedly correct. But at some point, the meeting would have to take a stand on the territories, at which point it was bound to alienate one section or the other. Virginia's James M. Mason assured Jefferson Davis that the gathering had "little prospect" of "agree[ing] on terms satisfactory" to his state. To the north, Greeley was equally pessimistic, noting that the "most influential statesmen and journals" of the lower South had "already expressed their contempt for any such attempt to patch up a truce between them and the United States." Illinois delegates made it clear from the start that they were attending only "as a matter of political necessity," and as the conference lacked the formal sanction of Congress, Henry Adams confided to his brother Charles Francis Jr. that their father doubted that "any great good can come from it, except to gain time." Most of all, if the delegates included some of the nation's leading names, most were like Tyler, older men who had been retired from public life for some years. "We have never had any faith in this heterogeneous assemblage of old political fossils," editorialized one New York newspaper, and journalists began to dub the group "the old gentlemen's convention."[46]

On February 7, Tyler led a handful of delegates to the White House to pay a call on Buchanan. According to one Vermont delegate who hoped to find evidence that the president was determined to contain secession, the tearful executive instead hugged each delegate and implored them to find some solution to the crisis. After they sat, Tyler pressed Buchanan not to take military action against the seceded states, and so desirous of appeasement was the aged president that he wondered if allowing federal troops in Washington to parade with militia volunteers would "arouse the susceptibilities of [southern] members of the Peace Convention." Discouraged northern delegates left the White House convinced that they might have to stand firm for the Union, since the president clearly would not. It was surely no coincidence that later that evening Republican delegates met and agreed not to support any convention action not endorsed by the party's congressional caucus.[47]

As had the Constitutional Convention of 1787, the Washington conference organized itself into a series of committees, the most important of which was the Committee on Resolutions, tasked with devising a series of recommendations or amendments to report to the full conference. Since the Virginia legislature had explicitly "embraced" the Crittenden plan as "the basis of such an adjustment of the unhappy controversy which now divides the States," the committee, which featured one delegate from each of the attending twenty-one states, began its discussions with the Kentuckian's resolutions. The southerners were especially anxious to adhere to Crittenden's protections for slavery in the Southwest, but as many Republicans in Washington feared, broad support for Crittenden's package could be found far beyond the capital's muddy boulevards. No less a figure than Robert Dale Owen, the utopian socialist and sometime Democratic Party activist, wrote from New Harmony, Indiana, to say "that if the Crittenden or any similar proposition be submitted as the recommendation of [the] Convention," it was sure to be endorsed by "two thirds at the least" of his state's voters.[48]

As ever, the possibility of agreement foundered on the question of the territories. Although a few slaveholding delegates couched their demands in terms of abstract rights and regional honor, a majority made it clear that their need to expand west was founded upon practical considerations. Unless Republicans proved willing to recognize the fundamental correctness of southerners' way of life, no compromise solution was possible. "We hold that these colored barbarians have been withdrawn from a country of native barbarism," James Seddon argued, "and under the benignant influence of Christian rule, of a Christian civilization, have been elevated, yes, *elevated* to a standing and position which they could never have otherwise secured." Such speeches, at least, had the virtue of disabusing Republicans of the myth that slavery could not survive in the New Mexico Territory, just as "the most terrible invectives" launched against Seward and Lincoln did little to motivate northern delegates to seek compromise. As one Virginian encouraged Tyler to explain to the convention, white southerners "do not resist the inauguration of Lincoln because he is a northern man," but rather because "their safety requires that they should not surrender" their right to own other Americans.[49]

On February 15, following what an increasingly weary Tyler described as "speech after speech," the Committee on Resolutions reported seven proposed constitutional amendments. The resolves most easily agreed to were ones that did not violate the Republican platform. Resolution four prevented states from passing personal liberty laws that hindered "the delivery of fugitives from labor," and resolution seven compensated masters in cases where federal marshals were "prevented" from recapturing runaways "by violence or intimidation." Resolution three denied Congress the "power to regulate, abolish, or control" slavery where it already existed. The longest and most contentious was resolution one, which carried the Missouri line to the Pacific; "neither Congress nor the Territorial government shall have power to hinder or prevent the taking to said territory persons held to labor or involuntary servitude." Unlike the Crittenden plan, the proposed amendment was largely silent about future acquisitions, although resolution two held that no new lands could be obtained unless agreed to "by four-fifths of all members of the Senate," effectively granting the North veto power over southern demands for Cuba or more of Mexico.[50]

The convention adjourned for a much-needed respite until February 25. The balloting, with each state receiving a single vote, took place the next day. The convention had agreed to vote on each resolution individually rather than considering them all as a package, and when the critical proposed amendment on the division of the territories came to the floor, several states abstained (including Missouri, its delegation displeased by resolution two), eleven voted no, and eight supported the scheme. The vote rendered the remainder of the resolutions superfluous, and surprised by the outcome, the glum conference adjourned for the day. Early the next morning, however, one moderate called for reconsideration when he heard that a New York Republican was absent, arguing a case before the Supreme Court. That deadlocked the New York delegation and canceled its vote. Missouri, Kansas, and Indiana again abstained, but this time two of the five Illinois delegates reversed their votes and supported the territorial solution. Chase voted no and won Ohio to his side. Virginia and North Carolina also voted no on the grounds that the package did not open future territory to slavery. But by a narrow margin of 9 to 8, the plan to extend the Missouri line passed, and the conference agreed to recommend a seven-part amendment to Congress. "Brightly breaks the morning," the *Albany Evening Journal* enthused.[51]

Just before noon, Tyler formally submitted the seven proposed amendments to Congress. Crittenden rose and asked that the package be referred to a new Senate commission, since the Committee of Thirteen had disbanded. The chamber agreed, and what became known as the Select Committee of Five—comprised of Crittenden, Trumbull, Seward, Democrat William Bigler of Pennsylvania, and New Jersey Democrat John Thomson—took the proposal under consideration. Since Lincoln's inaugural was less than a week away, Crittenden hoped to rush the package through Congress before the new president had the opportunity to urge his party to stand behind its historic devotion to territorial restriction.[52]

For radicals such as Chase, Lincoln could not arrive quickly enough, nor could the new Thirty-seventh Congress, to take their seats and replace the lame-duck moderates. Within weeks of the election, Chase had bluntly informed the wavering Seward that he would be "fully satisfied" if Lincoln maintained "the principles on which he was elected." Fearing that he could not get the peace proposals through Congress and off to the states by March 4, Crittenden also began to discuss the possibility of calling a constitutional convention, at which the package of amendments might be immediately incorporated into organic law. The aged Roger Baldwin of Connecticut, despite being a Republican, had been pushing for the idea of taking whatever came out of the Peace Conference to "a National Convention" for several weeks, and it was surely no accident that Baldwin was to retire from the Senate on March 4. In part because tossing the thorny issue into the first constitutional convention since 1787 provided Republican moderates with political cover, "nearly every member of the Peace Conference from New England" was "in favor of a constitutional convention," reported one New York journal, adding that "there is no doubt that Mr. Seward at the proper time will favor it." Crittenden did the cause little good, however, by announcing that the "dogma of [his] State is that she has as much right to go into the Territories with her slaves as you, who do not choose to hold such property, have to go without them."[53]

Northern moderates, and especially Democrats and Constitutional Unionists, having lost the previous November's election, gave every indication that they were willing to abandon the will of the voters in the name of sectional harmony. A large meeting in Boston's Faneuil Hall praised "the venerable patriot and statesman of Kentucky, John J. Crittenden" and endorsed any "plan of settlement" proposed by the Peace Convention. On March 1, Crittenden himself presented the Senate with a petition orchestrated by feminist and educator Emma Willard and signed by fourteen thousand women representing twelve states. The memorial, the pro-compromise *Washington National Intelligencer* gushed, "was rolled on a baton covered with sky blue silk, the whole enclosed in a silken bag, ornamented with tassels, bound with silk, emblematical of the ties that should bind the States together." Abolitionists were not impressed. In the House, Thaddeus Stevens denounced "concession, humiliation, and compromise," at least so long as southern states were "in open and declared rebellion against the Union," and Senator Sumner bluntly told Buchanan that he would see the republic "sink beneath the sea" rather than "adopt those propositions, acknowledging property in man & disfranchising a portion of her population."[54]

With four overlapping plans before the two chambers—the House and Senate committees', the Peace Convention package, and the drive to call a constitutional convention—the final days of the Thirty-sixth Congress collapsed into confusion. Virginia's Hunter tried to substitute Crittenden's original Senate plan for the Peace Convention's proposals, as it allowed for the future expansion of slavery, but the Kentuckian unexpectedly announced that his plan was off the table. Senator James Mason objected to any consideration of the House report over the peace plan, noting that he intended to vote against compromise solutions but wished to give Tyler's handiwork precedence "because it was due to the State of Virginia." Crittenden shouted that he "did not understand that sort of advocacy" but was interrupted by Texan Louis Wigfall, who laughed that he "felt no great interest in any thing relating to this Government, from which he expected to be altogether disconnected in a day or two."[55]

Buchanan publicly endorsed the peace proposals, and General Winfield Scott ordered a one-hundred-cannon salute of encouragement. Reading the Washington papers at home in Rochester, New York, Frederick Douglass feared that the Republicans were about to bargain away their November victory. They did not. When Ohio's Thomas Corwin finally forced a vote on February 28, most Republicans announced that they could only support an amendment protecting slavery where it yet existed. The House voted 133 to 65 in favor, but with so many southerners absent, legal experts wondered if the tally amounted to the two thirds of all elected members required by the Constitution. The Senate took up the proposed amendment at five in the morning on March 4, Inauguration Day. What would have become the Thirteenth Amendment if ratified by three fourths of the states passed by a margin of 24 to 12. Both chambers then took up the remaining peace proposals as a single package. The Senate voted no by 20 to 19; not a single Republican voted yes, although Seward and Cameron simply declined to answer when called. In the House, Charles Francis Adams defied his party and state and voted yes, but the measures failed there too.[56]

Democratic newspapers angrily placed the failure of conciliation squarely on both Lincoln's party and the president-elect. The crisis was advanced "by ultra republican Senators against compromise," editorialized the *Baltimore Sun*. "And why should the Republican party in Congress hesitate?" wondered the *New York Herald*. If New Mexico was admitted as a slave state, "the inexorable laws of climate, soil and emigration will ultimately establish" free soil. Like the modern scholars who describe Republicans as "shortsighted and unstatesmanlike" on the grounds "that slavery would never prosper" in the Southwest, these editors rarely paused to wonder why southern secessionists were willing to break up the Union rather than abandon the allegedly worthless territories to free soilers. Senator Benjamin Wade knew better. Annoyed at having to appear in the Senate at such an early hour but encouraged by the fact that the president-elect had arrived in Washington, Wade defended his vote against conciliation by observing, "Nothing could have induced a people to rise in rebellion with the deliberate purpose of subverting a Government like this, except it was the accursed institution that is now in question."[57]

When the Capitol was expanded in the 1850s, most of the work was performed by slaves and free black artisans. The original timber-framed dome was regarded as too small for the larger building, so Thomas U. Walter designed a "wedding cake" style cast-iron dome. The building, like the divided country, remained unfinished for Lincoln's first inaugural. Courtesy Library of Congress.

"To Act the Part of a Patriot"

March–April, 1861

T HE CAPITAL WAS a forlorn place in 1861, and not merely because so many southern politicians and their wives had abandoned the city for Montgomery. Visiting nineteen years before, Charles Dickens had described Washington as a "city of magnificent intentions," and little had changed in the past two decades to alter that. The "wide, half-built, unpaved streets [were] alternately oceans of mud or deep in dust," Charles Francis Adams Jr. complained. Workers high atop a forest of cranes labored to complete the new Capitol dome, and across the mall the Washington Monument sat unfinished, a white stump surrounded by discarded chunks of stone. Both ongoing projects, some visitors reflected, were apt metaphors for the broken, half-completed Union that Lincoln was about to inherit. As had been the case since Washington's founding, a good many of the workers who toiled on these projects were slaves. The city, if one counted the suburb of Georgetown, was home to 75,000 people, of whom 3,185 were slaves and 11,100 were free blacks; both groups were compelled to carry written passes or freedom papers. Nestled between the slave states of Maryland and Virginia, the capital "was altogether Southern in sympathy and in expression," a disapproving Adams observed.[1]

Lincoln's train pulled into the B&O Station minutes after dawn on

the morning of February 23. Because detective Allan Pinkerton's operatives had uncovered rumors of an assassination plot, Lincoln arrived in the
city ten hours ahead of schedule, and in contrast to the loving crowd in
Springfield that had seen him off, only a single person, Congressman
Elihu Washburne, waited on the station platform. Lincoln, Pinkerton,
and Washburne boarded a carriage for the Willard Hotel, which they
surreptitiously entered through the side "ladies' entrance" on Fourteenth
Street. Owner Henry Willard was up to greet the president-elect, and
within minutes Seward arrived to welcome his future superior and discuss Crittenden's proposals. After twelve days of travel, Lincoln was
"rather tired," and his mood was hardly lifted by an anonymous note
left at the Willard desk denouncing him as "nothing but a goddamn black
nigger." Shortly before, Mary Lincoln had received a similar missive
from South Carolina, containing a picture of Lincoln "with a rope around
his neck, his feet chained and his body adorned with tar and feathers."
Both Lincolns could be superstitious, and with the nation dissolving by
the day, it was difficult for the president-elect to laugh away such ill
omens.[2]

Lincoln checked in to the posh Parlor Number 6, but despite his long
travels, there was little time for rest. His first call was at the White House,
a courtesy stop to meet Buchanan. When Lincoln and Seward arrived, a
cabinet meeting was under way, but a doorkeeper handed the president
Lincoln's card. Shouting, "Uncle Abe is downstairs," Buchanan hurried
his entire cabinet down to the Red Room. Among them was Buchanan's
newest attorney general, Edwin Stanton. Years before, Lincoln and Stanton had faced off in the courtroom in a patent-rights case brought by
Cyrus McCormick, and the president-elect had not forgotten Stanton's
rude and mocking behavior. Neither had Lincoln failed to remember
Stanton's enormous ability and political resolve, and as it became clear
that Simon Cameron was not a wartime secretary, Stanton would increasingly come to mind. The two Republicans also paid a call on General
Winfield Scott, who was out seeing to the city's defenses. Returning
to the Willard by mid-morning, Lincoln was finally allowed a few hours'
sleep.[3]

As the day progressed, Lincoln received a number of visitors at the
Willard, some less welcome than others. John Sherman, soon to assume

Salmon Chase's seat in the Senate, met Lincoln for the first time. Noting Sherman's height, Lincoln insisted on his favorite game, in which the two stood back-to-back. "Well," Lincoln laughed, "I am taller than you." Scott arrived, returning Lincoln's call, and, despite his seventy-four years and vast bulk, managed a low bow, "sweeping his instep with the yellow plumes of his hat." Frank and Montgomery Blair also visited, as did Charles Sumner. But when Lincoln admired the senator's height and suggested that they too "measure backs" to see who was taller, Sumner stiffly declined on the grounds that it was "the time for uniting our fronts against the enemy and not our backs." More unpleasant still was a Missouri delegate to the Peace Convention, still meeting elsewhere in the Willard, who encountered Lincoln in the hallway and rudely dismissed him as "a man of no intelligence." When Mayor James G. Berret, one of the city's many slaveholders, welcomed the president-elect by ostentatiously urging him to remain "true to the instincts of constitutional liberty," Lincoln lost all patience. This was his first occasion to say "anything publicly within a region of country where the institution of slavery exists," Lincoln snapped, and he had no more desire "to withhold from you any of the benefits of the Constitution" than he would with any of his "own neighbors." Startled by the reply, the mayor soon afterward withdrew.[4]

Around four o'clock, the entire Illinois delegation called at the Willard. This meeting "was less formal," one newspaper reported, since Lincoln knew both senators and most of the congressmen and the Republicans in the group were old supporters. But Lincoln had not met Douglas since their final debate nearly three years before, and the press was eager to see how the two old foes, one of them recently humiliated in the electoral vote, would respond to each other. Rather to his surprise, a journalist thought the "interview between Mr. Lincoln and Mr. Douglas was particularly pleasant." Privately, however, Lincoln was shocked at Douglas's appearance, and the teetotaler concluded that the rumors of the senator's heavy drinking were true.[5]

After the Illinois contingent left, Lincoln joined Hamlin and Seward at the future secretary's house for dinner. Rather to Hamlin's dismay, Seward argued eloquently for his policy of non-coercion and conciliation, and he encouraged Lincoln to give serious consideration to the

Peace Convention's handiwork. Hamlin instead advocated taking a hard line against lower-South secessionists to check the movement for disunion in the border states. Lincoln listened quietly, but he had already decided on a position midway between the two policies. Given the need to retain Virginia and Maryland, he observed, coercion was to be adopted only if the administration was forced to do so by southern firebrands. Should war come, the responsibility must lie with those who no longer regarded themselves as part of the United States. Seward believed he had carried the argument, however, and he wrote Frances that Lincoln was "very cordial and kind toward me." Hamlin came to the same conclusion. He left the dinner disheartened by what he perceived to be Seward's undue influence over the untested president-elect.[6]

The weary Illinoisan's day was not yet over. Just before leaving for dinner, Lincoln had received a note from the delegates to the Peace Conference, requesting an audience. The group arrived at nine, led by Chase and Tyler. Lincoln welcomed the former president "with all the respect due his position," but it immediately became clear that Chase spoke for the minority in the group that evening. One delegate bluntly asked Lincoln if he intended to "yield to the just demands of the South," or whether he planned to "go to war on account of slavery." A second informed the president-elect that "everything now depends on you." Lincoln replied that he disagreed with such sentiments. "My course," he said, "is as plain as a turnpike road." He planned only to "preserve, protect, and defend the Constitution," and that could not happen "until it [was] enforced and obeyed in every part of every one of the United States." Although Tyler had come to the conclusion during the convention that his state would have to secede, the Virginian grasped what Seward had missed. The new president was determined to stand by his party's platform and prevent the further extension of slavery; in Lincoln's mind, no legitimate Confederacy existed or ever would. Tyler politely excused himself and made plans to return to his estate in Virginia.[7]

The rest of the week passed quickly for Lincoln. John Bell paid a call on February 24, and an hour later Vice President John C. Breckinridge did so as well. The meeting was awkward at first, but Mary played peacemaker, and the three talked of former days in Kentucky. When yet another delegation of Virginians arrived later in the afternoon, however,

Lincoln's testy response indicated that he was tiring of the repetition. One urged him to evacuate Fort Sumter and offer "satisfactory guarantees" to the border slave states still in the Union. Lincoln replied, yet again, that he could support the proposed amendment protecting slavery where it existed, but he would never consent to its expansion. And why should he not fly the flag over Sumter, he wondered, or collect customs revenues in all American ports?[8]

Douglas returned on February 26 for a private meeting. The Peace Convention was about to cast its final vote, and rumor had it that unless the delegates found some compromise wording, Maryland planned to secede immediately. The Democratic leader implored Lincoln to publicly embrace that or some other conciliation plan. Both men had children, Douglas said, and he begged Lincoln "in God's name, to act the patriot, and to save our children a country to live in." Lincoln "listened respectfully and kindly," and he assured his longtime opponent "that his mind was engrossed with the great theme which they had been discussing." Douglas failed to persuade the president-elect to reconsider his position on the territories, and Lincoln realized the absurdity at this late date of trying to convince the champion of popular sovereignty of the wisdom of free soil. Yet after an exchange lasting an hour, Douglas unexpectedly promised, "I am with you, Mr. President, and God bless you." Genuinely touched, Lincoln replied, "God bless you, Douglas," adding, "The danger is great, but with such words and friends why should we fear? Our Union cannot be destroyed."[9]

Lincoln had other matters to attend to. He had been thinking about his inaugural address almost since election night, and in early January he had asked Herndon to locate copies of Henry Clay's 1850 compromise address and Andrew Jackson's fiery proclamation denouncing nullification. Lincoln also asked David Davis and his longtime friend Orville Browning to read early drafts. Then, during the dinner at Seward's residence, he requested that the secretary-designate do the same. Given Seward's advice during the meal, it came as no surprise that the New Yorker counseled moderation, although the length and number of Seward's recommendations on the address—seven pages filled with forty-nine suggestions—served as a reminder that the New Yorker regarded himself as the administration's premier. As did Browning, Seward advised

Lincoln to omit threats to exert his full authority "to reclaim the public property and places which have fallen." No matter what their plans upon taking office, Seward hoped a less intimidating tone might hold the border states in place for the next few critical months. "Be sure that while all your administrative conduct will be in harmony with Republican principles and policy," Seward counseled, "you cannot lose the Republican Party by practicing in your advent to office the magnanimity of a victor."[10]

If Lincoln was honestly willing to accept most of Seward's suggestions, which altered not merely the phrasing of the speech but also the tone of the address, the final, eloquent touches flowed from the president-elect's pen. After long years in the Senate, Seward possessed the ability to speak for hours. As a successful courtroom attorney and an avid reader of novels and plays, Lincoln was skilled in swaying a jury with a few art-fully chosen phrases. Seward's final paragraph began with "I close" and asked that southern politicians "not be aliens or enemies but fellow countrymen and brethren." The "mystic chords which proceeding from so many battlefields" demanded the public to again "harmonize in their ancient music when breathed upon by the guardian angel of the nation." As Lincoln reshaped and rewrote Seward's draft, incorporating it into his earlier Springfield version, he perhaps remembered a line from *David Copperfield*, published ten years before, that instead invoked "the better angels of our nature."[11]

A strong gale hit Washington on the evening of March 3. By dawn, the "sun shone brightly," Charles Francis Adams Jr. scribbled into his diary, but it was cold and raw, and "a strong wind carried on it clouds of that Washington dust" from the unpaved streets. As many as twenty-five thousand visitors crowded the city, but only the lucky few secured hotel rooms. A group of Wide Awakes arrived at the Willard and shouted for Lincoln, and the manager, hoping to accommodate the president-elect's staunchest advocates, somehow scavenged 475 mattresses and laid them along the hallways. One editor guessed that the crowd was larger than at any previous inaugural by at least ten thousand people, "though there were less people from the South than usual on such occasions." So many northerners wished to glimpse the new president or obtain a job from the first-ever Republican administration that "swarms of dusty-looking chaps, bearing carpetbags, wandered forlornly about the town" looking for a room or a meal.[12]

Among those who had not slept was Winfield Scott, who had donned his first uniform a year before Lincoln's birth. Having been informed by Pinkerton and Seward of the alleged threat against Lincoln's life, the aged general organized 650 available soldiers, most of them regular army veterans, into a special "*posse comitatus*" to preserve the peace and protect the president-elect. Scott ordered one body of West Point sappers—specialists trained to impede enemy movements—to ride ahead of the presidential carriage. A second squadron was to ride on either side of the open barouche, while an infantry company planned to march behind. Scott also placed sharpshooters high atop buildings along the Pennsylvania Avenue parade route; other marksmen leaned out of the windows of the Capitol. Scott himself planned to observe the day's proceedings from a nearby rise, with a battery of light artillery stationed at his rear. Although a native of Virginia, Scott had held the title of general for a half century, and when he assured one subordinate that he intended to "blow to hell any secessionist who showed a head," nobody assumed him to be exaggerating.[13]

That morning, Lincoln rose at five o'clock. As he breakfasted, his son Robert read his inaugural address aloud, and Lincoln scratched out his final changes. Buchanan spent the morning at the Capitol, signing a last stack of bills, but just before noon he directed his driver toward the Willard to collect the president-elect. (Mary had left for the Capitol with Senator James Dixon thirty minutes before.) Wearing a new, Chicago-made black cashmere suit and holding his high silk hat and gold-tipped cane, Lincoln strode out of the hotel to applause and cheers, as a military band struck up "Hail to the Chief." Caught up in the enthusiasm of the moment, Lincoln forgot to pay his $773.75 hotel tab and had to be billed later. One witness thought the president-elect appeared "calm, easy, bland, self-possessed, yet grave and sedate," while Buchanan looked "pale and wearied." Assuming that the ride might be tense for the younger Republican and the aged Democrat, Senators Edward D. Baker and James A. Pearce joined them in the barouche. The outgoing president brightened enough to remark that if Lincoln was "as happy in entering the

White House" as he was in returning home to Pennsylvania, he would be "a happy man indeed." Few Americans had found much to admire in Buchanan's disastrous tenure, but Lincoln graciously replied: "Mr. President, I cannot say that I shall enter it with much pleasure, but I assure you that I shall do what I can to maintain the high standards set by my illustrious predecessors who have occupied it." With that, the four fell silent.[14]

In that era, the inaugural parade preceded the swearing-in ceremony. Federal marshals, dressed in blue and orange, rode at the head of the parade, and behind the infantrymen trailed a large wagon, drawn by four white horses. Emblazoned with the word UNION, it bore thirty-four "beautiful little girls, dressed in white," each representing a different state or territory. "This elegant car," reported one journalist, was "under the charge of ten Wide Awakes in full uniform." Not surprisingly, most observers thought the procession resembled a military operation more than a political pageant. Many of those who had journeyed to Washington to witness the ceremony were disappointed that they could barely see Lincoln behind a wall of mounted soldiers, and in fact Colonel Charles P. Stone, on Scott's orders, continually dug his spurs into his mount, so that the uneasy horse bucked enough to keep potential assassins from getting off an accurate shot.[15]

The party entered the Capitol from the north, allowing Lincoln to walk behind a high board fence constructed for the occasion. The Senate had adjourned that morning, and outgoing vice president Breckinridge thanked the chamber for its courtesies over the past four years. "The memory of all this will ever be cherished among the most gratifying recollections of my life," he promised. Hamlin stepped forward, glancing up at his wife, Ellen, who sat smiling in the packed gallery. "The experience of several years in this body has taught me something of the duties of the presiding officer," Hamlin assured the chamber, "and with a stern, inflexible purpose to discharge these duties faithfully, relying upon the courtesy and cooperation of the Senators, and invoking the aid of Divine Providence, I am now ready to take the oath required by the Constitution." Breckinridge administered the brief vow before crossing the chamber to shake hands with Seward. Although recently elected to the Senate to fill Crittenden's chair, the former vice president was soon to don Confederate gray.[16]

On the morning of March 4, Buchanan and the president-elect shared their
barouche with senators Edward D. Baker and James A. Pearce, whose job
it was to engage in polite conversation as the two men rode to the Capitol.
Soldiers lining the parade route used their bodies as shields against potential
snipers. Courtesy Library of Congress.

The official party proceeded outside to what young Adams described as
a "miserable scaffold" built above the portico, where Lincoln faced nearly
three hundred seated dignitaries and the bent, cadaverous, eighty-three-
year-old Chief Justice Roger Taney. On the grounds below, "every available spot was black with human beings," marveled one editor, "boys and

men clinging to rails, and mounting on fences, and climbing trees until they bent beneath their weight." Senator Baker stepped to the podium and shouted, "Fellow citizens, I introduce to you Abraham Lincoln, president-elect of the United States." The audience, filled mostly with Republicans, applauded as Lincoln pulled on his steel-rimmed spectacles. John Sherman sat close by, and he noticed that Douglas "stood conspicuous behind" the president-elect. As Lincoln began to speak, a gust of wind rattled his notes, and he fumbled with his stovepipe hat as he tried to hold his speech in place. Less than a year before, Douglas had confidently expected to be standing at the podium, but now he stepped forward, saying, "Permit me, sir." Douglas took the hat and, according to the ever-present Murat Halstead, "held it during the entire reading of the Inaugural." Lincoln then began to speak in "a clear, loud, and distinct voice."[17]

Over the past week, the two Illinois rivals, always respectful of each other's talents, had grown closer still. When told that morning of the rumored threats to Lincoln, Douglas responded that "if any man attacks Lincoln, he attacks me, too." As Lincoln began to read his address, the unsuccessful Democratic candidate, who may have had an advance look at the text, murmured "Good" and "That's so" and "Good again," loud enough for reporters to overhear. When later questioned by journalists as to what he had meant, Douglas simply replied with a phrase he was to use often in the coming weeks. "I mean, if I know myself, to act the part of a patriot, [and] I indorse it."[18]

Lincoln's address of thirty-six hundred words touched upon all of the points that he had made during his campaign and had repeated in correspondence and interviews since his election. He had no intention of "interfer[ing] with the institution of slavery in the States where it exists," he assured "the people of the Southern States," believing that he had "no lawful right to do so." But "the Union of these States is perpetual," Lincoln warned. Although he made no mention of recovering federal property seized by "insurrectionary or revolutionary" states, he dedicated his administration "to hold, occupy, and possess the property and places belonging to the Government and to collect the duties and imposts." There need be "no bloodshed or violence, and there shall be none unless it be forced upon the national authority," yet neither could he allow the government to dissolve over the question of "slavery in the Territories." The "central idea of secession is the essence of anarchy," Lincoln cautioned. "The rule of a minority, as a permanent arrangement, is wholly inadmissible; so that, rejecting the majority principle, anarchy or despotism in some form is all that is left."[19]

Having reaffirmed his position on upholding federal authority, Lincoln concluded. "I am loth to close. We are not enemies, but friends. We must not be enemies. Though passion may have strained it must not break our bonds of affection. The mystic chords of memory, stretching from every battlefield and patriot grave to every living heart and hearthstone all over this broad land will yet swell the chorus of the Union, when again touched, as surely they will be, by the better angels of our nature."[20]

As Lincoln finished speaking, Taney, resembling "a galvanized corpse," slowly rose to administer the oath. The chief justice had sworn in eight previous presidents, and some journalists thought that the architect of the Dred Scott decision appeared visibly "agitated" over Lincoln's remarks on the territories. After promising to "faithfully execute the office of President," the new president kissed the Bible. Below, those in the crowd cheered and tossed their hats in the air, as nearby cannons boomed in salute. Lincoln shook hands with Taney and then turned to find Douglas, his hand outstretched. Watching from a distance, General Scott sighed in relief, "Thank God, we now have a government."[21]

That evening was the inaugural ball, held in a temporary structure thrown up behind City Hall. Mary Lincoln, dressed in a blue silk gown and adorned with pearls, gold bracelets, and new diamonds, was offended by the crude building, as she was by the tradition that the president entered first, while she was to promenade behind with another partner. But Douglas extended his arm, and the woman who had once briefly considered the Illinois Democrat as a possible suitor waltzed into the hall to surprised applause. The senator's "genial manner [and] cordial sympathy with the personnel of the new Administration," observed one Republican journal, "won for himself many friends, and the gratitude of all the Republicans present." A Democratic newspaper saw it differently. Those at the ball who remarked that Mary "would have been a better match for Judge Douglas than 'Old Abe,' " the New York Herald snickered, must be alluding "to the fact that the Old Judge and the lady, as they walked together, appeared to be of nearly the same height and proportions."[22]

In the days following the inauguration, Douglas stubbornly defended Lincoln's speech to fellow Democrats, both those in the North and those along the southern border. The address was "a peace-offering rather than a war message," he assured one colleague, adding that the new president had "sunk the partisan in the patriot." Many of his old supporters, who suspected that Lincoln's calm tone masked a radical agenda, were dumbfounded by the senator's words. "What means this evident weakness of Mr. Douglas for Mr. Lincoln?" one wondered. Some assumed that Douglas was "playing a deep political game" and was already looking ahead to 1864. Southerners were more incredulous still. The Mobile *Register* expressed its "amazement" that "Douglas comes out like a man in support of President Lincoln." To this, Douglas responded that he had not altered a single position, and that he continued to endorse popular sovereignty in the West. "I expect to oppose [Lincoln's] administration with all my energy on those great principles which have separated parties in former times," the senator clarified. But "on this one question—that of preserving the Union by a peaceful solution of our present difficulties," he added, "I am with him."[23]

Confederate shore batteries opened fire on Fort Sumter on April 12, and dispatches telling of the garrison's surrender reached Washington two days later. Immediately upon hearing the news that Sunday, Douglas took a carriage to the White House, where he found Lincoln alone at his desk. The two former opponents spoke for several hours. Hoping for the support of the now-truncated nation's leading Democrat, Lincoln confided that he planned to call up 75,000 volunteers. "Make it 200,000," Douglas shot back. Having been denied his party's sole nomination, and perhaps also the presidency, owing to the machinations of fire-eaters, the senator had no doubts about the seriousness of the crisis. "You do not know the dishonest purposes of those men as I do," he insisted. Pointing to a map on the office wall, Douglas urged the president to reinforce Fortress Monroe, in eastern Virginia; Harpers Ferry; Cairo, Illinois; and Washington itself. Later that evening, Douglas discussed the meeting with former Massachusetts congressman George Ashmun. "I venture to say that no two men in the United States parted that night with a more cordial feeling of a united, friendly, and patriotic purpose than Mr. Lincoln and Mr. Douglas," Ashmun later remembered.[24]

So much time did the two former adversaries spend in consultation that Secretary Seward, increasingly aware that he was not fated to serve as puppeteer in a Lincoln administration, grew increasingly disturbed by the growing intimacy between the senator and the president. One of Douglas's close friends later claimed that he had it "by authority" that Lincoln intended to bring the senator into the cabinet, a not-improbable notion given the number of former Democrats already serving the president and Lincoln's growing awareness of Cameron's ineptitude. Less credible was the rumor published in several newspapers that "the President positively has a commission of Major General made out for Senator Douglas," as was the report that "he will accept it." Douglas was confident enough, however, to ask the president to find a position for James Madison Cutts Jr., his brother-in-law, whom he described as "a man of talent & attainment." (That turned out to be an understatement; Cutts later earned the Congressional Medal of Honor for his valor during the Wilderness Campaign of 1864).[25]

Unionists in the upper South who were horrified by what they decried as Lincoln's "coercion" in attempting to resupply Fort Sumter were aghast at Douglas's open support for administrative policies. One St. Louis resident cabled the senator in hopes of clarifying his position. "Do you endorse Lincoln's war policy?" James L. Faucett queried. "Missouri will not." Thomas H. Gilmer of Virginia was equally dismayed. "God forbid that I may ever live to see the day, when *S.A. Douglas* can stoop so low as to take by the hand, *such [men] as A. Lincoln and his cabinet*." Never one to back down from a scrap, Douglas fired back a response to Faucett that he knew would become public. "I depreciate war," he replied, "but if it must come, I am with my country and for my country, under all circumstances, and in every contingency." Unwilling to join those in his party who blamed the crisis on Lincoln, Douglas took out his fury on the southern extremists who had destroyed his campaign. "If I were president," he snapped at one supporter, "I'd convert or hang them *all* within forty-eight hours."[26]

Understanding that no other Democrat in the country possessed his influence with northern conservatives, Douglas devoted every waking hour to rallying his devoted supporters to victory. Having begged Lincoln to conciliate the South in late February, he now publicly called for the recapture of Sumter and the earliest possible invasion of the Confederacy. Angry Georgians denounced the senator as a "wretched political suicide" who supported "a war to compel the Sovereign States of the South, to place their own domestic and municipal institutions under the ban of the Federal Government." Northern editors thought otherwise and commended Douglas's "manly and patriotic" behavior, accurately noting that "by voice and pen [he] rallied his own State, and the country, to the support [of] his old rival." Lyman Trumbull agreed and cheerfully conceded that Douglas's "course had much to do in producing that unanimity in support of the Government which is now seen throughout the Loyal States."[27]

It was this volatile combination of patriotic devotion and wrath that carried Douglas on his final journey back to Illinois in late April of 1861. Emotional speeches in Springfield and Chicago further damaged his already injured health, and shortly after sunrise on June 3 he was dead. Douglas had "devoted everything, and, at last, his life," mourned one editor, "to the salvation of the Republic, the integrity of the Union, and the maintenance of the Constitution." Later that afternoon, United States and Confederate forces clashed in the first serious skirmish of the war, near the small town of Philippi, Virginia. Adele Douglas was to be just the first of far too many war widows.[28]

Old Washington hands responded as they always had when one of their own passed away. Partisan differences were forgotten, or at least set aside. In the Senate, Trumbull moved a resolution, which was unanimously adopted, calling on members of that chamber to mourn Douglas's death "by wearing crape on the left arm, for thirty days." Bishop James Duggan, who at last was allowed to say a few words over the body of the unrepentant agnostic, assured his listeners that never "was a public man so universally wept, or more sincerely mourned." Whatever the truth of that, or however little Republicans like Trumbull had thought of Douglas personally, Americans were right in fearing that his death was "a public calamity." As numerous observers fretted, the senator's absence denied the Democratic Party a viable leader. With southern fire-eaters gone and Douglas missing from the Senate, the Democrats drifted. Younger, untested congressmen, such as Ohio's racist Clement Vallandigham, tugged the party away from the center, depriving the Democrats, and the nation, of a responsible opposition leader. "The loss of such a statesman at any time would have been irreparable," worried one New England editor, "but how much more at such a time as this, when [Douglas's] far-seeing eye, and commanding powers of persuasion" were sadly needed by the now-minority party.[29]

Having announced his allegiance to a slaveholding republic in his "cornerstone" oration, Confederate vice president Stephens provided a suitably misinformed epitaph for his former friend. He wished that Douglas "had lived longer or died sooner." Had the Illinois Democrat somehow perished before the Charleston convention, Stephens mused, the Democrats could have united on Davis or Breckinridge. With no Republican in the White House, there would be no disunion. Having failed to observe that no proslavery Democrat could have captured the Electoral College, or that Yancey and the Rhetts had openly labored in hopes of a Republican victory, Stephens compounded his error by assuring his brother that Douglas would have allowed southern slaveholders to secede in peace. "Had he lived he might have exerted great power in staying the North from aggressive war," Stephens wrongly assumed. "He would have been for a treaty of recognition & for peace."[30]

An election that featured four major candidates and one potential spoiler marked 1860 as unique in American annals. But Douglas's refusal to abandon his long-held belief in popular sovereignty, even after it became clear that his convictions endangered his nomination, was equally unique, since the unfortunate tendency of politicians to abandon ideological positions in hopes of political advancement was already an old tradition. Whatever else one might say of Douglas, Lincoln, Gerrit Smith, and Breckinridge, their positions were as clear as they were unyielding. And try as the Constitutional Unionists did to avoid discussing the central issue in the campaign, even Bell occasionally hinted that he harbored real positions. Voters today complain that too often opposing candidates hold nearly indistinguishable positions. But the white and black men who flocked to the polls in 1860 were presented with a series of stark options, and the Republican strategy of nominating the allegedly moderate Lincoln hardly meant that the differences between the Illinoisan and both Breckinridge and Douglas were not readily apparent. As Lincoln stated repeatedly during the campaign—and again in his inaugural address—southern Democrats believed that "slavery is right and ought to be extended; we think it is wrong and ought to be restricted."[31]

The election was unique also in its wholly unexpected outcome. In some presidential contests, clear front-runners captured not only the nomination but also the White House. Discerning observers in 1828 or 1932, for example, expected Andrew Jackson and Franklin D. Roosevelt, respectively, to be both the nominee and the victor, and nobody was surprised when these predictions turned out to be correct. To the extent that most of the country in January 1860 anticipated a two-candidate race of Seward and Douglas, not only did the convention season run counter to the prevailing political wisdom, but the election itself demonstrated the curious reality of unintended consequences. Yancey and the Rhetts worked to destroy their party in hopes of electing Seward, convinced that the ensuing tidal wave of secession would be peaceful and successful. The Republican convention in Chicago caught Yancey off guard, and as he spoke around the country in October, he continued to focus on the unsuccessful New Yorker. In Cincinnati, one observer reported to Lincoln, Yancey "referred in bitter terms to the *black* republicans and made frequent contemptuous allusions to Senator Seward's late speeches in the N[orthwest,] but he did not once mention your name or that of any other presidential candidate." Yancey's death in late July of 1863 meant that he did not live to see the end of slavery or the Confederacy, but by then the Battle of Gettysburg was over, and the Alabaman was painfully aware that his schemes had gone badly awry.[32]

Challenging times demand great leaders. But democracies, in times of national crisis, also require responsible opponents of equal stature, and with Douglas gone, Lincoln lacked a seasoned, mainstream rival. A states' rights Jacksonian to the core, Douglas would surely never have endorsed Lincoln's slow march toward civil rights and black freedom. But finally aware of the corrosive dangers of human bondage and the threat it posed to the American political system, neither would he have engaged in the sort of ugly race-baiting and outright distortion that became the standard rhetoric of too many Democrats during the war years. Too far apart from Lincoln on crucial matters of constitutional interpretation and emancipation, Douglas might not have been comfortable, as was the grasping Andrew Johnson, replacing Hamlin on the ticket in 1864. Instead, an uncontested Democratic nomination was sure to have been his, and the republic might have been witness to a second set of great debates. Illumination often comes too late in life, if it comes at all, but in the wake of his greatest defeat, the Little Giant's understanding finally came to match his ambition. "If we hope to regain and perpetuate the ascendancy of our party," he wrote in his final, dictated letter, "we should never forget that a man cannot be a true Democrat unless he is a loyal patriot."[33]

1860 Election Scenarios and
Possible Outcomes

On the November 1992 morning after Governor Bill Clinton won the presidency with 43 percent of the popular vote, Senator Robert Dole, already looking ahead to 1996, reminded television viewers that Clinton was "a minority president," since 56.3 percent of American voters had cast their ballot for one of his two rivals. Victorious Democrats replied that the president-elect had captured 100 percent of the White House. Ecstatic Republicans responded much the same way in 1860. Preferring to ignore Lincoln's low popular vote of 39.8 percent (an unimpressive record that remains unbroken), Republicans gleefully pointed to the fact that their candidate had carried every northern state but New Jersey (which he split with Douglas). Lincoln took the new state of Oregon and picked up the four critical states—California, Illinois, Pennsylvania, and Indiana—that Frémont had failed to carry in 1856. His total electoral count reached 180 votes, 28 votes more than the 152 needed to win. In every state that he carried except California, Oregon, and New Jersey, Lincoln's popular vote exceeded those of his three major opponents combined, and California not yet being the populous electoral powerhouse it is today, the total electoral vote for those three states was only 14.[1]

Even so, a few historians have emphasized how close the vote was in several key states. Richard N. Current argues that a shift of 80,000 votes, or only 2 percent, in certain areas would have denied Lincoln his electoral majority. Since none of his many rivals could have captured the Electoral College either, that would have tossed the contest into the House of Representatives, where each state was to have a single vote. As the Constitution required none of the state delegations to adhere to the will of the voters—and especially since Republicans could claim no popular mandate—Harold Holzer has added that deals and "compromises would have remained a possibility," particularly if "Congress concluded that denying Lincoln the White House might preserve the Union."[2]

Other scholars dissent vigorously from this theory. Even if fusion tickets had united more effectively in New York or Pennsylvania, Lincoln won those states handily, carrying 53.7 and 56.2 percent of the popular vote, respectively. William E. Gienapp observed that since the combined electoral count of California, New Jersey, and Oregon amounted to only 14 votes, Lincoln could have lost those states and still held 169 electoral votes, 17 votes more than he needed to win. William C. Harris notes also that "the likelihood of a successful fusion was slim in the key states because of the deep-seated antagonisms among the various anti-Republican elements."[3]

But how might the math differ had Lincoln faced a united Democratic party, or had Bell not managed to win three critical states and 39 electoral votes? The electoral map suggests that even had it been possible for southern delegates at the Charleston and Baltimore conventions to ignore the fire-eaters' machinations and nominate Douglas with an electorally attractive running mate, the Democrats would have been unlikely to win. Douglas and Breckinridge's combined electoral vote stood at 84. A unified ticket was sure to have kept California in the Democratic camp, since the vote of the two Democrats in that state amounted to 71,968, or 33,235 votes more than Lincoln earned. That would also have been the case in Oregon, where their combined votes far surpassed Lincoln's tally. But that would have added only seven electoral votes, bringing the Democratic score to 91, leaving a unified party still 61 votes shy of the required figure, while not sufficiently damaging Lincoln's safe margin of victory.[4]

Nor did Bell play the role of spoiler. Even if the Democrats had fielded a single ticket, Bell could not have denied anybody the White House. The three states carried by the Constitutional Unionists were admittedly safe for the Democrats, at least in 1860. But even after adding Bell's electoral vote of 39 to that actually earned by Douglas and Breckinridge, the combined tally still reaches a mere 123. What Douglas needed to do was carry Missouri (the only state he won), *all* of Bell's states, *all* of Breckinridge's states, New Jersey's other 4 electoral votes, *plus* either Pennsylvania's 27 electoral votes (which would have given him 160) or *both* Indiana and Illinois (for a total of 157). That scenario was possible, but not probable. In Illinois, which Lincoln carried by only 50.6 percent of the popular vote, the vote for his combined rivals came to 167,460, which meant that had just 4,711 Lincoln voters remained with the Democrats, Douglas could have won his adoptive state. The same was true for Indiana, where Lincoln beat his three rivals by but 5,923 ballots.

But that also assumes that northern Bell voters, who gave his new party 5,306 votes in Indiana, 4,914 votes in Illinois, and an impressive 12,776 votes in Pennsylvania (where Lincoln won by a solid 56.2 percent), would have *all* cast their votes for Douglas rather than Lincoln. In the North especially, Bell and Everett appealed to former Whigs, and after Kansas-Nebraska, the Lecompton battle, and Dred Scott, the Democratic brand was badly tainted in states barely carried by Buchanan. As the elections of 1976 and 2008 suggest, even when a candidate is not to blame for his party's past transgressions, voter fatigue with corrupt or failed administrations can be hard to overcome. Douglas's task in 1860 was not impossible, but it was certainly unlikely.[5]

Still harder to determine is whether the fears voiced in the Wigwam by Henry S. Lane of Indiana and Andrew Curtin of Pennsylvania—that Seward could not carry their states—had any validity. Historian David M. Potter thought so. "Since Lincoln apparently gained a good many moderate votes that Seward might have lost," he argued, "there seems good reason to believe that the Chicago strategists were realistic in thinking that Lincoln was the only genuine Republican who could be elected." Seward surely would not have run as well in either Indiana or Illinois as did Lincoln, a western politician, and during the summer and early fall of 1860 the New Yorker was still perceived to be the more radical candidate (a misperception that began to dissipate over the course of the following winter). But even in those two states, Douglas would have required unified party support and all of Bell's backers, and then the architect of the Kansas-Nebraska fiasco would still have had to peel away 10,634 moderate Republican votes that *were* cast for Lincoln.[6]

If that scenario was at least theoretically possible, it remains very doubtful that Curtin was right to be worried about his Pennsylvania. During the October gubernatorial election, Curtin won by 32,000 votes, but in November, Lincoln nearly doubled that figure and carried the state by 59,628 votes over his combined opponents. Only in New England and Wisconsin, where Lincoln slightly bested his Pennsylvania figures with 56.6 percent, did he do better than in the Quaker State. Even native son Buchanan carried his home state in 1856 by only 51,301, so it is hard to see how Seward could have lost the 60,000 votes that Douglas would have needed to win the state and the election.[7]

In 2008, Illinois candidate Barack Obama launched his presidential bid in Lincoln's Springfield, and at his inauguration, he took his oath of office while resting his left hand on Lincoln's Bible. What made Obama's election possible, of course, is that women gained the right to vote in the century after 1860, and that black voters were no longer restricted to a handful of New England states. Interestingly, in each of the eleven states that became part of the Confederacy, Republican candidate John McCain won a larger share of the white male vote than he did nationwide. On average, the McCain-Palin ticket earned 55 percent of the white male vote. But from Florida (the lowest of the eleven with 56 percent) to Alabama and Mississippi (which tied at 88 percent), the Republicans handily won over white men in what once were the lower-South slave states. By comparison, McCain captured less than his national average in what were the free states, ranging from 54 percent of the white male vote in Indiana to just 31 percent of that group in Vermont. (In the five slave states that remained part of the United States, McCain ran from 57 percent in West Virginia to a low of 45 percent in Delaware.)[8]

ACKNOWLEDGMENTS

Finishing a book is always a satisfying moment, but perhaps the best part of that moment is getting to thank old friends for their help, advice, support, and when necessary, tough criticism. John Belohlavek, the last word on antebellum Democrats, and especially on northern doughfaces such as Cushing and Buchanan, read the early chapters with enormous insight and sensitivity. John has been a friend and supporter for more than two decades, and his knowledge of the period is matched only by his kindness, charm, and appreciation for vodka martinis.

Michael Morrison and Stanley Harrold, two leading authorities on the troubled decade of the 1850s, read the early chapters and saved me from more than a few foolish errors. Stan, in particular, is never shy in pointing out when we disagree on matters, but only a true friend will tell you when he thinks you are wrong. As is the case with virtually all of the colleagues and scholars listed in my acknowledgments, this book could never have been written had I not first read and profited from Michael's and Stan's important studies, articles, and biographies.

Sally E. Hadden and John Quist, American heroes both, read the later chapters and filled the margins with perceptive suggestions and comments. John knows as much about the antebellum South as he does the North, which marks him as an especially unique and valuable historian, and Sally's knowledge of early American law is unparalleled. Gary Kornblith also read portions of the manuscript, and his helpful remarks were intelligent and perceptive. Gary's understanding of counterfactual possibilities was a constant and useful reminder that there is no such thing as an inevitable election outcome.

Carol Lasser and Stacey Robinson both read some of the middle chapters and sent me several pages of detailed and insightful comments. They also allowed me to steal a marvelous story about Wide Awake marchers in Seneca Falls from their forthcoming book. Stacey informed me that she teared up when Lincoln's nomination was celebrated with blasts from a rooftop cannon high above Chicago's Wigwam, which demonstrates her excellent judgment when it comes to choosing candidates.

The sometimes troubled relationship between the Republican Party and the abolitionist movement was especially complicated, and I was fortunate to be able to call on the help of two old friends, both leading scholars of American antislavery. Richard S. Newman and James Brewer Stewart read the middle chapters, and I am grateful to them, and to their important, voluminous scholarship, for helping me to understand the shifting currents of these reform efforts. The fact that I have seen Rich, Jim, Carol, and John Quist in antebellum costume should probably be left unsaid.

Two dear friends, Donald R. Wright and Alan Gallay, read much of the manuscript, just as they have earlier manuscripts without complaint. It is now exactly thirty years from the day in 1980 when I met Alan in graduate school, and I have known Don for the two decades that I have lived in Syracuse. Both are an inspiration. Great scholars, wonderful writers, and kind and supportive friends, they make my work and life far better for their presence. Two other great pals, Clarence Taylor and Graham Hodges, also continue to inspire with their scholarship, prodigious output, friendship, and genuine decency. In a very different way, five other longtime companions—Eric, Paul, David, Pete, and Roger—also helped to make the road more enjoyable.

Alison Games filled the manuscript with her trademark indecipherable scribbles and original, brilliant insights. For somebody who pretends to know little about late antebellum period, Alison provided me with astonishingly smart ideas and editorial suggestions. The fact is, of course, that she knows a lot about everything, but as I've written before, that is not why I am so grateful to her.

As always, my two brilliant and beautiful Smithies, Kearney and Hannah, failed to read a single word of the manuscript, and when I carry on too long about things historical, they denounce me as a nerd. As a child, Kearney even had to leave the Seward house tour when her allergies acted up. But they are so completely wonderful otherwise, and their absolute perfection remains the one constant in my life.

My fantastic agent, Dan Green, believed in the project from the beginning. At Bloomsbury, Peter Ginna proved a marvelous editor and was supportive of my view that front-runners Douglas and Seward, rather than dark horse Lincoln, should be the central focus of this study. At Le Moyne College, research librarian Wayne Stevens tracked down more than a few obscure sources with skill and unfailing good humor. I am grateful also to the college's Committee on Research and Development for their generous support for the images included here.

During the fall of 2009 it was my privilege to have dinner with Senator George McGovern, whose *Abraham Lincoln* is a model for how to pack a long life into a short volume. His published insights into Lincoln's personality are as perceptive as were his comments that evening on the battle over health care and the war in Iraq. As did Lincoln in 1858, the senator knows what it feels like to lose a tough campaign, and for those of us who remember his principled 1972 run, it is some solace to know that both men now stand vindicated.

Douglas R. Egerton
Fayetteville, New York
March 2010

NOTES

Prologue

1 Russell McClintock, *Lincoln and the Decision for War: The Northern Response to Secession* (Chapel Hill, NC, 2008), 266; Robert W. Johannsen, *Stephen A. Douglas* (New
York, 1973), 862–63.

2 Johannsen, *Douglas*, 863–65; John Alexander Logan, *The Great Conspiracy: Its Origin
and History* (New York, 1886), 263.

3 Damon Wells, *Stephen Douglas: The Last Years, 1857–1861* (Austin, TX, 1974), 287–
88; Louis Howland, *Stephen A. Douglas* (New York, 1920), 368; *New York Tribune*,
May 1, 1861.

4 Johannsen, *Douglas*, 867–68; Bruce Catton, *The Coming Fury* (New York, 1961), 392–
93; Howland, *Douglas* (New York, 1920), 368; H. M. Flint, *Life and Speeches of
Stephen A. Douglas* (Philadelphia, 1863), 216; *New York Herald*, June 7, 1861.

5 Gerald M. Capers, *Stephen A. Douglas, Defender of the Union* (Boston, 1959), 224; *New
York Herald*, June 7, 1861; Stephen Douglas to Virgil Hickox, May 10, 1861, in *Letters of
Stephen A. Douglas*, ed. Robert W. Johannsen (New York, 1961), 511–12. The Tremont
House remains in business today as the Tremont Hotel, 100 East Chestnut Street.

6 *Baltimore Sun*, May 20 and June 7, 1861; *Macon (Georgia) Daily Telegraph*, June 18,
1861; *Middletown (Connecticut) Constitution*, June 19, 1861.

7 *Macon (Georgia) Daily Telegraph*, June 13 and June 18, 1861; *Milwaukee Sentinel*, June
13, 1861; *Middletown (Connecticut) Constitution*, June 19, 1861; *New York Herald*, June 4,
1861; *Wisconsin Daily Patriot*, June 3, 1861; *Brooklyn Eagle*, June 3, 1861.

8 *Washington National Intelligencer*, June 4, 1861; *New York Herald*, June 5 and June 7,
1861; *Wisconsin Daily Patriot*, June 4 and June 5, 1861.

9 R. J. Mernick to Abraham Lincoln, June 3, 1861, in Lincoln Papers, Library of Congress (hereafter LC); William H. Seward to Abraham Lincoln, June 3, 1861, ibid.;
Washington National Intelligencer, June 5, 1861.

10 Montgomery Blair to Abraham Lincoln, November 28, 1861, in Lincoln Papers, LC.
Roy Morris Jr. relates this story in *The Long Pursuit: Abraham Lincoln's Thirty-Year*

Struggle with Stephen Douglas for the Heart and Soul of America (New York, 2008), especially 14–15 and 216–17.

11 Johannsen, *Douglas*, 872–73; *New York Herald*, June 5, 1861; *Baltimore Sun*, June 7, 1861.

12 Jim Cullen, "The Wright Stuff: Stephen Douglas, Frederick Douglass, and the Blackened Reputation of Abraham Lincoln," *Common-place* 9 (October 2008); Morris, *Long Pursuit*, 43–44; *San Francisco Bulletin*, June 6, 1861; Abraham Lincoln, memorandum of meeting with Adele Douglas, November 27, 1861, in Lincoln Papers, LC.

13 Flint, *Life of Douglas*, 216–17; Allen Nevins, *The Emergence of Lincoln* (New York, 1950), 2:328–29. The literature on Civil War causation is vast, but for useful overviews one should start with Kenneth M. Stampp, ed., *The Causes of the Civil War* (Englewood Cliffs, 1992 ed.). Elizabeth R. Varon, *Disunion! The Coming of the American Civil War, 1789–1859* (Chapel Hill, 2008), 1–16, updates the debate between the so-called fundamentalists, who regard the war as "irrepressible," and the modern revisionists, who regard slavery as a critical issue, but also one embedded within a host of other issues. This volume, of course, places slavery and the southern desire to defend and expand it at the heart of the division between the two sections.

14 *Congressional Globe*, 36th Cong., 1st sess., 2154; William C. Davis, *Look Away: A History of the Confederate States of America* (New York, 2003), 22–23; *Montgomery (Alabama) Daily Confederation*, February 25, 1860. David S. Heidler, *Pulling the Temple Down: The Fire-Eaters and the Destruction of the Union* (Mechanicsburg, PA, 1994), 2, argues that there was no "conspiracy to dissolve the Union. There were instead some people who tried to compel individual states to secede from the Union," which may be a distinction without a difference.

15 Unsigned to Abraham Lincoln, February 7, 1861, in Lincoln Papers, LC; George H. Keith to Abraham Lincoln, July 23, 1860, ibid.

16 John Minor Botts, *The Great Rebellion: Its Secret History, Rise, Progress, and Disastrous Failure* (New York, 1866), 224–25; Logan, *Great Conspiracy*, v; Francis Pickens to Jefferson Davis, January 23, 1861, in *The Papers of Jefferson Davis*, ed. Lynda L. Crist (Baton Rouge, LA, 1992), 7:25; Elbert B. Smith, *The Presidency of James Buchanan* (Lawrence, KS, 1975), 113. John McCardell, *The Idea of a Southern Nation: Southern Nationalists and Southern Nationalism, 1830–1860* (New York, 1979), 325, writes that "Yancey and his disciplined troops came to Charleston determined to have their way or walk out." Having their way *meant* walking out.

17 *Montgomery (Alabama) Daily Confederation*, April 13, 1860; *Macon (Georgia) Daily Telegraph*, March 9, 1860; *Charleston Mercury*, November 1, 1860; *Washington National Intelligencer*, May 8, 1860.

18 Logan, *Great Conspiracy*, 115, 245; George Fort Milton, *The Eve of Conflict: Stephen A. Douglas and the Needless War* (New York, 1963 ed.), 396–97; *Washington National Intelligencer*, November 1, 1860.

19 *Montgomery (Alabama) Daily Confederation*, February 17, 1860; David M. Potter, *The Impending Crisis, 1848–1861* (New York, 1976), 500; William C. Davis, *Rhett: The Turbulent Life and Times of a Fire-Eater* (Columbia, SC, 2001), 380; Elting Morison,

"Election of 1860," in *History of American Presidential Elections*, ed. Arthur M. Schlesinger Jr. (New York, 1986), 1113; *Congressional Globe*, 36th Cong., 1st sess., 2154.

20 *Clarksville (Texas) Standard*, April 21, 1860; *Montgomery (Alabama) Daily Confederation*, April 13 and April 17, 1860. Eric H. Walther's otherwise excellent and thoughtful biography, *William Lowndes Yancey: The Coming of the Civil War* (Chapel Hill, NC, 2006), 243, argues that Yancey simply wished to "force the national convention to accept his slave plank or to nominate a proslavery candidate" and only belatedly realized "how close he had come [in Charleston] to destroying the party."

21 Richard H. Sewell, *A House Divided: Sectionalism and Civil War, 1848–1865* (Baltimore, 1988), 79; Davis, *Rhett*, 394.

22 Phillip S. Paludan, "The American Civil War Considered as a Crisis in Law and Order," *American Historical Review* 77 (1972): 1013; McClintock, *Lincoln and the Decision*, 3.

23 Walther, *Yancey*, 260; *Charleston Mercury*, February 13, 1861.

24 *New Jersey Atlantic Journal*, March 1, 1860.

25 Henricus Scholte to Elbridge G. Spaulding, April 4, 1860, in Seward Papers, University of Rochester (hereafter UR); Everett Banfield to William H. Seward, May 19, 1860, ibid.; Arthur W. Fletcher to William H. Seward, May 20, 1860, ibid.; Arthur Dexter to William H. Seward, May 19, 1860, ibid.

26 *Jamestown (New York) Journal*, May 11, 1860; William R. Bonner to William H. Seward, January 16, 1860, in Seward Papers, UR. The senator, curiously, requires a modern biographer: Glyndon G. Van Deusen, *William Henry Seward* (New York, 1967), is now more than forty years old, and the historiography of his upstate New York world has grown immeasurably; John M. Taylor, *William Henry Seward: Lincoln's Right Hand Man* (New York, 1991), devotes more pages to Seward's private life than did Van Deusen but otherwise disappoints.

27 Willard L. King, *David Davis, Lincoln's Manager* (Cambridge, MA, 1960), 134–36; Susan B. Anthony to Henry B. Stanton Jr., September 27, 1860, in *Antebellum Women: Private, Public, Political*, eds. Carol Lasser and Stacey Robertson (Lanham, 2010).

28 *New York Herald*, April 23, 1860; *Lowell Daily Citizen and News*, May 2, 1860; *Washington National Intelligencer*, May 11, 1860; Murat Halstead, *Three Against Lincoln: Murat Halstead Reports the Caucuses of 1860*, ed. William B. Hesseltine (New York, 1960), 170.

29 James E. Harvey to Abraham Lincoln, July 27, 1860, in Lincoln Papers, LC; Henry Mayer, *All on Fire: William Lloyd Garrison and the Abolition of Slavery* (New York, 1998), 513.

Chapter One: A Nation with Its "Hands Full": The Republic on the Eve of 1860

1 Charles Francis Adams Jr., *An Autobiography* (Boston, 1916), 47; Halstead, *Three Against Lincoln*, 119; Flint, *Life of Douglas*, 14.

2 Flint, *Life of Douglas*, 14.

3 John B. Boles, *The South Through Time: A History of an American Region* (Englewood Cliffs, NJ, 1995), 271; James M. McPherson, *Battle Cry of Freedom: The Civil War Era* (New York, 1988), 121–22; Potter, *Impending Crisis*, 151–52.

4 Michael F. Holt, *The Fate of Their Country: Politicians, Slavery Extension, and the Coming of the Civil War* (New York, 2004), 93–94; William E. Parrish, *David Rice Atchison of Missouri* (Columbia, MO, 1961), 142–43; Robert Y. Young, *Senator James Murray Mason: Defender of the Old South* (Knoxville, 1998), 53.

5 McPherson, *Battle Cry of Freedom*, 122; Holman Hamilton, *Prologue to Conflict: The Crisis and Compromise of 1850* (Lexington, KY, 1964), 172–74; Stephen Douglas to the editor of the *San Francisco National*, August 16, 1859, in *Letters of Douglas*, 458–59; Michael A. Morrison, *Slavery and the West: The Eclipse of Manifest Destiny* (Chapel Hill, NC, 1997), 142–43.

6 Potter, *Impending Crisis*, 158–59; Larry Gara, *The Presidency of Franklin Pierce* (Lawrence, KS, 1991), 91; Thomas L. Krannawitter, *Vindicating Lincoln: Defending the Politics of Our Greatest President* (Lanham, 2008), 56; William W. Freehling, *The Road to Disunion: Secessionists Triumphant, 1854–1861* (New York, 2007), 2:61–62.

7 Holt, *Fate of Their Country*, 102–3; Howland, *Douglas*, 194–95; Capers, *Douglas*, 94; *St. Albans (Vermont) Messenger*, February 23, 1854.

8 Johannsen, *Douglas*, 414–15; William C. Davis, *Jefferson Davis: The Man and His Hour, A Biography* (New York, 1991), 247–48; William C. Davis, *Breckinridge: Statesman, Soldier, Symbol* (Baton Rouge, 1992), 115; Roy F. Nichols, *Franklin Pierce: Young Hickory of the Granite Hills* (Philadelphia, 1958 ed.), 334; Nicole Etcheson, *Bleeding Kansas: Contested Liberty in the Civil War Era* (Lawrence, KS, 2006), 14.

9 James W. Sheahan, *The Life of Stephen A. Douglas* (New York, 1860), 201; Stephen Douglas to Charles H. Lanphier, August 25, 1854, in *Letters of Douglas*, 327; *Wisconsin Daily Patriot*, June 30, 1860.

10 Huston, *Douglas*, 53–54; Anita Clinton, "Stephen A. Douglas: His Mississippi Experience," *Journal of Mississippi History* 50 (Summer 1988): 56–88; *New Hampshire Farmer's Cabinet*, June 21, 1861; Flint, *Life of Douglas*, 15; Wells, *Douglas: Last Years*, 141–42 and n. 9. One of Douglas's campaign biographers, Sheahan, *Douglas*, 437–38, defended the senator's annuity on the grounds that he "was not blessed with an over abundance of treasure" at the time and might have instead "convert[ed the] plantations and slaves into cash at any moment" by selling them. Sheahan also quoted Douglas as insisting, dishonestly, that he had never "received and appropriated to my own use one dollar earned by slave labor."

11 Stephen B. Oates, *With Malice Toward None: The Life of Abraham Lincoln* (New York, 1977), 111; Capers, *Douglas*, 98–99; Johannsen, *Douglas*, 510. James A. Rawley, *Race and Politics: "Bleeding Kansas" and the Coming of the Civil War* (Lincoln, NE, 1979), 40, notes that this much-quoted phrase was used in private correspondence only and that "Douglas never publicly condemned slavery. Its morality did not disturb him."

12 Walther, *Yancey*, 181; Stephen Douglas to the editor of the *New Hampshire Concord*, February 16, 1854, in *Letters of Douglas*, 285–86; *St. Albans (Vermont) Messenger*, December 10, 1853; George Ticknor Curtis, *The Just Supremacy of Congress over the*

Territories (Boston, 1859), 14; Van Deusen, *Seward*, 152–53; Gara, *Presidency of Pierce*, 95.

13 Holt, *Fate of Their Country*, 94; Etcheson, *Bleeding Kansas*, 30; Freehling, *Road to Disunion*, 2:71–75; Phillip S. Paludan, "Lincoln's Firebell: The Kansas-Nebraska Act," in *The Kansas-Nebraska Act of 1854*, eds. John R. Wunder and Joann M. Ross (Lincoln, NE, 2008), 98–99; Boles, *South Through Time*, 274; *Washington National Era*, October 19, 1854.

14 *Washington National Era*, September 14, 1854, and October 19, 1854; Varon, *Disunion!*, 252–53; Richard H. Sewell, *Ballots for Freedom: Antislavery Politics in the United States* (New York, 1996), 296–97; David Herbert Donald, *Lincoln* (New York, 1995), 188.

15 Norman A. Graebner, "The Politicians and Slavery," in *Politics and the Crisis of 1860*, ed. Norman A. Graebner (Urbana, IL, 1961), 15–16; Richard H. Brown, "The Missouri Crisis, Slavery, and the Politics of Jacksonianism," *South Atlantic Quarterly* 65 (Winter 1966): 55–72; Sewell, *Ballots for Freedom*, 259–60.

16 Frederick J. Blue, *Salmon P. Chase: A Life in Politics* (Kent, OH, 1987), 93–94; Johannsen, *Douglas*, 418; Stanley Harrold, *Gamaliel Bailey and Antislavery Union* (Kent, OH, 1987), 159; Charles B. Going, *David Wilmot, Free Soiler* (New York, 1924), 447–48; William Gienapp, *The Origins of the Republican Party, 1852–1856* (New York, 1987), 88–89; McPherson, *Battle Cry of Freedom*, 126; *Albany (New York) Journal*, January 31, 1854.

17 Jefferson Davis, *The Rise and Fall of the Confederate Government* (New York, 1958 ed.), 50–51; *The Lincoln-Douglas Debates of 1858*, ed. Robert W. Johannsen (New York, 1965), 77–78; *New York Herald*, August 28, 1859.

18 Eric Foner, *Free Soil, Free Labor, Free Men: The Ideology of the Republican Party Before the War* (New York, 1995 ed.), 60–61; Kenneth M. Stampp, *The Imperiled Union: Essays on the Background of the Civil War* (New York, 1980), 108–11; Potter, *Impending Crisis*, 203.

19 Kevin R. C. Gutzman, "Abraham Lincoln, Jeffersonian: The Colonization Chimera," in *Lincoln Emancipated: The President and the Politics of Race*, eds. Brian R. Dirck and Allen C. Guelzo (DeKalb, IL, 2007), 68–69; Daniel Walker Howe, *The Political Culture of the American Whigs* (Chicago, 1979), 292; Gabor Boritt, "Did He Dream of a Lily-White America?," in *The Lincoln Enigma: The Changing Face of an American Icon*, ed. Gabor Boritt (New York, 2001), 11.

20 *Alexander H. Stephens, in Public and Private: With Letters and Speeches, Before, During, and Since the War*, ed. Henry Cleveland (Philadelphia, 1866), 719; Foner, *Free Soil*, 45–46; *Lincoln-Douglas Debates*, 52–53, 162–63.

21 McPherson, *Battle Cry of Freedom*, 227–28; David Donald, *Charles Sumner and the Coming of the Civil War* (New York, 1961), 235; Foner, *Free Soil*, 284–91; Abraham Lincoln, speech "on sectionalism," October 1, 1856, in *Complete Works of Abraham Lincoln*, eds. John G. Nicolay and John Hay (New York, 1894), 2:306–307.

22 Foner, *Free Soil*, 29–30, 46–47, 54–64; Graebner, "Politicians and Slavery," in *Politics and the Crisis*, 26–27; Donald, *Lincoln*, 234; Freehling, *Road to Disunion*, 2:327; *New York Herald*, August 28, 1859.

23 Allan Nevins, *Frémont: Pathfinder of the West* (New York, 1939), 432–33; Morris, *Long Pursuit*, 87–88; Michael F. Holt, *The Rise and Fall of the American Whig Party: Jacksonian Politics and the Onset of the American Civil War* (New York, 1999), 834; William E. Gianapp, "The Crisis of American Democracy: The Political System and the Coming of the Civil War," in *Why the War Came*, ed. Gabor S. Boritt (New York, 1996), 102–3.

24 Capers, *Douglas*, 148; Howland, *Douglas*, 253; Sheahan, *Douglas*, 447; Freehling, *Road to Disunion*, 2:100. The *New York Tribune*, November 7, 1856, incorrectly reported that Frémont had carried Illinois, which they believed would compel Douglas to resign "while a Republican takes his seat in the Senate."

25 Huston, *Douglas*, 122; *Wisconsin Daily Patriot*, June 4, 1861; Morris, *Long Pursuit*, 65–66.

26 Mary Chesnut, *Mary Chesnut's Civil War*, ed. C. Vann Woodward (New Haven, CT, 1981), 48; William Webb, *The History of William Webb, Composed by Himself* (Detroit, 1873), 13; David W. Blight, "They Knew What Time It Was: African-Americans and the Coming of the Civil War," in *Why the War Came*, 70.

27 Freehling, *Road to Disunion*, 2:104; Foner, *Free Soil*, 314–15; Howell Cobb, "Letter to the People of Georgia," 1860, in *Southern Pamphlets on Secession*, ed. Jon L. Wakelyn (Chapel Hill, NC, 1996), 88–90.

28 Morrison, *Slavery and the West*, 174; Robert Toombs to Alexander H. Stephens, February 10, 1860, in *Correspondence of Robert Toombs, Alexander H. Stephens, and Howell Cobb*, ed. U. B. Phillips (New York, 1970 reprint), 462; Potter, *Impending Crisis*, 477–78.

29 Freehling, *Road to Disunion*, 2:368–69; Stephanie McCurry, *Masters of Small Worlds: Yeomen Households, Gender Relations, and the Political Culture of the South Carolina Low Country* (New York, 1995), 279–80; Stampp, *Imperiled Union*, 241–42; Morrison, *Slavery and the West*, 175–76; Davis, *Look Away*, 30.

30 Eugene D. Genovese, *The Political Economy of Slavery: Studies in the Economy and Society of the Slave South* (New York, 1964), 244–47, remains the best discussion on the need for slavery's expansion. Herbert Fielder, *The Disunionist: The Evils of the Union* (Georgia, 1858), 72. Other historians, such as Daniel W. Crofts, *Reluctant Confederates: Upper South Unionists in the Secession Crisis* (Chapel Hill, NC, 1989), xix, hope to "challenge" historians like Genovese "who consider [the] North and South utterly distinct and antagonistic by the late antebellum period." Their argument, of course, is ultimately not with modern scholars but rather with southern fire-eaters like Fielder.

31 Genovese, *Political Economy of Slavery*, 256–57; Smith, *Presidency of Buchanan*, 135. Bertram Wyatt-Brown, *Yankee Saints and Southern Sinners* (Baton Rouge, 1985) 58, for example, wonders how "the Wilmot Proviso [would have] affect[ed] the ordinary planter in South Carolina" and suggests that "loss of honor was the great issue," but Rawley, *Race and Politics*, 49, convincingly argues that the explosion of slavery in Missouri during the 1850s proves the fallacy of the "natural limits" argument that slavery could never exist in Kansas.

32 Steven Channing, *Crisis of Fear: Secession in South Carolina* (New York, 1970), 149–50, and Freehling, *Road to Disunion*, 2:175–76, argue that secessionists used the debate as a tool to destroy the Democratic Party and the nation; the *Macon (Georgia) Daily Telegraph*,

March 9, 1860, argued the opposite; "Importation of African Laborers," *De Bow's Review*, May 1858, 422, demonstrates that the two positions were not mutually exclusive.

33 Stampp, *Imperiled Union*, 241; *Washington Constitution*, April 28, 1860.

34 Austin Allen, *Origins of the Dred Scott Case: Jacksonian Jurisprudence and the Supreme Court, 1837–1857* (Athens, GA, 2006), 142–43; Kenneth M. Stampp, *America in 1857: A Nation on the Brink* (New York, 1990), 82–83.

35 Smith, *Presidency of Buchanan*, 24–25; Don E. Fehrenbacher, *Slavery, Law, and Politics: The Dred Scott Case in Historical Perspective* (New York, 1981), 184; Boles, *South Through Time*, 279.

36 *Lincoln-Douglas Debates*, 15, 19; Paul Finkelman, *An Imperfect Union: Slavery, Federalism, and Comity* (Chapel Hill, NC, 1981), 320–21; Foner, *Free Soil*, 97–98; Allen, *Origins of Dred Scott*, 135.

37 McPherson, *Battle Cry of Freedom*, 180–81; Donald, *Lincoln*, 208; *Washington National Intelligencer*, April 18, 1860, and April 24, 1860; Sewell, *Ballots for Freedom*, 303–4; Finkelman, *Imperfect Union*, 296–97.

38 McPherson, *Battle Cry of Freedom*, 177–78; Donald, *Lincoln*, 201–2.

39 Freehling, *Road to Disunion*, 2:97–98; Jean H. Baker, *James Buchanan* (New York, 2004), 100; Drew Gilpin Faust, *James Henry Hammond and the Old South: A Design for Mastery* (Baton Rouge, LA, 1982), 344; Walther, *Yancey*, 208–9; Fehrenbacher, *Slavery, Law, and Politics*, 247.

40 McPherson, *Battle Cry of Freedom*, 166–67; Morrison, *Slavery and the West*, 197–98; Capers, *Douglas*, 166; Stephen Douglas to John W. Forney, February 6, 1858, in *Letters of Douglas*, 408–9.

41 Philip S. Klein, *President James Buchanan: A Biography* (Philadelphia, 1962), 301; Sean Wilentz, *The Rise of American Democracy: Jefferson to Lincoln* (New York, 2005), 717; Smith, *Presidency of Buchanan*, 40.

42 Alan C. Guelzo, *Abraham Lincoln: Redeemer President* (Grand Rapids, MI, 1999), 212; *New York Times*, December 19, 1857; Klein, *Buchanan*, 302; Smith, *Presidency of Buchanan*, 42; Freehling, *Road to Disunion*, 2:138–39; Holt, *Fate of Their Country*, 121–22.

43 Capers, *Douglas*, 172–73; Morrison, *Slavery and the West*, 196; *Kansas Freedom's Champion*, October 20, 1860; *Charleston Herald*, December 15, 1857.

44 Freehling, *Road to Disunion*, 2:279–80; "Southern Convention in Montgomery, Alabama," *De Bow's Review*, May 1858, 425; Walther, *Yancey*, 221–22.

45 Botts, *Great Rebellion*, 105; Davis, *Rhett*, 233–34, 379.

46 Donald, *Lincoln*, 214; Oates, *With Malice Toward None*, 138.

47 Abraham Lincoln to Thomas A. Marshall, April 23, 1858, in Lincoln Papers, LC; Abraham Lincoln to Elihu B. Washburne, April 26, 1858, ibid.; John H. Bryant to Abraham Lincoln, April 19, 1858, ibid.; Johannsen, *Douglas*, 640–41.

48 Donald, *Lincoln*, 84–85; Morris, *Long Pursuit*, 14–15; Oates, *With Malice Toward None*, 134; Wilentz, *Rise of American Democracy*, 736; Kenneth J. Winkle, "Paradox Though It May Seem: Lincoln on Antislavery, Race, and Union, 1837–1860," in *Lincoln Emancipated*, 18–19.

49 Oates, *With Malice Toward None*, 114, 134; Abraham Lincoln to Stephen Douglas, July 24, 1858, in Lincoln Papers, LC; Stephen Douglas to Abraham Lincoln, July 24, 1858, ibid.; Stephen Douglas to Abraham Lincoln, July 30, 1858, ibid.

50 Capers, *Douglas*, 186–87; Freehling, *Road to Disunion*, 2:272–73; *Lincoln-Douglas Debates*, 88–89.

51 *Lincoln-Douglas Debates*, 12; Benjamin P. Thomas, *Abraham Lincoln: A Biography* (New York, 1980 ed.), 202–3; William C. Harris, *Lincoln's Rise to the Presidency* (Lawrence, KS, 2007), 151.

52 Eugene D. Genovese, *From Rebellion to Revolution: Afro-American Slave Revolts in the Making of the Modern World* (Baton Rouge, LA, 1979), 81; David S. Reynolds, *John Brown, Abolitionist: The Man Who Killed Slavery, Sparked the Civil War, and Seeded Civil Rights* (New York, 2005), 288–308; Stephen B. Oates, *To Purge This Land with Blood: A Biography of John Brown* (Amherst, MA, 1984 ed.), 278–79.

53 Freehling, *Road to Disunion*, 2:209–10; Oates, *To Purge This Land*, 302.

54 John Stauffer, *The Black Hearts of Men: Radical Abolitionists and the Transformation of Race* (Cambridge, MA, 2002), 257; Genovese, *From Rebellion to Revolution*, 106; Boles, *South Through Time*, 283.

55 Donald, *Sumner*, 350; Potter, *Impending Crisis*, 372; Oates, *To Purge This Land*, 354; Mayer, *All on Fire*, 502.

56 McPherson, *Battle Cry of Freedom*, 211–12; Taylor, *Seward*, 121; Van Deusen, *Seward*, 214–15; Wells, *Douglas*, 196.

57 Lacy K. Ford, *Origins of Southern Radicalism: The South Carolina Upcountry, 1800–1860* (New York, 1988), 348–49; Philip Shaw Paludan, *The Presidency of Abraham Lincoln* (Lawrence, KS, 1994), 6; John Townsend, *The South Alone Should Govern the South and African Slavery Should Be Controlled by Those Only Who Are Friendly to It* (Charleston, 1860), 1–6.

Chapter Two: *"Douglas or Nobody": The Democrats*

1 Morris, *Long Pursuit*, 140–41; Halstead, *Three Against Lincoln*, 274–75.

2 William L. Barney, "William Lowndes Yancey," in *Encyclopedia of the Confederacy*, ed. Richard N. Current (New York, 1995), 1747; J. Mills Thornton, "William Lowndes Yancey," in *American National Biography*, ed. Mark C. Carnes (New York, 1999), 24:104; Ralph B. Draughton, "The Young Manhood of William L. Yancey," *Alabama Review* 19 (1966): 32–36; Eric H. Walther, *The Fire-Eaters* (Baton Rouge, LA, 1992), 50.

3 Thornton, "Yancey," 105–6; Walther, *Yancey*, 230.

4 Dwight Dumond, *The Secession Movement, 1860–1861* (New York, 1931), 24; Austin Venable, "William L. Yancey's Transition from Unionism to States' Rights," *Journal of Southern History* 10 (1944): 342; *Wisconsin Daily Patriot*, May 26, 1860.

5 Dumond, *Secession Movement*, 70–71; Catton, *Coming Fury*, 26. The nine resolutions were reprinted in *Official Proceedings of the Democratic National Convention at Charleston, 1860* (Cleveland, 1860), 56–57. Roy F. Nichols, *The Disruption of American Democracy* (New York, 1948), 279, notes that some of Yancey's enemies believed the plank was

designed to elevate him into the Senate. Forsyth, however, was surely more correct in guessing at Yancey's goals.

6 McCardell, *Idea of a Southern Nation*, 315–16; J. Mills Thornton, *Politics and Power in a Slave Society: Alabama, 1800–1860* (Baton Rouge, LA, 1978), 390–91.

7 William E. Gienapp, "The Crisis of American Democracy: The Political System and the Coming of the Civil War," in *Why the War Came*, 108; Robert Toombs to Alexander Stephens, February 10, 1860, in *Toombs, Stephens, Cobb Correspondence*, 461; "Presidential Candidates and Aspirants," *De Bow's Review*, July 1860, 98; Howland, *Douglas*, 346–47; McPherson, *Battle Cry of Freedom*, 195; Eli N. Evans, *Judah P. Benjamin: The Jewish Confederate* (New York, 1988), 106–7.

8 Potter, *Impending Crisis*, 403; Davis, *Davis*, 278–79; McPherson, *Battle Cry of Freedom*, 214; Sewell, *A House Divided*, 72–73.

9 Davis, *Rise and Fall*, 42–43; *Congressional Globe*, 36th Cong., 1st sess., 658; Jefferson Davis, "Resolutions on the Relations of the States," February 2, 1860, in *Papers of Davis*, 6:273–74. As Albert J. Von Frank, *The Trials of Anthony Burns: Freedom and Slavery in Emerson's Boston* (Cambridge, MA, 1998), 6–7, observes, the Fugitive Slave Act of 1850 did not allow runaways the benefit of counsel, since technically they were not charged with a crime.

10 Albert D. Kirwan, *John J. Crittenden: The Struggle for Union* (Lexington, KY, 1962), 342–43; Clement Eaton, *Jefferson Davis* (New York, 1977), 112–13; Morrison, *Slavery and the West*, 214; Nichols, *Disruption of American Democracy*, 283–84; William C. Cooper, *Jefferson Davis: American* (New York, 2000), 304–5.

11 Harris, *Lincoln's Rise*, 166–67; Stephen Douglas to J. B. Dorr, June 22, 1859, in *Letters of Douglas*, 446–47; *New Jersey Atlantic Journal*, March 1, 1860.

12 Freehling, *Road to Disunion*, 2:318; Stephen Douglas to James W. Singleton, March 31, 1859, in *Letters of Douglas*, 439; Robert Warden, *Life and Character of Stephen Arnold Douglas* (Columbus, OH, 1860), 6.

13 *San Antonio Ledger*, April 4, 1860; *Macon (Georgia) Daily Telegraph*, August 16, 1859; *Clarksville Texas Standard*, April 21, 1860; *Wisconsin Daily Patriot*, May 26, 1860.

14 *New York Herald*, March 16, 1860; *Montgomery (Alabama) Daily Confederation*, February 5, 1860.

15 *Boston Daily Courier*, June 27, 1859; *New York Herald*, April 23, 1860; Milton, *Eve of Conflict*, 373; *Macon (Georgia) Daily Telegraph*, March 9, 1860.

16 Cooper, *Davis*, 310; Eaton, *Davis*, 116; *Montgomery (Alabama) Daily Confederation*, April 13, 1860; *Lowell (Massachusetts) Daily Citizen and News*, May 2, 1860; *Washington Constitution*, April 14, 1860.

17 Davis, *Davis*, 280, flatly states that Davis's interest in the nomination by 1860 was "negligible," although he does concede that the New England tour was clearly political. Andrew Johnson to George W. Jones, March 13, 1860, in *The Papers of Andrew Johnson*, eds. LeRoy P. Graf and Ralph Haskins (Knoxville, TN, 1976), 3:466–67; John M. Belohlavek, *Broken Glass: Caleb Cushing and the Shattering of the Union* (Kent, OH, 2005), 297–98.

18 Nichols, *Disruption of American Democracy*, 278; Edward P. Crapol, *John Tyler, the Accidental President* (Chapel Hill, NC, 2006), 255–57; *Clarksville Texas Standard*, June 11, 1859; Davis, *Breckinridge*, 213–14.

19 "Presidential Candidates and Aspirants," *De Bow's Review*, 100; Hans L. Trefousse, *Andrew Johnson: A Biography* (New York, 1989), 45, 122–24.

20 Hu Douglas to Andrew Johnson, March 11, 1860, in *Papers of Johnson*, 3:460; Thomas J. Henley to Andrew Johnson, March 19, 1860, ibid., 3:476; Andrew Johnson to Robert Johnson, April 22, 1860, ibid., 3:573.

21 Thomas E. Schott, *Alexander Stephens of Georgia: A Biography* (Baton Rouge, LA, 1988), 285; *Lowell (Massachusetts) Daily Citizen and News*, April 14, 1860; John B. Hoge to Robert M. T. Hunter, February 19, 1860, in *Correspondence of Robert M.T. Hunter, 1826–1876*, ed. Charles H. Ambler (Washington, DC, 1918), 293; William W. Wick to Robert M. T. Hunter, May 6, 1860, ibid., 323; Charles Linsley to Robert M. T. Hunter, March 26, 1860, ibid., 306–7.

22 Schott, *Stephens*, 285; Potter, *Impending Crisis*, 323; "Presidential Candidates and Aspirants," *De Bow's Review*, 103.

23 Benjamin P. Thomas, *Stanton: The Life and Times of Lincoln's Secretary of War* (New York, 1962), 86–87; Morison, "Election of 1860," 1112–13; *Wisconsin Daily Patriot*, June 25, 1860; Milton, *Eve of Conflict*, 474; Freehling, *Road to Disunion*, 2:295; Davis, *Rhett*, 380.

24 Johannsen, *Douglas*, 747; Irving Katz, *August Belmont: A Political Biography* (New York, 1969), 62–63, 68.

25 Nichols, *Disruption of American Democracy*, 291; Johannsen, *Douglas*, 747; Milton, *Eve of Conflict*, 426; Walter J. Fraser Jr., *Charleston! Charleston! The History of a Southern City* (Columbia, SC, 1989), 239–40. On the Workhouse, see my *He Shall Go Out Free: The Lives of Denmark Vesey* (Lanham, MD, 2004 ed.), 32–33.

26 Halstead, *Three Against Lincoln*, xi, 7; Catton, *Coming Fury*, 24–25.

27 Davis, *Rhett*, 384; Channing, *Crisis of Fear*, 207–8.

28 Halstead, *Three Against Lincoln*, 12–13; Catton, *Coming Fury*, 6; Nevins, *Emergence of Lincoln*, 2:204; Katz, *Belmont*. The Hibernian Hall still stands at 105 Meeting Street, but its original Ionic arches were destroyed in the earthquake of 1886 and replaced with the Corinthian arches one sees today.

29 Halstead, *Three Against Lincoln*, 18–19; Nevins, *Emergence of Lincoln*, 2:212; *Official Proceedings of the Democratic Convention*, 3.

30 Freehling, *Road to Disunion*, 2:296–97; Nevins, *Emergence of Lincoln*, 2:207–8. On the creation of the two-thirds rule, which nearly cost Franklin Delano Roosevelt the nomination in 1932, see Glyndon G. Van Deusen, *The Jacksonian Era, 1828–1848* (New York, 1959), 68.

31 Wells, *Douglas*, 216; Potter, *Impending Crisis*, 408; Morison, "Election of 1860," 1113.

32 Nevins, *Emergence of Lincoln*, 2:205; Belohlavek, *Broken Glass*, 307; Halstead, *Three Against Lincoln*, 25–27.

33 Huston, *Douglas*, 163; Johannsen, *Douglas*, 751; Belohlavek, *Broken Glass*, 305; Michael T. Parrish, *Richard Taylor: Soldier Prince of Dixie* (Chapel Hill, NC, 1992), 86–87.

34 "Presidential Candidates and Aspirants," *De Bow's Review*, 99; Dick Nolan, *Benjamin Franklin Butler* (San Francisco, 1991), 50; Davis, *Breckinridge*, 218–19.

35 Halstead, *Three Against Lincoln*, 31–32; *New York Herald*, April 24, 1860; *Washington National Intelligencer*, April 26, 1860; *Lowell (Massachusetts) Daily Citizen and News*, April 30, 1860.

36 Halstead, *Three Against Lincoln*, 35–36, 50–51; Heidler, *Pulling the Temple Down*, 146; *Lowell (Massachusetts) Daily Citizen and News*, April 30, 1860.

37 *Washington National Intelligencer*, May 5, 1860, and April 27, 1860; *Lowell (Massachusetts) Daily Citizen and News*, April 27, 1860; *Official Proceedings of the Democratic Convention*, 32. There was, in fact, much discussion of reopening the Atlantic slave trade. Delegate W. B. Gaulden, a Savannah-based slave trader, claimed that the 1807 "prohibition of the slave trade had put an end to all hope of extending the area of slavery at the present time. There was but one remedy at present for the evils the South complained of, and that was to reopen the African slave trade." See Halstead, *Three Against Lincoln*, 89–90.

38 Nevins, *Emergence of Lincoln*, 2:224–25, suggests that the fire-eater "minority of the gathering . . . spoke for a minority of the party," but the fact that the post-1854 Democrats were a southern-based party is precisely why the slaveholding delegates in Charleston refused to consider a Douglas nomination. Huston, *Douglas*, 161; Davis, *Rhett*, 383.

39 Smith, *Presidency of Buchanan*, 106; Felicity Allen, *Jefferson Davis: Unconquerable Heart* (Columbia, MO, 1999), 249; Robert Toombs to Alexander Stephens, May 12, 1860, in *Toombs, Stephens, Cobb Correspondence*, 477; Robert Toombs to Alexander Stephens, May 5, 1860, ibid., 468.

40 *Houston Telegraph*, May 1, 1860; Wells, *Douglas*, 206; Smith, *Presidency of Buchanan*, 107; Potter, *Impending Crisis*, 411; Channing, *Crisis of Fear*, 204–5.

41 *Washington Constitution*, April 28, 1860; *Official Proceedings of the Democratic Convention*, 37; Dumond, *Secession Movement*, 46–49.

42 Wells, *Douglas*, 222–23; Logan, *Great Conspiracy*, 88; Halstead, *Three Against Lincoln*, 47.

43 Johannsen, *Douglas*, 753; *Washington National Intelligencer*, April 28, 1860; Morrison, *Slavery and the West*, 222; Halstead, *Three Against Lincoln*, 45.

44 *Washington Constitution*, April 28, 1860; Halstead, *Three Against Lincoln*, 8, 52–53.

45 Halstead, *Three Against Lincoln*, 53; Freehling, *Road to Disunion*, 2:301–2; Catton, *Coming Fury*, 31–32; *Washington National Intelligencer*, April 28, 1860.

46 Freehling, *Road to Disunion*, 2:283–84; Walther, *Yancey*, 216–17. On the 1820 law establishing illegal traffic in Africans as piracy, see my *Charles Fenton Mercer and the Trial of National Conservatism* (Jackson, MI, 1989), chap. 12.

47 Halstead, *Three Against Lincoln*, 54–55; *Lowell (Massachusetts) Daily Citizen and News*, April 30, 1828.

48 Walther, *Yancey*, 243; Parrish, *Taylor*, 105–6; Channing, *Crisis of Fear*, 162.

49 *Houston Telegraph*, May 1, 1860; Charles Mason to Robert M. T. Hunter, April 30, 1860, in *Correspondence of Hunter*, 322; Freehling, *Road to Disunion*, 2:305; Nevins, *Emergence of Lincoln*, 2:218.

50 William C. Davis, *"A Government of Our Own": The Making of the Confederacy* (New York, 1994), 10; Nevins, *Emergence of Lincoln*, 2:226–27.

51 Catton, *Coming Fury*, 34; McCardell, *Idea of a Southern Nation*, 326; *Washington National Intelligencer*, May 1, 1860, and May 17, 1860; Halstead, *Three Against Lincoln*, 74–75.

52 Walther, *Yancey*, 244; Heidler, *Pulling the Temple Down*, 153; Catton, *Coming Fury*, 77; Davis, *Rhett*, 385–86.

53 Johannsen, *Douglas*, 756; Morrison, *Slavery and the West*, 225.

54 Huston, *Douglas*, 165; Johannsen, *Douglas*, 759–60.

55 Dumond, *Secession Movement*, 56–57; Catton, *Coming Fury*, 38–39; Benson L. Lossing, *Pictorial History of the Civil War in the United States of America* (Philadelphia, 1866), 24.

56 *Macon (Georgia) Daily Telegraph*, April 30, 1860; Belohlavek, *Broken Glass*, 308; Dumond, *Secession Movement*, 39–40; *Washington National Intelligencer*, May 3, 1860; Wells, *Douglas*, 229. Word even arrived in Wisconsin that Douglas had received the nomination. See *Wisconsin Daily Patriot*, May 1, 1860, which added, "A thousand cheers for Douglas the next President."

57 *Official Proceedings of the Democratic National Committee*, 74; Catton, *Coming Fury*, 37; Halstead, *Three Against Lincoln*, 99; Morris, *Long Pursuit*, 151–52; Trefousse, *Johnson*, 124–25.

58 Halstead, *Three Against Lincoln*, 113–14; *Lowell (Massachusetts) Daily Citizen and News*, April 27, 1860.

59 Halstead, *Three Against Lincoln*, 66–67; Milton, *Eve of Conflict*, 436.

60 *Official Proceedings of the Democratic National Convention*, 90–91; *Washington National Intelligencer*, May 5, 1860; Halstead, *Three Against Lincoln*, 106–7.

61 Potter, *Impending Crisis*, 412; *Washington National Intelligencer*, May 5, 1860; Nichols, *Disruption of American Democracy*, 308.

62 Fraser, *Charleston!*, 246; Wells, *Douglas*, 231–32.

Chapter Three: Principles and the "Duty to Recognize" None: The Constitutional Union and Liberty Parties

1 *St. Albans (Vermont) Daily Messenger*, February 2, 1860; Kirwan, *Crittenden*, chaps. 1–3; Ann Mary Coleman, *The Life of John J. Crittenden* (Philadelphia, 1873), 1:13; *New York Times*, August 2, 1863.

2 Robert V. Remini, *Henry Clay: Statesman for the Union* (New York, 1991), 373; Allen E. Ragan, "John J. Crittenden, 1787–1863," *Filson Club Historical Quarterly* 18 (1944): 20–28.

3 Henry Clay to Cornelius C. Baldwin, August 28, 1838, in *The Papers of Henry Clay*, eds. Robert Seager and Melba P. Hay (Lexington, KY, 1988), 9:223; Glyndon G. Van Deusen, *The Life of Henry Clay* (Boston, 1937), 137; Coleman, *Crittenden*, 20; Kirwan, *Crittenden*, 344.

4 Arthur C. Cole, *The Whig Party in the South* (Washington, DC, 1914), 340; Kirwan, *Crittenden*, 345; Potter, *Impending Crisis*, 416.

5 Kirwan, *Crittenden*, 344–45.

6 Mayer, *All on Fire*, 509; *Liberator*, March 16, 1860. By 1860, African American men could vote in New England, but not in Lincoln's Illinois. In Seward's New York, blacks had to meet a property qualification not imposed upon white males. See Graham Russell Hodges, *Root and Branch: African Americans in New York and East Jersey, 1613–1865* (Chapel Hill, NC, 1999), 253.

7 Daniel Walker Howe, *What Hath God Wrought: The Transformation of America, 1815–1848* (New York, 2007), 510–12; Howe, *Political Culture*, 278–79; James Brewer Stewart, *Abolitionist Politics and the Coming of the Civil War* (Amherst, MA, 2008), 212; Donald, *Lincoln*, 234; Paludan, *Presidency of Lincoln*, 17.

8 Kirwan, *Crittenden*, 346; Milton, *Eve of Conflict*, 450–51; Morrison, *Slavery and the West*, 231.

9 Morrison, *Slavery and the West*, 247; Joseph H. Parks, *John Bell of Tennessee* (Baton Rouge, LA, 1950), 349. Harrison, in fact, remained the oldest man to be elected president until the election of Ronald Reagan in 1980.

10 *Staunton (Virginia) Spectator*, October 2, 1860; Parks, *Bell*, 347. Because Bell's holdings were diverse—typical of border Whigs—it is difficult to know precisely how many slaves he owned. His estate near Nashville was run by slaves, and he owned a tract of land in Louisiana. He was also the part owner of the Cumberland Iron Works in Tennessee, which owned or rented 365 slaves to work in the furnaces. See Parks, *Bell*, 340–41.

11 Kirwan, *Crittenden*, 350–51; Parks, *Bell*, 348–49; *Amherst (New Hampshire) Farmer's Cabinet*, April 4, 1860.

12 Stauffer, *Black Hearts of Men*, 20; Nevins, *Emergence of Lincoln*, 2:261; Catton, *Coming Fury*, 47–48; Harris, *Lincoln's Rise*, 201. Unfortunately, there remains no modern, scholarly biography of Smith. Norman K. Dann, *Practical Dreamer: Gerrit Smith and the Crusade for Social Reform* (Hamilton, NY, 2009), says nothing about the election of 1860; Stauffer, 5, agrees with other scholars that the oversight is due to Smith's utterly illegible handwriting.

13 *New York Herald*, March 10, 1860; Kirwan, *Crittenden*, 351–52. Since Crittenden clearly could have had the nomination had he wished, he was undoubtedly telling the truth in saying he had no interest in being a candidate.

14 *Washington National Intelligencer*, June 1, 1860; Marshall De Bruhl, *Sword of San Jacinto: A Life of Sam Houston* (New York, 1993), 386–89. The *Houston Telegraph* aptly described the Texas leader as a "people loving, Convention-hating Houston."

15 "Presidential Candidates and Aspirants," *De Bow's Review*, 93; Marvin R. Cain, *Lincoln's Attorney General: Edward Bates of Missouri* (Columbia, MO, 1965), 94–97; Timothy D. Johnson, *Winfield Scott: The Quest for Military Glory* (Lawrence, KS., 1998), 222; John S. D. Eisenhower, *Agent of Destiny: The Life and Times of General Winfield Scott* (New York, 1997), 344–45.

16 *Washington National Intelligencer*, May 10, 1860; *New York Herald*, May 9, 1860; Parks, *Bell*, 351–52; Kirwan, *Crittenden*, 354.

17 Kirwan, *Crittenden*, 354–55; *Concord New-Hampshire Patriot*, May 9, 1860; *Washington Constitution*, May 10, 1860; *Baltimore Sun*, May 10, 1860; Halstead, *Three Against Lincoln*, 122.

18 Jack Kelly, "John J. Crittenden and the Constitutional Union Party," *Filson Club History Quarterly* 48 (1974): 265–67; *Washington National Intelligencer*, May 15, 1860; *Lowell (Massachusetts) Daily Citizen*, May 19, 1860; Halstead, *Three Against Lincoln*, 122–23, 126.

19 *Wisconsin Daily Patriot*, May 9, 1860; *Daily Ohio Statesman*, May 10, 1860; Halstead, *Three Against Lincoln*, 124–25; *Washington National Intelligencer*, May 12, 1860.

20 *Washington National Intelligencer*, May 9, 1860; Halstead, *Three Against Lincoln*, 127.

21 Sherry Penney, *Patrician in Politics: Daniel D. Barnard of New York* (Port Washington, NY, 1974), 152–53; Nevins, *Emergence of Lincoln*, 2:270–80.

22 *Wisconsin Daily Patriot*, May 10, 1860; *New York Herald*, May 9, 1860.

23 *New York Herald*, May 9, 1860; *Lowell (Massachusetts) Daily Citizen*, May 10, 1860. On Houston and slavery, see De Bruhl, *Sword of San Jacinto*, 311, 339, 401.

24 Parks, *Bell*, 352–54; Kirwan, *Crittenden*, 353; *Wisconsin Daily Patriot*, May 4, 1860; *New York Herald*, May 9, 1860.

25 *Dallas Weekly Herald*, May 30, 1860; *Amherst (New Hampshire) Farmer's Cabinet*, May 16, 1860; *Wisconsin Daily Patriot*, May 10, 1860; *Washington National Intelligencer*, May 11, 1860.

26 *Washington National Intelligencer*, May 12, 1860; Halstead, *Three Against Lincoln*, 134–35.

27 *Dallas Weekly Herald*, May 30, 1860; *Washington National Intelligencer*, May 12, 1860; Parks, *Bell*, 355; John C. Waugh, *One Man Great Enough: Abraham Lincoln's Road to Civil War* (New York, 2007), 342. For several decades, Virginia women had been active participants in Whig politics and attended rallies, speeches, and processions. But they were drawn to the party's moral tone, not to Henry Clay's appearance. See Elizabeth Varon, *We Mean to Be Counted: White Women and Politics in Antebellum Virginia* (Chapel Hill, NC, 1998), 71–72.

28 *Washington National Intelligencer*, May 12, 1860.

29 Halstead, *Three Against Lincoln*, 135.

30 *Washington National Intelligencer*, May 16, 1860; Morris, *Long Pursuit*, 185.

31 Boles, *South Through Time*, 287. The *Washington National Intelligencer*, May 14, 1860, placed the number of supporters at six thousand, but the friendly newspaper also supported the Bell ticket.

32 Parks, *Bell*, 359–60; Halstead, *Three Against Lincoln*, 125; John Bell to Washington Hunt, May 21, 1860, in *A Political Text-Book for 1860*, eds. Horace Greeley and John F. Cleveland (New York, 1860), 213–14.

33 Edward Everett to Washington Hunt, May 29, in *Political Text-Book*, 214; *Washington National Intelligencer*, May 11, 1860; Parks, *Bell*, 357; Morrison, *Slavery and the West*, 236–37.

34 Davis, *Rise and Fall*, 52; John V. Mering, "The Slave-State Constitutional Unionists and the Politics of Consensus," *Journal of Southern History* 43 (1977): 401–2.

35 Dumond, *Secession Movement*, 94–95; McPherson, *Battle Cry of Freedom*, 222.

36 Parks, *Bell*, 357–58; Potter, *Impending Crisis*, 417. One notable exception is Carl N. Degler's classic *The Other South: Southern Dissenters in the Nineteenth Century* (New York, 1974), 158.

37 *New York Herald*, July 12, 1860; *Liberator*, March 9, 1860, and March 16, 1860; Mayer, *All on Fire*, 509; Dorothy Sterling, *Ahead of Her Time: Abby Kelley and the Politics of Antislavery* (New York, 1992), 327; Stacey M. Robertson, *Parker Pillsbury: Radical Abolitionist, Male Feminist* (Ithaca, NY, 2000), 120–21.

38 William C. Anderson to William C. Nell, April 1860, in *The Black Abolitionist Papers: The United States, 1859–1865* (Chapel Hill, NC, 1992), NC, 5:74–75; Thomas Hamilton, March 17, 1860, editorial in *Weekly Anglo-African*, ibid., 71–72.

39 Hodges, *Root and Branch*, 253; Leon Litwack, *North of Slavery: The Negro in the Free States, 1790–1860* (Chicago, 1961), 75–76; Christopher Malone, *Between Freedom and Bondage: Race, Party, and Voting Rights in the Antebellum North* (New York, 2007), 45–53.

40 Sewell, *Ballots for Freedom*, 340; Harrold, *Bailey*, 209; Frederick J. Blue, *The Free Soilers: Third Party Politics, 1848–1854* (Urbana, IL, 1973), 152–53; Stanley Harrold, *Subversives: Antislavery Community in Washington, D.C., 1828–1865* (Baton Rouge, LA, 2003), 114–15.

41 Donald, *Lincoln*, 100–101; Mayer, *All on Fire*, 486–87, 510.

42 Betty Fladeland, *James Gillespie Birney: Slaveholder to Abolitionist* (Ithaca, NY, 1955), 246; Hugh Davis, *Joshua Leavitt: Evangelical Abolitionist* (Baton Rouge, LA, 1990), 220; Morris, *Long Pursuit*, 39. Although Whigs remained livid about the election for years to come, the outcome was not as simple as Greeley and Lincoln believed. Out of 2,700,000 votes cast, Polk's margin of victory was only 38,175, while Birney garnered 62,103 votes across the North. The electoral vote, 170 to 105, was not as close, yet if Clay had carried New York and New Hampshire, the count would have been reversed in his favor, 147 to 128. But Clay carried pro-annexation Tennessee (and its 12 electoral votes) by a slim margin of only 123 votes; had he not shifted his position on Texas, which cost him votes in New York, he would certainly have lost Tennessee, and thus the Electoral College by 5 votes.

43 Harrold, *Bailey*, 206; William J. Watkins, September 24, 1860, editorial in *Weekly Anglo-African*, in *Black Abolitionist Papers*, 5:31–32.

44 Harrold, *Bailey*, 207; Foner, *Free Soil*, 302–3; Sewell, *Ballots for Freedom*, 341.

45 Nevins, *Emergence of Lincoln*, 2:300–301; Stauffer, *Black Hearts of Men*, 42; *Lowell (Massachusetts) Daily Citizen*, June 6, 1860; *Liberator*, June 1, 1860; *Albany (New York) Evening Journal*, June 5, 1860; William Lloyd Garrison to Samuel May, September 28, 1860, in *The Letters of William Lloyd Garrison*, ed. Louis Ruchames (Cambridge, MA, 1976), 4:694; *Washington Constitution*, July 26, 1850.

46 *New York Herald*, July 18, 1860; Elisabeth Griffith, *In Her Own Right: The Life of Elizabeth Cady Stanton* (New York, 1984), 105; Donald Yacovone, *Samuel Joseph May and the Dilemmas of the Liberal Persuasion, 1797–1871* (Philadelphia, 1991), 169; Mayer, *All on Fire*, 512.

47 *Liberator*, March 9, 1860; Robertson, *Pillsbury*, 120; James Brewer Stewart, *Wendell Phillips, Liberty's Hero* (Baton Rouge, LA, 1986), 210; James Oakes, *The Radical and the Republican: Frederick Douglass, Abraham Lincoln, and the Triumph of Antislavery Politics* (New York, 2007), 89; Williams S. McFeely, *Frederick Douglass* (New York, 1991), 208.

48 *Washington Constitution*, March 7, 1860; Stewart, *Phillips*, 210–11.

Chapter Four: "Moving Heaven and Earth": The Republicans

1   Stephen B. Oates, *Abraham Lincoln: The Man Behind the Myths* (New York, 1984), 34; Oates, *With Malice Toward None*, 102–3; Donald, *Lincoln*, 515; King, *Davis*, 71–72.

2   Oates, *Man Behind the Myths*, 36, 47; King, *Davis*, 14–52; Morris, *Long Pursuit*, 55. Seven years after Davis graduated, New Haven Law School became Yale Law School.

3   Morison, "Election of 1860," 1115; King, *Davis*, 126; David Davis to Abraham Lincoln, November 7, 1858, in Lincoln Papers, LC.

4   "Presidential Candidates and Aspirants," *De Bow's Review*, 102; Channing, *Crisis of Fear*, 230–31; Howell Cobb to Alexander H. Stephens, November 14, 1859, in *Toombs, Stephens, Cobb Correspondence*, 448.

5   William E. Gienapp, "Who Voted for Lincoln?," in *Abraham Lincoln and the American Political Tradition*, ed. John L. Thomas (Amherst, MA, 1986), 52–53; Don E. Fehrenbacher, "The Republican Decision at Chicago," in *Politics and the Crisis*, 41; Nevins, *Frémont*, 455–56.

6   *Jamestown (New York) Journal*, May 11, 1860; Nevins, *Emergence of Lincoln*, 2:240; William E. Baringer, "The Republican Triumph," in *Politics and the Crisis*, 92–93.

7   *Chicago Tribune*, May 15, 1860.

8   *Jamestown (New York) Journal*, May 11, 1860; John C. Underwood to William H. Seward, March 12, 1860, in Seward Papers, UR; William R. Bonner to William H. Seward, January 16, 1860, ibid.

9   Glyndon G. Van Deusen, *Thurlow Weed: Wizard of the Lobby* (Boston, 1947), 27; Van Deusen, *Seward*, 7; Taylor, *Seward*, 111–12; Richard Cross to Thurlow Weed, November 5, 1859, in Weed Papers, UR.

10 Van Deusen, *Seward*, 265–66; Charles Sumner to the Duchess of Argyll, May 22, 1860, in *The Selected Letters of Charles Sumner*, ed. Beverly Wilson Palmer (Boston, 1990), 2:23; Taylor, *Seward*, 113.

11 Van Deusen, *Weed*, 244; Harris, *Lincoln's Rise*, 174; *Columbus Ohio State Journal*, March 20, 1860; Josiah M. Lucas to Abraham Lincoln, January 26, 1860, in Lincoln Papers, LC.

12 Doris Kearns Goodwin, *Team of Rivals: The Political Genius of Abraham Lincoln* (New York, 2005), 213; *New York Herald*, May 23, 1860; *Congressional Globe*, 36th Cong., 1st sess., 911.

13 Goodwin, *Team of Rivals*, 214; *Liberator*, March 16, 1860; *Trenton (New Jersey) State Gazette*, March 19, 1860; George Ellis Baker to William Henry Seward, March 2, 1860, in Seward Papers, UR.

14 Taylor, *Seward*, 116; Van Deusen, *Weed*, 247; Henricus Scholte to Elbridge G. Spaulding, April 4, 1860, in Seward Papers, UR. Although the modern primary system also favors candidates from populous states, favorite sons and daughters from New York, California, and Texas first have to survive primaries and caucuses held in small and racially atypical states such as Iowa and New Hampshire.

15 Van Deusen, *Seward*, 222; Taylor, *Seward*, 117; Joseph Nunes to William Henry Seward, May 19, 1860, in Seward Papers, UR.

16 "Presidential Candidates and Aspirants," *De Bow's Review*, 94; Goodwin, *Team of Rivals*, 243; Allan Peskin, *Garfield* (Kent, OH 1978), 64.

17 Foner, *Free Soil*, 74; Davis, *Leavitt*, 266; Harrold, *Bailey*, 208.

18 Blue, *Chase*, 122–23; John Niven, *Salmon P. Chase: A Biography* (New York, 1995), 212.

19 Blue, *Chase*, 120–21; Niven, *Chase*, 214–17.

20 William E. Parrish, *Frank Blair: Lincoln's Conservative* (Columbia, MO, 1998), 84; Potter, *Impending Crisis*, 420–21; Glyndon G. Van Deusen, *Horace Greeley, Nineteenth Century Crusader* (New York, 1964), 242.

21 Nevins, *Emergence of Lincoln*, 2:328–29; Goodwin, *Team of Rivals*, 221; *Milwaukee Sentinel*, March 21, 1860; *New York Herald*, March 2, 1860, and March 29, 1860.

22 J. G. Randall, *Lincoln the President: Springfield to Gettysburg* (New York, 1945), 148; *New York Herald*, March 2, 1860; Theodore Little to Thurlow Weed, April 30, 1860, in Seward Papers, UR.

23 *Amherst (New Hampshire) Farmer's Cabinet*, May 16, 1860; Hans L. Trefousse, *Benjamin Franklin Wade: Radical Republican from Ohio* (New York, 1963), 122–25.

24 Hans L. Trefousse, *Thaddeus Stevens: Nineteenth Century Egalitarian* (Chapel Hill, NC, 1997), 101; Freehling, *Road to Disunion*, 2:328–29.

25 *Washington National Intelligencer*, May 19, 1860; Potter, *Impending Crisis*, 421; Thomas, *Lincoln*, 206.

26 Donald, *Lincoln*, 572; Oates, *Man Behind the Myths*, 35.

27 Ronald C. White Jr., *A. Lincoln: A Biography* (New York, 2009), 305; John A. Corry, *Lincoln at Cooper Union* (New York, 2003), 54; Abraham Lincoln to Jesse Fell, December 20, 1859, in Lincoln Papers, LC; Abraham Lincoln to Norman B. Judd, December 14, 1859, ibid.; Donald, *Lincoln*, 237; Goodwin, *Team of Rivals*, 228.

28 Donald, *Lincoln*, 237–38; Thomas, *Lincoln*, 213–14; Harold Holzer, *Lincoln at Cooper Union: The Speech That Made Abraham Lincoln President* (New York, 2004), 92–94.

29 Van Deusen, *Greeley*, 244; Holzer, *Lincoln at Cooper Union*, 105; Oates, *With Malice Toward None*, 172–73; Harris, *Lincoln's Rise*, 190; Wilentz, *Rise of American Democracy*, 760–61.

30 Oates, *With Malice Toward None*, 175–76; Guelzo, *Redeemer President*, 242; Paul F. Boller, *Presidential Campaigns: From George Washington to George W. Bush* (New York, 2004), 103; *Albany (New York) Evening Journal*, May 11, 1860.

31 Oates, *Man Behind the Myths*, 36; Donald, *Lincoln*, 245; Gienapp, "Who Voted for Lincoln," 60.

32 Catton, *Coming Fury*, 49; *Washington National Intelligencer*, April 23, 1860.

33 Niven, *Chase*, 217; Nevins, *Emergence of Lincoln*, 2:229, 247; Halstead, *Three Against Lincoln*, 142; Davis, *Rise and Fall*, 49; Stampp, *Imperiled Union*, 140–41.

34 Parrish, *Blair*, 83; Stampp, *Imperiled Union*, 144–45; Halstead, *Three Against Lincoln*, 142; King, *Davis*, 135–36; Jesse K. Dubois and David Davis to Abraham Lincoln, May 15, 1860, in Lincoln Papers, LC.

35 Niven, *Chase*, 218; *Washington National Intelligencer*, May 18, 1860; *Barre (Massachusetts) Gazette*, May 25, 1860; *New Albany (Indiana) Ledger*, May 17, 1860; Halstead, *Three Against Lincoln*, 145. (Halstead misidentified the governor as "Edmund" Morgan.)

36 *Barre (Massachusetts) Gazette*, May 25, 1860; *Lowell (Massachusetts) Daily Citizen*, May 17, 1860; Going, *Wilmot*, 528–29.

37 Stampp, *Imperiled Union*, 141; Going, *Wilmot*, 529–31.

38 Halstead, *Three Against Lincoln*, 145–46; Harris, *Lincoln's Rise*, 204; Randall, *Lincoln the President*, 1:155–56.

39 *Washington National Intelligencer*, May 18, 1860; Harrold, *Bailey*, 205; Stampp, *Imperiled Union*, 150; Don E. Fehrenbacher, "Republican Decision," 50–51; *National Republican Platform Adopted by the National Republican Convention*, May 17, 1860, in *Washington National Intelligencer*, May 19, 1860.

40 Foner, *Free Soil*, 175–76; Gienapp, "Who Voted for Lincoln?," 55–56; Elbert B. Smith, *Francis Preston Blair* (New York, 1980), 260; *National Republican Platform*.

41 Hans L. Trefousse, *Carl Schurz: A Biography* (Knoxville, TN, 1982), 85; Carl Schurz, *The Reminiscences of Carl Schurz* (New York, 1908), 2:180–81.

42 Sewell, *Ballots for Freedom*, 362–63; *Wisconsin Daily Patriot*, May 26, 1860; James Brewer Stewart, *Joshua Giddings and the Tactics of Radical Politics* (Cleveland, 1970), 272–73; Schurz, *Reminiscences*, 182.

43 Halstead, *Three Against Lincoln*, 159; Elbridge Spaulding to William Henry Seward, May 15, 1860, in Seward Papers, UR; H. Draper Hunt, *Hannibal Hamlin of Maine: Lincoln's First Vice President* (Syracuse, NY, 1969), 115.

44 Halstead, *Three Against Lincoln*, 161; Edwin D. Morgan to William Henry Seward, May 17, 1860, in Seward Papers, UR.

45 Halstead, *Three Against Lincoln*, 159–63; Foner, *Free Soil*, 181–82; Niven, *Chase*, 213–14.

46 Niven, *Chase*, 219; Blue, *Chase*, 124–25.

47 David Davis to Abraham Lincoln, May 17, 1860, in Lincoln Papers, LC; William E. Gienapp, *Abraham Lincoln and Civil War America: A Biography* (New York, 2002), 69; King, *Davis*, 134–36.

48 Stampp, *Imperiled Union*, 157; David Davis to Abraham Lincoln, November 19, 1860, in Lincoln Papers, LC; Halstead, *Three Against Lincoln*, 161.

49 Halstead, *Three Against Lincoln*, 149; Randall, *Lincoln the President*, 1:159; *Albany (New York) Evening Journal*, May 23, 1860; Glyndon G. Van Deusen, "Thurlow Weed's Analysis of William H. Seward's Defeat in the Republican Convention of 1860," *Mississippi Valley Historical Review* 34 (1947): 103; Elbridge G. Spaulding to William H. Seward, May 18, 1860, in Seward Papers, UR.

50 Van Deusen, "Thurlow Weed's Analysis," 104; Van Deusen, *Greeley*, 246; *New York Herald*, May 30, 1860; Fehrenbacher, "Republican Decision," 53–54.

51 Boller, *Presidential Campaigns*, 105; Morris, *Long Pursuit*, 160–61; Donald, *Lincoln*, 249; White, *A. Lincoln*, 325.

52 Halstead, *Three Against Lincoln*, 163; *Albany (New York) Evening Journal*, May 18, 1860; *Amherst (New Hampshire) Farmer's Cabinet*, May 23, 1860; Richard M. Blatchford to William Henry Seward, May 18, 1860, in Seward Papers, UR.

53 Waugh, *One Man Great Enough*, 325; Schurz, *Reminiscences*, 2:184–85.

54 Halstead, *Three Against Lincoln*, 165; *Albany (New York) Evening Journal*, May 18, 1860.

55 Halstead, *Three Against Lincoln*, 166–67; Randall, *Lincoln the President*, 1:166; Elbridge G. Spaulding to William Henry Seward, May 18, 1860, in Seward Papers, UR. Harris, *Lincoln's Rise*, 209, suggests that Weed believed he had secured "the rotten borough"

delegations from the South—states that no Republican could carry in November—in exchange for patronage. But the Virginians, like their Pennsylvania neighbors, concluded that Seward could not win and shifted their loyalties to the man who could give them federal jobs.

56 Halstead, *Three Against Lincoln*, 168–69; Fehrenbacher, "Republican Decision," 59; *Washington National Intelligencer*, May 19, 1860; *Albany (New York) Evening Journal*, May 18, 1860.

57 Van Deusen, *Weed*, 253; Trefousse, *Wade*, 127–28; Elbridge G. Spaulding to William Henry Seward, May 18, 1860, in Seward Papers, UR.

58 *Washington National Intelligencer*, May 19, 1860; Thomas, *Lincoln*, 225; *Amherst (New Hampshire) Farmer's Cabinet*, May 23, 1860; Halstead, *Three Against Lincoln*, 170–71.

59 *Washington National Intelligencer*, May 19, 1860; Hunt, *Hamlin*, 116–18; Halstead, *Three Against Lincoln*, 174–75; Jerry R. Desmond, "Maine and the Election of 1860," *New England Quarterly* 67 (1994): 461. Had Seward gotten the nomination, Clay almost certainly would have been selected as his running mate.

60 Halstead, *Three Against Lincoln*, 173; Catton, *Coming Fury*, 64–65; Schurz, *Reminiscences*, 186.

61 Van Deusen, *Seward*, 224–25; Edwin D. Morgan to William Henry Seward, May 18, 1860, in Seward Papers, UR.

62 J. J. A. Wilson to Abraham Lincoln, May 18, 1860, in Lincoln Papers, LC; George Ashmun to Abraham Lincoln, May 18, 1860, ibid.; Lincoln's response to the news and his remark about telling Mary come from Charles S. Zane, "Lincoln as I Knew Him," *Sunset Magazine*, October 1912, reprinted in *Journal of the Illinois State Historical Society* 14 (1921–1922): 83. *Daily Ohio Statesman*, May 25, 1860, reported a slightly different response from Lincoln. For three very different versions of Lincoln's comment regarding his wife, see Oates, *With Malice Toward None*, 179; Waugh, *One Man Great Enough*, 332–33; Donald, *Lincoln*, 251.

63 Desmond, "Maine and the Election," 460; Hunt, *Hamlin*, 118.

64 Milton, *Eve of Conflict*, 458; Johannsen, *Douglas*, 761; Harris, *Lincoln's Rise*, 212; Schuyler Colfax to Abraham Lincoln, May 18, 1860, in Lincoln Papers, LC.

65 Halstead, *Three Against Lincoln*, 173–74; *New York Herald*, May 21, 1860; Arthur Dexter to William Henry Seward, May 19, 1860, in Seward Papers, UR; Arthur Fletcher to William Henry Seward, May 20, 1860, ibid.; Lewis Benedict to William Henry Seward, May 19, 1860, ibid.

66 Everett Banfield to William Henry Seward, May 19, 1860, in Seward Papers, UR; Gilbert C. Davidson to William Henry Seward, May 18, 1860, ibid.; *Providence (Rhode Island) Journal*, May 22, 1860.

67 Roger L. Ransom, *Conflict and Compromise: The Political Economy of Slavery, Emancipation, and the American Civil War* (Cambridge, MA, 1989), 163; Samuel Wilkeson to William Henry Seward, May 16, 1860, in Seward Papers, UR.

68 David Davis to Abraham Lincoln, May 18, 1860, in Lincoln Papers, LC; Charles H. Ray to Abraham Lincoln, May 18, 1860, ibid.; Salmon P. Chase to Abraham Lincoln, May 17 [*sic*], 1860, ibid.; Abraham Lincoln to Salmon P. Chase, May 26, 1860, ibid.

Chapter Five: "Beyond the Power of Surgery": The Democrats, Again

1 Donald, *Lincoln*, 241; Holzer, *Lincoln at Cooper Union*, 14; *Speech of Hon. John C. Breckinridge, Vice-President of the United States, at Ashland, Kentucky, September 5th, 1860* (Washington, DC, 1860), 1.

2 *Washington Constitution*, June 28, 1960; Davis, *Breckinridge*, 8–45; Frank H. Heck, *Proud Kentuckian: John C. Breckinridge, 1821–1875* (Lexington, KY, 1976), 1–54; *New York Herald*, June 25, 1860.

3 Frank H. Heck, "John C. Breckinridge in the Crisis of 1860–1861," *Journal of Southern History* 21 (1955): 321; Davis, *Breckinridge*, 220–21.

4 Davis, *Breckinridge*, 228; *Speech of Breckinridge*, 1.

5 Milton, *Eve of Conflict*, 458; *Wisconsin Daily Patriot*, May 4 and June 16, 1860; *New Albany (New York) Daily Ledger*, June 6, 1859.

6 *Middletown (Connecticut) Constitution*, June 20, 1860; Howell Cobb to John B. Lamar, May 27, 1860, in *Toombs, Stephens, Cobb Correspondence*, 480; Hunt, *Hamlin*, 115.

7 Milton, *Eve of Conflict*, 451; *Congressional Globe*, 36th Cong., 1st sess., 2143–56; Davis, *Rise and Fall*, 45; Jefferson Davis, "Address to the National Democracy," May 7, 1860, in *Papers of Davis*, 6:292 and n. 2.

8 Johannsen, *Douglas*, 765; Huston, *Douglas*, 166–67; *Washington National Intelligencer*, May 29, 1860.

9 Parrish, *Taylor*, 94; Nevins, *Emergence of Lincoln*, 2:267–68.

10 *Wisconsin Daily Patriot*, June 16, 1860; Johannsen, *Douglas*, 762–63.

11 *Lowell (Massachusetts) Daily Citizen*, May 18, 1860; Davis, "Address to the National Democracy," 290–91; *Washington National Intelligencer*, May 21, 1860.

12 Nichols, *Disruption of American Democracy*, 313–14; Schott, *Stephens*, 290.

13 Faust, *Hammond*, 356. There remains a great deal of confusion about these slates. Nevins, *Emergence of Lincoln*, 2:266–67, writes that only South Carolina sent delegates to Richmond and, that "one-tenth of the Georgia convention" elected a separate slate of moderates for Baltimore. Potter, *Impending Crisis*, 412, insists that in Georgia, Douglas's forces "appointed new delegations to replace the delegations that had bolted in Charleston. Freehling, *Road to Disunion*, 2:317, argues that the walkout by the Douglas minority in Georgia represented 20 percent of the meeting, and he observes that Florida as well as South Carolina named slates for Richmond only.

14 Walther, *Yancey*, 248–49; *Washington National Intelligencer*, June 5, 1860; Thornton, *Politics and Power*, 395.

15 *Baltimore Sun*, October 19, 1860; Walther, *Yancey*, 249; *Washington Constitution*, October 19, 1860.

16 Halstead, *Three Against Lincoln*, 263–64.

17 Halstead, *Three Against Lincoln*, 178–79; William M. Mathew, *Edmund Ruffin and the Crisis of Slavery in the Old South: The Failure of Agricultural Reform* (Athens, GA, 1988), 50; Henry T. Shanks, *The Secession Movement in Virginia, 1847–1861* (New York, 1934), 107; Davis, *Rhett*, 388–89.

18 Halstead, *Three Against Lincoln*, 178; *Washington National Intelligencer*, June 14, 1860; *Montgomery (Alabama) Daily Confederation*, June 22, 1860.

19 Asia Booth Clarke, *The Elder and Younger Booth* (Boston, 1882), 145; Halstead, *Three Against Lincoln*, 185–86; *Official Proceedings of the Democratic Convention*, 90–91. Noel Ignatiev, *How the Irish Became White* (New York, 1995), 75, notes that as early as 1844 "the Irish were the most solid voting bloc in the country," uniformly casting their votes for the Democratic Party.

20 *Washington Constitution*, June 20, 1820; Belohlavek, *Broken Glass*, 310.

21 Catton, *Coming Fury*, 69–70; *Washington Constitution*, May 23, 1860; Thurlow Weed to Abraham Lincoln, June 10, 1860, in Lincoln Papers, LC.

22 Capers, *Douglas*, 206; Halstead, *Three Against Lincoln*, 230–31. Johannsen, *Douglas*, 770, observes that Douglas later insisted that he had Stephens in mind, but as the Georgian endorsed the Lecompton constitution, their positions on the frontier were hardly similar; Richardson published the letter only after Douglas's nomination was assured, and it appeared in the *Washington National Intelligencer*, June 27, 1860.

23 Milton, *Eve of Conflict*, 458; *Washington Constitution*, June 26, 1860; Belohlavek, *Broken Glass*, 309; Halstead, *Three Against Lincoln*, 203–4.

24 Milton, *Eve of Conflict*, 463–64; James W. Geary, "Clement L. Vallandigham Views the Charleston Convention," *Ohio History* 86 (1977): 132; Dumond, *Secession Movement*, 62–63.

25 *Washington Constitution*, June 26, 1860; Halstead, *Three Against Lincoln*, 238–39; Stephen A. Douglas to William A. Richardson, June 20, 1860, in *Letters of Douglas*, 492.

26 Huston, *Douglas*, 168; Wells, *Douglas*, 234–35; Johannsen, *Douglas*, 768.

27 Halstead, *Three Against Lincoln*, 197–98, 261–62; Katz, *Belmont*, 72; Milton, *Eve of Conflict*, 471.

28 *Official Proceedings of the Democratic Convention*, 111; *Washington National Intelligencer*, June 23, 1860. Thornton, *Politics and Power*, 396, writes that because of their "intransigence" the Douglas men bear "the immediate responsibility for the final disruption" of the convention, although he concedes that Yancey might well have "staged a second withdrawal" if the fire-eaters were not given the platform they desired. Since Yancey clearly wished to see the Republicans victorious in November, he almost surely would have led the Alabamans to bolt, even if they were granted the Tennessee platform. The unanswerable question is whether other delegations would have followed.

29 John A. Cobb to John B. Lamar, June 30, 1860, in *Toombs, Stephens, Cobb Correspondence*, 482 (Cobb was the son of Howell Cobb); *Official Proceedings of the Democratic Convention*, 116–17.

30 *Official Report of the Democratic Convention*, 146–47; Dumond, *Secession Movement*, 86–87; Davis, *Davis*, 282; Alexander Stephens to J. Henry Smith, September 12, 1860, in *Toombs, Stephens, Cobb Correspondence*, 495.

31 Johannsen, *Douglas*, 771; Morris, *Long Pursuit*, 168; Davis, *Breckinridge*, 222; *Baltimore Sun*, June 23, 1860. This point about the order of secession in both the conventions and in the country was first made by Potter, *Impending Crisis*, 414–15.

32 Belohlavek, *Broken Glass*, 310–11; Halstead, *Three Against Lincoln*, 244–45; *New York Herald*, June 24, 1860.

33 Halstead, *Three Against Lincoln*, 251; *Washington Constitution*, June 26, 1860; Garrison's *Liberator*, June 29, 1860, curiously, thought it worthy of mention that Douglas's delegate count was "short" of the required 202 votes.

34 *Columbus Ohio State Journal*, July 3, 1860; *Albany (New York) Journal*, June 25, 1860; *Baltimore Sun*, June 23, 1860; *Official Proceedings of the Democratic Convention*, 168–69; *Washington Constitution*, June 26, 1860.

35 Nichols, *Disruption of American Democracy*, 318–19; *Washington Constitution*, June 26, 1860; Schott, *Stephens*, 291.

36 *Albany (New York) Evening Journal*, June 25, 1860; *Washington National Intelligencer*, June 25, 1860; *Baltimore Sun*, June 23 and June 25, 1860; *Washington Constitution*, June 26, 1860.

37 Johannsen, *Douglas*, 772; Halstead, *Three Against Lincoln*, 233, 237, 252–53.

38 Halstead, *Three Against Lincoln*, 241, 265–66; Nevins, *Emergence of Lincoln*, 2:271–72. The hall burned in 1904 during the great Baltimore fire.

39 *St. Albans (Vermont) Daily Messenger*, June 28, 1860; Catton, *Coming Fury*, 76–77; Boles, *South Through Time*, 288–89; Morris, *Long Pursuit*, 169; Halstead, *Three Against Lincoln*, 267–68; *New York Herald*, June 24, 1860. Not surprisingly, Garrison's *Liberator*, June 29, 1860, editorialized that "the infamous Caleb Cushing, of Massachusetts, very properly [was chosen] to preside" at the southern Democratic convention.

40 Heck, "Breckinridge in the Crisis," 323; Nichols, *Disruption of American Democracy*, 319–20.

41 *St. Albans (Vermont) Daily Messenger*, June 28, 1860; *Concord New-Hampshire Patriot*, June 27, 1860; Heck, "Breckinridge in the Crisis," 323; Halstead, *Three Against Lincoln*, 274–75; *New York Herald*, June 24, 1860; "Presidential Candidates and Aspirants," *De Bow's Review*, 101.

42 *St. Albans (Vermont) Daily Messenger*, June 28, 1860; Nichols, *Disruption of American Democracy*, 320; *Washington Constitution*, June 27, 1860.

43 The events of that evening remain somewhat mysterious. Wells, *Douglas*, doubts that the proposal was ever made, and Davis, *Breckinridge*, 224–25, notes that the Kentuckian later insisted that *he* instigated the plan. But biographer Davis here and in his *Davis*, 283, argues that the scheme was formulated by the Mississippian. Belohlavek, *Broken Glass*, 311, adds that Cushing "likely assumed a prominent role in the plotting and planning." All that is known with any certainty is that the group was serenaded; see *Washington Constitution*, June 26, 1860.

44 Halstead, *Three Against Lincoln*, 277–78; *New York Times*, June 30, 1860.

45 Johannsen, *Douglas*, 772–73; Flint, *Life of Douglas*, 213. Douglas's draft letter to William H. Ludlow, June 27, 1860, in *Letters of Douglas*, 494–95, shows the evolution of his reply. Among other changes, Douglas first described the nominating body as the "Regular National convention," before dropping the word "Regular." He also stretched the truth a bit in listing the three previous platforms as supporting popular sovereignty. The 1848 platform did not openly do so, although certainly with the selection of popular sovereignty advocate Lewis Cass came his policy. And in 1852, the party promised only to stand by the Compromise of 1850, which used popular sover-

eignty to decide the question of slavery expansion in the New Mexico and Utah territories.

46 Katz, *Belmont*, 74–75; Johannsen, *Douglas*, 772, 775–76; *New Orleans Delta*, June 26, 1860.

47 Ransom, *Conflict and Compromise*, 163; *Washington Constitution*, June 28, 1860; Klein, *Buchanan*, 344; *Liberator*, June 29, 1860.

48 Willard Carl Klunder, *Lewis* (Kent, OH., 1996), *Cass* 302–3; *Daily Ohio Statesman*, June 24, 1860.

49 *New York Herald*, July 28, 1860; Thomas Palmer Jerman to John S. Palmer, July 27, 1860, in *A World Turned Upside Down: The Palmers of South Santee, 1818–1881*, ed. Louis P. Towles (Columbia, SC, 1996), 264.

50 *New York Herald*, June 29 and July 4, 1860; *Albany (New York) Evening Journal*, July 3, 1860; *New Orleans True Delta*, June 24, 1860; *Montgomery (Alabama) Daily Confederation*, June 22, 1860; Nevins, *Emergence of Lincoln*, 2:282–84.

51 *New York Herald*, June 25, 1860; Thurlow Weed to Abraham Lincoln, June 25, 1860, in Lincoln Papers, LC.

52 Mark W. Delahay to Abraham Lincoln, June 24, 1860, in ibid.; Edwin D. Morgan to Abraham Lincoln, July 10, 1860, in Lincoln Papers, LC; Abraham Lincoln to Simeon Francis, August 6, 1860, in *Collected Works*, 4:90.

53 *New York Herald*, July 28, 1860; Abraham Lincoln to Simeon Francis, August 6, 1860, in *Collected Works*, 4:90; James A. Harvey to Abraham Lincoln, June 25, 1860, in Lincoln Papers, LC.

Chapter Six: "Lincoln Is the Next President. I will Go South": The Campaigns

1 *St. Albans (Vermont) Daily Messenger*, June 14, 1860; *Kansas Freedom's Champion*, June 30, 1860; Catherine Clinton, *Mrs. Lincoln: A Life* (New York, 2009), 112; Jean H. Baker, *Mary Todd Lincoln: A Biography* (New York, 1987), 160; Morris, *Long Pursuit*, 180–81.

2 *Albany (New York) Evening Journal*, May 24, 1860; White, *A. Lincoln*, 340–41; Oates, *Man Behind the Myths*, 42; Baker, *Mary Todd Lincoln*, 37–39, 134–35.

3 *Lowell (Massachusetts) Daily Citizen*, May 24, 1860; *St. Albans (Vermont) Daily Messenger*, June 14, 1860; Varon, *We Mean to Be Counted*, 148. (Not surprisingly, one pro-Breckinridge newspaper responded that the ladies, dressed in black and white, represented Republican racial amalgamation.)

4 Huston, *Douglas*, 169; *New York Herald*, June 24, 1860.

5 Guelzo, *Redeemer President*, 246; Harris, *Lincoln's Rise*, 224; Gienapp, *Lincoln and Civil War America*, 74.

6 Oates, *With Malice Toward None*, 181; John Locke Scripps to Abraham Lincoln, June 2, 1860, in Lincoln Papers, LC; Horace White to Abraham Lincoln, June 27, 1860, ibid.; John Locke Scripps to Abraham Lincoln, July 17, 1860, ibid.

7 Michael Burlingame, *Abraham Lincoln: A Life* (Baltimore, 2008), 1:644–45; Thurlow Weed to Leonard Swett, June 7, 1860, in Lincoln Papers, LC; Leonard Swett to Abraham Lincoln, June 13, 1860, ibid.; Van Deusen, *Weed*, 255–56.

8 Edward C. Kirkland, *Charles Francis Adams, Jr., 1835–1915: The Patrician at Bay* (Cambridge, MA, 1965), 20; Adams, *Autobiography*, 64. Burlingame, *Lincoln*, 1:654, suggests that the "haughty New Yorker" demanded that Lincoln come to the depot, rather than their calling on him "at his house or office," but from Adams's comments, it appears likely that Lincoln chose to do it to make up for the fact that the local party did not wish Seward to address the city.

9 Waugh, *One Man Great Enough*, 345; *St. Albans (Vermont) Daily Messenger*, August 16, 1860; *Baltimore Sun*, August 11, 1860; Burlingame, *Lincoln*, 1:651.

10 Wilentz, *Rise of American Democracy*, 762; Griffith, *Elizabeth Cady Stanton*, 105; *New York Herald*, July 12, 1860; *New York Tribune*, July 9, 1860.

11 Mark E. Neely Jr., *The Boundaries of American Political Culture in the Civil War Era* (Chapel Hill, NC, 2009), 63–64; King, *Davis*, 154.

12 *Albany (New York) Evening Journal*, June 23, 1860; Catton, *Coming Fury*, 89, 96; Hunt, *Hamlin*, 125–26; Jon Grinspan, " 'Young Men for War': The Wide Awakes and Lincoln's 1860 Presidential Campaign," *Journal of American History* 96 (2009): 362, 375.

13 Grinspan, " 'Young Men for War,' " 375; Susan B. Anthony to Henry B. Stanton Jr., September 27, 1860, in *Antebellum Women*, forthcoming.

14 *New London (Connecticut) Chronicle*, July 6, 1860; *Baltimore Sun*, August 13, 1860; *Lowell (Massachusetts) Daily Citizen and News*, August 8, 1860; Taylor, *Seward*, 121–22; William H. Seward to Charles Francis Adams Jr., August 28, 1860, in Adams Family Papers, Massachusetts Historical Society (hereafter MHS); Adams, *Autobiography*, 60–61.

15 Van Deusen, *Seward*, 232; *Albany (New York) Evening Journal*, September 8, 1860; *Macon (Georgia) Daily Telegraph*, August 23, 1860.

16 Goodwin, *Team of Rivals*, 269; Adams, *Autobiography*, 62.

17 Taylor, *Seward*, 123; Adams, *Autobiography*, 65–66. When the Republican press began to depict "Douglas [as] a hard drinker," the *Madison Wisconsin Patriot*, October 15, 1860, insisted that there was "nothing in the appearance or habits of Judge Douglas to justify such an indecent and false attack."

18 Stampp, *Imperiled Union*, 130–31; Gienapp, "Who Voted for Lincoln?" 58–59; Morrison, *Slavery and the West*, 242.

19 Baringer, "The Republican Triumph," 102–3; Harris, *Lincoln's Rise*, 228; McPherson, *Battle Cry of Freedom*, 224; *New York Herald*, May 23, 1860.

20 Stanley Harrold, *American Abolitionists* (New York, 2001), 89; Lorman A. Ratner and Dwight L. Teeter Jr., *Fanatics and Fire-Eaters: Newspapers and the Coming of the Civil War* (Urbana, IL, 2004), 90–91; Davis, *"Government of Our Own,"* 6; Davis, *Rhett*, 390–91; Nichols, *Disruption of American Democracy*, 361.

21 Guelzo, *Redeemer President*, 248–49; Charles Sumner to the Duchess of Argyll, September 3, 1860, in *Letters of Sumner*, 34; Abraham Lincoln to Hannibal Hamlin, July 18, 1860, in *Collected Works*, 4:84.

22 Parks, *Bell*, 367–68; *Annapolis (Maryland) Gazette*, June 14, 1860.

23 Howe, *Political Culture*, 4; Varon, *We Mean to Be Counted*, 144–46.

24 Crofts, *Reluctant Confederates*, 76–77; *Houston Telegraph*, May 29, 1860; *Annapolis*

(Maryland) Ga{ette, June 14 and July 5, 1860; *Tallahassee Floridian and Journal*, May 26, 1860.

25 Kirwan, *Crittenden*, 360–61; *Annapolis (Maryland) Ga{ette*, May 31, 1860.

26 Parks, *Bell*, 361–62, 368–69; *New York Herald*, May 30, 1860.

27 Parks, *Bell*, 361; Randall, *Lincoln the President*, 1:144–45; *Columbus (Georgia) Daily Enquirer*, May 26 and May 29, 1860; *Macon (Georgia) Daily Telegraph*, May 25, 1860; *Lowell (Massachusetts) Daily Citi{en and News*, May 29, 1860; Morrison, *Slavery and the West*, 249.

28 Wells, *Douglas*, 244–45; Kirwan, *Crittenden*, 357–58; James E. Harvey to Abraham Lincoln, July 27, 1860, in Lincoln Papers, LC; *San Francisco Bulletin*, October 22, 1860; *Annapolis (Maryland) Ga{ette*, July 5, 1860.

29 Parks, *Bell*, 370–71; Kirwan, *Crittenden*, 358; Katz, *Belmont*, 80–81; Nichols, *Disruption of American Democracy*, 342; Michael P. Johnson, *Toward a Patriarchal Republic: The Secession of Georgia* (Baton Rouge, LA, 1977), 16; Shanks, *Secession Movement in Virginia*, 110–11; Thurlow Weed to Abraham Lincoln, August 13, 1860, in Lincoln Papers, LC.

30 *Barre (Massachusetts) Ga{ette*, July 27, 1860; Burlingame, *Lincoln*, 1:635.

31 Sewell, *Ballots for Freedom*, 341–42; Mayer, *All on Fire*, 513.

32 Davis, *Breckinridge*, 230; Belohlavek, *Broken Glass*, 312–13.

33 Heck, *Proud Kentuckian*, 86; Davis, *Breckinridge*, 231–32; John C. Breckinridge to Caleb Cushing, July 6, 1860, in *Political Text-Book*, 211–12.

34 Mering, "Slave-State Constitutional Unionists," 404; Heck, "Breckinridge in the Crisis," 328; Heck, *Proud Kentuckian*, 88.

35 Channing, *Crisis of Fear*, 233; Schott, *Stephens*, 297; Davis, *Breckinridge*, 232.

36 *Washington Constitution*, July 26, August 15, and August 17, 1860; Dumond, *Secessionist Movement*, 11; *New York Herald*, June 25, 1860.

37 Horace White to Abraham Lincoln, July 5, 1860, in Lincoln Papers, LC; Caleb B. Smith to Abraham Lincoln, July 20, 1860, ibid.; Jefferson Davis to William B. Sloan, July 8, 1860, in *Papers of Davis*, 6:356–57; Baker, *Buchanan*, 119.

38 Heck, *Proud Kentuckian*, 86; Morris, *Long Pursuit*, 184; Heck, "Breckinridge in the Crisis," 325; Davis, *Breckinridge*, 237. The Phoenix Hotel was finally demolished in 1987.

39 *New York Times*, September 6, 1860; *Washington National Intelligencer*, September 7, 1860; *Speech of Breckinridge*, 1–7. Davis, *Breckinridge*, 237, writes that the speech was "one of the most important, and in some degrees the most disappointing" of his career.

40 Johannsen, *Douglas*, 776; Milton, *Eve of Conflict*, 381–82.

41 Katz, *Belmont*, 74–75; Milton, *Eve of Conflict*, 489; Smith, *Presidency of Buchanan*, 122; Morris, *Long Pursuit*, 178–79; Nevins, *Emergence of Lincoln*, 292; Thurlow Weed to Abraham Lincoln, August 25, 1860, in Lincoln Papers, LC.

42 Baringer, "The Republican Triumph," 108–9; Robert W. Johannsen, "Stephen A. Douglas' New England Campaign, 1860," *New England Quarterly* 35 (1962): 184; Stephen A. Douglas to Nathan Pascall, July 4, 1860, in *Letters of Douglas*, 487; Stephen A. Douglas to Charles H. Lanphier, July 5, 1860, ibid., 498.

43 Johannsen, *Douglas*, 778–79; Huston, *Douglas*, 171; Johannsen, "Douglas' New England Campaign," 163; Milton, *Eve of Conflict*, 490, n. 31.

44 *New York Herald*, August 4, 1860; Johannsen, "Douglas' New England Campaign," 172; Jerry R. Desmond, "Maine and the Election of 1860," *New England Quarterly* 67 (1994): 464; George G. Fogg to Abraham Lincoln, August 18, 1860, in Lincoln Papers, LC.

45 Morrison, *Slavery and the West*, 232; Warden, *Life and Character of Douglas*, 106; Stephen A. Douglas to Charles H. Lanphier, July 5, 1860, in *Letters*, 498; Baringer, "The Republican Triumph," 104.

46 Johannsen, "Douglas' New England Campaign," 176–77; Burlingame, *Lincoln*, 1:639. Weed believed that Douglas preferred Lincoln's election "to that of Breckenridge or Bell," and that was probably true. See Thurlow Weed to Abraham Lincoln, July 27, 1860, in Lincoln Papers, LC.

47 *Lowell (Massachusetts) Daily Citizen and News*, October 10, 1860; Huston, *Douglas*, 176; Johannsen, *Douglas*, 797; Burlingame, *Lincoln*, 1:670; Harold Holzer, *Lincoln President-Elect: Abraham Lincoln and the Great Secession Winter 1860–1861* (New York, 2008), 12; Ward H. Lamon to Abraham Lincoln, October 10, 1860, in Lincoln Papers, LC. When Jefferson Davis got news of the October elections, he again urged Douglas and Breckinridge to withdraw in favor of Pierce, who vetoed the plan. See Nichols, *Pierce*, 513.

48 Ward H. Lamon to Abraham Lincoln, October 10, 1860, in Lincoln Papers, LC; Mark W. Delahay to Abraham Lincoln, October 10, 1860, ibid.; Alexander K. McClure to Abraham Lincoln, October 15, 1860, ibid.; Johannsen, "Douglas' New England Campaign," 186; Potter, *Impending Crisis*, 441.

49 Huston, *Douglas*, 172; Howland, *Douglas*, 352; Johannsen, *Douglas*, 791; Logan, *Great Conspiracy*, 95.

50 *Madison Wisconsin Patriot*, June 23, 1860; *Washington National Intelligencer*, September 7, 1860; *Daily Ohio Statesman*, July 4, 1860.

51 *Washington National Intelligencer*, October 31, 1860; *Hartford (Connecticut) Courant*, October 25, 1860.

52 Catton, *Coming Fury*, 100–101; Craig M. Simpson, *A Good Southerner: The Life of Henry A. Wise of Virginia* (Chapel Hill, NC, 1985), 234; *Washington National Intelligencer*, August 31, 1860.

53 Randall, *Lincoln the President*, 1:185–86; *Macon (Georgia) Daily Telegraph*, September 27, 1860; Waugh, *One Man Great Enough*, 352.

54 Morris, *Long Pursuit*, 193; Capers, *Douglas*, 200–201; Nichols, *Disruption of American Democracy*, 336; Wells, *Douglas*, 254–55; *Trenton (New Jersey) State Gazette*, November 5, 1860; *Baltimore Sun*, November 5, 1860.

55 Johannsen, *Douglas*, 801; Walther, *Yancey*, 252–53.

56 *Washington National Intelligencer*, September 8, 1860; *San Francisco Bulletin*, October 22, 1860.

57 *Washington National Intelligencer*, September 23, 1860; *San Francisco Bulletin*, October 9, 1860; Walther, *Fire-Eaters*, 76; *Madison Wisconsin Patriot*, August 9, 1860; *Albany*

(New York) Evening Journal, October 11, 1860; *Washington Constitution,* October 13 and October 17, 1860.

58 Walther, *Fire-Eaters,* 77; Walther, *Yancey,* 260. Thornton, *Politics and Power,* 398, writes that from Yancey's perspective "the vote for Breckinridge was not only not a vote for disunion, but was the final test of whether or not union was possible." Heidler, *Pulling the Temple Down,* 164–65, however, notes that during his tour Yancey consistently declined to answer when asked what southern whites should do if Lincoln won.

59 Mathew, *Ruffin,* 50; Waugh, *One Man Great Enough,* 353; Nevins, *Emergence of Lincoln,* 2:315–16. The Battle House was built in 1852 and burned in 1905; the current hotel of the same name on 26 North Royal Street was built in 1908.

60 *Philadelphia Public Ledger,* November 8, 1860; *Baltimore Sun,* November 8, 1860; White, *A. Lincoln,* 346; Burlingame, *Lincoln,* 1:677; *Lowell (Massachusetts) Daily Citizen and News,* November 9, 1860; Goodwin, *Team of Rivals,* 277.

61 Oates, *With Malice Toward None,* 191; Baker, *Mary Todd Lincoln,* 161–62; *New York Herald,* November 8, 1860; Holzer, *Lincoln President-Elect,* 39–40.

62 Griffith, *Elizabeth Cady Stanton,* 105; Sewell, *Ballots for Freedom,* 338–39; Burlingame, *Lincoln,* 1:683; David W. Blight, *Frederick Douglass' Civil War: Keeping Faith in Jubilee* (Baton Rouge, LA, 1989), 60.

63 Sterling, *Abby Kelly,* 329; *Liberator,* November 9, 1860; Davis, *Leavitt,* 266; Horace B. Sargent to William Henry Seward, November 7, 1860, in Seward Papers, UR; Ebenezer Gelaff to Charles Francis Adams Sr., November 7, 1860, in Adams Family Papers, MHS.

64 Gienapp, "Who Voted for Lincoln?," 62; Martin Duberman, *Charles Francis Adams, 1807–1886* (Palo Alto, CA, 1960), 222; *Albany (New York) Evening Journal,* November 8, 1860; *Washington Constitution,* November 8, 1860; Paludan, *Presidency of Lincoln,* 5.

65 Orville Vernon Burton, *The Age of Lincoln* (New York, 2007), 103; Gienapp, "Who Voted for Lincoln?," 68–69; Randall, *Lincoln the President,* 1:195; Oates, *Man Behind the Myths,* 53.

66 Thurlow Weed to David Davis, September 7, 1860, in Lincoln Papers, LC; Nevins, *Emergence of Lincoln,* 2:284–85; Wells, *Douglas,* 241–42; Parks, *Bell,* 385–86.

67 Ransom, *Conflict and Compromise,* 164–65; Capers, *Douglas,* 210.

68 William A. Link, *Roots of Secession: Slavery and Politics in Antebellum Virginia* (Chapel Hill, NC, 2003), 208; Crofts, *Reluctant Confederates,* 81; Shanks, *Secession Movement in Virginia,* 119; Gienapp, "Who Voted for Lincoln?," 62.

69 Stephen A. Douglas to Charles Lanphier, July 5, 1860, in *Letters of Douglas,* 498; Randall, *Lincoln the President,* 1:198–99; Robin E. Baker and Dale Baum, "The Texas Voter and the Crisis of the Union, 1859–1861," *Journal of Southern History* 53 (1987): 419; Freehling, *Road to Disunion,* 2:339.

70 Burton, *Age of Lincoln,* 105; Mering, "Slave-State Constitutional Unionists," 398; Oates, *Man Behind the Myths,* 81.

71 Alexander H. Stephens to J. Henly Smith, November 8, 1860, in *Toombs, Stephens, Cobb Correspondence,* 502; Walther, *Fire-Eaters,* 154; *New York Herald,* November 9, 1860; Fraser, *Charleston!,* 243; Logan, *Great Conspiracy,* 101; Catton, *Coming Fury,* 110–11.

Chapter Seven: "The Union Is Dissolved": The Lower South Secedes

1 Mathew, *Ruffin*, 48–50; Edmund Ruffin, *The Diary of Edmund Ruffin: Toward Independence, 1856–1861*, ed. William K. Scarborough (Baton Rouge, LA, 1972), 1:196, 367–68; *Macon (Georgia) Daily Telegraph*, March 13, 1860.

2 Edmund Ruffin, *Anticipations of the Future, to Serve as Lessons for the Present Time* (Richmond, VA, 1860); Ruffin, *Diary*, 554.

3 *Macon (Georgia) Daily Telegraph*, March 13, 1860; *New York Herald*, November 9, 1860; Logan, *Great Conspiracy*, 100; *Washington Constitution*, November 9, 1860.

4 *Madison Wisconsin Patriot*, April 27, 1861; *Philadelphia Inquirer*, August 6, 1861; Mathew, *Ruffin*, 53–55; Betty L. Mitchell, *Edmund Ruffin, A Biography* (Bloomington, IL, 1981), 255–56.

5 Walter Edgar, *South Carolina: A History* (Columbia, SC, 1998), 350; Manisha Sinha, *The Counterrevolution of Slavery: Politics and Ideology in Antebellum South Carolina* (Chapel Hill, NC, 2000), 232–33; Freehling, *Road to Disunion*, 2:391, 394; Fraser, *Charleston!*, 242; John Townsend, *The Doom of Slavery in the Union: Its Safety out of It* (Charleston, SC, 1860), 28.

6 Nichols, *Disruption of American Democracy*, 372–73; Davis, *Look Away*, 24–25.

7 Catton, *Coming Fury*, 105–6; Logan, *Great Conspiracy*, 96; McCardell, *Idea of a Southern Nation*, 328–29.

8 Henry A. Wise, *Seven Decades of the Union* (Philadelphia, 1872), 265; *Trenton (New Jersey) State Gazette*, January 8, 1861; Freehling, *Road to Disunion*, 2:347; Gienapp, "Crisis of American Democracy," 86; Wilentz, *Rise of American Democracy*, 772–73.

9 Huston, *Douglas*, 184; Channing, *Crisis of Fear*, 235–36; *Washington National Intelligencer*, November 1, 1860.

10 Faust, *Hammond*, 357; Channing, *Crisis of Fear*, 161; Guelzo, *Redeemer President*, 250. Gienapp, "Crisis of American Democracy," 119, laments the "refusal of Southerners to accept the inevitable end of slavery, however distant," but Genovese, *Political Economy of Slavery*, 266–67, rightly describes Lincoln's election as an "invitation to a (self-inflicted) beheading" and suggests that the assumption that the planter class could have accepted Republican policies of containment is plausible only to the extent "that men may agree to commit suicide."

11 Horace Greeley to William H. Herndon, December 26, 1860, in Lincoln Papers, LC; Milton, *Eve of Conflict*, 503; Freehling, *Road to Disunion*, 2:382; *Charleston Mercury*, February 13, 1861.

12 Ford, *Origins of Southern Radicalism*, 369–71; Davis, *Rhett*, 394.

13 Davis, *Rhett*, 396; *New York Herald*, November 9, 1860. The data on South Carolina's free blacks comes from Ira Berlin, *Slaves Without Masters: The Free Negro in the Antebellum South* (New York, 1974), 137.

14 Heidler, *Pulling the Temple Down*, 166; *New York Herald*, November 9, 1860; Mary A. DeCredico, *Mary Boykin Chesnut: A Confederate Woman's Life* (Lanham, MD, 2002), 44; Faust, *Hammond*, 358.

15 *Washington National Intelligencer*, November 12, 1860; Burton, *Age of Lincoln*, 130–31; Channing, *Crisis of Fear*, 277–78.

16 McPherson, *Battle Cry of Freedom*, 248; Thurlow Weed to Abraham Lincoln, November 7, 1860, in Lincoln Papers, LC; *New York Herald*, December 14, 1860.

17 Kenneth M. Stampp, *And the War Came* (Baton Rouge, LA, 1950), 54; McClintock, *Lincoln and the Decision*, 40; William N. Brigance, *Jeremiah Sullivan Black: Defender of the Constitution* (Philadelphia, 1934), 86–87; Klunder, *Cass*, 304.

18 Smith, *Presidency of Buchanan*, 148–49; Klein, *Buchanan*, 362–63; James Buchanan, "Message to the Senate and House," December 3, 1860, in *Congressional Globe: Senate Journal*, 36th Cong., 2nd sess., 7–32.

19 *Philadelphia Inquirer*, December 27, 1860; Holzer, *Lincoln President-Elect*, 131; Charles Francis Adams Sr. to Charles Francis Adams Jr., December 29, 1860, in Adams Family Papers, MHS; *Liberator*, December 21, 1860.

20 Logan, *Great Conspiracy*, 105; *Philadelphia Inquirer*, December 29, 1860; *San Francisco Bulletin*, December 29, 1860.

21 Baker, *Buchanan*, 124–25; Potter, *Impending Crisis*, 535–36; *Washington Constitution*, December 12, 1860.

22 Eisenhower, *Agent of Destiny*, 347–48; *Philadelphia Inquirer*, December 17, 1860; Stampp, *And the War Came*, 58–59.

23 Thomas, *Stanton*, 93–94; *Philadelphia Inquirer*, December 17, 1860, and January 7, 1861.

24 Charles Sumner to the Duchess of Argyll, December 14 and December 18, 1860, in *Letters of Sumner*, 38; Catton, *Coming Fury*, 131–32; Ralph Wooster, *The Secession Conventions of the South* (Princeton, NJ, 1962), 15–16; William H. Pease and Jane H. Pease, *James Louis Petigru: Southern Conservative, Southern Dissenter* (Athens, GA, 1995), 156.

25 Wooster, *Secession Conventions*, 19; Nevins, *Emergence of Lincoln*, 2:326; McPherson, *Battle Cry of Freedom*, 242–43.

26 Freehling, *Road to Disunion*, 2:398; Fraser, *Charleston!*, 244.

27 Dumond, *Secession Movement*, 140; Wells, *Douglas*, 231–32.

28 Leigh Fought, *Southern Womanhood and Slavery: A Biography of Louisa S. McCord, 1810–1879* (Columbia, MO, 2003), 152; *Madison Wisconsin Patriot*, December 29, 1860; *Philadelphia Inquirer*, December 21, 1860; DeCredico, *Chesnut*, 46; Johannsen, *Douglas*, 814; *Charleston Mercury Extra*, December 20, 1860.

29 Freehling, *Road to Disunion*, 2:422; Heidler, *Pulling the Temple Down*, 169; Pease and Pease, *Petigru*, 156. Bachman was sincere in his belief that whites had a solemn responsibility to care for African Americans, and in 1822 he attempted to counsel some of the rebels accused with black abolitionist Denmark Vesey. See my *He Shall Go Out Free*, 196.

30 *Madison Wisconsin Patriot*, December 22, 1860, and December 29, 1860.

31 *Philadelphia Inquirer*, December 25, 1860.

32 *Madison Wisconsin Patriot*, December 29, 1860; *Amherst (New Hampshire) Farmer's Cabinet*, December 28, 1860.

33 *Madison Wisconsin Patriot*, January 5, 1861; *Macon (Georgia) Daily Telegraph*, December 22, 1860; Belohlavek, *Broken Glass*, 316–17. Nevins, *Emergence of Lincoln*, 2:429, observes that none of the original seven Confederate states gave any reason for secession but slavery and the need to defend it.

34 Wooster, *Secession Conventions*, 22–23; *Lowell (Massachusetts) Daily Citizen and News*, December 27, 1860; *Madison Wisconsin Patriot*, January 5, 1861; *Concord New-Hampshire Patriot*, January 9, 1860; Francis Pickens to Jefferson Davis, January 23, 1861, in *Papers of Davis*, 7:25.

35 *Madison Wisconsin Patriot*, December 22, 1860; *Macon (Georgia) Daily Telegraph*, December 29, 1860; Potter, *Impending Crisis*, 540–41; James Buchanan, *Mr. Buchanan's Administration on the Eve of the Rebellion* (New York, 1866), 181.

36 Stampp, *And the War Came*, 72–73; Charles Francis Adams Sr. to Charles Francis Adams Jr., December 15, 1860; Waugh, *One Man Great Enough*, 362–63.

37 *Easton (Maryland) Gazette*, January 5, 1860; *Trenton (New Jersey) State Gazette*, January 5, 1860; Stampp, *And the War Came*, 80–81.

38 James A. Harvey to Abraham Lincoln, November 29, 1860, in Lincoln Papers, LC; Jefferson Davis to Robert Barnwell Rhett Jr., November 10, 1860, in *Papers of Davis*, 368–69; Nevins, *Emergence of Lincoln*, 2:321; Heidler, *Pulling the Temple Down*, 172–73.

39 Sewell, *A House Divided*, 78; Morrison, *Slavery and the West*, 258–59; Burton, *Age of Lincoln*, 120.

40 *Philadelphia Inquirer*, January 10, 1861; Davis, *Davis*, 291.

41 Davis, *Rise and Fall*, 227; Davis, *Davis*, 259; Eaton, *Davis*, 121; *Congressional Globe*, 36th Cong., 1st sess., 307; Jefferson Davis, *Remarks on the Special Message on Affairs in South Carolina*, in *Southern Pamphlets on Secession*, 126.

42 *Trenton (New Jersey) State Gazette*, January 8, 1861; *Macon (Georgia) Daily Telegraph*, January 8, 1861; *Baltimore Sun*, January 4, 1861; Larry E. Rivers, *Slavery in Florida: Territorial Days to Emancipation* (Gainesville, FL, 2000), 229.

43 *Macon (Georgia) Daily Telegraph*, January 1, 1860; Potter, *Impending Crisis*, 491; Walther, *Yancey*, 274.

44 *Macon (Georgia) Daily Telegraph*, January 9, 1861; Davis, "*Government of Our Own*," 8; Walther, *Yancey*, 272–73; Wooster, *Secession Conventions*, 58–59; Charles Pelham to Martha Coffin Wright, December 6, 1860, Osborne Family Papers, Syracuse University.

45 Heidler, *Pulling the Temple Down*, 174; Drew Gilpin Faust, *Creation of Confederate Nationalism: Ideology and Identity in the Civil War South* (Baton Rouge, LA, 1990), 35; Thornton, *Politics and Power*, 428.

46 Walther, *Fire-Eaters*, 78; Joel C. Dubose, *Alabama History* (Atlanta, 1915), 133–34; *New York Times*, January 12, 1861.

47 *Macon (Georgia) Daily Telegraph*, January 1 and January 9, 1861; Wooster, *Secession Conventions*, 80–81; Emory M. Thomas, *The Confederate Nation, 1861–1865* (New York, 1979), 52–53; *Albany (New York) Evening Journal*, January 8, 1861.

48 Heidler, *Pulling the Temple Down*, 154–55, 175; Schott, *Stephens*, 319; Howe, *Political Culture*, 252–53; Dumond, *Secession Movement*, 142–43; Logan, *Great Conspiracy*, 120.

49 Johnson, *Toward a Patriarchal Republic*, 47–48; *Macon (Georgia) Daily Telegraph*, January 1, 1861; Wilentz, *Rise of American Democracy*, 776.

50 Schott, *Stephens*, 316–17; *Macon (Georgia) Daily Telegraph*, January 1, 1861; Smith, *Presidency of Buchanan*, 138; Johnson, *Toward a Patriarchal Republic*, 63–64; *New Orleans Times Picayune*, January 10, 1861. Potter, *Impending Crisis*, 503–4, found that pattern true

in all of the seceding states. The "counties with the lowest ratios of slave population . . . gave only 37 percent of their vote for immediate secession, while the counties with the highest ratio of slaves were 72 percent for secession," he observes. "To a much greater degree than the slaveholders desired, secession had become a slaveholder's movement, toward which the people of the counties with few slaves showed a predominantly negative attitude."

51 *Easton (Maryland) Gazette*, January 5, 1860; Wooster, *Secession Conventions*, 91–92; Johnson, *Toward a Patriarchal Republic*, 117–18.

52 Wooster, *Secession Conventions*, 118–19; Nichols, *Disruption of American Democracy*, 442; *New Orleans Delta*, January 6, 1861; Charles B. Dew, "Who Won the Secession Election in Louisiana?," *Journal of Southern History* 36 (1970): 29; Freehling, *Road to Disunion*, 2:454; Ratner and Teeter, *Fanatics and Fire-Eaters*, 92.

53 Parrish, *Taylor*, 102–3; Dumond, *Secession Movement*, 208–9; Evans, *Benjamin*, 110; Charles P. Roland, "Louisiana and Secession," *Louisiana History* 19 (1978): 398; Johannsen, *Douglas*, 826; Lloyd Lewis, *Sherman: Fighting Prophet* (Lincoln, NE, 1993 ed.), 138.

54 Thomas, *Confederate Nation*, 55–56; Marquis James, *The Raven: A Biography of Sam Houston* (Austin, 1988 ed.), 406; De Bruhl, *Sword of San Jacinto*, 385, 389–90; Logan, *Great Conspiracy*, 134–35; Donald E. Reynolds, *Texas Terror: The Slave Insurrection Panic of 1860 and the Secession of the Lower South* (Baton Rouge, LA, 2007), 29, 116; Nevins, *Emergence of Lincoln*, 2:426–27.

55 Catton, *Coming Fury*, 234; De Bruhl, *Sword of San Jacinto*, 390–94; Wooster, *Secession Conventions*, 124–26.

56 Burlingame, *Lincoln*, 1:689; *Concord New-Hampshire Patriot*, January 9, 1861; *Baltimore Sun*, January 4, 1861.

57 McPherson, *Battle Cry of Freedom*, 254–55; *Philadelphia Inquirer*, January 15, 1861; Davis, *Look Away*, 36–37.

58 Potter, *Impending Crisis*, 506; Varon, *Disunion!*, 340; Shanks, *Secession Movement in Virginia*, 132–33; *Macon (Georgia) Daily Telegraph*, January 8, 1861.

59 John Tyler to Silas Reed, November 16, 1860, in John Tyler Papers, LC; Wooster, *Secession Conventions*, 140–41; Heidler, *Pulling the Temple Down*, 180.

60 Potter, *Impending Crisis*, 507; Varon, *We Mean to Be Counted*, 149; Simpson, *Wise*, 227, 239–40; Heidler, *Pulling the Temple Down*, 179; Charles B. Dew, *Apostles of Disunion: Southern Secession Commissioners and the Causes of the Civil War* (Charlottesville, VA, 2001), 60, 66–67.

61 Stampp, *And the War Came*, 124–25; *Dallas Weekly Herald*, January 9, 1861; Nichols, *Disruption of American Democracy*, 471–72; *Macon (Georgia) Daily Telegraph*, January 8, 1861; Huston, *Douglas*, 190.

62 *Brattleboro Vermont Phoenix*, January 10, 1861; *Dallas Weekly Herald*, January 9, 1861.

63 *Brattleboro Vermont Phoenix*, January 10, 1861.

64 Stampp, *And the War Came*, 8; Morrison, *Slavery and the West*, 262; James M. McPherson, *Lincoln and the Second American Revolution* (New York, 1991), 26–27; McPherson, *Battle Cry of Freedom*, 230–31; *Congressional Globe*, 36th Cong., 1st sess., 450–55.

65 Guelzo, *Redeemer President*, 252–53; George E. Ford to William H. Seward, January 12, 1861, in Seward Papers, UR; Blight, *Frederick Douglass' Civil War*, 62–63; Abraham Lincoln to Alexander H. Stephens, December 22, 1860, in *The Collected Works of Abraham Lincoln*, ed. Roy P. Basler (New York, 1953), 4:160.

Chapter Eight: "Others to Share the Burden": Two Governments Prepare

1 *Albany (New York) Evening Journal*, May 24, 1860; Taylor, *Seward*, 120; Van Deusen, *Seward*, 267.

2 Donald, *Lincoln*, 262; Goodwin, *Team of Rivals*, 280; McClintock, *Lincoln and the Decision*, 43.

3 Holzer, *Lincoln President-Elect*, 116; Helen Nicolay, *Lincoln's Secretary: A Biography of John G. Nicolay* (New York, 1949), 34–42; Potter, *Impending Crisis*, 555–56; Donald, *Lincoln*, 270; Thomas, *Lincoln*, 232.

4 Hunt, *Hamlin*, 126; Abraham Lincoln to Hannibal Hamlin, November 8, 1860, in Lincoln Papers, LC.

5 Oates, *With Malice Toward None*, 197; Randall, *Lincoln the President*, 1: 254–55; David M. Potter, *Lincoln and His Party in the Secession Crisis* (New Haven, CT, 1942), 152; Hunt, *Hamlin*, 127. Three white South Carolinians wrote a sarcastic letter to Lincoln offering to buy the "likely & intelligent mulatto boy" known "as Hanibal Hamlin." See A. J. Hause, J. D. Wright, and W. D. Hardy to Abraham Lincoln, November 27, 1860, in Lincoln Papers, LC.

6 Hunt, *Hamlin*, 128; Randall, *Lincoln the President*, 1:258–59; Burlingame, *Lincoln*, 1:721; Lyman Trumbull to Abraham Lincoln, December 2, 1860, in Lincoln Papers, LC; Smith, *Blair*, 271.

7 Hunt, *Hamlin*, 129; Abraham Lincoln to Lyman Trumbull, December 8, 1860, in Lincoln Papers, LC.

8 Hunt, *Hamlin*, 130–31; Donald, *Lincoln*, 263; Abraham Lincoln to Hannibal Hamlin, December 8, 1860, in Lincoln Papers, LC.

9 Taylor, *Seward*, 127; Abraham Lincoln to William H. Seward, December 8, 1860, in Lincoln Papers, LC; Abraham Lincoln to William H. Seward, December 8, 1860 (second letter of that date), ibid.

10 Van Deusen, *Seward*, 240; Waugh, *One Man Great Enough*, 370–71; William H. Seward to Abraham Lincoln, December 13, 1860, in Lincoln Papers, LC; Hannibal Hamlin to William H. Seward, November 17, 1860, in Seward Papers, UR; Frederick P. Stanton to William H. Seward, November 5, 1860, ibid.; Simon Cameron to William H. Seward, November 13, 1860, ibid.

11 Henry Adams to Charles Francis Adams Jr., January 11, 1861, in Adams Family Papers, MHS; William H. Seward to Abraham Lincoln, December 16, 1860, in Lincoln Papers, LC; Potter, *Lincoln and His Party*, 152; Clinton, *Mrs. Lincoln*, 118; King, *Davis*, 169.

12 White, *A. Lincoln*, 358; McClintock, *Lincoln and the Decision*, 91; John A. Gilmer to Abraham Lincoln, December 10, 1860, in Lincoln Papers, LC; Abraham Lincoln to John A. Gilmer, December 15, 1860, ibid.; Abraham Lincoln to William H. Seward, December 29, 1860, in *Collected Works*, 4:164

13 Thurlow Weed to Abraham Lincoln, December 23, 1860, in Lincoln Papers, LC; William H. Seward to Abraham Lincoln, December 28, 1860, in Seward Papers, UR.

14 Van Deusen, *Greeley*, 256; *Washington Constitution*, January 8, 1861; *New York Herald*, January 8, 1861, and February 21, 1861.

15 Burlingame, *Lincoln*, 1:727; Trefousse, *Stevens*, 104; King, *Davis*, 163; Simon Cameron to Abraham Lincoln, December 30, 1860, in Lincoln Papers, LC; Abraham Lincoln to Simon Cameron, December 31, 1860, in *Collected Works*, 4:168.

16 Smith, *Blair*, 270–71; Holzer, *Lincoln President-Elect*, 201; Henry Adams to Charles Francis Adams Jr., February 5, 1861, in Adams Family Papers, MHS; Samuel Galloway to John G. Nicolay, January 4, 1861, in Lincoln Papers, LC; Abraham Lincoln to Simon Cameron, January 3, 1861, ibid.

17 Burlingame, *Lincoln*, 2:54; Charles Francis Adams Sr. to John G. Palphrey, January 5, 1861, in Adams Family Papers, MHS; William H. Seward to Abraham Lincoln, January 13, 1861, in Lincoln Papers, LC; Henry Simons to Abraham Lincoln, January 14, 1861, ibid.; Leonard Swett to Abraham Lincoln, January 14, 1861, ibid.; Abraham Lincoln to Simon Cameron, January 21, 1861, ibid.

18 Francis Preston Blair Sr. to Abraham Lincoln, December 18, 1860, in Lincoln Papers, LC; Parrish, *Blair*, 89; *San Francisco Bulletin*, January 15, 1861; *Trenton (New Jersey) State Gazette*, March 1, 1861; *Baltimore Sun*, March 1, 1861. The elder Blair insisted, "I really liked [Cameron and Seward] but I do not like their ways." See Francis P. Blair Sr. to Francis P. Blair Jr., December 6, 1860, in Lincoln Papers, LC.

19 McClintock, *Lincoln and the Decision*, 124–25; *Albany (New York) Evening Journal*, February 28, 1861; *Washington Constitution*, January 8, 1861; William H. Seward to Abraham Lincoln, January 8, 1861, in Lincoln Papers, LC; John A. Gilmer to Abraham Lincoln, January 25, 1861, ibid.; John A. Gilmer to Abraham Lincoln, February 21, 1861, ibid.

20 Randall, *Lincoln the President*, 1:262–63; Goodwin, *Team of Rivals*, 286; Francis P. Blair Jr. to Abraham Lincoln, December 13, 1860, in Lincoln Papers, LC; Edward Bates to Abraham Lincoln, December 18, 1860, ibid.; Abraham Lincoln to Edward Bates, December 18, 1860, ibid.; *San Francisco Bulletin*, January 15, 1861.

21 Burlingame, *Lincoln*, 1:743; Hannibal Hamlin to Abraham Lincoln, December 29, 1860, in Lincoln Papers, LC; John Niven, *Gideon Welles: Lincoln's Secretary of the Navy* (New York, 1973), 320–21; *Philadelphia Inquirer*, March 4, 1861.

22 Oates, *With Malice Toward None*, 215; David Davis to Abraham Lincoln, November 19, 1860, in Lincoln Papers, LC.

23 Van Deusen, *Greeley*, 258; Abraham Lincoln to Salmon Chase, May 26, 1860, in Lincoln Papers, LC; Abraham Lincoln to Lyman Trumbull, January 7, 1861, ibid.

24 Guelzo, *Redeemer President*, 256; Burlingame, *Lincoln*, 1:737; *Baltimore Sun*, March 1, 1861; *New York Herald*, March 2, 1861; George G. Fogg to Abraham Lincoln, February 5, 1861, in Lincoln Papers, LC.

25 Abraham Lincoln to Salmon P. Chase, December 31, 1860, in *Collected Works*, 4:168; Oates, *With Malice Toward None*, 202–3; Niven, *Chase*, 222–23; James W. Stone to Abraham Lincoln, January 28, 1861, in Lincoln Papers, LC.

26 Jeremiah Nichols to Abraham Lincoln, January 22, 1861, in Lincoln Papers, LC; Anonymous to Abraham Lincoln, January 16, 1861, ibid. Blue, *Chase*, 131, calls Chase's response "sanctimonious," but given Lincoln's curious non-offer, Chase's injured answer is more than understandable.

27 Donald, *Lincoln*, 280–81; Henry M. Low to William H. Seward, January 10, 1861; Seward Papers, UR; Burlingame, *Lincoln*, 2:56; William H. Seward to Abraham Lincoln, March 2, 1861, in Lincoln Papers, LC.

28 White, *A. Lincoln*, 387; Abraham Lincoln to William H. Seward, March 4, 1861, in Lincoln Papers, LC; William H. Seward to Abraham Lincoln, March 5, 1861, ibid.

29 *Philadelphia Inquirer*, February 22, 1861; Burlingame, *Lincoln*, 2:58; *Lowell (Massachusetts) Daily Citizen and News*, March 1, 1861.

30 William W. Rogers, *Confederate Home Front: Montgomery During the Civil War* (Tuscaloosa, AL, 1999), 4–6; Davis, *"Government of Our Own,"* 22, 32.

31 Thomas, *Confederate Nation*, 39–40; Catton, *Coming Fury*, 204–5.

32 Thomas, *Confederate Nation*, 57–58; Avery O. Craven, *The Growth of Southern Nationalism, 1848–1861* (Baton Rouge, LA, 1953), 388; *Washington National Intelligencer*, February 9, 1861.

33 *New Orleans Times Picayune*, February 16, 1861; Edgar, *South Carolina*, 357; De-Credico, *Chesnut*, 48; George C. Rable, *The Confederate Republic: A Revolution Against Politics* (Chapel Hill, NC, 1994), 50–51.

34 McPherson, *Battle Cry of Freedom*, 258; Catton, *Coming Fury*, 208–9; Thomas, *Confederate Nation*, 64–65, 307–22 (for the entire document).

35 Rable, *Confederate Republic*, 52–53; *Charleston Mercury*, February 13, 1861; Davis, *"Government of Our Own,"* 87; Wooster, *Secession Conventions*, 48; *Washington National Intelligencer*, February 19, 1861.

36 DeCredico, *Chesnut*, 47–48; Sewell, *A House Divided*, 80–81; Rable, *Confederate Republic*, 44–45; *Clarksville (Texas) Standard*, March 2, 1861.

37 *Philadelphia Inquirer*, February 11, 1861; Cooper, *Davis*, 321; Davis, *Davis*, 302–3.

38 Catton, *Coming Fury*, 210–11; Howell Cobb to Mary Ann Cobb, February 6, 1861, in *Toombs, Stephens, Cobb Correspondence*, 537.

39 Catton, *Coming Fury*, 211; William Y. Thompson, *Robert Toombs of Georgia* (Baton Rouge, LA, 1966), 162; William C. Davis, *The Union That Shaped the Confederacy: Robert Toombs and Alexander H. Stephens* (Lawrence, KS, 2001), 100.

40 Chesnut, *Mary Chesnut's Civil War*, 6; Nichols, *Disruption of American Democracy*, 467–68.

41 Cooper, *Davis*, 322; Davis, *Rise and Fall*, 228; Chesnut, *Mary Chesnut's Civil War*, 6; Charles B. Flood, *Lee: The Last Years* (Boston, 1981), 220; *Macon (Georgia) Daily Telegraph*, February 21, 1861.

42 McPherson, *Battle Cry of Freedom*, 259; *Philadelphia Inquirer*, January 15, 1861; Rable, *Confederate Republic*, 66–67.

43 Catton, *Coming Fury*, 212; *Macon (Georgia) Daily Telegraph*, February 11, 1861, and February 21, 1861; Schott, *Stephens*, 331.

44 Eaton, *Davis*, 126; Schott, *Stephens*, 327.

45 James Ford Rhodes, *History of the United States from the Compromise of 1850* (New York, 1900), 3:209; Catton, *Coming Fury*, 212; Schott, *Stephens*, 328.

46 Allen, *Davis*, 267; Robert Toombs to Jefferson Davis, February 9, 1861, in *Papers of Davis*, 7:36; Varina Davis, *Jefferson Davis: A Memoir by His Wife* (New York, 1890), 2:17–19; Joan Cashin, *First Lady of the Confederacy: Varina Davis's Civil War* (Cambridge, MA, 2006), 102–3; Carol Berkin, *Civil War Wives* (New York, 2009), 157; *Macon (Georgia) Daily Telegraph*, February 16, 1861.

47 *Macon (Georgia) Daily Telegraph*, February 18, 1861; *New York Herald*, February 18, 1861; Davis, *Davis*, 306–7; Holzer, *Lincoln President-Elect*, 344; Cooper, *Davis*, 328–29; *Madison Wisconsin Patriot*, February 18, 1861.

48 Davis, *Look Away*, 76–77; Rable, *Confederate Republic*, 68–69; *Albany (New York) Evening Journal*, February 19, 1861; *New York Herald*, February 19, 1861; Jefferson Davis to Varina Davis, February 20, 1861, in *Papers of Davis*, 6:53; Howell Cobb to Mary Ann Cobb, February 20, 1861, in *Toombs, Stephens, Cobb Correspondence*, 544; Davis, *"Government of Our Own,"* 152–53.

49 *Washington National Intelligencer*, February 19, 1861; *Columbus (Georgia) Daily Enquirer*, February 19, 1861; *Baltimore Sun*, February 19, 1861; Davis, "Inaugural Address," February 18, 1861, in *Papers of Davis*, 7:45–48; *Macon (Georgia) Daily Telegraph*, February 19, 1861.

50 *Macon (Georgia) Daily Telegraph*, February 19, 1861. Davis, *Davis*, 308, makes this point nicely. Finally, in November 1861, a permanent government replaced the provisional Congress and presidency. Davis ran unopposed.

51 Davis, *Davis*, 182; Stampp, *Imperiled Union*, 192–93.

52 *Albany (New York) Evening Journal*, March 23, 1861; Herman Hattaway and Richard E. Beringer, *Jefferson Davis, Confederate President* (Lawrence, KS, 2002), 36; Ishbel Ross, *First Lady of the South: The Life of Mrs. Jefferson Davis* (New York, 1958), 108–9; Berkin, *Civil War Wives*, 159; Cashin, *First Lady of the Confederacy*, 103–4; Jefferson Davis to Varina Davis, February 20, 1861, in *Papers of Davis*, 6:54.

53 Walther, *Yancey*, 297; Davis, *Davis*, 311–12; Hattaway and Beringer, *Davis*, 32; Howell Cobb to Mary Ann Cobb, February 20, 1861, in *Toombs, Stephens, Cobb Correspondence*, 544.

54 *Pittsfield (Massachusetts) Sun*, February 21, 1861; *Macon (Georgia) Daily Telegraph*, February 21, 1861; Davis, *Rise and Fall*, 241–42; *Easton (Maryland) Gazette*, March 2, 1861.

55 *Albany (New York) Evening Journal*, February 23, 1861; Ford, *Origins of Southern Radicalism*, 178; Eaton, *Davis*, 129–30; *Baltimore Sun*, February 22, 1861.

56 Walther, *Yancey*, 297. The *Philadelphia Inquirer*, February 19, 1861, reported that the radicals complained that it would have been "far better for them to be in the United States of America than to be playing second fiddle to Jeff Davis and Aleck Stephens in a bogus Confederacy."

57 *Baltimore Sun*, March 9, 1861; *Macon (Georgia) Daily Telegraph*, February 22, 1861; Eaton, *Davis*, 130; Heidler, *Pulling the Temple Down*, 186. When Joseph Davis once expressed the hope that a southern Bonaparte might emerge, Mary Chesnut replied that it "would do no good. I do not think Walker would give him a commission." See *The*

Private Mary Chesnut: The Unpublished Civil War Diaries, eds. C. Vann Woodward and Elisabeth Muhlenfeld (New York, 1984), 99.

58 *Macon (Georgia) Daily Telegraph*, February 27, 1861; *Baltimore Sun*, February 26, 1861; Evans, *Benjamin*, 97; Davis, *Rise and Fall*, 242. The *New-Hampshire Sentinel*, February 21, 1861, enjoyed revealing that Benjamin never completed his studies at Yale and that he was suspected of theft while a student.

59 *New York Herald*, February 23, 1861; *New Orleans Delta*, February 28, 1861; Eaton, *Davis*, 128; Evans, *Benjamin*, vii.

60 Genovese, *Political Economy of Slavery*, 30; Hattaway and Beringer, *Davis*, 32; Evans, *Benjamin*, 32; 1860 Federal Census. Determining the number of slaves owned by Jefferson Davis is complicated by his joint operation with his brother Joseph and by their tax-roll undercount. By 1860, Joseph owned at least 345 slaves. See Janet Sharp Hermann, *The Pursuit of a Dream* (New York, 1981), 11.

61 *Macon (Georgia) Daily Telegraph*, March 12, 1861; Schott, *Stephens*, 334.

62 *Macon (Georgia) Daily Telegraph*, March 25, 1861; *Pittsfield (Massachusetts) Sun*, March 28, 1861.

63 *Macon (Georgia) Daily Telegraph*, March 25, 1861; *Liberator*, March 29, 1861.

64 *Milwaukee Sentinel*, March 25, 1861.

65 *New York Herald*, March 28, 1861; *Columbus (Ohio) Crisis*, April 4, 1861; *Lowell (Massachusetts) Daily Citizen and News*, March 29, 1861.

66 *Milwaukee Sentinel*, February 12, 1861. Donald, *Lincoln*, 272–73, and Oates, *With Malice Toward None*, 207, disagree as to whether Mary was still in Springfield or had traveled ahead to St. Louis. The *Madison Wisconsin Patriot*, February 11, 1861, reported that "Robert F. [*sic*] Lincoln" was traveling with the president-elect, while "Mrs. Lincoln remains in Springfield till next week."

67 *Madison Wisconsin Patriot*, February 11, 1861.

68 *Albany (New York) Evening Journal*, February 11, 1861. Holzer, *Lincoln President-Elect*, 298–301, notes that versions published that evening and the next day in newspapers varied slightly, depending on the stenographer. Lincoln himself promptly revised and condensed the speech for publication.

69 *Albany (New York) Evening Journal*, February 11, 1861; *Lowell (Massachusetts) Daily Citizen and News*, February 12, 1861; *Milwaukee Sentinel*, February 12, 1861; Holzer, *Lincoln President-Elect*, 302.

Chapter Nine: *"All Our Labor Is Lost"*: Compromise Committees and the Washington Peace Conference

1 Lynn Hudson Parsons, *John Quincy Adams* (Madison, 1998), 239–40; John Adams to Thomas Jefferson, February 3, 1821, in *The Adams-Jefferson Letters: The Complete Correspondence Between Thomas Jefferson and Abigail and John Adams*, ed. Lester Cappon (Chapel Hill, NC, 1959), 571; Duberman, *Adams*, 221–22.

2 Kirkland, *Adams*, 25–26; John David Smith, "Let Us All Be Grateful That We Have Colored Troops That Will Fight," in *Black Soldiers in Blue: African American Troops in the Civil War Era*, ed. John David Smith (Chapel Hill, NC, 2001), 4–5.

3 John Sherman, *Recollections of Forty Years in the House, Senate, and Cabinet: An Auto-biography* (New York, 1895), 1:214; McPherson, *Battle Cry of Freedom*, 250–51.

4 Duberman, *Adams*, 226–27; Nevins, *Emergence of Lincoln*, 2:405; *Congressional Globe*, 36th Cong., 2nd sess., 6.

5 Burlingame, *Lincoln*, 1:707; Smith, *Presidency of Buchanan*, 159; *Washington National Intelligencer*, December 14, 1861; *Congressional Globe*, 36th Cong., 2nd sess., 62.

6 Sherman, *Recollections*, 1:213; Paludan, *Presidency of Lincoln*, 31; Logan, *Great Conspiracy*, 107; Potter, *Impending Crisis*, 522–23.

7 Davis, *Davis*, 289–90; Allen, *Davis*, 250; Davis, *Rise and Fall*, 69; Potter, *Impending Crisis*, 530–31; Robert Toombs to the People of Georgia, December 23, 1860, in *Toombs, Stephens, Cobb Correspondence*, 525.

8 McPherson, *Battle Cry of Freedom*, 254; Stampp, *Imperiled Union*, 237–38; Paludan, *Presidency of Lincoln*, 34; Nevins, *Emergence of Lincoln*, 2:385–86.

9 Walther, *Yancey*, 288; Trefousse, *Johnson*, 134.

10 Stampp, *And the War Came*, 22; Silas A. Andrews to William H. Seward, December 4, 1860, in Seward Papers, UR; Lewis Benedict to William H. Seward, December 4, 1860, ibid.; Lahan Thompson to William H. Seward, December 8, 1860, ibid.

11 Charles Sumner to John Andrew, January 18, 1861, in *Letters of Sumner*, 2:43; Trefousse, *Wade*, 131–32.

12 Abraham Lincoln to John T. Hale, January 11, 1861, in Lincoln Papers, LC; Donald, *Lincoln*, 270.

13 Potter, *Lincoln and His Party*, 6–69; McClintock, *Lincoln and the Decision*, 57; Sewell, *A House Divided*, 82; Abraham Lincoln to Thurlow Weed, December 17, 1860, in *Collected Works*, 4:154.

14 Oates, *With Malice Toward None*, 199; Abraham Lincoln to James T. Hale, January 11, 1861, in Lincoln Papers, LC; Abraham Lincoln to Lyman Trumbull, December 10, 1860, in *Collected Works*, 4:149–50; Abraham Lincoln to William Kellogg, December 11, 1860, ibid., 150; Abraham Lincoln to Elihu B. Washburne, December 13, 1860, ibid., 151. Potter, *Lincoln and His Party*, 19, criticizes the "Republican failure to comprehend the reality of secession," but as Lincoln's letters indicate, the president-elect did not think that lower-South secessionists were bluffing.

15 Richard N. Current, *The Lincoln Nobody Knows* (New York, 1963), 91–92; Abraham Lincoln to James T. Hale, January 11, 1861, in Lincoln Papers, LC.

16 Worthington G. Snethen to Abraham Lincoln, December 8, 1860, in Lincoln Papers, LC; Stampp, *And the War Came*, 186–87; Charles Francis Adams Sr. to Charles Francis Adams Jr., December 15, 1860, in Adams Family Papers, MHS; Stampp, *Imperiled Union*, 165–66.

17 Boles, *South Through Time*, 298; Randall, *Lincoln the President*, 225; *Congressional Globe*, 36th Cong., 2nd sess., 112.

18 Cooper, *Davis*, 319; Potter, *Impending Crisis*, 531–32; *Congressional Globe*, 36th Cong., 2nd sess., 112.

19 McClintock, *Lincoln and the Decision*, 70; Stephen Douglas to August Belmont, December 25, 1860, in *Letters of Douglas*, 505; Stephen Douglas to Charles H. Lanphier, December 25, 1860, ibid., 504.

20 Johannsen, *Douglas*, 816; *Washington National Intelligencer*, December 26, 1860; Nevins, *Emergence of Lincoln*, 2:392; Capers, *Douglas*, 216–17.

21 *San Francisco Bulletin*, January 1, 1861; Nevins, *Emergence of Lincoln*, 2:392; *Lowell (Massachusetts) Daily Citizen and News*, January 8, 1861. "Oregon and California," *De Bow's Review*, January 1846, 68, argued that a "winter in this section of Oregon [was] not unlike that of some of our Southern States."

22 *New York Herald*, March 2, 1861; Wells, *Douglas*, 272–73; Burlingame, *Lincoln*, 1:697; Charles Sumner to John Andrew, February 8, 1861, in *Letters of Sumner*, 255.

23 *Philadelphia Inquirer*, January 9, 1861; Potter, *Lincoln and His Party*, 171.

24 Current, *Lincoln Nobody Knows*, 89–109; Van Deusen, *Seward*, 243; Cooper, *Davis*, 320. Thompson, *Toombs*, 152, insists that Toombs was prepared to vote for the Crittenden compromise "if the Republicans had done so." His demands made to the committee suggest otherwise.

25 Nichols, *Disruption of American Democracy*, 440–41; Kirwan, *Crittenden*, 392–93; Potter, *Impending Crisis*, 549; Nevins, *Emergence of Lincoln*, 2:401–2; *Easton (Maryland) Gazette*, January 5, 1860.

26 McClintock, *Lincoln and the Decision*, 115; *Washington National Intelligencer*, February 6, 1861; Stephen Douglas to Alexander Stephens, December 25, 1860, in *Letters of Douglas*, 506.

27 *New Orleans Delta*, January 8, 1861; Flint, *Life of Douglas*, 196; *Congressional Globe*, 36th Cong., 2nd sess., 35–42. Wells, *Douglas*, 262, rightly suggests that the speech was one of Douglas's worst.

28 *Madison Wisconsin Patriot*, November 24, 1860; Alexander Stephens to J. Henley Smith, December 31, 1860, in *Toombs, Stephens, Cobb Correspondence*, 526; Johannsen, *Douglas*, 817; Henry Adams to Charles Francis Adams Jr., February 13, 1861, in Adams Family Papers, MHS.

29 Potter, *Impending Crisis*, 563; Adams, *Autobiography*, 73; Kirwan, *Crittenden*, 397–98; Paludan, *Presidency of Lincoln*, 38; Taylor, *Seward*, 133–34.

30 *New York Herald*, January 8, 1861; "A Republican" to William H. Seward, January 10, 1861, in Seward Papers, UR; C. B. Taylor to William Henry Seward, January 28, 1861, ibid.; Gilbert C. Davidson to William H. Seward, January 11, 1861, ibid.; Charles Sumner to John Andrew, January 8, 1861, in *Letters of Sumner*, 2:40; Henry Adams to Charles Francis Adams Jr., December 22, 1860, in Adams Family Papers, MHS; Henry Adams to Charles Francis Adams Jr., January 26, 1861, ibid.

31 Henry Adams to Charles Francis Adams Jr., January 8, 1861, in Adams Family Papers, MHS; *Congressional Globe*, 36th Cong., 2nd sess., 341–44.

32 Champion S. Chase to William H. Seward, February 1, 1861, in Seward Papers, UR; J. H. Rhorer to William H. Seward, February 1, 1861, ibid.; Logan, *Great Conspiracy*, 109–10; Goodwin, *Team of Rivals*, 302.

33 Trefousse, *Wade*, 139; Samuel Grannis to William H. Seward, February 19, 1861, in Seward Papers, UR; Goodwin, *Team of Rivals*, 314; Charles Sumner to Salmon Chase, January 19, 1861, in *Letters of Sumner*, 44–45; Adams, *Autobiography*, 80–81; Wilentz, *Rise of American Democracy*, 780; McClintock, *Lincoln and the Decision*, 166.

34 Duberman, *Adams*, 228; *Baltimore Sun*, December 14, 1861.

35 Duberman, *Adams*, 231; Donald, *Sumner*, 374; *Liberator*, January 4, 1860; Henry Adams to Charles Francis Adams Jr., December 18, 1861, in Adams Family Papers, MHS.

36 Henry Adams to Charles Francis Adams Jr., December 9, 1861, in Adams Family Papers, MHS; *Washington Daily National Intelligencer*, December 30, 1860.

37 Duberman, *Adams*, 240–41; *New York Herald*, February 17, 1861; Donald, *Sumner*, 374, 380. Leaving aside the fact that southern promoters spoke often of using slaves to mine in the territories, the region was in fact well suited for cotton. One of my grandfathers, Clifton Egerton, grew cotton in Las Cruces, New Mexico, while the other, Frank Rogers, planted cotton in what is now suburban Phoenix, Arizona.

38 Stampp, *And the War Came*, 138–39; McClintock, *Lincoln and the Decision*, 138–39; Henry Adams to Charles Francis Adams Jr., December 22, 1860, in Adams Family Papers, MHS.

39 Sherman, *Recollections*, 1:206; *Philadelphia Inquirer*, January 1, 1861; Potter, *Lincoln and His Party*, 184–85; Erastus Hopkins to Charles Francis Adams Sr., December 10, 1860, in Adams Family Papers, MHS.

40 Charles Francis Adams Sr. to Charles Francis Adams Jr., December 21, 1860, in Adams Family Papers, MHS; *Washington National Intelligencer*, January 4, 1861; Joshua Giddings to Charles Francis Adams Sr., December 10, 1860, in Adams Family Papers, MHS; Thomas Corwin to Abraham Lincoln, January 16, 1861, in Lincoln Papers, LC.

41 Duberman, *Adams*, 245, 247; Nichols, *Disruption of American Democracy*, 453; *Albany (New York) Evening Journal*, January 12, 1861; Charles Francis Adams Sr. to Charles Francis Adams Jr., January 15, 1861, in Adams Family Papers, MHS.

42 Oliver P. Chitwood, *John Tyler: Champion of the Old South* (New York, 1939), 436–37; Potter, *Lincoln and His Party*, 61–62; Dumond, *Secession Movement*, 225–26; Wise, *Seven Decades of the Union*, 271; Klein, *Buchanan*, 399.

43 Potter, *Impending Crisis*, 546; Davis, *Rise and Fall*, 248; Botts, *Great Rebellion*, 184–85; Nichols, *Pierce*, 516; Logan, *Great Conspiracy*, 261–62; John Niven, *Martin Van Buren and the Romantic Age of American Politics* (New York, 1983), 610; Van Deusen, *Weed*, 268; Niven, *Chase*, 233; Duberman, *Adams*, 252.

44 Chitwood, *John Tyler: The Accidental President* (Chapel Hill, NC, 2006), 438–39; Robert Winthrop to John Tyler, February 12, 1861, in Tyler Papers, LC; Edward P. Crapol, *Tyler*, 253–54, 262.

45 *A Report of the Debates and Proceedings of the Secret Sessions of the Conference Convention, for Proposing Amendments to the Constitution of the United States*, ed. L. E. Chittenden (New York, 1864), 9, 12, 14; Wise, *Seven Decades of the Union*, 273–74; Chitwood, *Tyler*, 442–43; Johannsen, *Douglas*, 835.

46 Van Deusen, *Seward*, 248–49; Duberman, *Adams*, 252; James M. Mason to Jefferson Davis, February 12, 1861, in *Papers of Davis*, 7:39; Catton, *Coming Fury*, 237–38; Kirwan, *Crittenden*, 406; *Washington National Intelligencer*, March 4, 1861; Charles Francis Adams Sr. to Charles Francis Adams Jr., February 10, 1861, in Adams Family Papers, MHS; Henry Adams to Charles Francis Adams Jr., February 3, 1861, ibid.; *New York Herald*, February 20, 1861.

47 Craypol, *Tyler*, 259–60; Smith, *Presidency of Buchanan*, 162; James Buchanan to John Tyler, February 21, 1861, in Tyler Papers, LC.

48 Wise, *Seven Decades of the Union*, 277; *Report of the Debates*, 10; Robert Dale Owen to John Tyler, February 14, 1861, in Tyler Papers, LC.

49 *Philadelphia Inquirer*, February 18, 1861; *Report of the Debates*, 94; John Tyler to Julia Tyler, February 19, 1861, in Tyler Papers, LC; James Halyburton to John Tyler, January 25, 1861, ibid.

50 John Tyler to Julia Tyler, February 19, 1861, in Tyler Papers, LC; Logan, *Great Conspiracy*, 150–51; Kirwan, *Crittenden*, 409–10; *Report of the Debates*, 43–44; *Baltimore Sun*, February 15, 1861; *Washington National Intelligencer*, February 28, 1861.

51 McClintock, *Lincoln and the Decision*, 184; *New York Herald*, February 22, 1861; *Philadelphia Inquirer*, February 28, 1861; Holzer, *Lincoln President-Elect*, 427–28; *Albany (New York) Evening Journal*, February 28, 1861; *Washington National Intelligencer*, February 22, 1861. Craven, *Growth of Southern Nationalism*, 386, claims the conference "failed largely because the Republicans were determined to make no concessions." Not only did two Illinois Republicans break with the president-elect and their party platform, but two of the most influential southern states also voted no because they wanted *more* land beyond the current Southwest. In any case, the package *did* secure a majority vote.

52 *Washington National Intelligencer*, February 22 and March 1, 1861; Dumond, *Secession Movement*, 252–53; *Report of the Debates*, 584–85; *Congressional Globe*, 36th Cong., 2nd sess., 1254–55.

53 *New York Herald*, February 17 and February 21, 1861; Salmon Chase to William H. Seward, November 24, 1860, in Seward Papers, UR; McClintock, *Lincoln and the Decision*, 120.

54 *Washington National Intelligencer*, February 7 and March 2, 1861; Trefousse, *Stevens*, 106; Donald, *Sumner*, 370; Charles Sumner to John Andrew, February 3, 1861, in *Letters of Sumner*, 2:51.

55 Crofts, *Reluctant Confederates*, 248–49; *Washington National Intelligencer*, March 4, 1861.

56 Holzer, *Lincoln President-Elect*, 428–29; Blight, *Frederick Douglass' Civil War*, 64; Randall, *Lincoln the President*, 1:224; Kirwan, *Crittenden*, 420–21; Huston, *Douglas*, 185–86; *Lowell (Massachusetts) Daily Citizen and News*, March 1, 1861.

57 *Baltimore Sun*, February 15, 1861; *New York Herald*, December 14, 1860, and January 8, 1861. These historians include Kirwan, *Crittenden*, 383; Stampp, *And the War Came*, 156–57; and Trefousse, *Wade*, 142.

Epilogue: "To Act the Part of a Patriot": March–April, 1861

1 Charles Dickens, *American Notes* (New York, 1987 ed.), 116–17; Holzer, *Lincoln President-Elect*, 409; Adams, *Autobiography*, 49.

2 Ernest B. Furguson, *Freedom Rising: Washington in the Civil War* (New York, 2004), 44–45; Morris, *Long Pursuit*, 206–7; Goodwin, *Team of Rivals*, 306. Lincoln also received a telegram on November 8, 1861, informing him that he had been hanged in ef-

figy in Pensacola, Florida. See "A Citizen" to Abraham Lincoln, November 8, 1860, in Lincoln Papers, LC.

3 Margaret Leech, *Reveille in Washington, 1860–1865* (New York, 1941), 37; Eisenhower, *Agent of Destiny*, 353; *Washington National Intelligencer*, February 25, 1861.

4 Sherman, *Recollections*, 231; Donald, *Sumner*, 383; *Pittsfield (Massachusetts) Sun*, February 28, 1861; William Marvel, *Mr. Lincoln Goes to War* (New York, 2006), 10–11; Furguson, *Freedom Rising*, 56; *Albany (New York) Evening Journal*, February 28, 1861.

5 *Pittsfield (Massachusetts) Sun*, February 28, 1861; White, *A. Lincoln*, 383.

6 *Pittsfield (Massachusetts) Sun*, February 28, 1861; White, *A. Lincoln*, 383; Hunt, *Hamlin*, 145.

7 *Pittsfield (Massachusetts) Sun*, February 28, 1861; Catton, *Coming Fury*, 239; Craypol, *Tyler*, 262.

8 Davis, *Breckinridge*, 259; Donald, *Lincoln*, 280; Oates, *With Malice Toward None*, 214.

9 Burlingame, *Lincoln*, 2:43; Capers, *Douglas*, 220; James A. Rawley, "Stephen A. Douglas and the Kansas-Nebraska Act," in *Kansas-Nebraska Act*, 87.

10 McPherson, *Battle Cry of Freedom*, 262–63; Potter, *Impending Crisis*, 565; Stampp, *Imperiled Union*, 171–72; Douglas L. Wilson, *Lincoln's Sword: The Presidency and the Power of Words* (New York, 2006), 45; White, *A. Lincoln*, 383–84.

11 Wilson, *Lincoln's Sword*, 64; Holzer, *Lincoln President-Elect*, 444–45; Burlingame, *Lincoln*, 2:47.

12 Adams, *Autobiography*, 96; *New-Hampshire Sentinel*, March 7, 1861; Catton, *Coming Fury*, 258–59; Furguson, *Freedom Rising*, 58.

13 Johnson, *Scott*, 224–25; Waugh, *One Man Great Enough*, 403; Marvel, *Lincoln Goes to War*, 4, 12; Catton, *Coming Fury*, 259–60; Nevins, *Emergence of Lincoln*, 2:457–58; Eisenhower, *Agent of Destiny*, 354; *Liberator*, March 8, 1861.

14 Harris, *Lincoln's Rise*, 324; Holzer, *Lincoln President-Elect*, 447–48; *Washington National Intelligencer*, March 5, 1861. Accounts of Buchanan's deportment in the carriage vary depending on the writer's attitude toward the failed president. Oates, *With Malice Toward None*, 217, depicts Buchanan as "muttering" but otherwise silent, and Burlingame, *Lincoln*, 2:59, observes only that "Buchanan had little to say." By comparison, Klein, *Buchanan*, 402, describes the two as "chatting affably," while Smith, *Presidency of Buchanan*, 190, has the two "chatting amiably."

15 *Washington National Intelligencer*, March 5, 1861; *New-Hampshire Sentinel*, March 7, 1861; Randall, *Lincoln the President*, 1:294; White, *A. Lincoln*, 388; Donald, *Lincoln*, 283; Leech, *Reveille in Washington*, 43.

16 *Congressional Globe*, 36th Cong., 2nd sess., 1413, 1433; Nichols, *Disruption of American Democracy*, 494–95; Hunt, *Hamlin*, 146; Davis, *Breckinridge*, 260.

17 Morris, *Long Pursuit*, 210; Adams, *Autobiography*, 97; *Washington National Intelligencer*, March 5, 1861; *Liberator*, March 8, 1861; *New-Hampshire Sentinel*, March 7, 1861; Sherman, *Recollections*, 1:232. Allan Nevins resolves the old debate as to what

exactly Douglas did that afternoon in "He Did Hold Lincoln's Hat," *American Heritage* 10 (February 1959): 98–99.

18 Johannsen, *Douglas*, 844; "Reminiscences of Stephen A. Douglas," *Atlantic Monthly*, August 1861, 212.

19 *Washington National Intelligencer*, March 5, 1861; *Trenton (New Jersey) State Gazette*, March 5, 1861.

20 *Washington National Intelligencer*, March 5, 1861; *Trenton (New Jersey) State Gazette*, March 5, 1861.

21 Burlingame, *Lincoln*, 2:61; *Middletown (Connecticut) Constitution*, March 13, 1861; *Liberator*, March 8, 1861; *New-Hampshire Sentinel*, March 14, 1861; *Washington National Intelligencer*, March 5, 1861; Adams, *Autobiography*, 98; White, *A. Lincoln*, 394; Oates, *With Malice Toward None*, 218–219.

22 Baker, *Mary Todd Lincoln*, 178; *New York Herald*, March 6, 1861; "Reminiscences of Douglas," 212.

23 Johannsen, *Douglas*, 845; *Madison Wisconsin Patriot*, April 9, 1861; *Hartford (Connecticut) Courant*, April 26, 1861; *New-Hampshire Sentinel*, March 14, 1861; Nichols, *Disruption of American Democracy*, 500.

24 Wells, *Douglas*, 281; Capers, *Douglas*, 223; Johannsen, *Douglas*, 859.

25 Capers, *Douglas*, 222–23; *Hartford (Connecticut) Courant*, May 15, 1861; Stephen A. Douglas to Abraham Lincoln, April 29, 1861, in Lincoln Papers, LC.

26 Johannsen, *Douglas*, 860–61; Howland, *Douglas*, 366; Stephen A. Douglas to James L. Faucett, in *Letters of Douglas*, 510.

27 Wells, *Douglas*, 282; *Macon (Georgia) Daily Telegraph*, May 15, 1861; *Hartford (Connecticut) Courant*, June 4, 1861; Logan, *Great Conspiracy*, 264.

28 Wells, *Douglas*, 288–89; Morris, *Long Pursuit*, 216–17; *Madison Wisconsin Patriot*, June 15, 1861.

29 *Congressional Globe*, 37th Cong., 1st sess., 24; *Madison Wisconsin Patriot*, June 11, 1861; *Amherst (Massachusetts) Farmer's Cabinet*, June 7, 1861; *Middletown (Connecticut) Constitution*, June 5, 1861. Joel H. Silbey, *A Respectable Minority: The Democratic Party in the Civil War Era, 1860–1868* (New York, 1977), chap. 3, remains the best discussion of the party's plight following Douglas's death, which, however, he misdates at April 1861.

30 Catton, *Coming Fury*, 393–94.

31 Abraham Lincoln to John A. Gilmer, December 15, 1860, in Lincoln Papers, LC.

32 George W. Hazzard to Abraham Lincoln, October 21, 1860, ibid.

33 Huston, *Douglas*, 196, thinks it "probably best that he did not live to see the agony of his nation and the war's vast physical and human destruction," but Wells, *Douglas*, 297–98, makes a compelling argument that the "greatest chapter in Douglas' life remained unwritten." Nichols, *Disruption of American Democracy*, 511, notes that Douglas's death allowed for the unfortunate ascent of "Andrew Johnson, long an outsider," while Capers, *Douglas*, 225, wrongly, I think, believes Douglas "would probably have been chosen [as] Lincoln's running mate in 1864, and would thus have become President upon the assassination." Despite his growing respect for Lincoln, Douglas

remained aware of their ideological differences, which the more obtuse Johnson was willing to overlook in the cause of political advancement. Capers's biography also reveals its historiographical age by lamenting that Douglas might have been more successful than Johnson in preventing "the Radicals from exacting vengeance in the age of hate which followed the war."

Appendix: 1860 Election Scenarios and Possible Outcomes

1   Not only did Lincoln run far ahead of his rivals in New England, as the *Lowell (Massachusetts) Daily Citizen and News*, November 8, 1860, reported, his vote exceeded "that given for the state ticket," and he received 2,665 more votes than the popular Governor John Andrew.

2   Current, *Lincoln Nobody Knows*, 212; Holzer, *Lincoln President-Elect*, 42–43.

3   Gienapp, "Who Voted for Lincoln?," 62; Harris, *Lincoln's Rise to Power*, 243. The *Washington Constitution*, November 8, 1860, also emphasized that in Pennsylvania many Democratic voters "violated the solemn compact between them and the friends of Breckinridge and Lane, and cast their votes for a straight-out Douglas ticket."

4   *New York Herald*, November 7, 1860. Freehling, *Road to Disunion*, 2:339, notes that even after the ugly convention season, Douglas won one in seven popular votes in the South, which is true, but it still would not have been enough for a Democratic victory even had the party been united.

5   Morison, "Election of 1860," 1117, observes that "Bell and Douglas between them polled 100,000 more votes than Lincoln," but only in the border South did Bell carry states that might otherwise have gone to Douglas. There is no evidence to prove that Douglas could have captured Constitutional Union voters where he most needed them, in Indiana, Illinois, and Pennsylvania.

6   Potter, *Impending Crisis*, 430. In both Indiana and Illinois, Buchanan won only because third-party American Party candidate Fillmore ran a viable campaign. In both of those states, the combined vote of Frémont and Fillmore exceeded that of Buchanan. See *Dallas Weekly Herald*, November 7, 1860.

7   *Trenton (New Jersey) State Gazette*, November 8, 1860; *Philadelphia Inquirer*, November 8, 1860; *Dallas Weekly Herald*, November 7, 1860.

8   Robert S. McElvaine, "The Red, the Blue, and the Grey," *Washington Post*, February 8, 2009.